W

The
Nuclear
Turning Point

The
Nuclear
Turning Point

*A Blueprint for
Deep Cuts and De-alerting
of Nuclear Weapons*

HAROLD A. FEIVESON
editor

BRUCE G. BLAIR
JONATHAN DEAN
STEVE FETTER
JAMES GOODBY

GEORGE N. LEWIS
JANNE E. NOLAN
THEODORE POSTOL
FRANK N. VON HIPPEL

BROOKINGS INSTITUTION PRESS
Washington, D.C.

Copyright © 1999
THE BROOKINGS INSTITUTION
1775 Massachusetts Avenue, N.W.
Washington, D.C. 20036
www.brookings.edu

Library of Congress Cataloging-in-Publication data

Feiveson, Harold A.
  The nuclear turning point : a blueprint for deep cuts and de-alerting of
nuclear weapons / Harold A. Feiveson, ed.
  p.   cm.
Includes bibliographical references and index.

  ISBN 0-8157-0953-6 (paper)
  ISBN 0-8157-0954-4 (cloth)
  1. Nuclear arms control. 2. Nuclear weapons. 3. Security,
international. 4. Nuclear disarmament. 5. Nuclear weapons—United States. I.
Feiveson, Harold A. II. Title.
  JZ5665 .F45 1999   98-58149
  327.1'74—dc21   CIP

9 8 7 6 5 4 3 2 1

The paper used in this publication meets the minimum requirements of the
American National Standard for Information Sciences—Permanence of Paper for
Printed Library Materials, ANSI Z39.48-1984

Typeset in Sabon

Composition by Oakland Street Publishing
Arlington, Virginia

Printed by R. R. Donnelley and Sons
Harrisonburg, Virginia

ℬ THE BROOKINGS INSTITUTION

The Brookings Institution is an independent organization devoted to nonpartisan research, education, and publication in economics, government, foreign policy, and the social sciences generally. Its principal purposes are to aid in the development of sound public policies and to promote public understanding of issues of national importance.

The Institution was founded on December 8, 1927, to merge the activities of the Institute for Government Research, founded in 1916, the Institute of Economics, founded in 1922, and the Robert Brookings Graduate School of Economics and Government, founded in 1924.

The Board of Trustees is responsible for the general administration of the Institution, while the immediate direction of the policies, program, and staff is vested in the President, assisted by an advisory committee of the officers and staff. The by-laws of the Institution state: "It is the function of the Trustees to make possible the conduct of scientific research, and publication, under the most favorable conditions, and to safeguard the independence of the research staff in pursuit of their studies and in the publication of the result of such studies. It is not a part of their function to determine, control, or influence the conduct of particular investigations or the conclusions reached."

The President bears final responsibility for the decision to publish a manuscript as a Brookings book. In reaching his judgment on the competence, accuracy, and objectivity of each study, the President is advised by the director of the appropriate research program and weighs the views of a panel of expert outside readers who report to him in confidence on the quality of the work. Publication of the work signifies that it is deemed a competent treatment worthy of public consideration but does not imply endorsement of conclusions or recommendations.

The Institution maintains its position of neutrality on issues of public policy in order to safeguard the intellectual freedom of the staff. Hence interpretations or conclusions in Brookings publications should be understood to be solely those of the authors and should not be attributed to the Institution, to its trustees, officers, or other staff members, or to the organizations that support its research.

Foreword

The threat of nuclear war, which has been the inescapable backdrop to our lives for the past half century, has, unfortunately, far from disappeared. Although deliberate nuclear attacks by the United States and Russia on each other, the chief nuclear nightmare during the cold war, are now virtually unthinkable, other risks have become more apparent. Among these are the increasing danger that nuclear weapons and nuclear materials in a Russia in deep economic distress will find their way to other countries or terrorist groups; the continuing risks that U.S. and Russian strategic nuclear weapons, which remain on high alert, could be launched by accident or mistake; and the prospect of nuclear proliferation, a risk spotlighted by the Indian and Pakistani nuclear tests in May 1998.

These dangers have led some to counsel the complete abolition of nuclear weapons. The authors here do not believe that abolition is currently a realistic goal. As a consequence they have put forward a detailed political and technical blueprint for very deep nuclear reductions, which, while falling short of completely eliminating nuclear weapons, would nevertheless drastically reduce their dangers. The authors—from Brookings, the University of Maryland, the Massachusetts Institute of Technology, and Princeton University, and including two independent former ambassadors with wide experience in nuclear arms control—refined their thinking through a series of meetings held at Brookings and several rounds of drafts of the separate chapters of the book.

The authors wish to thank the experts from Russia, China, France, Germany, India, Pakistan, and Israel who have provided commentary (in the appendixes) on the program of deep cuts described in the book. They are grateful as well to many colleagues who reviewed drafts of the chapters, including notably Josh Handler and Oleg Bukharin of Princeton. They also thank Richard Haass, director of the Foreign Policy Studies program at Brookings, who commented extensively on the first complete draft of the manuscript; and other reviewers of the manuscript, including Richard Garwin.

Many persons contributed in bringing this book to publication. James Schneider edited the manuscript, Susan Jackson checked it for factual accuracy, Eloise Stinger proofread it, and Robert Elwood prepared the index. For all these contributions, the authors are grateful.

Generous financial assistance for the project was provided by the Ford Foundation and the John D. and Catherine T. MacArthur Foundation. In addition, the several authors wish to acknowledge support to their home institutions from these and other foundations, including the John Merck Fund and the W. Alton Jones Foundation.

The views in the book are solely those of the authors and should not be ascribed to any of the supporting foundations or to the trustees, officers, or staff members of the Brookings Institution.

MICHAEL H. ARMACOST
President

April 1999
Washington, D.C.

Preface

In the past decade the United States and Russia have made dramatic progress in shrinking their nuclear weapons arsenals. Numbers of deployed strategic nuclear weapons have been sharply reduced, almost all tactical nuclear weapons have been withdrawn from deployment and placed in storage, and for the first time since the onset of the cold war, U.S. and Russian production lines for new nuclear weapons systems are largely closed. Other countries also have sought to reduce the nuclear danger. In 1995 the parties to the Nuclear Non-Proliferation Treaty agreed to its indefinite extension; and in 1996 the nuclear weapon states and most other countries signed the Comprehensive Nuclear Test Ban Treaty (CTBT) to prohibit any future nuclear weapons tests. People were beginning to think that humankind was on a glide path to a world in which nuclear weapons no longer posed much of a problem.

The Indian and Pakistani nuclear tests in May 1998 shattered this illusion. At a stroke they destroyed the complacency that many were beginning to feel about the nonproliferation regime. And by focusing attention on the real possibility of a nuclear war in South Asia, they once again made the dangers of nuclear weapons vivid.

However, even before the tests the dangers of nuclear war had not disappeared. First, against all common sense the United States and Russia continue to deploy thousands of nuclear warheads on high alert on strategic ballistic missiles, with a substantial portion ready to launch simply on warning of an incoming attack. And although their tactical nuclear weapons are now mostly in storage, the two countries continue to reserve the right to employ thousands of nuclear weapons to repel a conventional attack. These are ingredients for accident, miscalculation, and nuclear escalation, risks heightened by political instability in Russia and conditions verging on economic collapse in much of its nuclear weapons complex.

In light of these dangers various knowledgeable groups, including many retired military officers, have forcefully argued that the weapons must be abolished. But the authors of this book do not believe that, at present, abolition is a politically realistic option; and in the summer of 1996 we began to meet to see if we could work out a strategy, short of abolition, to drastically reduce the nuclear threat.

This book, the result of an effort continued through the end of 1998, proposes a series of steps that would reduce the numbers of nuclear weapons in the arsenals of the nuclear weapon states over the next two decades from tens of thousands to hundreds, with almost all the weapons deactivated so that they could not be used without warning. At the end of this program of deep cuts, it should be possible for the international community to see more clearly the further steps necessary to achieve abolition.

The fundamental arguments of the book were hammered out in group meetings and through draft chapters. For each of the chapters, one or two members took primary responsibility, with the chapter drafts subjected to critiques by other members and then revised (typically, a procedure that took several rounds).[1]

Part I presents an overview of the deep cuts program. Chapter 1 describes the current arms control context, and chapter 2 summarizes the deep cuts proposal and the reasons for urgency in implementing the program.

Part II focuses on a deeply ingrained mindset in the United States (and to some extent in Russia) that will have to be overcome before the radical restructuring of nuclear forces that we advocate can go forward: the notion that nuclear weapons can realistically be used in a wide variety of contingencies. Chapter 3 examines the issue of no first use of nuclear weapons, and chapter 4 explores how strategic nuclear forces should be targeted. The central argument of the two chapters is that the function of nuclear weapons is to deter and, if necessary, to respond to the use of nuclear weapons by other countries, a role that could be filled by arsenals one-hundredth the size of those deployed by the United States and Russia today.

Part III describes and analyzes the deep cuts program. Chapter 5 examines the implications of the deployment of the national ballistic missile defense by the United States that is now being urged by a majority of the members of Congress. Such a defense appears likely to doom any program of deep cuts in strategic offensive nuclear forces, cuts that would provide a far surer and

---

1. The contributing authors are Harold A. Feiveson (chapters 1 and 2); Steve Fetter (chapters 3 and 4); George N. Lewis and Theodore Postol (chapter 5); Bruce G. Blair (chapter 6); George N. Lewis (chapters 7 and 8); James Goodby (chapter 9); Jonathan Dean (chapters 10 and 13); Harold A. Feiveson and Steve Fetter (chapter 11); and Janne E. Nolan (chapter 12). Frank N. von Hippel participated in the editing of all the chapters.

safer path to security against the threat of deliberate or mistaken ballistic missile attacks. With the progressive deterioration of the command-and-control system in Russia, it is clearly time for Washington and Moscow to end the policy of keeping nuclear missiles constantly ready to fire, and chapter 6 presents a practical prescription of methods by which such de-alerting and deactivation of nuclear forces could be accomplished. Chapters 7 and 8 describe in detail how strategic and tactical nuclear forces could be structured under a deep cuts program as the arsenals are progressively reduced and de-alerted. Chapter 9 describes how the deep cuts being advocated require a new focus for nuclear arms control—the verified dismantlement of nuclear warheads themselves, not only their delivery vehicles.

Chapter 10 expands on the details of the final stage of reductions to 200 warheads for each of the nuclear weapon states, explaining how Britain, France, and China, then India, Pakistan, and Israel, could be brought into the deep cuts program. Chapter 11 describes the essential elements of the verification system that will be required. Such a system will have to be comprehensive, including measures to monitor all nuclear material and nuclear warheads, and it will demand unprecedented transparency in the nuclear weapons programs. Chapter 12 analyzes two recent evaluations of nuclear weapons policies by the current U.S. administration, concluding that the deep cuts program could only be carried out if there is strong and sustained leadership by the United States with the active participation of the president.

Finally, in Part IV, chapter 13 sketches in a preliminary way (the only way now possible) the changes in the international system that will probably be required if the nuclear weapon states are to take the final steps to abolition.

In early 1999, as this book is going to press, and nearly six years after the signing of the START II Treaty by Presidents Bush and Yeltsin, the Duma of the Russian Federation has still failed to ratify the treaty (the U.S. Senate ratified in January 1996). At the same time, given its deteriorating conventional forces and inability to allocate the large sums needed to improve them, Russia has been placing more reliance on its nuclear weapons and has become less cooperative in its relationship with the United States than it had been in the early 1990s. Consequently, negotiation of U.S.-Russian disarmament agreements, like those that form the basis of the proposals in this book, will face fierce political obstacles.

In the long run, however, as the cold war nuclear confrontation recedes into history and pressures mount from nonnuclear states and from publics worldwide to reduce stocks of nuclear weapons, the United States, Russia, and the other nuclear weapon states will, we believe, increasingly support a program of arms reductions such as outlined here.

The validity of this view is affirmed by the perspectives of authors from Russia, China, France, Germany, India, Pakistan, and Israel that are included as appendixes. The authors do not accept completely all elements of our program, but generally their comments do suggest that there is a realistic prospect that the program can be negotiated and implemented once the United States takes the initiative to set it into motion.

THE DEEP CUTS STUDY GROUP

Contents

APPENDIXES

International Perspectives

PART ONE

Staged Reductions and De-alerting of Nuclear Forces

After going unheeded for several years, nuclear arms control now finds itself at a crossroads: along one path a prospect for very deep and continuing cuts in nuclear weapons; along the other the risk that the present arms control regime could unravel. This risk was made suddenly more tangible by the nuclear weapons tests of India and Pakistan in May 1998. These explosions shook the foundations of the nuclear nonproliferation regime that had been painstakingly constructed during the past quarter century, and they have revived calls in the United States for a national ballistic missile defense. Most important, they have made the prospect of nuclear war less abstract.

Chapter 1 looks at the factors that have placed the nuclear weapon states at this crossroads. It then describes the revolution in bilateral arms control wrought by the United States and Russia in the past decade, which, although it has stalled in recent years, has provided the basis for radical cuts in the nuclear arsenals. Chapter 2 outlines the program we advocate for the de-alerting and deep reductions of nuclear forces.

CHAPTER ONE

Nuclear Arms Control at a Crossroads

Nuclear arms control is at a crossroads. The old regime has been assaulted by the degradation of Russia's nuclear command and control and early warning network; a standstill in the development of U.S.-Russian cooperation on the securing and safety of nuclear weapons and fissile material stockpiles; China's ongoing development of strategic nuclear forces; new threats of nuclear proliferation from South Asia and North Korea; and a gathering opposition in Russia and the United States to a continuation of negotiations on strategic arms reductions that led to the START I and START II agreements.

The Danger of Accidental, Unauthorized, Mistaken Nuclear Launch

There is growing apprehension among experts that Russia's command, control, and intelligence system, including its network of radar installations for warning of a missile attack, is deteriorating in ways that could jeopardize the ability of the country's central authority to control nuclear weapons. This is deeply worrisome because U.S. and Russian command and control systems could interact in dangerous and unstable ways, given that both the United States and Russia maintain and regularly exercise a capability to launch on warning thousands of nuclear warheads after a missile attack is detected but before the incoming warheads arrive. The United States could launch approximately 2,700 strategic warheads within minutes; Russia 2,100. Even after the full implementation of the START I and START II Treaties, the United States would still be able to launch more than 1,600 warheads and Russia at least several hundred within a few minutes of an order to do so (see the tables at the end of chapter 7).

The early warning and nuclear release procedures for U.S. and Russian strategic nuclear missiles require a response time of fifteen to thirty minutes, allowing as little as three or four minutes for assessing attack information, and another three or four for top-level decisionmaking. Russia evidently initiated the early phases of the launch-on-warning procedures in January 1995 when the launch of a U.S. scientific rocket from Norway triggered a false warning of attack. This led to activation of President Boris Yeltsin's nuclear suitcase, an emergency telecommunications conference of the president and his nuclear advisors, and an alert broadcast to missile-launch control posts.

U.S. and Russian launch-on-warning postures are maintained for various reasons. First, their nuclear war plans are dominated by thousands of time-urgent military targets, particularly nuclear forces and associated command and control posts. Second, intercontinental ballistic missiles (ICBMs) in fixed silos or on mobile launchers in garrison and pier-side submarine-launched ballistic missiles (SLBMs) are vulnerable, which creates a strong incentive to fire them before they could be pulverized by incoming warheads. Finally, the command, control, and communications networks are themselves vulnerable, increasing pressures to use nuclear weapons early while the systems are still intact.

The only certain way to move the United States and Russia away from day-to-day reliance on launch on warning is to verifiably remove from alert as many nuclear weapons as possible, especially those that are vulnerable to attack. This de-alerting of nuclear forces is a centerpiece of our deep cuts program outlined later.

The Decline of Russia's Nuclear Forces

Many of Russia's nuclear weapons, both strategic and tactical, are approaching the end of their projected lifetimes, and the country's ability to refurbish them or to produce a new generation of weapons is increasingly in doubt. In an appendix to this book, Alexei Arbatov, a member of the Russian Duma and one of the most knowledgeable Russian nuclear weapons experts, projects the rapid decline of Russian nuclear forces over the next ten years and beyond under a variety of assumptions. Overall, it is clear that Russia will be unable to deploy more than about 2,000 strategic warheads by 2010 under a START II constraint that requires it to dismantle its multiple-warhead, silo-based intercontinental ballistic missiles, although START II allows up to 3,500 deployed warheads. (The START agreements are discussed more fully in the next section.) If its present very low deployment rate of new missiles and inadequate maintenance capability for existing forces persist, Russia would probably have to reduce its force to fewer than 600 total strategic warheads by 2010.[1]

The situation with respect to tactical nuclear weapons is similarly dramatic. Again referring to Arbatov, in 1991 the Soviet Union had about 22,000 tactical nuclear warheads. At present Russia probably has fewer than 4,000, most or all in military depots. If, as Arbatov believes, the manufacture of new weapons is proceeding very slowly, it is likely that Russia will have, after 2003, at most 1,000 tactical nuclear warheads, about the same number as the United States.

Despite this looming obsolescence of Russian forces (and, on a somewhat longer timetable, U.S. forces as well; see note 1), development and production of new nuclear weapons by the United States and Russia is at a virtual standstill. Russia began deployment in 1998 of a new ICBM, the SS-27, a single-warhead missile with both mobile and silo-basing options, to replace its SS-25 single-warhead missile. In 1996 it began construction of a new ballistic missile submarine, although this work is proceeding very slowly. Development work has commenced on a new solid-propellant missile to be deployed on the new submarines.[2] And Russian military leaders talk vaguely about a new strategic bomber sometime in the next decade. That is it. Although the United States is modernizing its present systems, it has no entirely new strategic weapon system in assembly. "For the first time since the beginning of the Cold War, the assembly lines for submarines, missiles, and bombers are largely idle."[3]

1. U.S. forces also will eventually face obsolescence. In the spring of 1998 the U.S. Strategic Command released a viewgraph titled "The Brick Wall" that showed schematically the expected lifetimes of U.S. and Russian strategic weapons. Although the schematic did not label the weapon systems, it is possible to decode the figure, as was done by Chuck Ferguson of the Federation of American Scientists. The figure with Ferguson's decoding indicates "rust-out" dates for U.S. weapons as follows: Trident submarines and missiles, 2023 (subsequently increased to 2040); B-52 bombers, 2033; B-2 bombers, 2040; Minuteman III missiles, 2025. Estimated rust-out dates for Russia are also given, but in light of comments by Arbatov and other Russians, they may assume an unrealistic longevity. They are as follows: Delta III submarine, 2006; Typhoon submarine, 2014; Delta IV submarine, 2015; Bear bomber, 2015; Blackjack bomber, 2020; SS-19 ICBM, 2006; SS-24, 2005; SS-18, 2012; SS-25, 2015; and SS-27, 2030. Charles Ferguson, Federation of American Scientists, private communication, June 1998.

2. Paul Podvig, "The Russian Strategic Forces: Uncertain Future," *Breakthroughs*, Security Studies Program, Massachusetts Institute of Technology (February 1998).

3. William Arkin, "What's 'New'?" *Bulletin of the Atomic Scientists* (November-December 1997).

One could argue that the decline in Russian forces and the pause in the development of new weapons reduce the urgency for the United States to seek agreed reductions in nuclear weapons. But this view is short-sighted. Although Russia's current economic crisis does not realistically allow significant deployment of new weapons, economic recovery and a worsening of U.S.-Russia relations could in the future spur Moscow to undertake a new round of nuclear arms production. By 2000, with the first enlargement of NATO mostly implemented, a second wave of candidates, including the Baltic states, might be pressing for admission. Russia may also be faced by then with a U.S. decision to deploy a nationwide ballistic missile defense system. Both developments would increase political pressures on Russia to reinforce its nuclear deterrent.

In any case, given the long gestation required to develop and deploy new strategic weapon systems, Russia very soon, and the United States not long after, will have to begin planning their next generation of weapons. The United States, for example, is already investigating a host of technologies for a next generation of ballistic missile submarines, reentry vehicles, ICBMs, and submarine-launched ballistic missiles. It also has an active "stockpile stewardship" program to maintain capabilities in the national weapons laboratories that could lead eventually to the development of new nuclear warheads.[4]

U.S. policy at present is to hedge against the eventuality of a resurgent and hostile Russia by maintaining a large nuclear arsenal with a capacity for relatively rapid expansion if necessary. It would be far wiser for Washington to catch the moment of decline in Russian nuclear forces to secure binding U.S.-Russian agreements for irreversible deep cuts in nuclear arms.

U.S. and Russian Cooperation on Nuclear Security

The state of cooperative U.S.-Russian programs to secure and dispose of weapons and fissile material in Russia is also at a crossroads, with formal negotiations on transparency in warhead dismantlement and warhead and fissile-material storage at a standstill, but with enough work now done at a technical level to allow rapid progress in the negotiations if there is a political decision to move forward.

The dangers of diversions of nuclear weapons and materials in Russia

4. C. E. Paine and M. G. McKinzie, "Does the U.S. Science-Based Stockpile Stewardship Program Pose a Proliferation Threat?" *Science and Global Security*, vol. 7, no. 2 (1998).

are recognized by the Russian government, which has taken steps to strengthen security. It has consolidated stocks of tactical warheads and warheads removed from missiles and bombers, once dispersed over several hundred sites, into about eighty sites.[5] And it is dismantling excess and obsolete warheads.

The United States is providing vital assistance in upgrading the security of fissile materials and warheads. The cooperative effort includes both government-to-government programs, in which technical and financial assistance are channeled to Russia through formal agreements between U.S. and Russian government agencies, and lab-to-lab programs in which the critical cooperation is directly between U.S. and Russian national laboratories. Modern material protection, control, and accounting systems are now being installed in virtually all Russian facilities where weapons-usable materials are used for nonmilitary purposes and in many other facilities as well, including weapons design labs. Excess weapon-grade uranium is also being blended down to the low enrichment used in power reactor fuel and sold to the United States. With assistance from the U.S. Cooperative Threat Reduction (Nunn-Lugar) program under which the United States provides financial support for disarmament efforts in the former Soviet Union, a high-security storage facility for excess fissile material recovered from weapons is under construction near Chelyabinsk 65, a once closed nuclear weapons manufacturing city in the Ural Mountains.

During 1994–95 the United States proposed a transparency and irreversibility regime that would include U.S.-Russian exchanges of detailed information on aggregate stockpiles of nuclear warheads and fissile materials, reciprocal inspections to confirm the stockpiles of highly enriched uranium and plutonium recovered from nuclear weapons, cooperative measures to confirm reciprocal declarations of fissile material stocks, and exchanges of fissile material production records and visits to production sites. A U.S.-Russian working group was established to examine these ideas, but Russia cut off negotiations in November 1995. (The failure of the transparency negotiations is discussed in chapter 9.)

It is critical that Russia and the United States continue to move steadily and in parallel to eliminate most or all tactical and strategic warheads removed from deployment and to embrace a transparency regime that will provide greater assurance to each other and to the international community that the nuclear weapons and materials are secure.

5. Department of Defense, *Proliferation: Threat and Response* (November 1997), p. 43.

The Future of Chinese Nuclear Forces

China has relatively few nuclear weapons compared with the United States and Russia, but it is unlikely to remain content with this disparity. It will also have to decide how to respond to possible U.S. deployment of a national ballistic missile defense or high-altitude theater defenses that could be redeployed as national defenses. Either could bring into question the deterrent value of its small strategic missile force. Although resources that can be devoted to new weapons systems are still limited in China, in the long run, given its rapidly growing economy, such constraints may weaken.

A worrisome sign is an apparent rise of interest among Chinese strategists in concepts introduced by the United States and Russia during the height of their cold war confrontation, including counterforce options and even the development of launch-on-warning capabilities.[6] China today does not have the capabilities to target a significant fraction of U.S. or Russian nuclear forces and apparently has kept its nuclear forces essentially de-alerted. But it is believed to have used its final nuclear tests during 1994–96 to develop more compact warheads, which could be used either to equip existing missiles with multiple warheads or to make possible a transition from large ICBMs and intermediate-range ballistic missiles to smaller, single-warhead, solid fuel mobile missiles.

Whether a U.S.-Russian program of deep reductions and adherence to the Anti-Ballistic Missile Treaty would be sufficient to get China to formally cap its forces at current levels is unclear, but such a program appears to be an essential precondition for it to do so and a precondition for its eventually joining an arms reduction regime.

The Shaky Nonproliferation Regime

The international community has responded to the Indian and Pakistani nuclear tests by demanding that the testing moratorium informally adopted by the two countries be converted into a formal obligation under a Comprehensive Test Ban Treaty (CTBT) and that the two countries not deploy their nuclear weapons. It has also pressed them to enter into negotiations on a Fissile Material Cutoff Treaty to ban production of highly enriched

---

6. Alastair Ian Johnston, "China's New 'Old Thinking': The Concept of Limited Deterrence," *International Security*, vol. 20 (Winter 1995–96), pp. 5–42.

uranium and plutonium for weapons. India and Pakistan have now agreed to participate in negotiations on a cutoff. Immediately after its tests, India indicated a willingness to be similarly forthcoming on the CTBT but soon reverted to its demand that it be coupled to commitments by the nuclear weapon states to eliminate their nuclear weapons by a specified date, a linkage that most of the charter nuclear weapon states are not willing to accept.

It is too early to know how far negotiations to include India and Pakistan in a test ban and cutoff will go, but it is clear that India certainly and Pakistan probably will insist on being treated as members of the nuclear weapons club. With Iran and Iraq waiting in the wings (Israel informally joined the club long ago), the international community is naturally reluctant to do so.

A program of deep cuts in nuclear weapons, such as the one put forward in this book, could provide a way out of this impasse by making it more credible that final negotiations on nuclear disarmament will not be put off indefinitely. And because of the end of the cold war and the unprecedented support for nuclear disarmament among senior retired military officers and ministers in the United States, Russia, and elsewhere, for the first time in many years very deep cuts in nuclear weapons forces appear politically realistic. The following section summarizes briefly the recent history of nuclear arms control, which for all its shortcomings has nevertheless prepared the ground for a deep cuts program.

The Interrupted Revolution in Nuclear Arms Control

From 1986 to 1992 the United States and the Soviet Union (and, in the last stage, Russia) took dramatic initiatives to reduce the dangers of nuclear war. In December 1987 they signed the Intermediate Nuclear Forces (INF) Treaty, which eliminates all ground-launched missiles with ranges between 500 and 5,500 kilometers. They followed this success by completing and signing START I in July 1991 and in May 1992 negotiating the Lisbon Protocol to START I, which committed Belarus, Kazakhstan, and Ukraine to eliminate the strategic nuclear weapons left within their territories after the breakup of the Soviet Union. In January 1993 the United States and Russia signed START II. This treaty has not yet been ratified by Russia, but if it eventually enters into force, it will reduce U.S. and Russian actively deployed strategic nuclear warheads to roughly one-third of their 1990 levels by 2003 (box 1-1).

Along with the START negotiations and in the wake of the August 1991

Box 1-1. START I and START II

START I is a multilateral treaty between the United States, Russia, Ukraine, Kazakhstan, and Belarus.[1] It limits the United States and Russia to 1,600 strategic nuclear delivery vehicles each and places a ceiling on each country of 6,000 "accountable" warheads.[2] It also requires Russia to limit the number of its heavy ICBMs in fixed silos to half the number possessed by the former Soviet Union. And it requires Ukraine, Kazakhstan, and Belarus to become free of nuclear weapons, which they have.[3] The reduction of weapons called for under START I is to be completed seven years after the treaty entered into force (that is, by December 2001). Currently, all the parties are ahead of schedule. When completed, START I will have accomplished a 30 to 40 percent reduction in the strategic nuclear arsenals deployed at the time of the treaty signing.

START II is a bilateral treaty between the United States and Russia.[4] Its main elements are a ban on all land-based, multiple-warhead ballistic missiles by January 1, 2003, with an overall ceiling on deployed strategic warheads of 3,500 by 2003, and a limit on sea-based ballistic missile warheads of 1,750. START II, which is to be implemented simultaneously with START I, would reduce the deployed strategic offensive arsenals of the United States and Russia by roughly two-thirds compared with the level at the beginning of the START process. START II was ratified by the U.S. Senate in January 1996, but it has not yet been ratified by the Russian Duma.

1. *The START Treaty*, report of the Senate Committee on Foreign Relations (Government Printing Office, September 1992).

2. START I attributes an agreed number of accountable warheads to a weapon system for purposes of counting toward the maximum aggregate limits provided for in the treaty, whether or not the system actually carries that number of warheads. The biggest disparity between the treaty's accounting and reality involved strategic bombers not equipped to carry long-range cruise missiles; each bomber was counted as carrying only one accountable warhead, although it could actually carry sixteen. In START II, bombers have attributed to them the maximum number of warheads that they are actually equipped to carry.

3. Ukraine completed its nuclear disarmament in June 1996 when its remaining strategic nuclear warheads were loaded on a train and sent to Russia for destruction. Kazakhstan completed its shipment of nuclear weapons to Russia in 1995; Belarus completed its by the end of 1996. "START I Aggregate Numbers of Strategic Offensive Arms as of July 1, 1996," U.S. Arms Control and Disarmament Agency release, October 2, 1996.

4. U.S. Arms Control and Disarmament Agency, *Treaty between the United States of America and the Russian Federation on Further Reduction and Limitation of Strategic Offensive Arms—START II*, January 3, 1993.

Moscow coup, Presidents George Bush and Mikhail Gorbachev took parallel actions to remove most tactical nuclear weapons from deployment. These unilateral but reciprocal actions resulted in all the Soviet Army's short-range nuclear weapons being relocated to storage sites within Russia by June 1992, the denuclearization of the U.S. and Soviet Armies, the removal to storage of all nuclear weapons from U.S. and Russian surface ships and attack submarines, and the dismantling of a significant fraction of the warheads withdrawn from deployment.[7]

The United States and Russia also took significant steps to accelerate the pace of the START I reductions by deactivating the nuclear weapons that were to be eliminated. The United States took 450 Minuteman II missiles off alert by removing the launch keys from their underground control posts and installing pins in each missile silo to physically block the possibility of first-stage rocket motor ignition. It also took all strategic bombers off alert and unloaded their warheads to storage in nearby depots. Russia responded by announcing that it would deactivate 503 intercontinental ballistic missiles and pledging to keep its bomber force at a low level of readiness. Both countries also took off alert the ballistic missile submarines that were to be retired by the START I Treaty.

Since 1995, however, the pace of bilateral nuclear arms reductions has slowed. In part this was due to the unwillingness of the Russian Duma to ratify START II. The Duma was reluctant first because START II requires

7. As announced by Bush and Gorbachev, the United States would withdraw all nuclear artillery shells and all nuclear warheads for short-range ballistic missiles to the United States. These and any similar warheads stored in the United States would be dismantled and destroyed. All tactical nuclear weapons, including nuclear-armed cruise missiles, would be withdrawn from U.S. surface ships and attack submarines. Nuclear weapons associated with land-based naval aircraft also would be removed. Many of these weapons would be dismantled and destroyed and the remainder placed in secure central storage areas. All strategic bombers would be removed from day-to-day alert and their weapons returned to storage areas. All ICBMs scheduled for deactivation under START I would be taken off alert status. The single-warhead ICBM would be the sole remaining U.S. ICBM modernization program; certain other nuclear weapon programs would be terminated. President Bush called on the Soviet Union to take comparable although not identical measures. "White House Fact Sheet," September 27, 1991, published in *NATO Review*, no. 5 (October 1991).

All Soviet nuclear artillery ammunition and nuclear warheads for tactical missiles would be destroyed. Nuclear warheads of antiaircraft missiles would be removed from the army and stored in central bases; part of them would be destroyed. All nuclear mines would be eliminated. All tactical nuclear weapons would be removed from surface ships and multipurpose submarines. These weapons, as well as weapons from ground-based naval aviation, would be stored and part would be destroyed. *Novosti* report of President Gorbachev's televised address of October 5, 1991, published in *Survival*, vol. 33 (November-December 1991).

that Russia dismantle by 2003 all its multiple-warhead ICBMs, except for 105 SS-19 missiles, which must be downloaded to one warhead each. This would leave the country about 1,000 warheads below the START II ceiling. However, the Helsinki Summit, which established a framework agreement for START III, may have effectively addressed this Russian concern.

Second, with the elimination of its multiple-warhead ICBMs, Russia will be unable to match the U.S. capability under START II to load stockpiled warheads onto missiles and bombers that are not themselves eliminated under the treaties. By reloading 500 Minuteman III ICBMs with 3 warheads each (up from the START II limit of 1 warhead), reloading back from 5 to 8 warheads on each of the 336 Trident II submarine-launched ballistic missiles, and reconverting B-1B bombers to nuclear missions, the United States would be able to regenerate a strategic force roughly double that permitted by START II. By contrast, Russia's principal hedge would be to reload from 1 to 6 warheads each its 105 remaining SS-19 missiles.

Perhaps most important, NATO's decision to expand eastward into central Europe, ratified in the spring of 1998, has been invoked by some members of the Duma as political grounds to oppose ratification of START II. The NATO/Russia Founding Act, signed on May 27, 1997, sought to reassure Moscow that the members of NATO had "no intention, no plan, and no reason to deploy nuclear weapons on the territory of new members, nor any need to change any aspects of NATO's nuclear posture or nuclear policy—and do not foresee any future need to do so."[8] But this reassurance has not completely allayed Russian concerns, especially among Russian hardliners who denounced the agreement at Paris as a complete collapse in the face of Western aggression and the NATO expansion itself as the aggressive action of a hostile military bloc. Even if START II is soon ratified, the subject of NATO expansion is sure to remain active as long as there is a prospect of membership for the Baltic States. According to Alexei Arbatov, NATO expansion is "universally perceived in Russia (by some with grief, by others with malevolence) as a major defeat of Moscow's policy of broad partnership with the West. It is considered a great setback for Russian democrats, whose domestic political positions, commitments, and reform plans are largely predicated on such cooperation."[9]

8. *Founding Act on Mutual Relations, Cooperation, and Security between NATO and the Russian Federation*, Paris, May 27, 1997.

9. Alexei Arbatov, "As NATO Grows, START 2 Shudders," *New York Times*, August 26, 1997.

Box 1-2. Helsinki Summit on the START III and ABM Treaties

At their summit of March 21, 1997, Presidents Bill Clinton and Boris Yeltsin reached an understanding that START III will establish by December 31, 2007, a ceiling of 2,000–2,500 strategic nuclear weapons for each of the parties. They also agreed that START III will include measures relating to the transparency and destruction of nondeployed inventories of strategic nuclear warheads.

To deal with imbalances in U.S. and Russian post–START II forces, they further agreed to extend the START II deadline for eliminations to the START III deadline of December 31, 2007, but agreed that all systems scheduled for elimination under START II would be deactivated by December 31, 2003. In addition the presidents agreed to explore measures relating to limitations on long-range nuclear sea-launched cruise missiles and tactical nuclear systems.

Finally, they reaffirmed their commitment to the Limitations of Anti-Ballistic Missile Systems (the ABM Treaty), but President Yeltsin accepted the U.S. view that effective theater missile defenses (TMD) were necessary and agreed that any ground-based missile defense system not tested against a target with a speed exceeding 5 kilometers per second or a range exceeding 3,500 kilometers would be regarded as a TMD system and exempt from any ABM Treaty limits. However, the subsequent TMD demarcation agreement concluded in September 1997 only stated that TMD systems with interceptors with speeds less than 3 kilometers per second that obeyed this testing limit would be compliant, leaving the compliance of higher-speed systems unresolved. (See chapter 5 for discussion of these systems and the meaning of the demarcation of TMD systems).

Nuclear reductions also slowed because a go-slow approach was adopted in 1994 as a result of the U.S. Defense Department's Nuclear Posture Review (NPR). The NPR recommended that Washington delay making any commitments to post–START II reductions, a recommendation later endorsed in a presidential decision directive. (The internal bureaucratic struggle that shaped the NPR is discussed in chapter 12.)

This policy of delay began to change in late 1996 as the United States considered commiting to further reductions as a way to encourage Duma ratification of START II. At the March 1997 Helsinki Summit, President

Clinton committed to a follow-on START III agreement that would reduce the START II limit of 3,500 deployed strategic warheads to 2,000–2,500 by the end of 2007 (box 1-2). However, the United States is refusing to negotiate START III before the Duma ratifies START II.

CHAPTER TWO

A Strategy of Staged Reductions and De-alerting of Nuclear Forces

Almost all the elements of a framework for agreements on deeper bilateral cuts are in place. This framework can now be used, if the nuclear weapon states have the political will to do so, to cut the numbers and military significance of nuclear weapons steadily and drastically. It is not yet possible to describe in detail the far-reaching changes that will probably have to be made in the international system to allow complete abolition. But it is possible to map a road that would go far enough to achieve critical intermediate objectives: the elimination of fears of large-scale surprise nuclear attacks, near elimination of risks of accidental and unauthorized uses of nuclear weapons, drastic reduction in the possibility of the use of nuclear weapons in regional conflicts, elimination of almost all the world's stockpiles of warheads and fissile materials, and construction of arrangements that will forestall renewed buildups of nuclear arsenals and nuclear weapons proliferation.

This book describes a three-stage program of deep cuts in which all the weapons remaining at each stage are de-alerted and a large part are deactivated. By de-alerting, we mean measures that substantially increase to hours or days the time required to launch nuclear weapons in the active operational forces. Deactivation means that most weapons are unusable for weeks or months. This could be achieved, for example, by removing the warheads from ballistic missiles. Because they are reversible, de-alerting and deactivation measures require less formal negotiation than nuclear reduction treaties and can be put into place more rapidly. Figure 2-1 shows schematically the three-stage reductions.

In the first stage (our version of START III) the United States and Russia would ratify the Comprehensive Test Ban Treaty, reaffirm their commitment to the Treaty on the Limitation of Anti-Ballistic Missile Systems

Figure 2-1. U. S. and Russian Staged Reductions in Nuclear Weapons[a]
Nuclear Warheads in Operational Forces

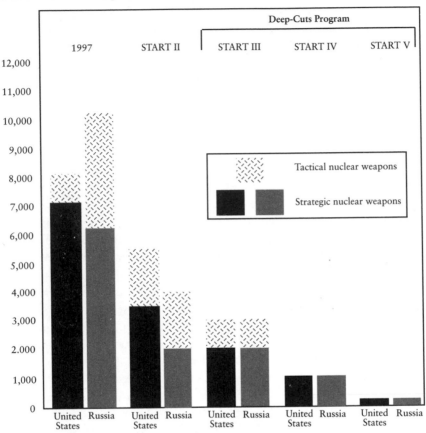

a. Under the plan advocated here, U.S. and Russian strategic arsenals would be reduced in stages from approximately 8,000 deployed strategic warheads today to 2,000 under START III, to 1,000 in START IV, and 200 in START V. Tactical nuclear weapons would largely be eliminated by START IV.

(the ABM Treaty), eliminate most of their tactical nuclear weapons, reduce to 2,000 operational strategic warheads each, de-alert or deactivate their strategic forces, and begin to put into place a comprehensive bilateral accounting system for warheads and fissile materials. All warheads withdrawn from deployment (or a specified proportion) would be dismantled, with their fissile material transferred to monitored storage; and all missiles and launchers withdrawn from the operational forces would be destroyed. This first stage is compatible with the START III framework agreed to by Presidents Clinton and Yeltsin at the Helsinki Summit.

In the second stage, which we call START IV, a verified ceiling of 1,000 each would be imposed on the total number of warheads (stored as well as deployed) held by Russia and the United States. By this time Britain, France, and China, and it is hoped, India, Pakistan, and Israel, would be engaged in the nuclear arms control process. And in the third stage, START V, the United States, western Europe, Russia, and China would each reduce their nuclear weapons stockpiles to 200 warheads or fewer, with most of these deactivated, primarily by verified separation of nuclear warheads from their delivery vehicles. This is not complete abolition, but it amounts to the longest steps in that direction that can be realistically projected under current international conditions.

There is a close relationship between the two central strands of our program directed at strategic nuclear forces: the stand-down from high alert of the forces and deep cuts in deployed nuclear weapons. First, we propose that where possible the strategic systems destined to be eliminated under START II, START III, and subsequent treaties be deactivated years earlier in anticipation of their eventual destruction. It was already agreed at the Helsinki Summit that multiple-warhead silo-based ICBMs will be deactivated five years before they have to be eliminated under START II. Although they might for a few years be considered as a hedge force that could be reconstituted, deactivated nuclear weapons would no longer be included in U.S. and Russian strategic plans. Second, we propose that at every stage of the deep cuts program the launch readiness of the remaining ballistic missiles would be decreased in a manner that does not increase their vulnerability.

Although technically each stage could probably be completed within about five years, their timing will have to take into account political as well as technical issues. In particular, it cannot now be specified with any certainty how much time will be required for the United States and Russia to gain confidence that they can monitor and control nondeployed warheads. Nevertheless, it will be important for the two countries to make clear at the outset that the objective of the deep cuts program is to reduce nuclear arsenals to very low numbers and to verifiably de-alert most or all of the remaining nuclear forces.

The First Stage

Even the first stage of this program will include many contentious elements. Carrying it out will therefore require sustained and extraordinary leadership by the United States. Successful implementation will, however, be a historic achievement. Although complete implementation may take until the end of the first stage, each element should be put in motion as soon as possible.

Limitations on Ballistic Missile Defenses

Continued adherence by the United States to the ABM Treaty will be controversial and politically difficult. Supporters of a limited national ballistic missile defense for the United States point, as we have, to the possibility that Russian ballistic missiles may be launched by mistake or accident. They also argue less plausibly that countries such as North Korea, Iran, and Iraq may soon be able and willing to launch a few nuclear ballistic missiles at the United States. However, deployment of a ballistic missile defense could provoke Russia to move to even more dangerous operational practices. A more effective protection against mistaken launch would be to de-alert most ballistic missiles and then eliminate them, the focus of the program advanced in this book.

With respect to North Korea, Iran, and Iraq, it is not clear how soon a combined threat to the United States from ballistic missiles and weapons of mass destruction could arise. However, the use of such weapons would be strongly deterred by the threat of retaliation.

Of course, no one can state for certain that the United States will never face a limited missile attack. Any responsible political leader would welcome a national defense, if an effective one were available and the costs and risks acceptable. However, despite technical advances, the same arguments about the ease of countermeasures that discredited previous proposals of ballistic missile defense systems are still valid.

The ABM Treaty, in order to facilitate reductions in offensive forces, explicitly prohibits national missile defenses. Advocates of national missile defense (NMD) argue that the treaty could be amended to allow such a defense if the system employed only a small number of interceptors. However, even such a light system could provide the basis for a *major* breakout from the terms of the ABM Treaty, especially if combined with mobile long-range missile interceptors for theater defense, which are now being developed by the United States. These include the high-altitude interceptor systems, Army Theater High Altitude Area Defense (THAAD) and Navy Upper Tier. If adapted to use the data from proposed space-based sensors, these systems could provide nationwide coverage from a small number of sites, perhaps three or four ships off the U.S. East and West Coasts in the case of the Upper Tier system. It would also be possible for early warning radar to be used for battle management.

Although a system relying on exoatmospheric intercept could be easily overwhelmed by the use of simple decoys, worst-case analysis would make Russian planners reluctant to reduce their offensive forces in the presence of even a very light U.S. national defense, especially if it could rapidly be converted into a thick defense.[1] Indeed, the Russian government has warned repeatedly that Russian ratification of START II will require a U.S. commitment of strict adherence to the ABM Treaty. Overall, it seems highly probable that the deployment of a national ballistic missile defense system by the United States would interfere with implementation of START II, and it would almost certainly imperil deep cuts in nuclear forces beyond those negotiated in START II. As long as states rely on ballistic missiles as a central component of their deterrent forces, they will not be willing to reduce the forces to low levels in the face of missile defense deployments by potential adversaries. It would be a poor trade-off for the United States to deploy a ballistic missile defense system of doubtful effectiveness if that meant forgoing the opportunity to eliminate thousands of Russian ballistic missiles and ballistic missile warheads and de-alert most of the rest.

De-alerting and Deactivation of Nuclear Forces

The United States and Russia should almost immediately stand down most or all of their nuclear forces to reduce the dangers inherent in their current launch-on-warning postures. Of course, in doing so it will be essential to keep in mind the concerns of U.S. and Russian nuclear planners about the possibility that vulnerabilities or instabilities might be created. Our de-alerting scenario, summarized briefly below and in detail in chapter 6, has been designed to minimize these concerns.[2]

PUT U.S. MX AND W88 WARHEADS IN STORAGE. First, to induce Russia to take its silo-based ICBMs off high alert (and thus off launch on warning), it is critical that the United States reduce its first-strike threat to this portion of the Russian forces. This could be done by removing the 500 W87 warheads on the 50 MX intercontinental ballistic missiles and replacing the

1. George Lewis and Theodore Postol, "Future Challenges to Ballistic Missile Defenses," *IEEE Spectrum* (September 1997).
2. A version of the following discussion of de-alerting appeared in "Nuclear De-Alerting: Taking a Step Back," *UNIDIR NewsLetter,* no. 38 (Summer 1998).

approximately 400 accurate high-yield W88 warheads deployed on submarine-based Trident II missiles by lower-yield W76 warheads.

DEPLOY U.S. SUBMARINES IN A LESS THREATENING MANNER. As additional confidence-building measures the United States, Britain, and France should announce that they plan to keep their attack submarines well away from Russia's ballistic missile submarine bases, and the United States should announce that its ballistic missile submarines will patrol out of range of targets in Russia.

DEACTIVATE U.S. AND RUSSIAN FORCES TO START III LEVELS. Reducing the threat to Russia's silo-based missiles in the ways proposed should then make it possible for Russia to agree to deactivate the weapons that would be eliminated by START III. The United States and Russia agreed at the March 1997 Helsinki Summit to deactivate by the end of 2003 the missiles that are to be eliminated under START II. They should go further and deactivate to the START III level of 2,000 warheads.

DE-ALERT REMAINING U.S. AND RUSSIAN MISSILES AND KEEP BOMBERS DEACTIVATED. The missiles that would remain operational should be configured so that they could not be launched on short notice. This could be done in various ways. In both the United States and Russia strategic bombers are already kept at a low level of combat readiness and without nuclear payloads. Additional steps to increase the time and visibility necessary for their regeneration should be taken.

IMMEDIATELY ELIMINATE LAUNCH-ON-WARNING OPTIONS FROM U.S. AND RUSSIAN NUCLEAR WAR PLANS. This would follow from the above actions, but could be undertaken at once. Initially, such committments would not be verifiable; but because deterrence does not require the ability to launch on warning, transparency is not essential.

Confidence in many of these de-alerting measures could be increased through the random on-site inspections already agreed to in START I. These inspections, for example, could be used by mutual agreement for verification that W88 warheads are no longer deployed on U.S. Trident II missiles, that the aerodynamic shrouds had been removed from the silo-based missiles, and so forth. Remotely monitored tamper-proof devices could be installed to verify that such measures were not being reversed between inspections.

Mobile systems such as submarines and truck-mounted missiles could not be continuously monitored when away from their bases because the monitoring could reveal their locations and compromise their survivability. However, at spaced intervals a random submarine or missile launcher could be asked to allow the electronic seals on de-alerted equipment to send a coded status report. The exact location of the system could also be concealed in various ways.

Even without new types of verification measures, the de-alerted postures proposed here ensure that enough warheads can be kept survivable to deter any surprise attack. This would also protect against any significant advantage accruing to a country that decided to realert first or was able to realert most rapidly.

It is noteworthy that the British Ministry of Defence, in its recently completed public report, *Strategic Defence Review*, noted that the "vast improvement in current strategic conditions since the end of the cold war permits us to adopt a reduced day-to-day alert state. . . . We will have only one submarine on patrol at a time. . . . The submarine's missiles will not be targeted and it will normally be at several days notice to fire."[3]

Reduce to 2,000 Deployed Warheads

The first stage of the post–START II staged reductions proposed here is similar to the outline of the START III Treaty the Clinton administration proposed at the Helsinki Summit in an effort to secure Russian ratification of START II. In our scheme the United States and Russia would reduce to a total of 2,000 operational warheads by 2007. For the United States such a reduction could be achieved, for example, by

—reducing the number of Minuteman III ICBMs from 500 under START II to 300,

—further downloading the Trident II SLBMs from 5 to 4 warheads each, and

—reducing to 10 the number of ballistic missile submarines from the projected START II level of 14.

At the 2,000-warhead level, Russia would be expected to retain some silo-based single-warhead ICBMs, several hundred mobile ICBMs, a reduced submarine ballistic missile force, and possibly a small force of strategic bombers. The detailed trade-offs to be considered in designing the reduced

3. UK Ministry of Defence, *Strategic Defence Review* (July 9, 1998), chap. 4.

forces are discussed in chapters 7 and 8. Most of the missiles and warheads withdrawn from deployment would be destroyed to make the reductions irreversible and to reduce concerns that each side might harbor regarding the upload potential of the other.

Eliminate Most Tactical Nuclear Warheads

The United States and Russia possess tactical nuclear weapons such as nuclear bombs for tactical bombers and warheads for sea-launched cruise missiles. Many tactical weapons were eliminated pursuant to the U.S and Soviet initiatives of 1991, but thousands remain (although at present in storage).

There should be deep reductions in these tactical weapons as well. The willingness of the United States and Russia to undertake such reductions was already signaled in the Helsinki Summit statement, which committed the two countries to explore "possible measures relating to nuclear long-range sea-launched cruise missiles and tactical nuclear systems, to include appropriate confidence-building and transparency measures."[4]

Unlike their discussions on strategic weapons, the United States and Russia have had no data exchanges on the numbers and locations of tactical weapons. The first step to bring these weapons into a deep reductions process would be to begin such exchanges. This would allow each side to verify that the tactical weapons taken out of deployment in 1991 and afterwards were indeed dismantled or placed in secure storage. It would then set the stage to begin to eliminate remaining warheads.

Establish a Comprehensive Warhead Verification System

The ultimate objective of the U.S.-Russian nuclear reductions program we envisage is to bring total numbers of warheads, nondeployed as well as deployed, down to a few hundred for each country. A deep reductions program, therefore, will require Russia and the United States to find an agreed method of reducing warheads under verifiable conditions to make the elimination irreversible and to find a way to confirm how many nondeployed warheads exist. Large numbers of nondeployed warheads would present a serious breakout potential, especially if means of delivery are readily available. The disposition of nondeployed warheads has not been a concern of arms control negotiations in the past, partly because agreement on on-site

4. Office of the Press Secretary, "Joint Statement on Parameters on Future Reductions in Nuclear Forces, March 21, 1997 (http://www.usis.hu/helspara.htm).

verification was impossible. Such verification now seems more negotiable, although sensitivities about revealing warhead design information remain.

The United States and Russia should start by exchanging declarations of the numbers and locations of all their nuclear warheads and identify each warhead by a unique serial number. Building confidence in these declarations and ensuing reductions would be gained through exchanges of production records, monitoring arrangements to confirm that warheads are being dismantled and their fissile materials placed in secure storage, and additional measures such as challenge inspections. Since in all likelihood it would take several years to secure a reasonable level of confidence that all nondeployed warheads are accounted for, it seems probable that in the first stage of disarmament the United States and Russia would wish, for a time, to maintain substantial reserves of warheads. For this reason, we propose a warhead ceiling on *operational* warheads in the first stage, not on total warheads, including spares and reserves.

However, the proposed warhead-verification system would create a framework for a sustained program of deep reductions in nondeployed as well as deployed nuclear warheads at later stages. And it is critical that verification begin early in the first stage. Because by the time the number of allowed nuclear weapons falls to the hundreds, states are likely to have far more confidence in a declaration whose accuracy has been verified for several years and for tens of thousands of nuclear warheads, than in one whose verification had begun recently and only after thousands of warheads had already been dismantled.

The Second Stage: Reductions to 1,000 Total Warheads

The second stage of reductions could set a verified ceiling of 1,000 each on total U.S. and Russian warheads, stored as well as deployed. All additional warheads would be dismantled under bilateral monitoring arrangements and the recovered fissile materials placed in internationally monitored storage until used for nuclear reactor fuel or otherwise disposed of permanently.

Although reductions by the United States and Russia to 1,000 warheads—roughly equal to the combined arsenals of China, France, and the United Kingdom today—does not require the full participation of the other nuclear weapon states, they should be deep enough to bring these states into the process. At this stage, or preferably even earlier, all the nuclear weapon states, including India, Pakistan, and Israel, should be brought into an international agreement to cut off all production of fissile material for weapons. This would effectively cap other countries' nuclear arsenals as the United

States and Russia are cutting their own. We believe it should also be possible to secure at least a tacit undertaking by these countries to maintain their nuclear weapons in a de-alerted status.

Reductions of the U.S. and Russian arsenals to 1,000 warheads could be carried out in a variety of ways. The United States could, for example, eliminate the remainder of its ICBM force and rely on a submarine-based force consisting of 10 submarines, each carrying 16 four- warhead Trident II missiles, for a total of 640 warheads, and a small bomber force, perhaps just its 20 B-2s, with all B-52s converted to nonnuclear status. Alternatively, the United States could retain a few hundred silo-based ICBMs with the warheads demated and stored singly in hardened sites along with sea-based ballistic missiles and bombers.

Russia might choose to abandon the strategic bomber leg of its triad, a direction in which it appears already heading. Its strategic forces could then be divided between approximately 600 warheads deployed on 8 ballistic missile submarines, perhaps 4 Delta-IVs and 4 new submarines and 400 warheads on single-warhead mobile ICBMs.

British and French nuclear forces would presumably be deployed as today predominantly on four ballistic missile submarines for each country, although France may continue to deploy some air-delivered weapons. Much less is known about China's plans for its future forces.

The Third Stage: Reductions to 200 Warheads

In the third stage of reductions the United States, Russia, China, and Britain and France in combination could each reduce their nuclear warhead stockpiles to 200 or fewer, with most of the warheads deactivated. The 200-warhead level would still allow nuclear force structures large and diverse enough to ensure high survivability.

For the United States, one possibility would be to divide its 200 warheads between SLBMs and bombers. Eight Trident submarines could each carry three 4-warhead Trident missiles or 12 small single-warhead missiles, for a total of 96 warheads. The bomber force could remain at 20 B-2s with 5 warheads each (on a reconfigured rotary launcher) for a total of 100. Russia could similarly deploy eight ballistic missile submarines with 12 warheads each, for a total of 96 warheads; 80 warheads could be deployed on mobile single-warhead missiles and the remaining 24 warheads could be bombs assigned to a small force of tactical bombers.

If Britain and France agreed to a combined limit of 200 warheads, the west European nuclear force would equal that of the United States, Russia, or China. Such a combined limit would be helpful in reducing the disparity between the forces of Russia and the combined forces of its former European adversaries. Assuming that Britain and France continued to operate four ballistic missile submarines each, with 16 warheads per submarine, each country would have 64 warheads, for a combined total of 128. If necessary, Britain and France could each keep two of their submarines at sea at all times, which would provide them with a highly survivable deterrent. Their remaining 72 permitted warheads could be deployed on air-to-ground missiles. Alternatively, all their warheads could be deployed on submarines with 24 warheads per submarine.

It is very difficult to predict how China might choose to structure its forces under a 200-warhead limit. However, it seems likely that it would try to preserve a diverse force based on mobile or cave-based missiles, SLBMs, and air-delivered weapons.

Most of the nuclear weapons in these third-stage arsenals would be deactivated so that they could not be used without warning. The deactivation could be effected in various ways but would most likely be accomplished by separating the nuclear warheads from their launchers and placing both in storage on the territory of the owner state under monitoring. Agreed rules would govern how these immobilized forces could be regenerated. In general, warheads and delivery systems could be withdrawn from storage and assembly sites by owner governments only in extraordinary situations and would have to be done with notification to other parties to the deep cuts regime.

As in the earlier stages, some portion of the 200-warhead force of each country would be based in a survivable manner—for example, in ballistic missile submarines at sea. This force, which would be de-alerted, should be large enough to retaliate devastatingly against a surprise attack, but not large enough to destroy other weapon states or their residual arsenals in a surprise attack of its own. The size of this portion of the force, which would have to be negotiated by the parties, might be 10 to 20 warheads.

Stability

Deep reductions and de-alerting of nuclear forces will not happen unless relations between the nuclear powers improve steadily as reductions proceed. Nevertheless, one cannot rule out the possibility that at some point during the reductions, relations between the United States and Russia (or, at the final stage, between any of the nuclear weapon states) might deteriorate. Because of this possibility, we need at the outset of the reductions to address questions of crisis stability.

Overall, our program seeks to ensure stability by first taking off high alert the weapons systems that are the most vulnerable and therefore the most tempting to place on launch on warning—silo-based MIRVed missiles, submarines at pier side, and mobile missiles in garrison—leaving as large a fraction as possible of deployed strategic weapons in basing modes that are highly survivable, such as submarines at sea.

The critical point is this: at all stages of our deep cuts program, each nuclear weapon state will maintain a core of invulnerable weapons, for example on submarines at sea. In such circumstances, whether one country's forces could be brought to full alert before another should not be decisive, and there should not be severe pressure to race to realert weapons systems, even in a deep and protracted crisis. These issues of crisis stability are analyzed further in chapters 7 and 8.

The Politics of Deep Cuts and De-alerting

This book does not systematically explore the international and domestic politics of a program of deep cuts and de-alerting except in chapter 12, which argues that in the United States such a program must be initiated and strongly supported by the president and cannot be left to the nuclear weapons bureaucracy. However, we have tried to make clear throughout the book how our program furthers the security interests of the United States and other countries. And the various country perspectives in the appendixes, including those from Russia and China, Europe, and India, Pakistan, and Israel, indicate that there could be very wide international support for the program of deep cuts and de-alerting that we propose.

Conclusion

The combination of deep cuts and de-alerting would go far to eliminate the possibility of any use of nuclear weapons. It would eliminate fears of massive surprise nuclear attacks and all but eliminate risks of accidental and unauthorized uses of nuclear weapons. It would drastically reduce the possibility of the use of nuclear weapons in regional conflicts and incentives to threaten the use of nuclear weapons. It would contribute materially to a much tighter nonproliferation regime. It would eliminate large stockpiles of warheads and materials that could be stolen by black marketers or terrorist groups. Finally, the reductions achieved would be to low enough levels to allow the nuclear states to focus on the steps necessary for the total elimination of nuclear weapons.

PART TWO

Nuclear Strategy

Strategy is the art of matching the instruments of national power—in this case nuclear weapons and related doctrines—to the goals of national policy. Any comprehensive discussion of U.S. nuclear policy must examine the role of nuclear weapons in achieving U.S. foreign policy and defense policy goals.

Opinion about the appropriate role of nuclear weapons is sharply divided. Some observers see them as valuable instruments of statecraft, the foundation of global stability, useful for deterring a wide range of threats to U.S. interests. Indeed, the United States still reserves the right to use nuclear weapons first, although the logical basis for that policy evaporated with the end of the cold war. Even the promise not to use nuclear weapons against countries that do not possess them has been severely eroded in recent years as nuclear forces have been considered for deterring or responding to attacks by chemical or biological weapons. Finally, and most important to our deep cuts and de-alerting proposals, official U.S. policy clings to cold war concepts that emphasize the importance of constantly standing ready to deliver a quick and massive attack against opposing nuclear forces.

We believe that such policies are fundamentally misguided. The overriding goal of U.S. policy should be to prevent the use, threat of use, or further spread of nuclear weapons. In the long term this can be accomplished only if the United States demonstrates by its own actions and policies that nuclear weapons are not useful instruments of military power. The United States should make clear in both its declared policy and operational doctrine that it possesses nuclear weapons only to deter the use of nuclear weapons by other states. Accordingly, it should promise never to initiate the use of nuclear weapons. Rather than plan and practice massive rapid attacks against Russian nuclear forces, the United States should strengthen its ability to delay retaliation and to design responses that are tailored to unique and unforeseeable circumstances.

This discussion focuses on the United States, not because other states are unimportant but because the United States is best placed to take the lead in developing and presenting a vision for the role of nuclear weapons in the post–cold war world. As the first country to develop and the only country to use nuclear weapons, and as the country with the most secure and sophisticated nuclear arsenal, the United States has a unique responsibility to take the lead. The U.S. government is more open and responsive to pressure for change in this area than are the governments of most of the other nuclear weapon states. These other states will, of course, make their own judgments about how nuclear weapons serve their interests, but their reasoning and conclusions should be similar to those given here for the United States.

Chapter 3 focuses on the overall question of what nuclear weapons are for. Chapter 4 explores nuclear strategy and targeting doctrine for strategic nuclear weapons.

Limiting the Role
of Nuclear Weapons

A t the risk of oversimplification, U.S. foreign policy goals are to foster an international environment that protects and improves the welfare and prosperity of U.S. citizens and to promote the spread of democracy, respect for human rights, the rule of law, and other basic American values. To achieve these goals, the United States has entered into alliances with important countries in western Europe, East Asia, and the Middle East. Protecting the security of these states has also become a goal of U.S. foreign policy.

During the cold war, nuclear weapons were viewed as useful, and perhaps essential, tools for achieving U.S. foreign and defense policy goals. The Soviet Union and China were considered potent threats to U.S. interests, with large armies that were thought to be ready, willing, and able to subjugate most of Eurasia. The United States believed that the independence of states in this region, particularly industrial powers such as Japan, Germany, France, Italy, and the United Kingdom, was vital to its security and prosperity. Initially, policymakers believed that the atomic bomb would serve as the ultimate trump card that would force Soviet leaders to bend to U.S. desires in Europe and Asia.[1] But they came to realize that the utility of nuclear threats was very limited, both because of the enormously destructive nature of the threat and because the Soviet Union quickly developed a nuclear arsenal of its own.

After the United States lost its nuclear monopoly, nuclear weapons nevertheless remained central in its foreign policy as a deterrent to overwhelming attacks on allies who, it was argued, could not be defended by conventional means alone. However, because of the inherent difficulty in convincing the

---

1. See, for example, Gregg Herken, *The Winning Weapon: The Atomic Bomb in the Cold War, 1945–1950* (Vintage Books, 1981).

Soviet Union and U.S. allies that the United States would risk its own destruction by using nuclear weapons to defend its allies, the United States searched constantly for options that would improve the credibility of its nuclear umbrella.[2]

U.S. reliance on nuclear weapons helped spur massive growth in the Soviet nuclear arsenal, and for the first time in more than a century America became vulnerable to devastating attacks by a foreign power. It sought to deter this threat with a strategy that would deny any advantage to the Soviet Union in a nuclear war of any size or duration. To this end, new warheads, missiles, and bombers were deployed and maintained at high states of readiness. The resulting situation, in which both superpowers continuously maintained forces capable of instant and immense destruction, was considered by many Western policymakers an unavoidable, albeit regrettable, price of preserving a favorable world order.

The foundation of U.S. nuclear policy crumbled with the breakup of the Warsaw Pact and the Soviet Union. Russia and China are no longer considered immediate threats to U.S. interests, and nuclear weapons are no longer needed to deter attacks by hostile countries with superior armies. The military and economic strength of the United States and its allies far exceeds that of all potential adversaries.[3] Most U.S. allies can defend themselves against any plausible nonnuclear external threat, and those that cannot can rely on the conventional military strength of the United States and other allies.

Although the benefits once attributed to nuclear weapons have waned, the weapons continue to pose a real and present danger to U.S. security. Nations armed with a few tens of nuclear weapons can destroy the United States. Nuclear weapons are the great equalizer. They allow small and otherwise weak countries to threaten much larger and more powerful countries. This observation led former U.S. Secretary of Defense Les Aspin to conclude that the United States would be better off if nuclear weapons did not exist.[4]

2. See Lawrence Freedman, *The Evolution of Nuclear Strategy* (London: Macmillan, 1989).

3. OECD countries, most of which are in security alliances with the United States, account for more than 60 percent of world military spending and 80 percent of world economic output. Potential adversaries—Algeria, China, Cuba, Iran, Iraq, Libya, North Korea, Russia, and Syria—together account for less than 25 percent of world military spending and 5 percent of economic output. If other U.S. allies are included (Poland, Hungary, Israel, Taiwan, Saudi Arabia, and others), the balance is even more overwhelming. *Military Balance 1996* (London: International Institute for Strategic Studies, 1996).

4. "The United States has undergone a fundamental shift in its interest regarding nuclear weapons. In fact, it is a complete reversal. The United States has relied on nuclear weapons to

Nuclear weapons cannot be disinvented, of course, but the taboo on their use can be strengthened. They have not been used since the bombings of Hiroshima and Nagasaki more than fifty years ago. On those increasingly rare occasions when U.S. officials have made threats, they have been vague and oblique and have omitted the word "nuclear," referring instead to "the strongest possible response," "devastating force," or "any capability available to us."[5] An international norm has developed against the use or explicit threat of use of nuclear weapons. The United States is a primary beneficiary of this taboo, and it compromises the taboo at its own peril.

A related but weaker norm has developed against the spread of nuclear weapons. The five nuclear weapon states, the only countries that admit to deploying the weapons, first acquired them between 1945 and 1964. The four countries that subsequently developed nuclear weapons—Israel, India, Pakistan, and South Africa—did so in secret, partly because they feared international sanctions if they announced their nuclear status.[6] A number of states considered but abandoned the nuclear option, including Sweden, South Korea, and Taiwan. The nonproliferation norm was strengthened greatly during the 1990s as Iraq, North Korea, South Africa, Brazil, Argentina, Ukraine, Kazakhstan, and Belarus were impelled, were induced, or volunteered to forsake a nuclear weapon capability.

The centerpiece of efforts to stop the spread of nuclear weapons is the Non-Proliferation Treaty (NPT), in which the five nuclear weapon states agree

---

offset numerical inferiority in conventional warfare. But we are now the only conventional superpower and our interests in this regard are dramatically reversed. . . . Suppose, somehow, that we had been offered a magic wand that would wipe out all nuclear weapons and the knowledge of their construction . . . we'd wave it in a nanosecond. A world without nuclear weapons would not be disadvantageous to the United States. In fact, a world without nuclear weapons would actually be better.

Nuclear weapons are still the big equalizer, but now the United States is not the equalizer but the equalizee." Les Aspin, "Three Propositions for a New Era Nuclear Policy," commencement address delivered at the Massachusetts Institute of Technology, June 1, 1992.

5. These phrases were used by U.S. officials in response to questions about whether the United States would use nuclear weapons against Iraq and were widely interpreted as meaning that the United States might use nuclear weapons. Brian Hall, "Overkill Is Not Dead," *New York Times Magazine*, March 15, 1998, p. 42; and Kenneth Bacon, Pentagon Spokesperson, January 27, 1998.

6. India conducted a nuclear test in May 1974. Publicly, however, it referred to the test as a "peaceful" explosion, denied any interest in deploying nuclear weapons, and insisted that it favored nuclear disarmament. In May 1998 India and Pakistan conducted several nuclear tests, but both countries continue to maintain that they have no plans to deploy nuclear weapons. The strong and widespread international reaction against the Indian and Pakistani tests, even though it was widely believed that both countries had long before acquired the capability to build nuclear weapons, is further evidence of strength of the nonproliferation norm.

not to help countries acquire nuclear weapons and all other parties promise not to acquire such weapons. To secure support for the treaty and its indefinite extension in 1995, the nuclear weapon states made three important promises. First, they promised not to use nuclear weapons against nonnuclear weapon states that are parties to the NPT.[7] Second, they pledged to act immediately to provide assistance to such states if they are the victim of, or are threatened with, aggression involving nuclear weapons.[8] Third, they agreed to pursue nuclear arms control and disarmament.[9] Partly as a result of these assurances, the NPT has been a remarkable success: only four countries—Cuba, India, Israel, and Pakistan—have not signed the treaty. In addition to their NPT-related pledges, the nuclear weapon states have agreed to respect nuclear weapon–free zones in Latin America, Africa, the South Pacific, and Southeast Asia, in which they may not deploy, use, or threaten to use nuclear weapons.

The international norms that have developed against the use or the further spread of nuclear weapons are extremely valuable to U.S. security. Strengthening these norms should be the central goal of U.S. nuclear policy. Whatever benefits one might imagine could be derived from using, threatening to use, or reserving the right to use nuclear weapons in a particular situation must be weighed against the long-term costs of weakening the taboos on the use or the spread of nuclear weapons.

To maintain and strengthen these norms, U.S. nuclear weapons should

7. This "negative security assurance" was first offered by the United States, the United Kingdom, and the Soviet Union in 1978. These three states, together with France, issued nearly identical statements in connection with UN Security Council resolution 984 (April 11, 1995). The only exception to the nonuse pledge is for attacks carried out or sustained by a nonnuclear weapon state in association or alliance with a nuclear weapon state. China has maintained an even stronger commitment that it would not "be the first to use nuclear weapons at any time or under any circumstances" and that it "undertakes not to use or threaten to use nuclear weapons against nonnuclear weapon states or nuclear weapon free zones at any time or under any circumstances." International Court of Justice, "Legality of the Threat of Use of Nuclear Weapons," Dissenting opinion of Judge Shingeru Oda, 1995.

8. This "positive security assurance" was first offered in UN Security Council resolution 255 (June 19, 1968), and was restated in resolution 984 (April 11, 1995) as follows: "The Security Council, and above all its nuclear-weapon State permanent members, will act immediately . . . in the event that [nonnuclear weapon states that are parties to the NPT] are the victim of an act of, or object of a threat of, aggression in which nuclear weapons are used," and will seek "to provide, in accordance with the Charter, the necessary assistance to the State victim."

9. Article VI of the NPT states that "each of the Parties to the Treaty undertakes to pursue negotiations in good faith on effective measures relating to cessation of the nuclear arms race at an early date and to nuclear disarmament, and on a Treaty on general and complete disarmament under strict and effective international control." This commitment was reiterated by the five nuclear weapon states in 1995.

be strictly limited to what the U.S. National Academy of Sciences refers to as the "core function" of nuclear weapons: deterring their use against the United States and its allies.[10] Accordingly, the United States should promise never to use nuclear weapons first. Even this function may atrophy if U.S. relations with Russia and China continue to improve. The mere existence of nuclear weapons inevitably introduces an element of caution into all possible military interactions, but explicit posturing of nuclear forces to deter other than nuclear threats is unnecessary and detrimental to U.S. security and international stability.

Unfortunately, more expansive roles for nuclear weapons have been advanced in the post–cold war world.[11] The most recent official reviews of U.S. nuclear policy, the Nuclear Posture Review and presidential decision directive 60, concluded that the targeting and declaratory doctrines developed during the cold war, which emphasize early and large attacks against nuclear forces and permit the first use of nuclear weapons, continue to be valuable in deterring threats to U.S. interests.[12] Others have argued that the role of nuclear weapons should be expanded to include deterring and responding to the use of chemical or biological weapons, and high officials have hinted that U.S. policy has indeed moved in that direction.[13] In the rest of this chapter we examine, and reject, potential roles for U.S. nuclear weapons beyond that of deterring the use of nuclear weapons by others.

Deterring Chemical and Biological Weapons

Prominent in post–cold war discussions is the perceived need to deter the use of chemical and biological weapons (CBW), which according to current fashion are lumped together with nuclear weapons as "weapons of mass destruction." Some analysts argue that because of their great destructive

10. Committee on International Security and Arms Control, National Academy of Sciences, *The Future of U.S. Nuclear Weapons Policy* (Washington: National Academy Press, 1997), pp. 3, 15, 26.

11. See, for example, Thomas C. Reed and Michael O. Wheeler, "The Role of Nuclear Weapons in the New World Order," study prepared for the Joint Strategic Target Planning Staff of the Strategic Air Command, 1991; and J. J. Martin, "U.S. Nuclear Targeting: A Historical Inquiry into Lessons for the Future," study prepared for U.S. Strategic Command, December 13, 1995.

12. William M. Arkin and Hans Kristensen, "Dangerous Directions," *Bulletin of the Atomic Scientists*, vol. 54 (March-April 1998).

13. See Stephen I. Schwartz, "Miscalculated Ambiguity: U.S. Policy on the Use and Threat of Use of Nuclear Weapons," *Disarmament Diplomacy* (February 1998).

potential, the use of chemical and biological weapons cannot be deterred by the threat of conventional retaliation alone.[14] Because the United States, as a signatory to the Chemical Weapons Convention and the Biological Weapons Convention, has forsworn such weapons, the analysts argue that nuclear weapons should be used to deter and, if necessary, respond to CBW attacks. They often cite the apparent success of veiled nuclear threats in deterring Iraqi CBW use during the Persian Gulf War. However, these arguments seem unconvincing.

First, they are based on the mistaken notion that the effects of chemical and biological weapons are morally, militarily, and politically equivalent to those of nuclear weapons. It is extremely difficult to protect people against nuclear weapons, but defenses against CBW (shelters, protective gear, vaccines, antidotes) can be highly effective. In fact, U.S. and NATO troops are equipped and trained to operate effectively under CBW attack. Even against unprotected people, a well-executed chemical attack would, under most circumstances, be about as lethal as a well-placed truck bomb.[15] An attack with biological weapons could kill far more—perhaps as many as a nuclear weapon—if the deadliest agents were distributed with high efficiency against unprotected urban populations during periods of extreme atmospheric stability. Fortunately, it would be technically and operationally difficult to achieve such high numbers of casualties with biological weapons, and no nation is known to possess weapons so effective. Unlike nuclear weapons, CBW leave roads, airports, hospitals, sewers, telephones, and supplies of water, electricity, and natural gas intact, making it easier to cope with the effects of attacks. In most contingencies, threats of nuclear retaliation would appear disproportionate and would lack credibility.

Second, there are strong moral and legal arguments against using or threatening to use nuclear weapons in response to CBW attacks. It would shatter the taboo against the use of nuclear weapons and the pledge not to use or threaten to use nuclear weapons against states without nuclear weapons.[16] It would, moreover, probably violate generally accepted laws

14. See, for example, David C. Gompert, "Rethinking the Role of Nuclear Weapons," *Strategic Review*, no. 140 (May 1998), pp. 1–5.

15. For a discussion of the effects of CBW, see Steve Fetter, "Ballistic Missiles and Weapons of Mass Destruction: What Is the Threat? What Should Be Done?" *International Security*, vol. 16 (Summer 1991), pp. 5–42.

16. Under the doctrine of "belligerent reprisal," normally illegal actions (for example, the use of nuclear weapons against non-nuclear weapons states) can be rendered legal by a prior illegal act such as the use of CBW by the state against which the reprisal is directed. Even then, any use or threat of use of nuclear weapons would be subject to generally accepted laws and principles governing the use of force. See George Bunn, "Expanding Nuclear Options: Is the U.S. Negating Its Non-Use Pledges?" *Arms Control Today* (May-June 1996), pp. 7–10.

and humanitarian principles governing the use of force.[17] According to these laws and principles, any threat or use of nuclear weapons must be limited to, and necessary for, self-defense; must not be directed at civilians and must be capable of distinguishing between civilian and military targets; and must not cause unnecessary suffering to combatants or harm greater than that unavoidable to achieve legitimate military objectives. Attacks in which the purpose is pure retribution or vengeance are not permitted. If a country launches a biological weapons attack against a U.S. city and kills a hundred thousand civilians, this would not give the United States the right to retaliate with nuclear weapons against one of the attacker's cities. Populations should not be punished for the deeds of their leaders.

It is difficult to imagine effective uses of nuclear weapons that would not violate the laws and principles governing the use of force. Nuclear attacks against military targets would be difficult to justify unless it could be demonstrated that they were necessary to achieve legitimate military objectives, that they would not cause unnecessary suffering, and that the objectives could not be achieved by conventional means. Nuclear weapons might be capable of destroying deeply buried shelters containing the leaders who are ordering or directing chemical or biological weapons attacks, but it would be difficult to justify nuclear attacks if these shelters were located in or near large cities, or if the entrances to the shelters could be destroyed with conventional weapons. Nuclear weapons could incinerate and render harmless stockpiles of chemical and biological agents, but it is unlikely that the effects of nuclear explosions would be, and would be seen as, less hazardous than the chemical or biological contamination that might result from conventional attacks. Moreover, conventional attacks can be designed to minimize the dispersal of agents, and U.S. troops could protect themselves against such contamination.

There are also practical political reasons for not using nuclear weapons to respond to chemical or biological weapons attacks. Domestic pressure for revenge might be strong in the wake of an attack, but a wise leadership would weigh this against the damage nuclear reprisal would do to U.S. security. In the short term, nuclear attacks could turn world opinion against the United States rather than against the country that had initiated the chemical or biological attack. This could make a collective response against the offender difficult or impossible. The long-term effects would be more pro-

17. The International Court of Justice, in an advisory opinion, unanimously agreed that the threat or use of nuclear weapons is subject to these generally accepted laws and principles. "International Court of Justice: Advisory Opinion on the Legality of the Threat or Use of Nuclear Weapons," *International Legal Materials*, vol. 35 (1996), p. 831.

found. Nuclear strikes could damage U.S. leadership and its alliances with other countries. Such attacks would certainly undermine the nonproliferation regime, legitimizing the acquisition of nuclear weapons by states that face threats from chemical or biological weapons. If the United States must resort to nuclear weapons to deter or respond to such attacks, weaker states might easily conclude that they have even more need of nuclear weapons. Nuclear use or threats of use to counter chemical or biological weapons also could encourage countries to consider them a poor man's nuclear bomb, thereby stimulating their spread. Although it is sometimes claimed that a nuclear response would set a useful precedent by demonstrating that CBW attacks would not be tolerated, a successful response without nuclear weapons would set a more valuable precedent about the inutility of these weapons.

Even if the use of nuclear weapons might under certain extreme circumstances be morally, legally, militarily, and politically justifiable, explicit nuclear threats, or policy statements that reserve the right to use nuclear weapons, add little to the deterrence of chemical or biological attacks and undermine nonproliferation goals. Adversaries would be aware of the strong arguments that would weigh against a nuclear response by the United States. More fundamentally, it is doubtful that any statement or policy could substantially bolster or detract from the existential deterrence that derives from the mere possession of nuclear weapons. Even if the United States had announced that it would not retaliate with nuclear weapons, adversaries would be deterred by the possibility that attacks resulting in great loss of American lives might trigger nuclear retribution. A decision to use nuclear weapons would be so momentous that what had been said about it in advance would be of secondary importance. In any case, most adversaries are unlikely to put much stock in public pronouncements or official promises about the circumstances under which the United States would or would not use nuclear weapons.

Some believe that the risk of attack from chemical or biological weapons is so great that it would be unwise to forgo the "sharp deterrence" provided by explicit threats to use nuclear weapons in response.[18] Rather than promise never to use nuclear weapons first, they advocate a pledge not to initiate the use of weapons of mass destruction. Few can argue with the desire to deter CBW attacks, but it would be foolish to issue threats that, if carried out, would be counter to one's own interests. Threats have a way of becoming

18. Gompert, "Rethinking the Role of Nuclear Weapons," p. 4.

self-fulfilling prophesies. Although policymakers might be content with ambiguity, military organizations would develop detailed contingency plans and standard operating procedures that would dominate their thinking about how to respond in a crisis. Having issued the threat of a nuclear response, policymakers would worry that U.S. credibility and resolve would be called into question if they did not follow through, even if they believed that doing so would be unnecessary or imprudent. The marginal value of explicit threats is so small, and the wisdom of carrying out such threats is so dubious, that it makes no sense to change U.S. policy in this way.

Contrary to common belief, it is not clear that U.S. nuclear threats deterred the use of chemical or biological weapons during the Persian Gulf War.[19] Although Iraq's foreign minister, Tariq Aziz, told Rolf Ekeus, the UN official in charge of dismantling Iraqi chemical and biological weapons, that Iraq refrained from using them because it feared U.S. nuclear retaliation, Ekeus believed that such statements were self-serving, since they depicted Iraq as the victim of U.S. nuclear coercion.[20] There is evidence that Iraq was unable, rather than unwilling, to use its chemical weapons. Just before the start of the war, it moved chemical and biological bombs to airfields and filled warheads with chemical and biological agents, but the rapid and widespread destruction of Iraqi airfields, command and control systems, and lines of communication by the allied bombing campaign would have prevented Iraq from mounting an attack.

It is worth noting that President Bush's threat of "the strongest possible response" (which many understood to be nuclear) if Iraq used its chemical weapons applied equally to the destruction of Kuwait's oilfields, which Iraq did with impunity.[21] U.S. officials threatened more privately to escalate the war in ways that did not involve nuclear weapons, and these threats may have been more important than the implicit nuclear threat.[22] We do not know

19. For a more complete discussion of this issue, see William M. Arkin, "Calculated Ambiguity: Nuclear Weapons and the Gulf War," *Washington Quarterly*, vol. 19 (Autumn 1996).

20. Schwartz, "Miscalculated Ambiguity."

21. The last paragraph of a letter from President Bush to President Hussein, delivered by Secretary of State James Baker to Iraqi Foreign Minister Tariq Aziz on the eve of the Persian Gulf War, stated, "the United States will not tolerate the use of chemical or biological weapons, support of any kind of terrorist actions, or the destruction of Kuwait's oilfields and installations. The American people would demand the strongest possible response. You and your country will pay a terrible price if you order unconscionable action of this sort." "Confrontation in the Gulf: Text of Letter from Bush to Hussein," *New York Times*, January 13, 1991.

22. On the eve of the Persian Gulf War, General Colin Powell drafted the following warning to Saddam Hussein: "Only conventional weapons will be used in strict accordance with the Geneva Convention and commonly accepted rules of warfare. If you, however, use chem-

why Iraq did not use chemical or biological weapons, but the balance of evidence does not support the conclusion that it was solely or even largely because of veiled U.S. threats to use nuclear weapons.

Relying on the threat or use of nuclear weapons to deter or respond to CBW use is a policy of weakness, not of strength, an unnecessary crutch that interferes with a serious effort to deal with the possibility of their use. A better policy would begin by pressing for the widest possible adherence to, and enforcement of, the Chemical Weapons and Biological Weapons Conventions. If countries violate these conventions and produce such weapons, they should be sanctioned by the UN Security Council, which has ruled that possession of them is a threat to international peace and security. Sanctions could include military action to destroy CBW production and storage sites. If these steps fail and the United States becomes embroiled in a conflict with a country having the weapons, production and storage sites and delivery vehicles could be destroyed preemptively in the first phase of the war. The use of any surviving chemical and biological weapons could be deterred through the threat of expanded conventional attacks, culminating with the occupation of the country, removal of the government, and trial of the authorities responsible for ordering the attacks.[23] If deterrence fails, massive conventional assaults against military targets could limit the scope of CBW attacks, while civil defenses could reduce casualties dramatically.

Military and political objectives should be achieved without using nuclear weapons if at all possible. In some cases the use of nuclear weapons might be expected to reduce U.S. casualties and end the war more quickly. It would be wrong, however, to think of nuclear weapons simply as a more efficient

---

ical or biological weapons in violation of treaty obligations we will: destroy your merchant fleet, destroy your railroad infrastructure, destroy your port facilities, destroy your highway system, destroy your oil facilities, destroy your airline infrastructure." He added that, if driven to it, "we would destroy the dams on the Tigris and Euphrates rivers and flood Baghdad, with horrendous consequences." Note that Powell believed that even this last action would be preferable to using nuclear weapons. Colin L. Powell, *My American Journey* (Random House, 1995), p. 504.

In addition, U.S. Secretary of State James Baker delivered the following threat to Tariq Aziz on the eve of the Persian Gulf War: "If the conflict starts, God forbid, and chemical or biological weapons are used against our forces, the American people would demand revenge, and we have the means to implement this. This is not a threat, but a pledge that if there is any use of such weapons, our objective would not be only the liberation of Kuwait, but also the toppling of the present regime. Any person who is responsible for the use of these weapons would be held accountable in the future." Lawrence Freedman and Efraim Karsh, *The Gulf Conflict: 1990–1991* (London: Faber and Faber, 1993), p. 257.

23. See, for example, the statements by General Powell and Secretary of State Baker in note 22.

way of winning a war. It may seem callous, but the first use of nuclear weapons would over the long term damage U.S. security far more than the loss of thousands of American lives, unless, as seems highly unlikely, international opinion would consider nuclear use justified in those circumstances.

Nuclear Weapons in Conventional Conflicts

A central role of U.S. nuclear weapons during the cold war was to deter and, if necessary, defeat conventional attacks against U.S. allies in Western Europe and Northeast Asia. Although such attacks did not occur, it is impossible to say to what extent "extended" nuclear deterrence was responsible.[24] The propensity of the Soviet Union to have launched such attacks is not known, and many factors other than nuclear deterrence were at work in preventing war between the major powers.[25] Even if one discounts these other factors, the active practice of extended deterrence—stationing nuclear weapons in Europe, developing plans for their use to counter a Soviet invasion, and the associated public pronouncements designed to make their use seem credible—probably was less important than the deterrence provided by the mere existence of the U.S., British, and French nuclear arsenals and their indestructible capacity to destroy the Soviet Union. It is important to note, however, that nuclear weapons did not deter a great number of smaller conflicts, largely because the use of nuclear weapons would not have been credible or militarily effective in those circumstances.[26]

Regardless of the value of nuclear weapons in deterring major conventional war in the past, this value has diminished greatly in importance. During the cold war, nuclear weapons were thought to be an essential counterweight to superior Soviet conventional forces; now the United States

24. As the term is used here, "extended deterrence" signifies an extension of the deterrent threat both in geography (from using nuclear weapons to deter attacks on the United States to using them to deter attacks on allies) and in the type of behavior that is deterred (from deterring nuclear attacks to deterring conventional attacks).

25. These included the memory of the devastation wrought by two world wars, the substantial and qualitatively superior conventional military capabilities of the United States and its allies, the development of collective security arrangements, such as NATO, and of shared political and economic institutions that helped cement and sustain these alliances, the advent of modern intelligence and surveillance systems that facilitate accurate assessments of military capabilities and make surprise attacks less likely to succeed, and the growth of information-based economic systems that do not depend on or benefit from territorial conquest.

26. U.S. nuclear weapons did not deter North Korea and China from attacking South Korea (with Soviet assistance), North Vietnam from attacking South Vietnam (with Soviet assistance),

has conventional superiority. No threat to the territorial integrity of the United States and its close allies exists that could not be countered effectively by their combined conventional military strength, nor is such a threat likely to emerge. In short, nuclear weapons are not needed to deter or respond to conventional attacks on vital U.S. interests.

Nevertheless, some analysts have suggested that nuclear weapons might be useful in future conventional conflicts.[27] For example, only nuclear weapons would be capable of destroying deeply buried hardened bunkers. Alternatively, U.S. or allied forces may find themselves in a situation in which defeat is imminent or victory is impossible using conventional forces. To give a frequently cited example from the Persian Gulf War, if the Iraqi army had invaded Saudi Arabia before sufficient allied forces had been deployed on the ground, Iraq may have been able to capture Saudi oil fields and inflict heavy casualties on U.S. troops. In such situations, it is claimed, the use of nuclear weapons might be the only way to prevent a military defeat.

The arguments against using nuclear weapons in a conventional conflict are similar to those outlined in the previous section. Using them in response to conventional military attacks would raise very difficult moral, legal, political, and diplomatic problems. To adversaries familiar with American political culture, nuclear threats would not be credible unless truly vital U.S. interests were threatened or unless the loss of American lives had been (or promised to be) massive. In such circumstances the deterrence provided by the mere existence of nuclear weapons is sufficient. Any attempt to improve deterrence by making explicit threats to respond to conventional attacks with nuclear weapons would damage the nonproliferation regime, and the actual use of nuclear weapons could destroy it.

Furthermore, from a purely military point of view the battlefield utility of nuclear weapons is limited, and it is unlikely that situations would arise

---

Soviet suppression of revolts in Hungary and Czechoslovakia, or Iraq from attacking Kuwait. Similarly, British nuclear weapons did not deter Argentina from occupying the Falkland Islands, Soviet nuclear weapons did not deter attacks by China or Afghan rebels, and Chinese nuclear weapons did not deter attacks by Vietnam. Nuclear weapons may have been important in deterring the United States and Russia from challenging each other's vital interests in Europe, the Middle East, and Cuba, but it is much easier to identify situations in which deterrence failed than those in which it succeeded. For a more complete discussion of the efficacy of U.S. nuclear threats in cold war crises, see Richard K. Betts, *Nuclear Blackmail and Nuclear Balance* (Brookings, 1987).

27. See Thomas W. Dowler and Joseph S. Howard III, "Countering the Threat of the Well-armed Tyrant: A Modest Proposal for Small Nuclear Weapons," *Strategic Review* (Fall 1991), pp. 34–40; and Thomas F. Ramos, "The Future of Theater Nuclear Forces," *Strategic Review* (Fall 1991), pp. 41–47.

in which nuclear weapons could achieve military goals that could not be realized through conventional means. The key difficulty in destroying chemical or biological weapons or political and military leaders is not being able to destroy the bunkers (the entrances can be destroyed with conventional weapons), but knowing the location of the bunker they are in. Concentrations of heavy armor can be destroyed with conventional airpower and precision-guided weapons, but "to do serious damage to just one armored division dispersed in the desert would require a considerable number of small tactical nuclear weapons."[28] The most obvious way to avoid heavy casualties without resort to nuclear weapons is not to put troops into situations in which the only hope is to use nuclear weapons. But even if U.S. troops were in grave danger, we cannot foresee any circumstances in which the short-term benefits of using nuclear weapons would outweigh the long-term costs. As in the case of CBW use, heavy conventional losses could be deterred or responded to by intensifying conventional strikes and expanding war aims.

That said, the existence of nuclear arsenals moderates the behavior of states. The arsenals engender fear that a crisis or conflict might spin out of control and lead to the use of the weapons. States therefore tend to avoid war and to limit their means and aims in war, particularly when the vital interests of a nuclear weapon state might be threatened. This moderating effect derives from the mere existence of survivable nuclear weapons, not from particular force deployments, war plans, doctrines, or explicit threats to use these weapons under certain circumstances. Our argument is not that nuclear weapons are irrelevant to the prevention or moderation of conventional conflicts, but that declaratory doctrines and operational plans that permit the use of the weapons in such conflicts are unnecessary and counterproductive.

Deterring the Use of Nuclear Weapons

The principal purpose for U.S. nuclear weapons is to deter and, if necessary, respond to the use of nuclear weapons against the United States or its allies. Fortunately, only a handful of potentially hostile countries have nuclear

28. Powell, *My American Journey*, p. 486. "I told Tom Kelly to gather a handful of people in the most secure cell in the building to work out nuclear strike options. The results unnerved me. . . . I showed this analysis to [Secretary of Defense] Cheney and then had it destroyed. If I had any doubts before about the practicality of nukes on the field of battle, this report clinched them."

weapons, and few if any additional countries are likely to acquire them in the future. Thus the potential for challenges to vital U.S. interests by nuclear-armed countries is limited.

Besides the United States, only four countries admit to deploying nuclear weapons: Russia, China, the United Kingdom, and France. Britain and France are, of course, close allies of the United States, and U.S. relations with Russia and China are better than at any time since World War II. If Russia or China should again become overtly hostile, it should be easy to deter direct nuclear attacks on the United States because no strategic nuclear exchange could benefit the country that initiated it. Based on the cold war experience, it also should be possible to deter nuclear attacks on countries in which the United States has much stronger interests than Russia or China. This would include those having U.S. security guarantees (the NATO countries, Japan, and South Korea), most other industrial democracies, and other countries in the Western Hemisphere. The United States should not, however, extend nuclear guarantees to areas where they would not be credible or reliable. It would be difficult, for example, to deter the use of nuclear weapons in situations where nuclear-armed adversaries believed that their vital interests were threatened much more than those of the United States— by Russia in the case of former republics of the Soviet Union, for example, or by China in the case of Taiwan. In such a situation nuclear threats would either be empty or would contain the seeds for Armageddon.[29] This is one reason why it is unwise to expand NATO to Russia's border.

Looking beyond the five declared nuclear powers, the three additional states thought to have nuclear weapons—Israel, India, and Pakistan (the latter two having tested)—do not challenge vital U.S. interests. Rather than engage in any confrontation with the United States, it is far more likely that they might become embroiled in a conflict with their neighbors, leading to the threat of use or actual use of nuclear weapons. For Israel this might involve Syria, Iraq, or Iran; for India and Pakistan it could involve each other and perhaps China. U.S. motives for intervening in such conflicts would be mostly humanitarian, together with a desire to preserve the non-

29. Some analysts reject this line of reasoning, which they believe would consign such areas to Russia's or China's sphere of influence and invite domination by them. But the United States cannot guarantee the security, backed with the threat to use nuclear weapons, of every state. It is important not to create situations in which hostile nuclear weapon states promise to use, or believe that they should or could use, nuclear weapons to defend their interests. This does not mean that the United States must simply acquiesce if Russia or China violates the sovereignty of its neighbors. Such actions can be opposed by a variety of diplomatic, economic, political, and nonnuclear military means.

proliferation regime and the taboo on the use of nuclear weapons. U.S. nuclear weapons are not likely to be instrumental in accomplishing these objectives. It seems extremely unlikely that the United States would use its nuclear arsenal to deter or respond to Israeli, Indian, or Pakistani nuclear strikes.

All other countries (except Cuba) are members of the Nuclear Non-Proliferation Treaty. Chances are reasonably good that no additional countries will join the nuclear club. Today's list of potential proliferators is short: North Korea, Iraq, and Iran. Major shifts in the political and technical environment may cause this list to grow, but it is difficult to see a positive role for U.S. nuclear weapons beyond the relatively straightforward one of deterring direct attacks on the United States or its close allies.[30] In fact, the deterrence relationship between the United States and potentially hostile proliferators most likely would run stronger in the opposite direction: new nuclear nations would use their arsenals to deter U.S. intervention in regional affairs.

Summary: The Role of Nuclear Weapons

The overriding goal of U.S. nuclear policy is to prevent the use or threat of use of nuclear weapons against the United States and its allies and to prevent the further spread of the weapons. Over the long term this will be possible only if the United States demonstrates by its own actions and policies that nuclear weapons are not useful or usable. U.S. nuclear weapons should be deployed only to deter or respond to the use of nuclear weapons by other states, and the United States should promise never to initiate the use of nuclear weapons. The threat or use of nuclear weapons in other situations or against nonnuclear weapon states, including those that may be armed with chemical or biological weapons, is not necessary to achieve short-term political and military objectives and would harm long-term U.S. interests in nonproliferation and the stability of the international order. The existence of U.S. nuclear weapons undoubtedly will serve to deter nonnuclear attacks on vital U.S. interests, but this effect need not and should not be bolstered by explicit threats or plans to use the weapons in response to such attacks.

30. Scenarios that could add significantly to the number of potential proliferators include a breakdown of civil and military authority in Russia or China, leading to the widespread theft or sale of nuclear weapons and fissile materials, or the emergence of serious conventional or nuclear threats to Germany, Japan, or South Korea, coupled with the real or imagined collapse of credible U.S. security guarantees to these countries. The probability of either scenario coming to pass can be reduced substantially through intelligent U.S. policy.

CHAPTER FOUR

Nuclear Strategy and
Targeting Doctrine

As long as the United States maintains a nuclear arsenal, a doctrine is needed to guide its operation and possible use. It is not enough to have a nuclear capability; the United States needs a conceptual framework to guide decisions about how many and what type of weapons are required and how its arsenal would be operated in various military and political situations. Even if all nuclear weapons were taken off alert and placed in storage, plans would still exist for how to ready the weapons for use and against what targets they should be aimed.

Counterforce Targeting

U.S. nuclear doctrine has two primary objectives: to deter nuclear attacks on the United States and its allies and to limit damage if deterrence fails. During the cold war the first objective was achieved by maintaining forces of sufficient size and capability to hold at risk a range of assets Soviet political and military leaders valued. These included nuclear forces and related command-and-control targets, conventional military forces, political and military leadership, and defense industries. This doctrine was developed to deter Soviet political and military leaders who were believed to be implacable, aggressive, and risk-taking adversaries that valued the perpetuation, expansion, and aggrandizement of their regime more than the lives of millions of ordinary citizens.

If deterrence failed or seemed about to fail, the second objective, limiting damage to the United States, would be achieved in three ways: by limiting the scope of initial nuclear attacks, avoiding attacks on Soviet cities while holding in reserve weapons to destroy them, and degrading the Soviet capacity to execute nuclear attacks by destroying its nuclear forces, command-and-control assets and, ultimately, its political and military leadership. Thus the United States would give the Soviet Union the incentive to avoid attacks on U.S. cities through the threat of retaliation in kind, even while degrading the Soviet ability to attack. The Soviet policy also appeared to emphasize early and massive counterforce attacks, as evidenced by the huge ICBM force it fielded during the 1970s.

Cold war nuclear strategy was complicated enormously by the U.S. threat to use nuclear weapons first in defense of allies facing superior Soviet and Chinese forces. To make such threats credible, the United States sought ways it could initiate the use of nuclear weapons that would not lead to an all-out nuclear war and the destruction of American cities. In the beginning this was accomplished through a massive supremacy in strategic weapons that gave the United States a reasonable prospect of a disarming first strike. As the Soviet Union attained nuclear parity in the 1960s, however, the threat of a massive U.S. response to limited Soviet attacks was no longer credible. The United States responded by bolstering the conventional defense of its allies, developing limited and selective nuclear options, and deploying thousands of warheads of greater accuracy to improve the prospects for successful counterforce attacks.

Some military and civilian nuclear strategists believe that cold war nuclear doctrine continues to be relevant and appropriate. This was the basic conclusion of the Nuclear Posture Review that was completed by the U.S. Defense Department in September 1994. The review concluded that the United States should retain existing purposes and missions for nuclear weapons and that it should maintain an ability to upload its nuclear forces rapidly to double the START II limits as a hedge against the "possible emergence of a hostile government in Russia or failure of the arms control process in the [former] Soviet Union."[1] Although the more recent presidential review directive 60, which cleared the way for cuts down to 2,500 deployed strategic warheads, reportedly eliminated the requirement to prevail in a protracted nuclear war, it nevertheless maintained the basic structure of U.S. nuclear doctrine and targeting plans.[2]

The decisive argument for maintaining thousands of strategic nuclear warheads, even after the end of the cold war, was that U.S. nuclear forces must maintain a capability to threaten a wide spectrum of targets in Russia and other countries that might become hostile to the United States. As General

1. *Nuclear Posture Review: Press/Public Version*, September 22, 1994.
2. William M. Arkin and Hans Kristensen, "Dangerous Directions," *Bulletin of the Atomic Scientists*, vol. 54 (March-April 1998).

John Shalikashvili, then chairman of the U.S. Joint Chiefs of Staff, stated during the START II hearings, "It was our view that with the 3,500 warheads allowed under this treaty, we would remain capable of holding at risk a broad enough range of high value political and military targets to deter any rational adversary from launching a nuclear attack against our nation or our allies."[3]

A previous nuclear policy review, known as the Reed-Wheeler report after its principal authors, was more explicit about what should constitute a broad range of targets: nuclear forces, general-purpose military forces, hostile leaderships, and war-supporting industries and supporting infrastructures.[4] Particularly prominent in the target list are Russian nuclear forces, including missile silos, bomber and submarine bases, nuclear warhead storage sites, air and ballistic missile defense sites, communications centers, and nuclear command sites from launch control facilities up to the military and political leaderships, perhaps 3,000 targets in all.[5]

A counterforce retaliatory doctrine demands large strategic forces on hair-trigger alert, which increases the risks of escalation or accidental use during crises. We believe that these risks made the doctrine unwise even during the cold war. But whatever its appropriateness in the past, the balance of nuclear risks has shifted decisively. It is no longer sensible that the focus of U.S. nuclear doctrine should be the deterrence of a deliberate, massive attack against U.S. nuclear forces or the limitation of damage in a war involving the detonation of thousands of warheads. Today, the most important risks are accidental, unauthorized, or erroneous attacks triggered by a breakdown in the Russian command-and-control system.

3. U.S. Senate Committee on Foreign Relations, *Report on the START II Treaty*, 104th Congress, Exec. Report 104-10, December 15, 1996, p. 11.

4. Thomas C. Reed and Michael O. Wheeler, "The Role of Nuclear Weapons in the New World Order." The report was commissioned by General George Butler (then commander in chief of the Strategic Air Command). Reed was a former secretary of the air force (1976–77) and assistant to the president for national security policy (1982–83), and Wheeler was former special assistant to three chairmen of the Joint Chiefs of Staff and executive secretary of the National Security Council (1982–83). See also R. Jeffrey Smith, "U.S. Urged to Cut 50% of A-Arms," *Washington Post*, January 6, 1992.

5. The Reed-Wheeler report (pp. 26–27) recommended targeting "bomber bases, [ballistic missile submarine] ports, ICBM support bases, mobile ICBM garrisons, nuclear storage bunkers, and other command nodes." With regard to ICBM silos, it states that "in a START environment, where the silo force of possible adversaries will be no larger than 200 to 250 silos, there is not a high penalty paid in terms of number of U.S. weapons in targeting a weapon against each silo." As described in Janne E. Nolan, *Guardians of the Arsenal: The Politics of Nuclear Strategy* (Basic Books, 1989), there has been very little change in U.S. targeting strategy over the decades.

Counterforce doctrine increases the risk of accidental or erroneous strikes. A policy of targeting opposing nuclear forces for rapid destruction puts pressure on the other side to be ready at all times to launch vulnerable forces (particularly ICBMs and pier-side SLBMs) on short notice before they are destroyed. This hair-trigger posture could lead to a launch of Russian nuclear forces in response to a false warning or a massive U.S. response to a small accidental or unauthorized Russian attack. A doctrine that provides for the rapid launch of nuclear forces during peacetime simply cannot be justified in the post–cold war security environment where the probability of an accidental, unauthorized, or erroneous launch is far greater than the probability of a deliberate nuclear attack. Even an *option* to launch under attack is unwise because it forces political and military leaders to make momentous decisions in a few minutes with incomplete information on the nature or origin of the attack.

Although the goal of counterforce attacks is to limit damage by destroying an opponent's nuclear forces, such attacks are more likely to have the opposite effect because an opponent may launch forces upon warning of attack rather than wait while they are destroyed. Thus a counterforce attack may do little more than trigger the launch of opposing forces. Counterforce attacks cannot achieve the objective of damage limitation in any case because nuclear forces sufficient to destroy U.S. cities almost certainly would survive.[6]

Targeting command and control and political and military leadership does

6. This certainly is true for Russia. Some analysts claim that retaliatory or second-strike counterforce attacks can limit damage to the United States by, for example, destroying ICBMs that malfunctioned or destroying Russia's capacity to reload silos for a second round of nuclear strikes. First, such attacks would likely prompt the launch of any remaining Russian forces that are vulnerable to a U.S. attack. Other types of responses might be able to avoid or deter the launch of these forces, limiting damage far more effectively. Second, malfunctions and reloads are unlikely to be important compared with the capacity of submarines at sea or dispersed mobile missiles, which cannot be eliminated by a counterforce attack, to destroy U.S. cities. Third, if reloads are worrisome, the possession of extra missiles above some nominal level could be prohibited by agreement.

Damage-limiting counterforce attacks may, however, be possible against China or some other country that acquires nuclear weapons. In these cases a disarming first strike might be contemplated if one was convinced that a nuclear attack was imminent. But even in the early 1960s, when the Soviet strategic nuclear force was much smaller than the U.S. force and extremely vulnerable, the U.S. military did not believe that it could prevent the destruction of many U.S. cities. See "Briefing for the President, SIOP–62," quoted in Scott D. Sagan, "SIOP–62: The Nuclear War Plan Briefing to President Kennedy," *International Security*, vol. 12 (Summer 1987), p. 22. Nor does a counterforce *second* strike make sense, since it would easily prompt these countries to use their small residual forces—most likely against U.S. cities—rather than see them destroyed. If the leaders of these countries had initiated nuclear attacks against the United States, one must presume that they would be prepared to go all the way.

not make sense either. The point is often made that deterrence is improved if the leaders who might order and carry out nuclear attacks know that they are targeted. But leaders who fear for their own survival would be tempted to launch the forces under their command if they believed—perhaps mistakenly—that they were under attack. They also would be more inclined to delegate launch authority to lower-level officers, increasing the probability of unauthorized use and making attacks more difficult to control and terminate. If erroneous or unauthorized use is more worrisome than deliberate attack, it makes sense not to target leadership or command and control. Even in the event of deliberate attack, it would be foolish to kill enemy leaders and destroy their capacity to order a cease fire unless the United States had already been destroyed. Leadership should be targeted last, if at all.

A counterforce doctrine perpetuates the misperception that large numbers of nuclear weapons are needed for deterrence. Even today, after the collapse of the Warsaw Pact, the breakup of the Soviet Union, and substantial reductions in Russian nuclear forces, thousands of potential counterforce targets remain in Russia, including hundreds of ICBM silos, launch control centers, and mobile missile garrisons; dozens of strategic bomber and submarine bases; hundreds of air defense, nuclear weapon storage, and command-and-control targets; and hundreds of leadership targets. The reluctance of many U.S. defense officials to endorse deep reductions is due in large part to their continued attachment to counterforce doctrine.

It will not be easy to break out of cold war thought patterns regarding the use of nuclear weapons. War plans are carefully guarded secrets, and changes in them can at best be verified only indirectly and over time through corresponding changes in force posture. Nuclear doctrine is important, however, because it is the basis for force structure and operations and could largely determine how the entire nuclear command system would react in a crisis. An evolving dialogue between U.S. and Russian military leaders on this subject would be useful and could help pave the way toward very deep reductions in nuclear forces.

The United States could take the lead by announcing that the only purpose of U.S. nuclear weapons is to deter nuclear attacks on the United States and its allies, adopting a policy of no first use of nuclear weapons and renouncing counterforce targeting. These changes in doctrine and declaratory policy would be a natural complement to efforts to reduce the role, size, and readiness of nuclear forces and to reinforce the nonproliferation regime. In repudiating counterforce the United States would acknowledge that damage could not be limited to any meaningful extent by destroying

Russia's nuclear forces and the means to control them. The best hope for limiting damage is to prevent the use of nuclear weapons in the first place or, if nuclear weapons are used, to end their use as soon as possible.

Countervalue Targeting

The traditional alternative to counterforce is countervalue targeting, in which the use of nuclear weapons is deterred by threatening to destroy cities and industry. Deterrence based on countervalue targeting is sometimes called minimum deterrence because relatively few weapons are needed to utterly destroy the cities and economy of even the largest country.

Perhaps the best-known formulation of countervalue deterrence is the "assured destruction" criterion set forth by Secretary of Defense Robert McNamara: U.S. strategic forces surviving a Soviet first strike should be capable of destroying 50 percent of Soviet industry and 20 to 25 percent of the Soviet population. The Department of Defense estimated that this level of destruction would require 200 to 400 one-megaton explosions.[7] More recent estimates for Russia indicate that this level of destruction could be caused by the detonation of about 100 U.S. warheads.[8] Another criterion might be the number of warheads needed to inflict casualties on the scale of history's most deadly war, World War II, which was responsible for the deaths of 20 million Soviet citizens and about the same number of Chinese. This level of death and destruction could be caused by the detonation of as few as 15 warheads on Russian cities or 5 on Chinese cities.[9]

7. Alain C. Enthoven and K. Wayne Smith, *How Much Is Enough? Shaping the Defense Program, 1961–1969* (Harper and Row, 1971), p. 207.

8. More than 50 percent of Russian industry and 35 percent of Russian population are concentrated in fifty cities, which could be destroyed completely by about one hundred U.S. strategic nuclear warheads. Roger D. Speed, "Potential CIS/Russian Targets," UCRL-ID-111040 (Livermore, Calif.: Lawrence Livermore National Laboratory, June 1992).

9. A simple calculation illustrates the destructive potential of a small number of nuclear weapons. Large Russian cities have average population densities ranging from 10,000 to 15,000 per square kilometer. An urban population of 20 million would therefore occupy a total area of 1,300 to 2,000 square kilometers, or about 1,500 square kilometers if one focuses on city centers. The U.S. warheads most likely to constitute a small, surviving force are the 100-kiloton W-76 and the 475-kiloton W-88 SLBM warheads. Detonation of the lower-yield W-76 warhead would destroy an urban area of 35 to 60 square kilometers; the area of destruction for the high-yield W-88 would be 100 to 150 square kilometers. The smaller areas are for blast effects alone, while the larger include the area potentially destroyed by fire. Thus the complete destruction 1,500 square kilometers of urban area could be accomplished with 25 to 40 W-76 or 10 to 15 W-88 warheads.

The Reed-Wheeler report argued that a countervalue targeting doctrine would lack credibility, both with potential adversaries and with U.S. allies, since the threat to use nuclear weapons against another country's cities would be credible only in response to an attack on U.S. cities. Thus, it was argued, the United States would not be able to deter or respond to other, more limited nuclear attacks against itself. But a countervalue doctrine seems to have been adequate for the three "medium" nuclear powers, even during the cold war. Each seems to have been satisfied with the deterrent effect of its force, and only a fool would test the resolve of British, French, or Chinese leaders to use nuclear weapons in retaliation for any sort of nuclear attack against their territory.

In addition, the Reed-Wheeler report argued that a countervalue strategy would be unable to deter the use of nuclear weapons against U.S. allies because it is not credible to threaten to destroy enemy cities—and thereby trigger the destruction of one's own cities—in response to a nuclear attack on an ally. Thus a countervalue strategy might be appropriate for China but not for the United States. Because allies also would doubt the credibility of a countervalue deterrent, the report argued that a move in this direction might trigger the acquisition of nuclear weapons by these states. "The concept of a minimum deterrent based upon a few hundred weapons or less is unrealistic. . . . No non-nuclear industrial power is going to believe security guarantees from a nation with this posture. They would be increasingly inclined to seek nuclear capabilities of their own."[10]

It is not so obvious, however, that the United States could not deter nuclear attacks on allies if it adopted a countervalue doctrine. The United Kingdom has for many years placed some of its weapons under NATO command, and France reportedly has considered offering nuclear guarantees to other European states. It is not necessary that potential adversaries be absolutely convinced that nuclear attacks on U.S. allies would trigger a nuclear response by the United States, but only that such a response could not be ruled out. Given the close and long-standing ties between the United States and its allies covered by nuclear security guarantees, this degree of credibility should not be difficult to maintain regardless of the doctrine that is adopted.

Chinese cities have population densities up to 45,000 per square kilometer. Twenty million people live in the four most densely populated Chinese cities, which have a combined area of only 530 square kilometers. These four cities could be destroyed by 10 to 15 W-76 or 5 W-88 warheads.

10. Reed-Wheeler report, p. 28.

Finally, the Reed-Wheeler report argued that there are moral problems with targeting cities: "No responsible observer doubts that a major nuclear exchange would result in millions of casualties, including civilian casualties, whatever the targeting doctrine. However, the differences between intentionally attacking civilians, and attacking other targets. . . which will unavoidably result in civilian casualties, has been critical in Western thought on what is legitimate in warfare."[11] The claim that counterforce is morally superior to countervalue targeting rings hollow inasmuch as the human consequences of counterforce attacks, which necessarily would involve a much larger number of warheads and attacks against targets near cities, would not be significantly different from attacks that explicitly targeted cities. Nevertheless, a countervalue doctrine is clearly at odds with established international humanitarian law, which requires that threats or uses of force must never be directed at civilians.

Counterpower Targeting

A third option is to target conventional military forces and defense industries critical to supporting a war effort.[12] This counterpower strategy would avoid the instabilities associated with counterforce, because neither side would fear for the safety of its nuclear force, while offering credible retaliatory options other than the immoral and suicidal one of destroying cities. Options for retaliatory strikes could be designed to minimize civilian casualties in order to limit the pressure for escalation and allow political leaders time to negotiate an end to nuclear attacks. Such targets might include major military bases and storage areas and possibly energy infrastructure

11. Reed-Wheeler report, p. 25. For detailed estimates of civilian casualties from counterforce attacks see, for example, William Daugherty, Barbara Levi, and Frank von Hippel, "The Consequences of 'Limited' Nuclear Attacks on the United States," *International Security*, vol. 10 (Spring 1986), pp. 3–45; and Barbara G. Levi, Frank von Hippel, and William H. Daugherty, "Civilian Casualties from 'Limited' Nuclear Attacks on the USSR," *International Security*, vol. 12 (Winter 1987–88), pp. 168–89. For START II forces, the attacks and consequences would be somewhat reduced. In particular, there would be fewer missile silos to attack. Nevertheless, the *direct* civilian fatalities would still be on the order of 10 million each in the United States and Russia.

12. For a discussion of counterpower strategies, see Jeffrey Richelson, "The Dilemmas of Counterpower Targeting," in *Strategic Nuclear Targeting*, edited by Desmond Ball and Jeffrey Richelson (Cornell University Press, 1985); Bernard Albert, "Constructive Counterpower," *Orbis*, vol. 20 (Summer 1976); and Bruce Russett, "Assured Destruction of What? A Countercombatant Alternative to Nuclear MADness," *Public Policy*, vol. 22 (Spring 1974).

(refineries or transmission nodes for gas and electricity) located away from major cities. Unlike counterforce, counterpower targeting would require at most a hundred warheads, enough to hold at risk the most valuable conventional military and energy targets located outside cities.

A possible drawback to counterpower targeting is that a nuclear attack against conventional military targets could be misinterpreted as an attempt to win the war rather than an attempt to retaliate in ways that minimize the potential for escalation. This concern is strengthened by the likelihood that nuclear weapons would be used only after the outbreak of a conventional war. Any use of nuclear weapons should be, and should be seen as, a political act designed to discourage additional nuclear attacks, not as a military attack designed to influence the outcome of a battle. Nuclear attacks against conventional military targets risk blurring the line between nuclear and conventional war and between strategic and tactical goals.

An alternative that has received relatively little attention is to retaliate with conventional rather than nuclear weapons, at least initially. This would be particularly appropriate against countries with clearly inferior conventional capabilities and without effective air defenses. In the Persian Gulf War the United States and its allies used a combination of stealth aircraft, cruise missiles, and smart munitions to disable Iraq's air defenses, destroy its communications systems, and disrupt its electricity and transportation networks. Not only did these actions by themselves inflict great damage on Iraqi military capability, but they left Iraq open to even more punishing strikes and to possible occupation. It is not clear, however, that a purely conventional retaliation could punish the attacker sufficiently while deterring further nuclear attacks. Even though the United States might attempt, at least initially, to limit its response to using conventional force, it should have plausible nuclear retaliatory options available that do not involve the suicidal or escalatory options of attacks on cities or nuclear forces.

Adaptive Targeting

Rather than simply replace one set of targets with another, the United States should give serious thought to doing away with fixed nuclear war plans altogether. The title of the current U.S. nuclear war plan—the Single Integrated Operations Plan (SIOP)—implies a degree of focus and preplanning that is inappropriate today. The SIOP was constructed to coordinate a rapid attack consisting of thousands of warheads against a well-defined enemy.

But Russia is no longer an enemy of the United States, and a deliberate attack by Moscow is almost unthinkable. Why then should the United States have detailed plans, which it updates and exercises regularly, to destroy Russia on a few minutes notice? As the size and alert status of nuclear forces are reduced and as the probability of a massive Russian attack becomes vanishingly small, it is no longer necessary or desirable to have standing plans for a massive, unidirectional U.S. response. Moreover, it no longer is technically necessary to have preprogrammed war plans; the technology exists to devise an attack and target missiles in a matter of hours.

The circumstances in which the United States might seriously consider the use of nuclear weapons are so uncertain and unforeseeable that it makes little sense to focus on a handful of preplanned options. A U.S. president who found himself in such a situation would likely find these options unsatisfactory. At that point he undoubtedly would want to begin to consider afresh how, in that particular situation, U.S. nuclear forces could best be used—or not used—to protect the security of the United States and its allies. For this reason it would be wise to create a process that would encourage deliberation and allow the creation of options tailored to a particular situation.

Adaptive or ad hoc targeting would not mean an end to war planning. Instead, the U.S. Strategic Command would be directed to rethink how nuclear weapons might be used within the confines of the limited role assigned to them and to subject the resulting concepts to periodic review by policymakers. At the operational level the ability to develop and execute plans in response to hypothetical scenarios would be exercised regularly. Contingency planning should be guided by several assumptions:

—the United States will not use nuclear weapons first;

—the United States will not use nuclear weapons in haste (no launch on warning or launch under attack);

—any U.S. nuclear retaliatory strike would be tailored to the circumstances and would be designed to facilitate a cease-fire and to minimize the risk of additional nuclear attacks, particularly against U.S. or allied cities; and

—the retaliatory strike would be directed at military targets and be designed to minimize civilian casualties.

As noted earlier, these criteria could be satisfied with strikes against carefully selected military supply depots and transportation or energy targets located outside cities. It is not our intention to specify detailed options for retaliatory strikes here but simply to outline the political constraints and principles that should guide the formulation of such options.

Summary: Targeting Doctrine

There is no satisfactory solution to the problem of how best to plan to use nuclear weapons in response to a nuclear attack on the United States or its allies. Plans to attack nuclear forces and command-and-control systems exacerbate crisis instabilities and risks of accidental, unauthorized, or inadvertent use. Plans to attack cities are suicidal and violate established humanitarian principles. Plans to attack conventional military forces risk sending the wrong message. Because a deliberate nuclear attack against the United States is almost unthinkable, we cannot foresee the circumstances under which the United States might use nuclear weapons. War planners should therefore create a process that presumes that any use of nuclear weapons would be tailored to a particular set of possibly unforeseeable circumstances. Planning would continue, guided by the general principles we have laid out, but it would not focus on a single, integrated operations plan.

Guidelines for Force Size and Structure

The size and composition of nuclear forces should be dictated by the concepts, doctrines, and plans that are developed for their use. However, there should be no fixed plans for using nuclear weapons. Rather the U.S. nuclear arsenal should be regarded as a flexible contingency force for the very limited purpose of deterring or responding to the use of nuclear weapons against the United States and its allies.

How large should this contingency force be? Even if one rejects countervalue targeting, the threat to destroy another country's society is the inescapable core of deterrence. No sane adversary would believe that any political or military advantage would be worth a significant risk of the destruction of his own society. As noted earlier, the delivery of one hundred U.S. warheads would be sufficient to destroy the society and economy of Russia or China, and as few as ten detonations could kill more people than have ever been killed in any country in any previous war. Thus ten to one hundred survivable warheads should be more than enough to deter any rational leader from ordering an attack on the cities of the United States or its allies.

Retaliating against cities would be suicidal unless one's own cities had already been destroyed. If the United States suffered less than all-out nuclear attack and a nuclear response was deemed necessary, the president should have options to use nuclear weapons on targets other than an opponent's cities, and thereby minimize the probability of escalation and mutual suicide. Ten to one hundred survivable warheads should be sufficient for such contingencies. Against Russia, for example, one hundred nuclear explosions would be enough to destroy all major air and naval bases, staging areas, command centers, and logistics centers that might be used to support a conventional attack.[13] Alternatively, one hundred explosions would be sufficient to destroy all major energy and industrial targets located outside cities.[14] It is, however, difficult to imagine that one hundred nuclear weapons could be used against an opponent, even in a manner that avoided cities, without triggering an all-out response. Indeed, ten warheads probably is closer to the upper limit of what would be interpreted by an adversary as a limited retaliatory attack.

Possible force structures and readiness postures during the various stages of reductions are discussed in more detail in later chapters. Here we note only that, however many weapons the United States decides are required for deterrence, a substantial fraction should not be vulnerable to attack either by nuclear or conventional means. In this context, "survivable" excludes targetable weapons, such as silo-based ICBMs and pier-side SLBMs.[15] A considered nuclear retaliatory response, tailored to the circumstances of the attack and designed to minimize the risks of additional attacks on U.S. cities, would not be possible if nuclear forces and their command-and-control systems were not capable of surviving a nuclear attack.

13. Speed, "Potential CIS/Russian Targets."

14. Fifty generating stations account for 50 percent of Russian electricity production, and twenty refineries account for 70 percent of its petroleum. Most of these and other major industrial and energy facilities are located in or near major cities, and attacks would be virtually indistinguishable from an attack on the population. The number of major industrial targets located outside major cities is almost certainly less than one hundred. See Speed, "Potential CIS/Russian Targets."

15. Two arguments are often made for retaining relatively large numbers of silo- based ICBMs. First, if such missiles are armed with a single warhead, no advantage could be obtained by attacking the silos because no more than one warhead could be destroyed by each attacking warhead. This does not mean that both sides would not plan to destroy silos, however, just as they do today. Thus the existence of silo-based missiles will inevitably create pressures for quick decisions.

Second, it is argued that the existence of numerous silos ensures that a counterforce attack would have to be large, which would make adversaries more reluctant to attempt such attacks. But any adversary that was foolish and risk taking enough to attempt a first strike against the United States, knowing that submarines at sea could not be destroyed, could just as easily avoid the silos. It is difficult to imagine circumstances in which the existence of silo-based missiles would make a significant difference in the calculations of an adversary about whether to launch a first strike.

Although nuclear forces must be survivable, they need not be capable of rapid retaliation. Time would be required to evaluate a nuclear attack on the United States and prepare an appropriate response. A potential attacker would not be less deterred if a retaliatory response was delayed by an hour or a day because the attacker could not, during such a delay, expect to gain a political or military advantage that would in any way blunt or offset a devastating retaliatory strike.

Finally, there is no compelling military or strategic rationale for linking the size of U.S. nuclear forces to those of other nuclear weapon states. As long as the United States has enough survivable warheads to deter and respond to nuclear attacks, it should not matter how many weapons other countries have. If based and operated properly, the survivability of U.S. weapons would be insensitive to the size of other nuclear arsenals. Even a 10,000-warhead force could not nullify a 200-warhead force based on submarines at sea. Relative numbers will, of course, retain considerable symbolic political value because they will be viewed as making a statement about the relative stature of the countries. It is primarily for this reason, and not for purposes of maintaining strategic stability, that the relative sizes of nuclear forces would be an important factor in a deep cuts agreement.

PART THREE

The Deep Cuts and De-alerting Program

CHAPTER FIVE

Ballistic Missile Defenses
and Deep Reductions

D uring the cold war the possibilities for limiting and reducing U.S. and Soviet offensive nuclear forces were based on the fundamental assumption that defenses against offensive forces would be strictly limited. This assumption was codified in the Anti-Ballistic Missile (ABM) Treaty of 1972, which banned the deployment of nationwide strategic missile defenses.

Since the end of the cold war, arguments have been made that the ABM Treaty is obsolete and unnecessary, that there is a threat to the United States of accidental or inadvertent Russian launches, that there is a growing danger that China or other developing countries could threaten U.S. territory with missile attacks, and that theater ballistic missiles (TBMs) pose a serious and increasing threat to U.S. forces and allies. Missile defense proponents argue that new missile defense systems are needed to deal with these threats and that the ABM Treaty either need not or should not be allowed to stand in the way. At present, the United States is pursuing a vigorous theater missile defense (TMD) program and is moving closer to a decision on deployment of a national missile defense (NMD).

U.S. missile defense activities, however, raise concerns that they will interfere with efforts to reduce offensive nuclear forces. Although the September 1997 signing of the U.S.-Russia TMD Demarcation Agreement has reduced the probability that U.S. missile defense activities will interfere with the ratification of START II, they could interfere with future efforts to reduct offensive nuclear forces, including the actual implementation of the START II Treaty.

We focus here on the impact of potential U.S. missile defense activities because the United States has by far the most advanced and comprehensive ballistic missile defense program. The chapter begins by reviewing the relationship between nuclear weapons and strategic missile defenses during the cold war and the role played by the ABM Treaty. It then discusses current and likely future ballistic missile threats, current U.S. programs for both national and theater missile defenses, and the changes to the ABM Treaty agreed to by the United States and Russia in their September 1997 TMD agreement.

The next sections discuss the effectiveness of ballistic missile defenses, particularly in the face of countermeasures, the compatibility of missile defenses and nuclear reductions, and finally the possibility of scenarios (albeit ones improbable in the near term) in which the deployment of strategic-capable defense might not interfere with deep cuts.

Overall, the chapter argues that unless a fundamental change in deterrence relationships occurs *before* the deployment of significant levels of strategic-capable defenses, their deployment will almost certainly prevent the attainment of the deep reductions this book advocates. The chapter concludes with a discussion of how and to what extent the ballistic missile threat can be met without deploying defenses that might imperil the attainment of deep nuclear reductions.

The ABM Treaty, Missile Defenses, and Cold War Arms Control

The Anti-Ballistic Missile Treaty has long been considered the foundation of strategic nuclear arms control.[1] The signing of the treaty resulted from the recognition by the United States and the Soviet Union that neither side could hope to build an effective defense against a strategic ballistic missile attack by the other, given their large offensive nuclear forces and their ability to expand these forces and employ countermeasures to overwhelm a defense at a relatively low cost. They also recognized that the seemingly inevitable offense-defense competition that would result from the deployment of defenses would be wasteful and harmful to the security of both countries. The U.S. reaction to the 1960s deployment of the Galosh missile defense system around Moscow is illustrative. This system posed no real threat to U.S. deterrent capabilities because it could have been easily destroyed by a small number of U.S. warheads. Nevertheless, Galosh was a crucial factor in the U.S. decision to vastly increase the number of its strategic missile warheads by deploying multiple independently targeted reentry vehicles (MIRVs).

1. For the text of the treaty and analysis see Matthew Bunn, *Foundation for the Future: The ABM Treaty and National Security* (Washington: Arms Control Association, 1990).

Another reason for agreeing to limit ballistic missile defenses was concern that defenses could increase the incentive to strike first. This could be destabilizing because defenses would be more effective against a ragged retaliatory strike than a first strike.

By signing the ABM Treaty the United States and the Soviet Union each agreed "not to deploy ABM systems for a defense of the territory of its country and not to provide a base for such a defense." The original treaty permitted each country to deploy up to two limited strategic defense sites—one at the national capital and one at an ICBM silo field—each with a maximum of one hundred interceptors. The 1974 protocol to the treaty reduced this to only one site each. This single permitted site must be located at either the national capital or an ICBM launcher field and is limited to covering only an "individual region" of each country. Thus despite claims to the contrary by some national missile defense advocates, it is not possible to deploy a treaty-compliant single-site defense of the entire United States. Moreover, from a purely technical view a single-site defense cannot provide coverage of the entire United States (or Russia) because the curvature of earth prevents a centrally located radar from seeing missiles attacking the coasts.[2] The Soviet Union built its permitted ABM system around Moscow, and Russia operates an upgraded version of that system today. Recent reports indicate that it may have been converted from nuclear-armed to conventionally armed interceptors.[3] In the mid-1970s the United States built its permitted system (Safeguard) near a missile silo field at Grand Forks, North Dakota, but closed the system down after only a few months of operation.

Other treaty provisions, such as limits on the permitted locations of large phased-array early warning radars and a prohibition on developing, testing, or deploying mobile strategic defense systems or components, are intended to ensure that neither country could break out of the treaty's limits and rapidly deploy a nationwide defense. The treaty was not intended to limit theater missile defenses or air defenses. However, to prevent strate-

2. Lisbeth Gronlund and David C. Wright, "Limits on the Coverage of a Treaty-Compliant ABM System," *Physics and Society*, vol. 21 (April 1992), pp. 3–6. Pop-up infrared sensors launched into space from the ground on warning of attack, might in principle be able to provide sensor coverage from a single site. However, since such a sensor would be an ABM component based on other physical principles and substituting for an ABM radar, it could not be deployed under the ABM Treaty unless the parties agreed. A space-based sensor system, such as the low-earth-orbit component of the planned U.S. space-based infrared system, could also provide the needed sensor coverage. However, the deployment of such a system would also require changing the ABM Treaty because it currently prohibits the deployment of space-based ABM components.

3. "Newsbreaks," *Aviation Week and Space Technology*, March 2, 1998, p. 21.

gic defenses from being deployed under the guise of being theater defenses or air defenses, the treaty bans giving such systems capabilities to counter strategic missiles or testing them against strategic missiles.

During the cold war, the ABM Treaty not only made it possible to avoid a potentially costly, wasteful, and dangerous offense-defense arms race, but by providing a predictable strategic environment, it made possible agreements controlling or reducing strategic offensive forces, culminating in START I and II. Because each country could be certain that the other could not rapidly deploy a national defense, they could retain confidence in the retaliatory capabilities of their strategic offensive forces even while reducing the size of the forces.

The Ballistic Missile Threat

The focus of U.S. missile defense activities is no longer a large-scale, deliberate missile attack by Russia. The major concerns now cited by missile defense advocates are protecting overseas U.S. troops and allied cities from attacks by theater ballistic missiles, protecting the U.S. homeland from accidental or unauthorized Russian missile launches, and protecting U.S. territory from deliberate missile attacks by China or other developing countries that might acquire intercontinental ballistic missiles. In the discussion that follows, we classify ballistic missiles as either short-range (less than 500 km), medium-range (500 to 5,500 km), or intercontinental (greater than 5,500 km).[4]

The largest missile threat, at least in terms of numbers, to deployed U.S. forces and the cities of U.S. allies, is from short-range TBMs, with ranges up to about 300 km with a 1-ton payload. Roughly twenty–five developing countries have such missiles. However, of these countries, only five— North Korea, Iran, Iraq, Syria, and Libya—are generally regarded as being hostile to the United States. These five have received Scud-B missiles with a range of 300 km from the Soviet Union, although most or all of Iraq's missiles were destroyed following the Gulf War.[5] North Korea has also been

4. "Ballistic Missiles and the World Security Environment," *Ballistic Missile Defense Organization Fact Sheet* no. DSI 9801 (July 1998); and "Executive Summary" (the full report is classified), *Report of the Commission to Assess the Ballistic Missile Threat to the United States.* The summary is available on-line at http://www.fas.org/irp/threat/bm-threat.htm

5. Lisbeth Gronlund and David Wright, "Threat Assessment Part A: Third World Missiles," in *The Last Fifteen Minutes: Ballistic Missile Defense in Perspective* (Washington: Coalition to Reduce Nuclear Dangers, 1996), pp. 16–21.

able to produce and export (to Iran and Syria) a reverse-engineered version of the Scud-B.[6]

The only other currently deployed short-range missile threat of concern to the United States is the possibility of Chinese missile attacks on Taiwan. Although China possesses missiles with intercontinental range, no part of Taiwan is more than 400 km from mainland China, and thus any Chinese missile attacks on the island are unlikely to involve long-range missiles. The missiles fired by China into waters near Taiwan in March 1996 were reportedly 600-km-range DF-15s (also known as M-9s).[7]

A smaller number of countries possess missiles with ranges of about 600 km. In particular, North Korea has produced and reportedly exported a modified Scud, known as the Scud-C, with a maximum range of about 600 km, although reaching this range apparently required reducing the weight of its warhead to well below 1 ton. The characteristics of the Scud-C may be similar to those of the Iraqi Al-Hussein missiles, which were modified Scud-Bs, used during the Gulf War.[8] Table 5-1 lists known or suspected medium-range missile programs.

Recent concerns over medium-range missile proliferation have centered on the North Korean missile program, on the possibility that Iran is developing medium-range missiles with assistance from Russia or China or both, and a possible missile competition between India and Pakistan in the wake of their nuclear tests.

North Korea has been developing a missile with a range of about 1,000 km, which would enable it to reach much of Japan. Known as the Nodong and apparently based on Scud technology, it has been flight-tested only once, in May 1993, and only to a maximum range of about 500 km.[9] However the U.S. Department of Defense declared in 1998 that the Nodong was operational, although given the lack of full-range flight tests, it is unclear what this determination means.[10] It is believed that North Korea has sold missiles or missile technology or both to countries such as Iran, Pakistan, and Syria.

6. David C. Wright, "Will North Korea Negotiate Away Its Missiles?" *Breakthroughs* (MIT Security Studies Program), vol. 7 (Spring 1998), pp. 29–36.

7. Michael A. Dornheim, "DF-15 Sophisticated, Hard to Intercept," *Aviation Week and Space Technology*, March 18, 1996, p. 23.

8. David C. Wright and Timur Kadyshev, "An Analysis of the North Korean Nodong Missile," *Science and Global Security*, vol. 4, no. 2 (1994), pp. 129–60.

9. For a description and analysis of the Nodong and other shorter-range North Korean missiles, see Wright and Kadyshev, "An Analysis of the North Korean Nodong Missile," pp. 129–60.

10. Bill Gertz, "Pentagon: N. Korea's Missiles Operational," *Washington Times*, June 10, 1998, p. 9.

Table 5-1. Known or Suspected Medium-Range Missile Programs, by Country

Missile	Range (km)	Payload (kg)	Status	Flight tests
Bulgaria				
SS-23	500	450	operational	?
China				
DF-3	3,000	2,000	operational	yes
DF-21	1,800	600	operational	yes
M-9	600	500	operational	yes
DF-25	1,700	2,000	cancelled?	?
JL-1	1,700	600	operational	?
Czech Republic				
SS-23	500	450	operational	?
Egypt				
Vector	700	?	?	?
India				
Agni	1,500–2,500	1,000+	under development	three
Iran				
Scud-C	500	700	operational	yes?
Shahab-3	1,300	?	under development	yes
Shahab-4	2,000	?	under development	no
Israel				
Jericho-1	500	500	operational	yes
Jericho-2	1,500	1,000	operational	yes
Libya				
Al-Fatah	1,000	500	under development?	no
North Korea				
Scud-C	500	700	operational	yes
Nodong	1,000	1,000	operational?	once
Taepodong-1	1,500–2,000	500	under development	once
Taepodong-2	4,000–6,000	1,000	under development?	no
Pakistan				
Hatf-3	600	500	under development	once?
Shaheen-1	700	?	under development?	no
Shaheen-2	2,000	?	under development	no
Ghauri	1,000+	700	under development	once
Ghaznavi	2,000+	?	under development	no
Saudi Arabia				
DF-3	3,000	2,000	operational?	no
Slovakia				
SS-23	500	450	operational	?
Syria				
Scud-C	500	700	operational	?
Taiwan				
Tien Ma	600–950	?	under development?	no
Ukraine				
SS-23	500	450	operational	?

Sources: "Artillery Rocket, Ballistic Missile, Sounding Rocket and Space Launch Capabilities of Selected Countries," *Nonproliferation Review* (Fall 1996), pp. 177; and Bill Gertz, "Pentagon Confirms Details on Iranian Missiles," *Washington Times*, March 27, 1998, p. 10.

In August 1998 North Korea carried out its first flight test of its two-stage Taepodong-1 missile, the second stage of which overflew Japan.[11] The Taepodong-1 is believed to be a modified Scud missile mounted on top of a Nodong. The test flight apparently included a small third-stage booster for deploying a small satellite. Although this third stage apparently failed, the test did demonstrate a successful two-stage missile, a significant technical advance for North Korea. According to one estimate, the Taepodong-1 can likely deliver a 1,000 kg payload to a range of 2,500 km and a 500 kg payload to 4,100 km.[12] If the third stage problem is corrected, it could potentially deliver a small payload to intercontinental range.

North Korea is reported to be working on the Taepodong-2 with a range possibly as great as 6,000 km.[13] A North Korean missile with that range would be able to reach parts of western Alaska and far western Hawaii. However, there has been no flight test of the Taepodong-2 and such a missile would likely require the development of a more powerful rocket booster or the clustering together of Nodong engines.

Iran is believed to be developing two medium-range missiles, the Shahab-3, with a range of 1,300 km and the Shahab-4, with a range of 2,000 km.[14] Russia and China are believed to have provided technical assistance to these development programs. The Shahab-3, which is believed to be a North Korean Nodong, was first tested in July 1998.[15] These missiles could be operational in the first half of the next decade.

India's two main ballistic missile programs, the short-range Prithvi and the medium-range Agni, have been in development since at least the mid-1980s.[16] The Prithvi exists in several variants with ranges between 150 and 350 km (the longer-range versions have reduced payloads), and at least the shorter-range version is now operational. The Agni, intended to have a range of about 1,500 km, was originally described by India as a technology demonstration program and underwent three flight tests before testing ended in 1994. However, Pakistan's 1998 test flight of its medium-range Ghauri

11. Rowan Scarborough and Bill Gertz, "N. Korea Fires Missile over Japan," *Washington Times*, September 1, 1998, p. 1.

12. David Wright, "An Analysis of the North Korean Missile Launch of 31 August 1998," *INESAP Information Bulletin*, no. 16 (November 1998), pp. 23–25.

13. Scarborough and Gertz, "N. Korea Fires Missile over Japan," p. 1.

14. Bill Gertz, "Pentagon Confirms Details on Iranian Missiles: Russia, China Provided Technology," *Washington Times*, March 27, 1998, p. 10.

15. Bill Gertz, "Iran Tests Medium-Range Missile," *Washington Times*, July 23, 1998, p. 1.

16. Timothy V. McCarthy, "India: Emerging Missile Power," in William C. Potter and Harlan W. Jencks, eds. *The International Missile Bazaar* (Boulder, Colo.: Westview Press, 1994), pp. 201–34.

missile has revived the Agni. It is likely that deployment of the Agni or an extended-range version, the Agni-II with a range of about 2,000–2,500 km, will take place within a few years.[17]

Pakistan has been developing several medium-range ballistic missiles, apparently with assistance from China and North Korea. In 1997 Pakistan may have conducted a test launch of its 600-km-range Hatf-3 missile, which is believed to be based on Chinese technology. In April 1998 it flight-tested a missile, the Ghauri, that has been reported to have a range of 1,500 km but may actually be considerably less, perhaps 700 to 1,100 km.[18] It is believed that the Ghauri too is based on the North Korean Nodong missile.[19] A follow-on, the Ghaznavi (sometimes spelled Ghanzi), with double the range of the Ghauri, may be under development as well. Pakistan is also reported to be developing two medium-range solid-fuel ballistic missiles, the Shaheen-1, with a range of 700 km, and the Shaheen-2, with a range of 2,100 km.[20] Neither has been flight-tested, and their status is unknown.

Before the possible transfer of Nodong missiles by North Korea to Pakistan (and it is unclear if entire missiles or just technology was transferred), the only transfer of missiles with ranges greater than 600 km (excluding U.S. sales of submarine-launched ballistic missiles to Britain) was China's sale in 1988 of 3,000-km-range DF-3 missiles to Saudi Arabia. This sale contributed to efforts to strengthen antiproliferation measures such as the Missile Technology Control Regime (MTCR). Aside from the five declared nuclear nations and as noted earlier, Saudi Arabia and possibly North Korea, the only other countries possessing missiles or space launchers with ranges greater than about 1,000 km are Japan, Israel, and India.[21]

The missiles we have described are primarily a concern to the United States because they could threaten U.S. forces deployed abroad or the cities of U.S. allies and because they might represent steps toward developing missiles with intercontinental ranges. There is no currently deployed ICBM outside of the charter nuclear weapon states that is able to reach the U.S. homeland. A November 1995 national intelligence estimate (NIE) concluded that there is

17. Vivek Raghuvanshi, "India to Prepare Nuclear Doctrine, Arsenal for Deployment," *Defense News*, vol. 13 (June 1–7, 1998), p. 14.

18. David C. Wright, "An Analysis of the Pakistani Ghauri Missile Test of April 6, 1988," *Science and Global Security*, vol. 7 (1998), pp. 227–36.

19. Tim Weiner, "U.S. Says N. Korea Helped Develop New Pakistani Missile," *New York Times*, April 11, 1998, p. 3.

20. Umer Farooq, "Pakistan Needs Up to 70 Nuclear Warheads," *Jane's Defence Weekly*, June 10, 1998, p. 3.

21. Gronlund and Wright, "Threat Assessment Part A," pp. 16–21.

little chance that a third-world ICBM threat to the contiguous forty-eight United States would develop in the next fifteen years.[22] Although this estimate was criticized by some congressional missile defense advocates as being politicized, a congressionally mandated independent review panel "found no evidence of politicization and is completely satisfied that the analysts' views were based on the evidence before them and their substantive analysis." The review panel, headed by former Director of Central Intelligence Robert M. Gates, concluded that the authors of the NIE could have made an even stronger case for their findings than they actually did.[23]

In contrast, the congressionally established Rumsfeld Commission to Assess the Ballistic Missile Threat, in a report released in July 1998, argued that the ballistic missile threat was "broader, more mature, and evolving more rapidly than has been reported in estimates and reports by the intelligence community."[24] The report raised the possibility that within five years of deciding to do so Iran or North Korea might be able to develop and deploy a missile capable of reaching the United States. The report further argued that the warning times of new missile threats were being reduced and that under certain circumstances the United States might have little or no warning of the deployment of a missile threat. But following the release of the Rumsfeld report, the intelligence community reiterated that it stood by its assessment and that "it remains the view of the [intelligence community] that it is unlikely that countries other than Russia, China, and perhaps North Korea will deploy an ICBM capable of reaching any part of the U.S. before 2010."[25]

The only currently deployed ballistic missile threat to the U.S. homeland is a deliberate attack or an accidental or unauthorized launch by Russia or China. However, the long-range missile capabilities of a number of potentially hostile developing countries are gradually increasing, and a missile

22. The estimate is available on-line at http://www.fas.org/spp/congress/ 1996_hr/s961204p.htm (on the Federation of American Scientists' Star Wars homepage, maintained by John Pike).

23. The panel's report stated, "But, based on our investigation and study of relevant documents, perhaps the most serious deficiency is that the Intelligence Community's conclusions in the NIE with respect to the intercontinental ballistic missile threat to the United States are based on a stronger evidentiary and technical case than was presented in the Estimate." The unclassified version of the review panel's report is available on the Federation of American Scientists' homepage at http://www.fas.org/irp/threat/missile/oca961908.htm.

24. "Executive Summary," *Report of the Commission to Assess the Ballistic Missile Threat to the United States*. The summary is available on-line at http://www.fas.org/irp/threat/bm-threat.htm.

25. "Ballistic Missile Threat and U.S. Policy," July 14, 1998. Available on-line at http://www.fas.org/irp/news/1998/07/980714-threat.htm.

threat to U.S. territory from one of them could develop in the next decade. With the end of the cold war, a deliberate Russian attack is generally not regarded as a serious threat. However, concerns are sometimes raised that China might threaten such an attack if a military conflict arose over Taiwan.[26] As discussed in chapter 7, China has at most twenty long-range missiles capable of reaching U.S. territory. However, they are apparently maintained unfueled and without warheads, and as long as this remains the case, there is no danger of an accidental or unauthorized launch.[27] Conditions in Russia have raised concern that the danger of an accidental or unauthorized Russian launch may be growing. The scale of such a launch could range from a single ICBM warhead to a 200-warhead launch from a Typhoon SSBN to an even larger launch resulting from a failure of Russia's early warning system or a breakdown at the highest levels of the Russian command.

The U.S. National Missile Defense Program

The Republican-controlled U.S. Congress has pushed for a decision to deploy a national missile defense system by a fixed date. The 1996 Defense Authorization Bill passed in December 1995 would have required the deployment of a nationwide defense by 2003. Primarily because of its missile defense provisions, the bill was vetoed by President Clinton. The so-called Defend America Act, introduced by Senate and House leaders in March 1996, similarly would have required deployment of a nationwide system by 2003. Faced with a presidential veto as well as an estimate by the Congressional Budget Office that the deployment and operation of the defense called for could cost up to $116 billion, the act was never brought to a vote.[28] Similarly, the National Missile Defense Act of 1997, which also required deployment by 2003, was never brought to a vote. But Congress continues to push: a bill that would require the deployment of a national missile defense "as soon as technologically possible" twice failed by a single vote in the Senate in 1998.

The Clinton administration's position has been that there is no threat justifying the deployment of a national missile defense system, but under con-

26. Barton Gellman, "U.S. and China Nearly Came to Blows," *Washington Post*, June 21, 1998, p. 1.

27. Walter Pincus, "U.S., China May Retarget Nuclear Weapons," *Washington Post*, June 16, 1998, p. 10.

28. For an analysis of why congressional Republican efforts to force the deployment of a nationwide system by 2003 have so far failed, see Joseph Cirincione, "Why the Right Lost the Missile Defense Debate," *Foreign Policy* (Spring 1997), pp. 39–55.

tinuing pressure from Congress it developed a "3 + 3" plan for national missile defense that it describes as moving the United States over a period of three years from a technology readiness program to a deployment readiness program.[29] Under this plan a thin NMD system (that is, a system intended to deal with only small-scale attacks) would be developed by 2000 and could be deployed in an additional three years if a decision was made that a threat justifying deployment had arisen. If after the first three years of the program a decision to deploy was not made, development and testing would continue so that the United States would maintain a capability to deploy a thin NMD system within three years. Concerns have been expressed, however, that the tight timelines required under the 3 + 3 plan either cannot be met or will result in the deployment of an inadequately tested system.[30]

The deployment of an NMD system that can cover only part of the United States is politically implausible. Thus the 3 + 3 plan and other proposed thin NMD architectures are designed to provide coverage of the entire country, including Alaska and Hawaii. In an attempt to avoid a direct conflict with the ABM Treaty, NMD supporters have claimed that because the 3 + 3 system and other similar architectures would deploy at most one hundred interceptors at single site, they are permitted by the treaty. However, to achieve nationwide coverage, all these architectures require placing sensors at multiple locations or in space to obtain needed target tracking information and are thus illegal. A defense of the entire United States, whether from a single site or multiple sites, is banned by the ABM Treaty. To deploy a nationwide NMD system, the United States must either successfully renegotiate the treaty or violate or withdraw from it.

The 3 + 3 program would initially deploy about twenty very-high-speed (greater than 7 km per second) ground-based interceptors in Alaska or at the former U.S. Safeguard missile defense site near Grand Forks, North Dakota.[31] Intercept tests for the interceptor kill vehicle as well as an integrated test of the entire NMD system are to take place in 1999. The number of interceptors could be increased to one hundred. It may be technically

29. "National Missile Defense Program Evolution," *Ballistic Missile Defense Organization Fact Sheet* JN-98-04 (March 1998).

30. Bradley Graham, "Review of Missile Defense Programs Follows Warning of 'Rush to Failure,'" *Washington Post*, March 25, 1998, p. 5.

31. The Safeguard system was built in the early 1970s as the single-site strategic defense system permitted under the ABM Treaty to protect a nearby ICBM launcher field. Safeguard briefly became operational before being closed down because its limited effectiveness was not judged to justify its cost of operation.

feasible for such high-speed interceptors at a single site to cover all fifty states against an attack by full-range ICBMs. However, a single-site system cannot defend against missiles launched by offshore submarines or ships because of the potentially very short flight times. If interceptors were based at multiple sites, better coverage against off-shore missiles would be possible, although more interceptors would be required for a given level of coverage because each interceptor site would have to be capable of meeting the full threat. Such an expansion to a multiple-site system is a future "evolutionary option" for the 3 + 3 defense.

The primary sensor for the 3 + 3 program is ground-based radar (GBR), which will be deployed at the same site as the interceptors. To overcome the limitations imposed by the earth's curvature, current plans envision the use of either upgraded early warning radars or new large X-band phased-array radars to provide tracking information on attacking missiles that are not visible to the GBR.

The planned deployment of the low-earth-orbit component of the Space-Based Infrared System (SBIRS-LOW) (formerly known as the Space and Missile Tracking System and before that as Brilliant Eyes) will also provide the capability to track missile targets that are out of view of ground-based radar. SBIRS-LOW satellites will be placed in low earth orbits so as to be able to detect warm warheads against the cold background of space. They could in fact provide tracking information adequate for interceptor guidance completely independent of the GBR network (and thus could not only supplement but actually replace the national missile defense system's ground-based sensors). SBIRS-LOW is also intended to support U.S. theater missile defense systems and will be able to provide tracking data for exoatmospheric TMD systems deployed anywhere in the world. Deployment of SBIRS-LOW is scheduled to begin in 2004.[32]

The U.S. Theater Missile Defense Program

The Clinton administration has declared theater missile defense to be its top missile defense priority and is vigorously pursuing a range of systems.[33] These

32. Statement of Paul G. Kaminski to the House Committee on National Security, Subcommittee on Military Research and Development and Subcommittee on Military Procurement, 105 Cong. 1 sess., May 15, 1997.

33. Office of the Assistant Secretary of Defense (Public Affairs), DoD News Briefing, Secretary of Defense William J. Perry, February 16, 1996.

Table 5-2. Primary U.S. Theater Missile Defense Programs

System	Description	Intercept
Patriot PAC-3	Major upgrade of Patriot PAC-2 used in Gulf War. Uses new interceptor missile, the PAC-3	Endoatmospheric
Navy Area	Modifies Aegis air defense system on U.S. Navy ships to give it some capability against short-range missiles	Endoatmospheric
MEADS	Joint U.S.-European program to protect troops in the field from short-range missile threats. Replaces Hawk	Endoatmospheric
THAAD	U.S. Army system to defend large areas from missiles with ranges up to 3,500 km	Exoatmospheric
Navy Theater Wide	High-altitude, wide-area system based on Navy Aegis ships	Exoatmospheric
Airborne Laser	Megawatt-class laser on a Boeing 747 airliner. Range of 300–500 km	Boost phase

Source: David E. Mosher, "The Grand Plans," *IEEE Spectrum* (September 1997), pp. 28–39.

include endoatmospheric (that is, intercepting within the atmosphere) lower-tier systems that are intended to protect relatively small areas against relatively short-range missiles. These systems are the Patriot PAC-3 (ERINT), the Navy Area Defense system, and the Medium Extended Air Defense System (MEADS). The major U.S. theater missile defense systems are summarized in table 5-2.

The Patriot PAC-3 is an extensive upgrade to the Patriot system, which was unable to intercept successfully the Iraqi Al-Hussein missiles during the 1991 Gulf War, primarily because of the inadvertent breakups and resulting unpredictable maneuvers of the Iraqi missiles during their reentry.[34] In the PAC-3 upgrade, the original Patriot missile with its high-explosive warhead will be replaced by a new and much more maneuverable hit-to-kill missile. The Navy's Area Defense system (formerly known as Navy Lower Tier) involves modifying the Standard antiaircraft missiles and Aegis radars on its Aegis cruisers and Arleigh Burke destroyers to enable them to intercept relatively short range theater ballistic missiles. MEADS, a system being developed in cooperation with several western European countries, is intended to be a highly mobile system that would be able to accompany forces in the field and provide 360° coverage against short-range missile threats.

34. George N. Lewis and Theodore A. Postol, "Video Evidence on the Effectiveness of Patriot during the 1991 Gulf War," *Science and Global Security*, vol. 4, no. 1 (1993), pp. 1–64.

All three programs are intended to protect relatively small areas (with dimensions measured in tens of kilometers) against relatively short-range theater ballistic missiles. The maximum distance of the missile threats these systems are intended to counter has not been publicly stated but is probably 1,000–1,500 km.[35] The systems appear to be true TMD systems, with little or no effectiveness against strategic ballistic missiles, and their deployment does not appear to pose any significant problems for future reductions in strategic forces. The Clinton administration has stated that to put greater missile defense capabilities into the field as soon as possible, Patriot PAC-3 and Navy Area Defense will be its top theater missile defense priorities.[36]

The missile defense program also includes two theaterwide area defenses, the army's Theater High Altitude Area Defense (THAAD) System and the navy's Theater Wide System (formerly known as the Navy Upper Tier System). Both are designed to intercept targets above or in the upper layers of the atmosphere (that is, they are exoatmospheric), and are intended to protect areas with dimensions of hundreds of kilometers from attacks by missiles with ranges up to about 3,500 km.

The THAAD system, designed to be air transportable, has been the central element of the administration's wide-area TMD program. As currently designed, the system's hit-to-kill interceptor guided by infrared sensor would have a peak speed of about 2.6 km per second and would make intercepts at altitudes ranging from the upper layers of the atmosphere (20–40 km is a reasonable estimate) up to more than 100 km. Until recently plans called for a single prototype THAAD User Operational Evaluation System (UOES) battery, consisting of about two radars and forty missiles, to become available for field testing, and overseas deployment if needed, by 2001, with full-scale deployment to begin about 2006. However, in the first five THAAD intercept tests, the most recent of which was in May 1998, the interceptor failed to hit its target.[37] These failures will certainly delay deployment and have thrown the future of the system into doubt.

The Navy Theater Wide system, like the Navy Area Defense system, will

35. The upper limit of target ranges against which these systems can be expected to have a significant capability is determined by the reentry speed of the target missile, which increases with the missile's range. All else being equal, a greater reentry speed will decrease the defense's response time, increase the intercept closing speed, and possibly lead to greater target maneuverability in the atmosphere.

36. Prepared Statement of General Joseph W. Ralston, vice chairman, Joint Chiefs of Staff, before the Senate Armed Services Committee, 105 Cong. 2 sess., October 2, 1998.

37. Bradley Graham, "Antimissile Test Yields 5th Failure in a Row," *Washington Post*, May 13, 1998, p. 1.

Box 5-1. Boost-Phase Defenses

The United States is also investigating defenses that can intercept theater ballistic missiles in their boost phase because a missile armed with conventional, chemical, or biological weapons could have its payload packaged as small submunitions that could be released immediately after the end of the missile's boost phase. Such a simple step would defeat all of the terminal TMD systems discussed here simply by overwhelming them. The leading boost-phase concept at the moment is the air force's airborne laser, which would deploy a megawatt-class laser on a Boeing 747 airliner.[1] Other boost-phase approaches being investigated include space-based lasers and interceptor missiles carried on unpiloted aircraft. All of these systems currently under consideration would have at least a theoretical capability against strategic missiles whose launch locations were predictable to within several hundred kilometers. Their potential against Russian SLBMs deployed on submarines in their "bastion" deployment areas could, therefore, raise ABM Treaty compliance concerns.

1. See Geoffrey E. Forden, "'The Airborne' Laser," *IEEE Spectrum*, September 1997, pp. 40–49.

be built around Aegis-equipped ships. However, Navy Theater Wide will use a much higher speed exoatmospheric interceptor, most likely a Standard missile with an extra booster stage and a Lightweight Exo-Atmospheric Projectile (LEAP) kill vehicle, with a peak speed of about 4.5 km per second. Navy Theater Wide will not be able to intercept as low in the atmosphere as THAAD and will only be able to intercept targets at altitudes above about 80–100 km.[38] Navy Theater Wide is not as far along in development as THAAD, and its deployment schedule is still uncertain. The earliest deployment date for the production version appears to be about 2007.

38. The minimum intercept altitude for both the THAAD interceptor and Navy Theater Wide's LEAP kill vehicle is likely set by atmospheric heating of the windows of their infrared seekers, which can blind the seekers. The higher minimum intercept altitude for Navy Theater Wide presumably is due to LEAP's having a less effective system for protecting its window from heating as well as the higher speed of the Navy Theater Wide's interceptor. In addition, however, the LEAP kill vehicle is not aerodynamically shaped and would be unstable in an atmospheric of any significant density.

The 1997 TMD Demarcation Agreement

Both THAAD and Navy Theater Wide are based on the same technologies that would be used in ground-based nationwide missile defense systems, and both will use interceptors with inherent strategic capabilities. In fact, Navy Theater Wide supporters have specifically called for using it as the basis for a national missile defense system.[39] Both systems raise serious concerns with respect to the ABM Treaty's prohibition on giving TMD systems capabilities to counter strategic missiles. Although the Clinton administration initially stated that the deployment of THAAD would require agreement by Russia on changing the treaty, it later declared that both the testing and deployment of THAAD and Navy Theater Wide were fully compliant with the treaty.[40] At the same time, the administration launched negotiations with the Russians aimed at changing the ABM Treaty so that the deployment of systems such as THAAD and Navy Theater Wide Treaty would be clearly compliant.

These TMD demarcation negotiations to allow more capable defense systems began with a U.S. proposal in late 1993 that any missile defense sys-

39. For example, see David Hughes, "Former SDIO Leaders Back Navy Upper Tier," *Aviation Week and Space Technology*, June 19, 1995 (the "Former SDIO Leaders" are among the authors of *Defending America: A Near- and Long-Term Plan to Deploy Missile Defenses* (Washington: Heritage Foundation, 1995), which advocated using Navy Theater Wide as the basis of a rapidly deployable NMD system); and Elaine M. Grossman and Thomas Duffy, "BMDO Briefs Capitol Hill on Sea-Based National Missile Defense Concept," *Inside Missile Defense*, May 1, 1996, p. 1.

40. In late 1993 and early 1994 a wide range of administration officials stated that THAAD could not be tested or deployed unless an agreement on modifying the ABM Treaty was reached with Russia. However, as it became apparent that Russian agreement was not going to be forthcoming and the planned date of the first THAAD test approached, the U.S. administration changed its position to one in which testing of THAAD could begin but deployment was still illegal. Finally, in mid-1996, with no sign of an agreement with the Russians in sight, the United States simply declared THAAD to be fully treaty compliant. See George Lewis, "The ABM Treaty and the Future of Arms Control and Non-Proliferation," *Breakthroughs*, MIT Security Studies Program (Spring 1996), pp. 11–18. The administration's position on Navy Theater Wide has always been that it is compliant and that it has absolutely no capability to intercept strategic missiles. According to then Deputy Defense Secretary John Deutch, "Since the Upper Tier System [as Navy Theater Wide was then called], as built, has no capability against a strategic ballistic missile, it is not covered by the ABM Treaty, and you can build as many of them as you want without reference to the ABM Treaty, and that's the position of our department" (Bill Gertz, "Navy Missile Defense Shouldn't Be Issue in Talks; Deutch Asserts Upper Tier Legal under ABM Treaty," *Washington Times*, April 14, 1995, p. 3). This conclusion apparently was based on an assessment that Navy Theater Wide's radar would be unable to detect a strategic target in time to intercept it before it reached Navy Theater Wide's minimum intercept altitude.

tem that was not tested against a target with a maximum speed greater than 5 km per second (corresponding to a range of about 3,500 km) would be defined to be a TMD system and not limited in any way by the treaty. Russia appeared to be willing to accept this U.S. proposal but insisted on an additional limit of 3 km per second on the maximum interceptor speed. This limit would have allowed THAAD but would have prohibited Navy Theater Wide and possibly some types of boost-phase systems. The United States was unwilling to accept this limit, and the talks deadlocked for several years. With no agreement in sight the Clinton administration made it clear that it would make its own judgments on ABM Treaty compliance and that the absence of a Theater Missile Defense Demarcation Agreement would not prevent it from proceeding with its planned TMD systems.

Following the March 1997 Clinton-Yeltsin summit in Helsinki, it was announced that Russia had essentially accepted the U.S. position and agreed that TMD systems would comply with the treaty as long as they were not tested against targets with speeds greater than 5 km per second or ranges greater than 3,500 km, clearing the way for both THAAD and Navy Theater Wide.[41] A formal TMD Demarcation Agreement was signed in September 1997. This agreement actually consisted of several related agreements, including separate ones covering low-speed systems (with interceptor speeds not greater than 3 km per second) and high-speed systems (interceptor speeds greater than 3 km per second) and an agreement on confidence-building measures (box 5-2).[42] Both the high- and low-speed agreements stated that legal TMD systems could not be tested against targets with a speed greater than 5 km per second or with a range greater than 3,500 km. The lower-speed agreement unambiguously declared that missile defense systems with interceptor speeds no greater than 3 km per second would be legal as long as they obeyed this test target speed limit.

However, the higher-speed agreement reflected the inability of the two countries to come to agreement about higher-speed systems and only said

---

41. Thomas W. Lippman, "Clinton, Yeltsin Agree on Broad Arms Cuts," *Washington Post*, March 24, 1997, p. 1. The text of the summit statement is reprinted in *Arms Control Today*, March 1997, p. 20.

42. The demarcation agreement also included a memorandum of understanding stating that the parties to the treaty will be the United States, Russia, Ukraine, Kazakhstan, and Belarus and provided for an exchange of (nonbinding) statements regarding plans to conduct certain types of tests. The text of the demarcation agreements, other related agreements, and State Department fact sheets and press releases are available on the Internet at http://www.acda.gov/missdef1.htm. For an analysis of the TMD Demarcation Agreement, see Lisbeth Gronlund, "ABM: Just Kicking the Can," *Bulletin of the Atomic Scientists*, vol. 54 (January-February 1998), pp. 15–16.

Box 5-2. Confidence-Building Measures in the
1997 TMD Demarcation Agreement

The TMD Demarcation Agreement also included an agreement on confidence-building measures.[1] These measures apply to higher-speed systems (in the U.S. case, THAAD and Navy Theater Wide) and require declaration of test ranges where interceptor launches will take place and notification of interceptor test flights in which a target is used. Each party also committed to provide "assurances that it will not deploy systems subject to this Agreement in numbers and locations so that these systems could pose a realistic threat to the strategic nuclear force of another Party." These assurances are to include an assessment of each missile defense program with respect to the ballistic missile threat; some technical details on each system, such as maximum radar power-aperture product and the dimensions of interceptor missiles; information on the general concept of operations of each defense system; the status of plans and operations; and for systems being tested, the number of units each country plans to possess. The agreement also states that any party could voluntarily release any other information or arrange demonstrations of its systems or components.

The agreement on higher-speed systems states that among the principles that served as a basis for the agreement are that the high-speed defenses deployed by one country will not pose a realistic threat to the strategic nuclear force of the other country, that they will not be deployed for use against the other country, and that the scale of deployments in terms of number and geographic scope will be consistent with the theater missile threat facing the country.

Although these agreements may be useful as political statements, they in no way limit the capability of the higher-speed TMD systems or, given the great mobility of these systems, the ways they could be used.

1. "Agreement on Confidence-Building Measures Related to Systems to Counter Ballistic Missiles Other than Strategic Ballistic Missiles," September 26, 1997; http://www.acda.gov/factshee/missdef/abm_cbm.htm.

that systems with interceptor speeds above 3 km per second that obey the test target speed limit would be subject to consultations and discussions, thereby setting the stage for future disputes. Although Russia will almost certainly interpret this statement as requiring mutual agreement on the deployment of higher-speed systems, the United States immediately announced that determining the compliance of a high-speed system will be a unilateral national decision.[43] The high-speed agreement also stated as a "principle" underlying the agreement that the permitted TMD systems may be deployed as long as they do not "pose a realistic threat to the strategic nuclear force of another Party and which will not be tested to give such systems that capability," reflecting U.S. interest in moving to a "force-on-force" criterion for assessing treaty compliance.[44]

Although the signing of the TMD Demarcation Agreement may have removed one of the primary obstacles to Russia's ratification of START II, it also severely weakens the ABM Treaty. It eliminates the treaty's prohibition on giving a TMD system capabilities to intercept strategic missiles, replacing it with a very weak limitation on the speed of targets it can be tested against.[45] In fact, at least under the U.S. interpretation of this agreement, there are no limits whatsoever on the capabilities of any system defined as a TMD system by these criteria. The only limit on the overall capability of a defense would be the highly ambiguous force-on-force criterion that it not pose a realistic threat to the other party's entire nuclear force. This criterion represents not only a very serious weakening of the treaty but creates a potential source of disputes over what constitutes a "realistic threat."

Effectiveness of Defenses

The effectiveness of any ballistic missile defense system will depend primarily on its ability to deal with countermeasures employed by the attacking missiles as well as with any unexpected natural variability in the targets. The primary concern here is with countermeasures that operate outside the atmosphere because national missile defense systems, as well as advanced wide-area TMD systems such as THAAD and Navy Theater Wide, will attempt to intercept their targets above the atmosphere. A wide range of potentially very effective countermeasures (only a few of which will be men-

43. U.S. Department of State, Office of the Spokesman, "Fact Sheet: Second Agreed Statement of September 26, 1997, Relating to the ABM Treaty," September 26, 1997.

44. http://www.acda.gov/factshee/missdef/abm_scc2.htm.

45. For a discussion of why this test target speed limit does not pose a significant barrier to the development of TMD systems able to intercept strategic missile warheads, see Lisbeth Gronlund and others, "Highly Capable Theater Missile Defenses and the ABM Treaty," *Arms Control Today* (April 1994), pp. 3–8, and George Lewis and Theodore Postol, "Portrait of a Bad Idea," *Bulletin of the Atomic Scientists* (July-August 1997).

tioned here) are available to defeat such defenses.[46] Exoatmospheric defenses' vulnerability to countermeasures has long been recognized as their greatest weakness; there is no reason to expect this situation to change.[47]

Although certain types of exoatmospheric countermeasures could defeat a defense by causing its interceptors to miss their target, many simply aim to prevent the defense from identifying the target until it is too late to intercept. Most of these techniques rely on the fact that in the vacuum of space, very light objects and heavy objects travel on identical trajectories. As a result, at the end of its boost phase an attacking missile could deploy large numbers of lightweight decoys such as metalized balloons. These balloons could be replica decoys shaped to mimic the actual warhead, or more likely and probably more effectively would be spherical balloons, with the real warhead enclosed in an identical balloon. The balloons could be equipped with small heaters and other devices to prevent the defense from using thermal, vibrational, or rotational signatures to identify the balloon containing the warhead. The defense would be unable to identify the real target until it reentered the atmosphere and the lightweight decoys were rapidly decelerated by air resistance, at which point it could be too late to make an intercept.

Another example, but still potentially effective, countermeasure against missile defense radars would be for the missile to deploy clouds of chaff and hide the warhead in one of these clouds. Such chaff would consist of inch-long pieces of wire or metal-coated glass.[48] Depending on its orientation relative to the radar, each piece of chaff could have a radar cross-section comparable to that of a warhead properly shaped to reduce radar reflections. Because a pound of chaff could contain millions of chaff strands, an attacking missile could deploy many chaff clouds, only one of which would

46. For a more detailed description of some of these countermeasures, see George N. Lewis and Theodore A. Postol, "Future Challenges to Ballistic Missile Defenses," *IEEE Spectrum* (September 1997), pp. 60–68.

47. Richard L. Garwin and Hans A. Bethe, "Anti-Ballistic-Missile Systems," *Scientific American*, vol. 218 (March 1968), pp. 19, 21–31, with supplemental material printed in May 1968, pp. 7–8.

48. The figures cited in this paragraph assume a radar operating in the X-band frequency range at roughly 10 GHz. Both the THAAD TMD radar and the NMD radar the United States is currently developing will operate in the X band; see Lewis and Postol, "Future Challenges to Ballistic Missile Defenses." For maximum effect, pieces of chaff should be cut to a length equal to one-half the radar wavelength, in this case 1.5 centimeters, or about 0.6 inches. If used against early warning radars, chaff could be even more effective because of the relatively poor resolution and discrimination capabilities of these radars, which operate at frequencies of 450 MHz. Although the chaff strands would have to be longer (about 13 inches), they would also have a greater radar cross-section because the radar cross-section of a tuned chaff strand is proportional to the square of its length.

contain the warhead, thereby preventing the defense from locating the warhead until the atmosphere stripped away the chaff.

An alternative would be to reduce the signatures of the warhead so that the defense would be unable to detect it in time to intercept. Both the radar cross-section and the thermal signature of the warhead could be greatly reduced by enclosing it in a thin metal shroud with a pointed nose and rounded back end, which could be cooled using a small quantity of liquid nitrogen.[49]

Such simple countermeasures, which could certainly be implemented by any country capable of building a long-range ballistic missile, could be used to defeat an NMD or exoatmospheric TMD system.[50] Thus any country deploying such a defense system is unlikely to be able to attain any significant degree of confidence that the system will be able to protect it reliably.

Defenses that operate within the atmosphere, such as Patriot PAC-3, can generally wait until the atmosphere has filtered out any exoatmospheric countermeasures (at least against the relatively slow, shorter-range missiles these systems are generally intended to counter). However, these systems too are vulnerable to countermeasures. For attacks using conventional high explosive, chemical, or biological weapons, dividing the payload of the missile into submunitions can defeat any terminal or midcourse defense (including exoatmospheric ones) simply by overwhelming it. For missiles armed with nuclear warheads, which cannot be subdivided beyond a certain point, the most important countermeasure against defenses that operate in the atmosphere is likely to be intentional atmospheric maneuvers. These could be similar to or even more vigorous than the inadvertent maneuvers, such as the corkscrew reentry trajectories, that enabled Iraq's Al-Hussein missiles to defeat Patriot PAC-2s during the 1991 Gulf War. Such maneuvers

49. Shaping to reduce the radar cross-section would not be effective at the long wavelengths used by current early warning radars. If early warning radars were the primary concern, the radar cross-section of the warhead could be greatly reduced simply by enclosing it in a plastic bag filled with radar absorbing foam. This bag would be destroyed on reentry, but by then its mission would be accomplished.

50. So severe are the difficulties posed by such countermeasures that during the era of the Strategic Defense Initiative interactive discrimination techniques, such as space-based particle beams, were seriously raised as being necessary to address this problem. (For a technical discussion of the feasibility of such interactive discrimination, see the American Physical Society's Directed Energy Weapons Study: N. Bloembergen and C.K.N. Patel, and others, "Report to the American Physical Society of the Study Group on the Physics and Technology of Directed Energy Weapons," *Reviews of Modern Physics*, vol. 59, No. 3, part II (July 1987), pp. S156-S169.) Such vastly expensive and technically questionable approaches will certainly play no role in the more modest NMD systems now under consideration.

Box 5-3. Cruise Missiles

The deployment of a national ballistic missile defense will not defend U.S. territory against cruise missiles. The Gates Panel review of the November 1995 national intelligence estimate on the ballistic missile threat to the United States stated, "By contrast, the Panel believes the Estimate did not give nearly enough attention to the potential for land-attack cruise missiles launched from within several hundred miles of U.S. territory." Similarly, the Rumsfeld Commission, while it did not examine the cruise missile threat in detail, concluded that "cruise missiles have a number of characteristics which could be seen as increasingly valuable in fulfilling the aspirations of emerging ballistic missile states."[1] The widespread availability of Global Positioning System data greatly simplifies what is probably the most difficult problem of developing such cruise missiles, that of guidance.[2] In addition, cruise missiles are likely to be much more effective as a means of dispersing chemical and biological weapons than ballistic missiles.

1. "Executive Summary," *Report of the Commission to Assess the Ballistic Missile Threat to the United States.* The summary is available on-line at http://www.fas.org/irp/threat/bm-threat.htm.
2. For a general discussion of the cruise missile threat (and possible responses to it), see Dennis M. Gormley, "Hedging Against the Cruise Missile Threat," *Survival* (Spring 1998), pp. 92–111.

may be difficult to counter, but in contrast to the situation with exoatmospheric countermeasures, at least it is clear to the defense designer what steps, such as increasing the maneuverability of the interceptor, must be taken to deal with this situation.

Finally, it is important to remember, particularly in the context of national missile defense, that even a perfect defense does not end the threat posed by nuclear weapons. There are many ways—by air, sea, and ground—that a determined nation or even subnational group could deliver a nuclear weapon into U.S. territory. An intercontinental ballistic missile, which involves significant technical difficulties and leaves a clear "return address" for retaliation, may not even be high on the list of preferred delivery means.

The Compatibility of Missile Defenses and Nuclear Reductions

During the cold war the ABM Treaty's constraints on strategic ballistic missile defenses enabled agreements to limit and eventually reduce strategic offensive forces. Has the end of the cold war broken this connection between limits on defenses and offensive reductions?

Although there have been many changes, two fundamental facts have not changed: nuclear deterrence remains the policy underlying the nuclear security policy and nuclear forces of all five charter nuclear nations, and ballistic missiles and the nuclear weapons they carry remain central to the nuclear arsenals of these nations. Until this situation changes, the United States and Russia will be unwilling to reduce their ballistic missile forces if they believe that doing so could allow missile defenses to threaten the deterrent capabilities of these forces. Acting otherwise would require, for example, that Russia accept that a U.S. defense deployment could potentially nullify its strategic deterrent. This would not be acceptable to Russia (or to the United States if the circumstances were reversed) and would lead to Russian efforts to boost the capabilities of its offensive forces to ensure that a retaliatory attack could defeat the defense. This is precisely the situation the ABM Treaty was intended to prevent. And it is apparently the reason Russian officials have repeatedly linked ratification of START II and the implementation of both START I and II to continued U.S. adherence to the ABM Treaty.

This lack of fundamental change in deterrence does not mean that reductions will be impossible if any defenses are deployed. Missile defenses and offensive nuclear reductions can be compatible as long as the defenses are limited enough that they are not considered threatening to the reducing countries' deterrent capabilities.

The true effectiveness of a defense system will be determined primarily by its ability to deal with countermeasures, and potentially very effective countermeasures must be expected to be present if defenses are deployed. But even defenses that to their deployer might not appear to have much capability could still undermine confidence in deterrence. Military planners in countries that believe they might have to face defenses that can counter strategic missiles will analyze whether and under what conditions the defenses could reduce the retaliatory capability of their strategic nuclear forces below levels that they believe are required for deterrence. Assessing the potential impact of defenses on the retaliatory capability of nuclear forces is a complicated task filled with both technical and policy ambiguities. The findings of such analyses would almost certainly result in widely varying and often inflated estimates of the capabilities of defenses, both because their effectiveness is difficult to assess reliably in advance and because attackers and defenders will form very different assessments. Analytical uncertainties can be exploited by bureaucracies and other organizations with vested interests to overstate the threats posed by defenses. This can in turn have an important effect on the ability of political leaders to engage in further reductions in strategic nuclear forces.

These circumstances indicate that although it will be difficult for the defender to have great confidence in the effectiveness of its defense, countries facing such a defense are likely to overrate its capabilities. Even if technical analysts could agree on the capabilities of defense deployments, political reactions may not reflect actualities. In addition, deployment of a thin defense could set up the infrastructure that would allow a rapid breakout to a thick defense. Thus a defense must be judged based not only on its current capabilities but on its potential for future upgrades and expansions. Even though a U.S. NMD system may not be intended to counter Russian strategic offensive forces, Russian analysts will without doubt view it in terms of its current and possible future potential to intercept their strategic missiles. Given conservative assessments by each side, a U.S. NMD system that is viewed by its deployers as hopelessly inadequate against a deliberate Russian attack could easily be seen by Russia as a serious threat to its nuclear retaliatory deterrent.

If the U.S. deployment of missile defenses is not to provoke Russian reluctance to proceed with further offensive nuclear force reductions, Russia must be convinced that these systems do not threaten its retaliatory capability. Russia must also believe that the defenses could not be rapidly expanded to a level at which they could threaten Russian retaliatory capabilities sooner than Russia could effectively respond. In the next two sections we consider the extent to which U.S. national and theater missile defenses systems currently being developed might be able to meet these criteria.

Limited U.S. National Missile Defenses and Russia

The primary focus of U.S. national missile defense activities is no longer a large-scale, deliberate attack by Russia. In addition, many of the threats that advocates of a national missile defense now cite would involve relatively few warheads. Could a thin NMD system be deployed to counter such smaller threats without interfering with U.S.-Russian strategic reductions and future deep cuts?

After the START II reductions, Russia could in principle field enough survivable forces to overwhelm a thin U.S. NMD system even following a U.S. first strike. This conclusion probably would not be much changed even by reductions to force levels well below those of START II. Russia might be unhappy, however, about the cost of keeping a significant part of its forces out of port or garrison and might instead choose to increase the number of its survivable warheads by keeping mobile missiles in garrisons and SLBMs in port ready to launch on warning, actions contrary to one of the crucial objectives advocated in this book.

More important, Russia may balk at further reductions because of the potential for a thin NMD system to be rapidly expanded. The Defend America Act of 1996, although not enacted, called for the initial defense to be "augmented over time to provide a layered defense against larger and more sophisticated ballistic missile threats as they emerge." Even the less aggressive approach to national missile defense advocated by the Clinton administration envisions the deployment of more interceptors and sensors at multiple sites as possible "evolutionary options" for its NMD program.

Any nationwide defense system, even a very thin one, will provide most or all of the infrastructure and testing needed for a thicker system. In particular, it will provide the needed sensor capabilities, which have always been regarded as the long lead time element of a strategic missile defense (although some of these sensor capabilities, particularly modified early warning radars on the U.S. periphery, may be quite vulnerable to attack). For the NMD system now being developed by the United States, this will be particularly true once the SBIRS-LOW space-based tracking system has been deployed. The time required to convert a thin NMD system to a thicker one could be very short, potentially much shorter than the time it would take for Russian strategic offensive forces to be reconstituted.

The deeper offensive reductions become, the more serious the problem of defense breakout. Steps that might accompany deep reductions of nuclear offensive forces, such as the required destruction of reduced nuclear warheads and even more the disposal of the fissile material they contain, could further extend the offensive buildup time and make defensive breakout a more severe problem.

Such considerations would almost certainly cause Russian planners to be cautious about reducing their offensive forces in the presence of even a limited U.S. NMD system. Would Russia's Galosh ABM system at Moscow similarly cause U.S. concern about reducing its strategic forces? Clearly this is not a concern at START II levels and probably would not be a concern even at the lower levels of 1,000 warheads each. However, for reductions to very low levels it could become a concern and it should be eliminated.

The level of forces to which Russia ultimately might be willing to reduce in the presence of a limited NMD system cannot be predicted with any certainty. However, it is almost certainly higher than the 200 mostly nondeployed warheads that this book proposes. Indeed, Russian expressions of concern about defenses in connection with START II ratification and START I implementation indicate that this level could be much higher and that U.S. deployment of a national missile defense system might well pose a serious barrier to even the first steps toward the deep cuts proposed in this book.

Theater Missile Defenses and Strategic Offensive Reductions

Two exoatmospheric systems, THAAD and Navy Theater Wide, are important elements of the current U.S. theater missile defense program. The United States appears to be committed to deploying large numbers of such advanced interceptors and radars. Both systems, although nominally intended for use as theater defenses, involve interceptors that are, except for a lower burnout speed, similar to those that would be used in a national missile defense system. These systems' combination of large numbers of radars and interceptors, high mobility, intrinsic strategic capability, and upgrade potential would almost certainly raise concern about their use for national missile defense.

Consider the capabilities of THAAD against an ICBM warhead fired from Russia. If provided only with launch-point cuing, such as is currently available from the Defense Support Program (DSP) early warning satellites, each defense battery would be able to cover an area the size of the metropolitan area of a major city.[51] In practice, however, much better cuing information will certainly be available.

51. Cuing information is data provided by other sensors that helps the defense system predict the direction in which to look for an incoming warhead. This information generally allows the defense to detect targets at greater distances and thus enables it to protect a larger area. Launch-point cuing means the defense is provided only with information on an attacking missile's launch location. Better cuing information could include data on the trajectory of the missile after its launch.

On coverage see Lisbeth Gronlund and others, "Highly Capable Theater Missile Defenses and the ABM Treaty," *Arms Control Today* (April 1994), pp. 3–8.

Sources of improved cuing data include existing (or in the future, upgraded) early warning radars that provide coverage around the continental United States, new early warning satellites scheduled to replace the current DSP satellites early in the next century, or the planned SBIRS-LOW space-based tracking system. It is also possible that DSP satellites can already provide much better cuing data than just the launch point. With better cuing data each defense battery could cover a larger area. For example, if cuing data from current early warning radars were used, each THAAD battery might be able to cover an area with dimensions of hundreds rather than tens of kilometers against an ICBM.

Other types of long-range tracking sensors, such as SBIRS-LOW satellites or the planned X-band radars, could be used to guide THAAD or Navy Theater Wide interceptors directly to targets without their radars ever detecting the targets. With such guidance, each THAAD battery would be able to defend an area comparable to that covered by the U.S. Safeguard system briefly deployed in the 1970s. The faster Navy Theater Wide interceptor would be able to defend an even larger area: the entire continental United States could potentially be covered from no more than three or four Navy Theater Wide ships.

There does not appear to be any practical way to prevent systems such as THAAD or Navy Theater Wide from using existing early warning radar or other cuing data to expand greatly their coverage area. Even if the United States pledged not to use such data, from the Russian perspective the verifiable breakout time to using the data would be essentially zero. Thus the deployment of THAAD or Navy Theater Wide would almost inevitably shake Russia's confidence in its retaliatory capability at some point in the process of reducing its strategic ballistic missile force to very low levels.

This conclusion would hold even more strongly if both wide-area TMD systems and an NMD system were deployed. Any national missile defense system, even a very thin one, would provide essentially all the sensor coverage and at least some of the battle-management capabilities needed for a thick nationwide defense. The THAAD or Navy Theater Wide interceptors could potentially be inserted into this infrastructure relatively quickly. Given currently discussed procurement levels, this could result in a national defense with 1,000–2,000 interceptors. It is difficult to envision any scheme that could verifiably prevent such TMD interceptors from being incorporated into an NMD system and tested against strategic targets much more quickly than the time it would take Russia to deploy significant numbers of additional warheads or missiles.

Reaction of China, Britain, and France to Missile Defenses

Other countries, notably China, will also be affected by U.S. deployment of missile defenses. Because China could in effect veto deep reductions by refusing to participate, its attitude toward possible ballistic missile defense deployments and the future of the ABM Treaty cannot be ignored.

Even a limited U.S. (or Russian) national missile defense would threaten China's very small ICBM force. The thin defense systems currently under discussion in the United States are intended to be able to counter an attack by a number of warheads approximately equal to the number that Beijing has deployed. At a minimum, it must be expected that China will respond by deploying countermeasures. China also appears to have a substantial capability to enlarge its strategic forces, either by building additional ICBMs or MIRVing existing and new ones or both.[52]

It is difficult to see how such a buildup of China's intercontinental nuclear force could be anything but harmful to U.S. security. Although a buildup might not directly affect U.S. and Russian reductions to START II or START III levels, it could pose a significant problem for further reductions and for the involvement of the other smaller nuclear weapon states in reductions. Moreover, a Chinese buildup to the equivalent of one hundred or more warheads capable of reaching the United States would undermine one of the crucial stated reasons for a limited U.S. national missile defense system and might force an enlargement of it.

China is also concerned about potential sales of advanced theater missile defense systems such as THAAD to other Asian countries.[53] Most of

52. The nuclear tests China conducted before signing the Comprehensive Test Ban Treaty were reportedly intended to test smaller warheads that could be used as MIRVs or on small mobile ICBMs. Steven Mufson, "Chinese Nuclear Test; U.S., Japan Join Protests," *Washington Post*, May 16, 1995, p. 1; and "New Nuclear Weapons Said Goal of Current Tests," in Foreign Broadcast Information Service, *Daily Report: China*, November 13, 1995, p. 29.

53. "The so-called Theatre Missile Defense system (TMD) which certain countries are [going] all-out to develop will in fact possess the capacity to intercept strategic missiles, thus breaking the limits imposed by the Anti-ballistic Missile Treaty (ABM) and rendering the treaty virtually meaningless. The development of such a system will constitute an impediment to the further reduction of nuclear weapons by the major nuclear powers, touch off a new round of the arms race, and destabilize the global strategic equilibrium. It will also inevitably raise concerns among other countries, and dampen their enthusiasm to participate in the global process of arms control and disarmament. In addition, the so-called cooperation among certain countries in the development of TMD systems will also lead to the proliferation of advanced missile systems and the related technologies, thus posing a threat to regional and even global security and stability." Statement by Sha Zukang, ambassador of the People's Republic of China for disarmament affairs at the First Committee of the Fifty-First Session of the United Nations General Assembly, October 1996.

China's missiles have ranges shorter than the nominal range these systems are designed to counter. The United States has made it clear that it is interested in selling advanced TMD systems to countries such as Japan, South Korea, and Taiwan. The sale of highly capable systems to Japan, which some Chinese view as a latent nuclear state given its large stockpiles of plutonium, is likely to be of particular concern because it could be viewed as the shield to complement a potential future nuclear sword.

The likely Chinese response to U.S. ballistic missile defense activities could cause other problems for arms control and nonproliferation efforts. China may become reluctant to become involved in control measures that might limit its options if the potential proliferation of defenses was creating uncertainties about its nuclear requirements. It could, for instance, decline to participate in a fissile material cutoff to leave open the option of producing more material for additional warheads.

The other two charter nuclear nations, Britain and France, are unlikely to be directly worried about U.S. deployment of a thin NMD system or advanced TMD systems. However, they are concerned that such U.S. deployments, coupled with the loosened controls necessary to deploy such missile defense systems, would eventually lead Russia to deploy similar systems, possibly even nuclear-armed ones, thus threatening their deterrent capabilities.[54] For this reason, they have strongly supported the ABM Treaty and opposed U.S. deployment of national missile defenses. Large-scale deployment of strategic-capable missile defenses could make them reluctant to participate in negotiated nuclear reductions. However, this possibility is probably of only secondary significance because in such a situation it would be unlikely that the United States and Russia would reduce their forces to levels that would allow Britain, France, and China to join in the reductions.

Cooperation on Missile Defenses

Is it possible that U.S.-Russian cooperation on missile defenses could pave the way for the deployment of strategic-capable defenses that would not provoke offensive responses?

54. A June 25, 1996, letter from Russian Foreign Minister Yevgeny Primakov to U.S. Secretary of State Warren Christopher stated that one of the guidelines for the continuing TMD demarcation talks should be that nuclear-armed TMD interceptors would not be prohibited. Excerpts from the letter appeared in Bill Gertz, "Russia Wants New Curbs on US Defenses," *Washington Times*, July 15, 1996, p. 1.

Cooperation on defense could take many forms: information exchanges, technology sharing, joint development of defenses, and even joint defense deployments. Early warning systems would seem to be particularly promising for such cooperation. To the extent cooperation can occur, it is probably better than the same activities occurring in an adversarial manner. There was considerable discussion of the possibilities for cooperation on defenses during 1991–92, and in 1995 Presidents Clinton and Yeltsin reaffirmed their interest in it. But little has happened since.[55]

China would almost certainly view U.S.-Russian cooperation on ballistic missile defenses as directed against it and as an even more serious threat than unilateral U.S. defense activities. In response a Chinese buildup of offensive forces would be expected. This problem could possibly be ameliorated, at least from a psychological if not a military perspective, by including China in a program of cooperation on ballistic missile defenses.

More generally, a U.S. commitment to worldwide cooperation on missile defenses, perhaps beginning with a global early warning system and leading to standardized missile defenses available to all participating nations, could reduce concerns about at least the early phases of U.S. missile defense deployments. The deployment of an internationally controlled ballistic missile defense system (to provide worldwide coverage, it would probably have to be space-based), might similarly be less threatening if the difficult problems underlying how to deploy and control it could be resolved. But not only does extensive cooperation on such defenses appear improbable, alone it cannot solve the underlying problem: that defenses that threaten to nul-

55. At the end of their May 1995 meeting in Moscow, Presidents Clinton and Yeltsin issued a statement that reaffirmed the commitment of the United States and Russia to the ABM Treaty. The statement went on to say, "The Presidents confirmed the interest of the sides in the development and fielding of effective theater missile defense systems on a cooperative basis. The sides will make every effort toward the goal of broadening bilateral cooperation in the area of defense against ballistic missiles. They will consider expanding cooperative efforts in theater missile defense technology and exercises, study ways of sharing data obtained through early warning systems, discuss theater missile defense architecture concepts, and seek opportunities for joint research and development in theater missile defense." The text of the joint statement on missile defenses is reprinted in "Select Documents from the Moscow Summit," *Arms Control Today,* vol. 25 (June 1995), pp. 24–25. Reports on earlier discussions of cooperation on ballistic missile defenses include John D. Morrocco, "Soviets Endorse U.S. Effort to Cooperate on ABM Systems," *Aviation Week and Space Technology,* October 14, 1991, pp. 20–21; Henry F. Cooper, "From Confrontation to Cooperation on Ballistic Missile Defenses," *Armed Forces Journal International* (January 1992), pp. 16-17; James F. Asker, "Bush to Offer Yeltsin Concept for Global Missile Defense," *Aviation Week and Space Technology,* May 25, 1992, p. 81; and Michael R. Gordon, "U.S. Team Going to Moscow to Push Joint Missile Defense," *New York Times,* July 12, 1992, p. 12.

Box 5-4. Point Defenses

Strategic defenses that are expressly designed to be able to protect only very small areas against strategic ballistic missile attacks might not raise serious problems for nuclear arms reductions. Such point defenses could even aid in achieving reductions if a strictly limited number were deployed to protect nuclear warhead storage sites or the bases of nuclear forces. Point defenses would have to be carefully designed with limits on the capabilities of their interceptors or controlling sensors so that they could not be easily converted to covering large areas (one way might be to restrict interceptors to maneuvering only via aerodynamic forces so that they could not operate above the atmosphere). But whether they could be made effective enough against a nuclear attack to justify their cost is at best highly uncertain.

lify a country's deterrent will provoke offensive reactions. Only a fundamental change in deterrence relationships can address this.

Thus although U.S.-Russian, or even multinational, cooperation on ballistic missile defenses might be helpful in reducing Russian objections to U.S. missile defense activities while strategic forces are at the START II level or even somewhat lower, it does not appear to be able to eliminate the problems such defenses pose for obtaining deep reductions.

Strategic-Capable Ballistic Missile Defenses and Deep Cuts

Not all types of missile defense deployments pose problems for deep cuts. The endoatmospheric TMD systems that the U.S. is now developing, such as the Patriot PAC-3, have little ability to threaten strategic forces and cannot be easily upgraded or expanded to do so. Given the potential effectiveness of exoatmospheric countermeasures, such systems, or similar systems with greater capabilities, could be nearly as effective as can be realistically expected against the currently existing shorter-range TMD threat. But these systems will not be able to satisfy those who seek a multiple-layer, wide-area defense against longer-range theater missiles by adding exoatmospheric defenses. However, any additional protection that might be provided by exoatmospheric layers must be weighed against their potential effect on efforts to reduce the threat that the continued deployment of large numbers of nuclear weapons poses to the United States. This trade-off is even more apparent in considering the defense of the U.S. homeland against strategic ballistic missiles.

The analysis in this chapter indicates that, as long as the political and deterrent situation among the nuclear weapon states remains unchanged, the deployment of strategic-capable defenses on any significant scale would almost certainly interfere with efforts to obtain deep reductions in strategic nuclear forces. This book argues for a reduction in nuclear forces to a level of 200 warheads per country, with only a few of these weapons deployed. Our assumption is that if the nuclear weapons states are not willing to reduce to below this level, it is because they continue to believe that the few remaining weapons still constitute an important deterrent. Given the small size of these nuclear forces, virtually any deployment of strategic-capable defenses would threaten their deterrent capability. Thus the situation would be essentially the same as today except that the smaller size of the nuclear forces would make them even more sensitive to the deployment of defenses. The small nuclear forces proposed in this book are clearly incompatible with significant strategic-capable ballistic missile defense deployments, at least in the context of the current reliance on nuclear-armed ballistic missiles for deterrence.

Nevertheless, it is useful to consider under what changed conditions it might become possible to deploy wide-area strategic-capable ballistic missile defenses while simultaneously attaining deep reductions in offensive forces. Such a result would require that the deployment of a strategic-capable defense by one country does not pose a threat to a vital offensive capability of another. Albeit unlikely in the near future, there are possible situations in which these deployments might not provoke offensive responses.

First, the major nuclear powers might decide to eliminate ballistic missiles as strategic nuclear delivery vehicles in favor of bombers, cruise missiles, or some other type of delivery system (or do away with nuclear weapons altogether). In the INF, START I, and START II Treaties the United States and Russia agreed to eliminate a significant portion of their missile forces, and a U.S.-Russian or global agreement to eliminate ballistic missiles (or missiles that could travel beyond a given range limit) is not inconceivable even if it seems improbable in the near future. In such a situation strategic ballistic missile defenses would appear to be limited to deterring the future deployment of ballistic missiles by parties to the agreement (that is, guarding against breakout from the agreement to eliminate ballistic missiles) and guarding against the presumably small numbers of long-range nuclear ballistic missiles held by countries outside the agreement. Assuming that the technical problem of making defenses effective against even small ballistic missile attacks could be solved, ballistic missile defenses could be a stabilizing factor. But the threat posed by nuclear or other weapons of mass destruction would still exist because other methods for delivering the weapons would exist. Such a world might simply replace the problem of offensive reductions and ballistic missile defenses with the problem of offensive reductions and air defenses.

A second instance in which defenses would not provoke offensive ballistic missile reactions would be if missile defenses achieved complete dominance over missile offenses. In such a world efforts to build up missile forces to counter the defenses would be futile. But there are serious problems with this vision. First, it is technically implausible. It is much easier to build countermeasures to defeat strategic defenses than it is to build defenses to deal with countermeasures. This has been the case since ballistic missiles were first deployed, and there is no reason to believe the situation will change. Second, aside from the question of technical feasibility, there is no apparent way to reach such a situation. Currently, ballistic missile offenses hold a large advantage over defenses. Unless there is a fundamental change in the U.S.-Russia deterrence relationship, any attempt to approach a defense-dominant world by deploying strategic-capable defenses would be met by offensive responses that would drive the relationship away from defense dominance.[56]

A third possible situation is that relations between the United States, Russia, and China might evolve into something similar to what now exists between the United States, Britain, and France, in which it is considered inconceivable that nuclear weapons could be used against each other. Indeed the deep reductions argued for in this book probably require at least some movement in this direction. In such a situation the nuclear weapon states might be able to abandon nuclear deterrence in its present form. They could adopt a policy in which the mere existence of small stocks of nondeployed but survivable nuclear weapons would deter any country from threatening to use or actually using nuclear weapons, turn over all remaining stocks of nuclear weapons to an international authority, or simply eliminate nuclear weapons. Ballistic missile defenses could discourage breakout and hedge against hidden stocks. Defenses could also discourage attacks by any nations

56. A defense deployment by one country could in principle be met by a defense deployment by the other country instead of an offensive buildup. Assuming that defenses could be made effective, one could imagine a series of such defensive buildups without offensive countermeasures resulting in a defense-dominant world. However, reaching this world would require both countries to accept, at some point in the defense buildup, that their offensive missile forces would soon no longer be able to provide a deterrent capability toward the other country. That is, they would have to abandon the concept of deterrence *before* reaching the defense dominant world.

that chose to retain nuclear weapons—presumably a small number, because if any nation retained large numbers of nuclear weapons, this approach would likely break down. But whether the benefits provided by such defenses, which would still be vulnerable to defeat by countermeasures, would be enough to justify the costs of deploying them is unclear.

Although these three visions suggest that strategic-capable ballistic missile defenses and deep reductions in nuclear weapons could coexist, they also emphasize the key argument of this chapter: ballistic missile-based nuclear deterrence as practiced today and significant levels of strategic-capable ballistic missile defenses are fundamentally incompatible. As long as nuclear deterrence remains a central aspect of the relationship between the nuclear weapon states, strategic defenses will prevent deep cuts. Reaching any of the three imagined worlds requires abandoning ballistic missile-based deterrence, at least as now practiced by the nuclear weapon states, *before* defenses are deployed.

The attainment of deep cuts requires a cooperative effort among the United States, Russia, China, and other countries. If the United States deploys strategic-capable ballistic missile defenses, the ultimate decision on whether and when such defenses will interfere with nuclear reductions lies not with Washington but with decisionmakers in Moscow and Beijing. Deep cuts will require at least tacit agreement across a reasonably broad spectrum of opinion in Russia and China that U.S. missile defense activities do not pose an unacceptable threat as nuclear arsenals are reduced. Achieving such agreement depends on more than just hardware; it depends on the whole strategic environment. But given the pace of the current U.S. missile defense program, it is possible that substantial strategic defense capabilities will be deployed before any fundamental change in nuclear deterrence relationships could occur. This would greatly diminish the prospects for achieving deep cuts.

Meeting the Ballistic Missile Threat

Can the threats posed by ballistic missiles be countered without interfering with efforts to achieve deep cuts in nuclear forces? A defense that could protect against a deliberate nuclear attack by Russia is not a realistic possibility, and current U.S. ballistic missile defense efforts are not being justified on these terms. The only way to protect against such an attack is to make sure it does not occur. This is now accomplished by the deterrent effect of

Box 5-5. The Missile Technology Control Regime

The Missile Technology Control Regime was established in 1987 to restrict the proliferation of ballistic and cruise missiles, unpiloted air vehicles, and related technologies. The MTCR is not a formal treaty but a voluntary agreement among a group of countries to apply export controls to a common list of complete missiles, missile subsystems and components, and missile-related technologies. The regime originally was aimed at nuclear-capable missiles, defined as those able to carry a 500 kg payload 300 or more kilometers. In 1993 the minimum payload was eliminated (so that the MTCR was now aimed at all missiles with ranges greater than 300 km) to address missiles capable of delivering chemical and biological weapons. The regime has twenty-nine members, including the United States, Russia, Britain, and France. A number of other countries, including China, while not members, have agreed to adhere to its guidelines.[1]

1. U.S. Arms Control and Disarmament Agency, "The Missile Technology Control Regime," Factsheet, September 15, 1997.

the threat of certain and devastating retaliation. Deterrence remains the best (and indeed only, short of the abolition of nuclear weapons) answer to deliberate nuclear attack by Russia.

U.S. missile defense activities are primarily justified in terms of three threats: an accidental or unauthorized launch of Russian missiles, a deliberate attack by China or a third world country against U.S. territory, and attacks on U.S. forces deployed abroad or the cities of U.S. allies by shorter-range theater ballistic missiles.

The deep cuts proposed in this book would largely eliminate the first threat by slashing the number of Russian warheads and removing the remaining weapons from a ready-to-launch posture. This is a better and more effective way to deal with the threat than reliance on ballistic missile defenses. Indeed, defenses that could interfere with efforts to remove weapons from rapid-launch postures would keep the danger of accidental or unauthorized launches unnecessarily high without providing assured protection.

A national missile defense system also cannot be expected to provide protection against a deliberate Chinese attack. Although the number of Chinese ICBMs capable of reaching the United States is now small, this situation will almost certainly change if the United States deploys a national missile defense. Defenses that could provoke China to expand its nuclear capabilities while not providing reliable protection would be counterproductive.

There is no currently deployed third world ballistic missile threat to U.S. territory, although it is possible that one could appear in the next decade. As noted by the Rumsfeld Commission, such a threat might first appear in the form of short-range missiles launched from ships or from missiles carrying chemical or biological submunitions. National missile defenses of the type currently under consideration would be ill–suited to countering such threats. A full-size third world intercontinental range missile capable of carrying a nuclear weapon to U.S. territory, if such a weapon is ever deployed, would likely be equipped with countermeasures that would cast serious doubt on the effectiveness of a national missile defense.

Given that a third world missile threat to U.S. territory may or may not appear, and that national missile defenses of the type now under consideration do not appear to be capable of providing reliable protection against missiles, it is far from clear that the near-term deployment of such defenses can be justified, given their likely adverse consequences for future efforts to reduce nuclear weapons.

Certainly the United States should continue to make every effort to limit the spread of long-range ballistic missiles. In particular, it should bring China and Russia into rigorous compliance with arms control regimes such as the Missile Technology Control Regime and other measures covering weapons of mass destruction. It should also work to halt the missile programs of key developing countries, which it is currently attempting to do in negotiations with North Korea. Even if such efforts fail, the U.S. ability to retaliate will strongly deter use of missiles against it. However, the fundamental point here is that the consequences of the near-term deployment of national missile defenses of questionable effectiveness must be carefully weighed against their likely adverse consequences for efforts to reduce nuclear weapons and the dangers these weapons pose.

The real ballistic missile threat lies in the large numbers of short- and medium-range missiles held by countries considered hostile to the United States. The United States is developing ballistic missile defense systems to counter such missiles—Patriot PAC-3, Navy Area Defense, and MEADS— that operate within the atmosphere and do not appear to raise problems for strategic arms reductions.

Summary

Strategic missile defenses will, as during the cold war, inhibit reductions in strategic offensive forces because all the declared nuclear powers rely on missile-delivered nuclear weapons for deterrence. As long as this reliance continues, strategic defenses will impede reductions below a certain level. Thus, if one is concerned with achieving deep offensive force reductions, ballistic missile defense deployments should be approached with great caution.

Even a very limited nationwide missile defense system could pose serious problems for reductions because its deployment could provide the infrastructure needed to rapidly expand the system into a thick defense. Although the precise offensive force levels at which a limited system would prevent further force reductions cannot be predicted with certainty, without a fundamental change in the deterrent role of ballistic missiles, the deployment of such a defense would certainly prevent achieving the very low force levels advocated in this study. The development and deployment of advanced exoatmospheric TMD systems, particularly if coupled with the deployment of space-based tracking systems, could similarly prevent deep cuts.

Given current trends, it appears entirely plausible and perhaps even likely that the United States will deploy within the next ten years or so a nationwide missile defense system, the THAAD and Navy Theater Wide exoatmospheric theater missile defense systems and the SBIRS-LOW space-based tracking system. It is difficult to imagine any other step that it could take that would create a greater obstacle to achieving deep cuts in nuclear forces.

CHAPTER SIX

De-alerting Strategic Nuclear Forces

Neither the United States nor Russia has changed its nuclear targeting or alert practices since the end of the cold war. The former adversaries still keep thousands of warheads on their strategic missiles poised for immediate launch and aimed at each other. The daily alert postures permit a massive preemptive first strike to be initiated or a quick second strike to be launched before incoming missiles reach their targets. The latter—launch on warning—in fact remains the centerpiece, the main option, of each side's strategy. It allows only a few minutes for detecting and assessing a missile attack, only a few for making a decision to retaliate, and only a few for disseminating and carrying out the order. In short, both sides still keep their strategic missile forces in an alert posture that creates the inherent risk of accidental nuclear war and impedes the normalization of U.S.- Russian relations.

To render these postures safer and less threatening, the United States and Russia need to supplant the 1994 detargeting agreement, which was to stop aiming strategic forces at each other's countries, an action that can be reversed in seconds, by practical measures that lower the daily launch readiness of the forces.[1] De-alerting means lengthening the fuse on nuclear weapons by increasing the preparation time needed to launch the weapons. It seeks first to eliminate the hair-trigger option of launch on warning. Then it seeks to extend the launch preparation time to days, weeks, or longer through graduated reciprocal measures instituted by the two parties.

1. For detailed discussions of U.S. and Russian detargeting and retargeting, see John Donnelly, "U.S. ICBMs No Longer Target China, Expert Says," *Defense Week*, vol. 19 (June 22, 1998), p. 1; Bruce Blair, "Where Would All the Missiles Go?" *Washington Post*, October 15, 1996, p. A15; and Blair, *Global Zero Alert for Nuclear Forces* (Brookings, 1995). General Eugene Habiger, commander of U.S. Strategic Command in 1996–98, contends that Russia needs more than ten minutes to retarget its strategic missiles. See "Department of Defense News Briefing, June 16, 1998" (available at http://www.defenselink.mil/news/Jun1998/t06231998_t616hab2.html). Russian experts from the Strategic Rocket Forces told Bruce Blair in personal communications that Habiger's figure applies only to the time needed to insert completely new target coordinates into missiles and that preprogrammed coordinates in missile memory can be activated in ten to fifteen seconds.

De-alerting offers a quick way to reduce the strategic arsenals in an operational sense while preserving the legal prerogative and capacity to reverse gears if either party concludes that its national security requires doing so. The major difference between de-alerting and traditional arms reductions (the START process) is that de-alerting is legally and technically reversible while arms reductions require permanent cuts in the arsenals.

From a U.S. perspective the main benefit of de-alerting Russian forces is that it would help prevent a breakdown of Russian nuclear control and mitigate the consequences were such a breakdown to occur. De-alerting would delay the Russian capacity for launch and reduce the risks of accidental, inadvertent, or unauthorized launch. De-alerting thus addresses the main current security threat to the United States: the progressive deterioration of Russian nuclear command and control and early warning networks at a time of heavy and growing reliance of the country on nuclear weapons. It also constrains the technical capacity for initiating a deliberate sudden massive attack, however remote such a threat has become.

The main benefit to Russia from the de-alerting of U.S. forces is the alleviation of vulnerability to surprise attack. Standard calculations show that a systematic U.S. counterforce attack could destroy most of Russia's strategic nuclear forces except for those carried by one or two ballistic missile submarines at sea and perhaps a single regiment of single-warhead, mobile missiles deployed out of garrison. Russia depends on launch on warning to offset the vulnerability associated with its low submarine and mobile missile deployment levels despite a deficient early warning system that makes this quick-draw posture an unreliable deterrent and a safety hazard. Thus by drastically diminishing the U.S. capacity to launch a sudden overwhelming attack, the de-alerting of U.S. forces could relieve the operational burdens on the Russian command system, eliminate Russia's overdependence on launch on warning, and restore stability to the strategic balance.

Taking missiles off alert would also help rectify an acute imbalance in strategic arsenals that will otherwise emerge within the START II framework. Although neither side's arsenal can exceed 2,500 weapons by the end of 2007, Russia cannot afford a modern arsenal nearly this large, as noted in chapter 1 and in Alexei Arbatov's comment in the appendix. Without real military reform and an economic turnaround that boosts defense spending, Russia's strategic arsenal could shrink dramatically, possibly to 700 weapons or less (compared with 6,000 today) within ten years, and 500 or less within fifteen years.[2]

2. Bruce Blair, "The Changing Strategic Landscape of Nuclear Policy," Testimony before the Subcomittee on Strategic Forces, Senate Armed Services Committee, March 31, 1998; Elaine

These circumstances put Russia in a quandary. They leave few choices other than to accelerate the output of its missile factories at enormous expense (probably economically infeasible); negotiate a new agreement establishing much lower ceilings than those contemplated for START III (desirable but politically difficult and time consuming); abandon strategic arms control and attempt to preserve the aging multiple- warhead ICBMs that are to be eliminated by START II (undesirable in practically every respect); fulfill its treaty commitments and lapse into numerical inferiority (politically unattractive); or stand down its nuclear missiles in parallel with the United States to a sustainable level (desirable and technically feasible).

In sum, nuclear security depends on ironclad control over U.S. and Russian forces, but the high alert status of these forces undermines such control as the Russian military establishment as a whole deteriorates.

Deterioration of Russian Nuclear Control

Russia's official line denies that serious problems of nuclear control exist, and the Clinton administration generally echoes the assessment despite some intelligence reports that contradict it. The denial in both camps ignores abundant signs of technical and organizational decay and human duress.

Designers of command systems in Russia went to extraordinary lengths to ensure strict central control over nuclear weapons, a core value of Soviet political and military culture. During the cold war they built an impressive command system whose safety features often exceeded U.S. standards.[3] Nevertheless, they failed to anticipate a host of dangers that developed after the Soviet empire dissolved: coups, secession of member republics, severe civil-military tensions, slashes in defense spending, difficult working and living conditions even for elite nuclear units, a drastically reduced level of training exercises, declining proficiency in the safe handling of weapons, widespread corruption and incompetence within the senior ranks, and pervasive demoralization among the rank and file officers and enlisted per-

---

Grossman, "'It's Too Early' to Name START IV Treaty Figures, Says White House Aide," *Inside the Pentagon*, vol. 14 (February 26, 1998); "Strategic Command Chief Sees Long Road Ahead to START IV," *Inside the Pentagon*, vol. 14 (March 5, 1998); "Experts Diverge on U.S. Response to Shrinking Russian Nuclear Force," *Inside the Pentagon*, vol. 14 (April 16, 1998); David Hoffman, "Downsizing a Mighty Arsenal: Moscow Rethinks Role as Its Weapons Rust," *Washington Post*, March 16, 1998, p. A1; and David Hoffman, "Troubles Invigorate Debate on START II: Russian Crisis Saps Budget for Missiles," *Washington Post*, November 19, 1998, p. A42.

3. Bruce G. Blair, *The Logic of Accidental Nuclear War* (Brookings, 1993).

sonnel.[4] As if these burdens were not enough, the aging nuclear control system needs extensive repair and modernization. However effective the safeguards have been, the trends pertinent to the functioning of the system are downward in physical, organizational, and human terms, casting serious doubt on its ability to endure the strain indefinitely.[5]

In February 1997 the institute responsible for designing the sophisticated command, control, and communications systems for Russia's Strategic Rocket Forces (SRF) staged a one-day strike to protest pay arrears and the lack of resources to trouble-shoot and upgrade their equipment. This institute was also losing some of its best designers to the private sector. Three days later, Defense Minister Igor Rodionov asserted that "if the shortage of funds persists . . . Russia may soon approach a threshold beyond which its missiles and nuclear systems become uncontrollable." Prime Minister Viktor Chernomyrdin responded not with increased resources but with the reassurance that "Russian strategic missile forces are . . . in reliable hands."[6] President Boris Yeltsin soon fired Rodionov for failing to shrink and reform the military.

Rodionov's warning may have been in part a maneuver to muster support for greater defense spending, but he emphatically repeated it after his resignation, and recent reports by the U.S. Central Intelligence Agency indicate that the SRF and other elite nuclear units have indeed fallen on hard times.[7] These reports cite frequent malfunctions of command-and-control equipment and intermittent spontaneous switching to a combat mode for no apparent reason. Power to key nuclear weapons installations has been cut off numerous times for nonpayment of bills, and on seven occasions during autumn 1996, operations at some nuclear facilities were disrupted because thieves were "mining" communications cables for valuable metals. Technical safeguards against unauthorized use of nuclear weapons have weakened or become inoperable due to inadequate maintenance. And

4. A good overview of the state of Russia's military is David Hoffman, "Russian Forces Disintegrating," *Washington Post*, October 5, 1996, p. Al. A more recent review is Mark Galeotti, "Crisis Continues for Russia's Army," *Jane's Intelligence Review*, vol. 10 (June 1998), p. 3.

5. This section draws on Bruce G. Blair, Harold A. Feiveson, and Frank N. von Hippel, "Taking Nuclear Weapons Off Hair-Trigger Alert," *Scientific American* (November 1997), p. 5.

6. "Last Chilling Warning on Russian Nuclear Safety and Security," *Disarmament Diplomacy*, no. 13 (London: Acronym Institute, 1997), p. 48. See also David Hoffman, "Cold-War Doctrines Refuse to Die: False Alert after '95 Rocket Launch Shows Fragility of Aging Standards," *Washington Post*, March 15, 1998, p. A1.

7. Two pertinent CIA reports leaked to the press are discussed in Bill Gertz, "Russian Renegades Pose Nuke Danger," *Washington Times*, October 22, 1996, p. A1; and Gertz, "Mishaps Put Russian Missiles in 'Combat Mode,'" *Washington Times*, May 12, 1997, p. A1.

although launch crews normally need special unlock codes held by the General Staff, the highest echelon of military command, to fire their missiles, the CIA report warned that these codes may be distributed fairly widely to alternative command centers and that some submarine crews may possess autonomous launch capability for the ballistic missiles on board.[8]

The Russian early warning network constructed by the former Soviet Union to detect a ballistic missile attack is perhaps the most neglected component of the strategic posture.[9] Many ground radars no longer operate or routinely suffer power outages and other afflictions; only three of Russia's nine modern radars (large phased-array radars) are working at all. Three have been deactivated or never completed, and three are inoperable or barely functional. Seven out of ten older, less capable Hen House radars sit outside Russia in former Soviet republics; a key station in Latvia recently shut down for political reasons, leaving a gaping hole in Russia's coverage of a major submarine missile attack corridor. Two of the nine slots in Russia's constellation of early warning satellites that observe U.S. land-based missile fields from elliptical orbits are empty; of the seven occupied slots, only three satellites are operating normally, reducing coverage to about fifteen hours a day. Furthermore, for technical reasons Russia appears to lack satellite coverage of the ocean areas from which U.S. (or British or French) submarine missiles could be launched. This glaring deficiency in missile attack early warning evidently stems from technological difficulties in designing satellite infrared sensors capable of looking down at the oceans (as opposed to looking down at small areas or monitoring the earth limb with cool dark space as the background).[10] In consequence Russia lacks "dual phenomenology" (detection using two different types of sensors) for many potential missile attack corridors and thus has no way to check rapidly a potentially false report issued by a single sensor.

8. According to a Russian Navy admiral still on active duty, this launch autonomy applied only to older Yankee class ballistic missile submarines, which have been recently retired. Newer submarines must receive a special unlocking code in order to fire. Regarding the distribution of the unlock codes for Russian strategic forces, Bruce Blair believes that they are held exclusively by the General Staff operations directorate at the main and alternative war rooms (at Moscow, Chekhov, and Penza) under normal peacetime conditions, though options exist to distribute them more extensively down the chain of command during a nuclear crisis.

9. This discussion of early warning draws heavily on personal communications with U.S. government analysts. Also, an excellent article is David Hoffman, "Cold-War Doctrines."

10. For an original and detailed assessment of Russia's satellite early warning problems, see Theodore A. Postol, "The Nuclear Danger from Shortfalls in the Capabilities of Russian Early Warning Satellites: A Cooperative Russian-US Remedy," MIT Security Studies Program, March 1998. See also David Hoffman, "Russia's Myopic Missile Defense: Gaps in Early-Warning Satellite Coverage Raise Risk of Launch Error," *Washington Post*, February 10, 1999, p. A1.

The aging command system and communications networks that support nuclear operations, including launch on warning, are also crumbling. These networks are typically five or more years past due for overhaul and modernization; some components are ten or more years past their design life.[11] Their performance is deteriorating, raising the question of whether they will fail safe or deadly. Even the famous nuclear suitcases that receive early warning information and accompany the president, defense minister, and chief of the General Staff are falling into disrepair.[12]

The latest concern is that the millenium computer bug (the so-called Y2K problem) may well cause Russia's missile attack early warning or other nuclear controls to crash or go haywire. After earlier denials, Russian officials now acknowledge that their nuclear warning systems have this bug. U.S. defense officials regard the hazard as serious enough to justify offering Russia a backup source of missile attack warning from U.S. early warning sensors.[13]

Russia's nuclear weapons establishment also suffers from a host of human and organizational problems. Crews receive less training than they once did because of broken equipment and budget cutting, which translates into less adherence to safety rules. Their motivation to follow the rules diligently can also be doubted in view of their poor working conditions. Despite President Yeltsin's promises to improve conditions, endemic housing and food shortages have led to demoralization and disaffection within the elite Strategic Rocket Forces, the strategic submarine fleet, and the custodians of Russia's vast stockpiles of nuclear weapons. As a result, the suicide rate among officers rose sharply in 1997 and 1998. The likelihood also increases that desperate low-level commanders would flaunt safety rules or, worse still, might take unauthorized control of nuclear weapons, something that a deteriorating central command system might be unable to detect or counter. These afflictions, particularly pay arrears, led the newly elected governor of Krasnayarsk, General Alexander Lebed, to express his willingness to take over from Moscow the SS-18 intercontinental land rockets at Uzhur.

Even at the top, control over nuclear weapons could splinter along polit-

11. Personal communication with Russian command system designers, August 1997.

12. Bill Gertz, " Mishaps Put Russian Missiles in 'Combat Mode': Defense Minister Vexed by Breakdowns Due to Short Funds," *Washington Times*, May 12, 1997, p. A1.

13. For pertinent testimony on this problem by John Hamie, the deputy secretary of defense, and Lieutenant General Kenneth Minihan, the director of the National Security Agency, see *Hearing to Receive Testimony on the Future Threats to the Department of Defense Information Systems, Including the Year 2000 Problems and the Sale of the Frequency Spectrum,* Hearing before the Senate Committee on Armed Services, June 4, 1998, transcript provided by Alderson Reporting Company.

ical fault lines. Authority in Moscow depends today far more on personal allegiances than on institutional bonds, and military leaders disaffection with politicians cast a shadow over the military's loyalty. Physical control of the nuclear weapon unlock and launch authorization codes resides with the military, and cohesion at the apex may be difficult to maintain during periods of political turmoil.[14] The General Staff's direct access to the launch codes enables its members to initiate a missile attack with or without the permission of political authorities. In fact, during the August 1991 coup against President Gorbachev, for three days Defense Minister Dimitriy Yazov and Chief of the General Staff Mikhail Moiseyev had usurped the power to launch nuclear weapons.

Nuclear command might splinter down other political fault lines. A CIA report considered the possibility that the Far East region of Russia, or the military district or Pacific fleet located there, might secede along with the nuclear weapons stationed there.[15] Ukraine's secession and subsequent prolonged temptation to seize control over nuclear weapons on its territory represent an instructive precedent.

The list of possible scenarios for a breakdown of nuclear control leading to a mistaken or illicit launch is long and growing. Although the risks cannot be precisely measured, it is not unreasonable to fear a serious, even catastrophic, failure of Russian nuclear control. All the trends are adverse. What remains uncertain is how close to the precipice Russia has come and how much if any margin of safety exists.

The Nuclear Hair Trigger

While Russian control erodes, both Moscow and Washington try to maintain the bulk of their strategic missile forces on hair-trigger alert. Although bombers no longer stand alert in peacetime, the daily launch readiness of missiles is high. Within just a few minutes after receiving the order to fire, a large fraction of the U.S. and Russian land-based rockets armed with 2,000 and 3,500 warheads, respectively, would begin their 25-minute flight over the North Pole to their wartime targets. Within 20 minutes after ordering the attack, strategic submarines would empty their launch tubes. Four alert

14. Blair, *Global Zero Alert*.

15. Bruce Blair, notes taken from CIA report "Prospects for Unsanctioned Use of Russian Nuclear Weapons," September 1996. See also Bill Gertz, "Russian Renegades Pose Nuke Danger: CIA Says Arsenal Lacks Tight Controls," *Washington Times*, October 22, 1996, p. A1.

U.S. Trident submarines (out of a fleet of eighteen) could send more than 600 warheads on their way, and several alert Russian submarines (out of a fleet of twenty-six) at sea or dockside would dispatch perhaps 300 to 400 warheads. In sum, the daily alert postures enable the nuclear superpowers to launch within 20 minutes about 5,000 nuclear weapons aimed at military installations and cities.[16]

Given the weakening control over Russian forces, the unintentional use of nuclear weapons is a more serious threat than is a failure of deterrence leading to a calculated act of nuclear aggression. The United States and Russia are running a growing risk of stumbling into an inadvertent war in order to deter a vanishing risk of deliberate attack. This situation is worrisome even under normal conditions. It could rapidly become extremely dangerous if the Russian command system came under any immediate pressure from an internal or international crisis. Nevertheless, the misplaced priorities in both countries' nuclear weapons establishments leave them fixated on the remote specter of a cold-blooded massive attack.

In hedging against this threat, military planners naturally assume that their counterpart's first strike would be designed to produce the maximum possible damage to their retaliatory capabilities: the missile launchers, nuclear bombers, and the command system that directs these forces. To deter such a strike, they strive to project a convincing threat to strike back and destroy the attacker's military forces, leadership, and war-supporting industry. Planners thus saddle their strategic arsenals with a demanding requirement that is virtually identical in scope to mounting a first strike: guarantee the second-strike destruction of thousands of enemy targets spread across a distant continent. This is a classic case of the security dilemma in which defensive preparations appear to the opponent as offensive preparations, fueling a tense interaction that sustains high-level alert on both sides.

To meet this demand for comprehensive target coverage, both the United States and Russia plan to launch on warning—launching a massive retaliatory missile salvo after detecting an enemy missile attack but before the incoming warheads arrive 15 to 30 minutes later. (The shortest flight times would be from close-in submarines; the longest from land-based rockets on home territory). Although it has thousands of warheads securely deployed at sea, even the United States adheres to this quick-draw stance because of

16. Alert rates for Russian forces are author's estimates. Rates for U.S. forces are estimates based in part on data provided by the U.S. Strategic Command to Bruce Blair, Hal Feiveson, and Frank von Hippel.

the vulnerability of its missile silos and command apparatus, including its political and military leadership in Washington.[17]

Russia also plans to launch missiles on warning. The General Staff knows that if Russia's strategic forces are not launched immediately, only a small number, perhaps only tens of missiles carrying fewer than 200 weapons (out of a total arsenal of 6,000 warheads), would be able to respond after absorbing a systematic attack. This estimate partially reflects the vulnerability of the silos housing most of Russia's land-based missiles to attack by accurate U.S. missiles, especially the U.S. MX Peacekeeper land-based missile, and the Trident II submarine missile armed with high-yield W88 warheads.

Russia's current inability, because of budgetary and manpower constraints, to deploy many of its submarines survivably at sea and mobile land-based rockets in the field amplifies this worry. A lack of resources and qualified personnel have forced the Russian Navy to keep on average only two of its twenty-six ballistic missile submarines at sea on combat patrol at any time—typically, a Delta IV submarine in the northern fleet and a Delta III in the Pacific. Many weeks of the year no missile submarines are deployed at sea.

Similar constraints prevent Russia from hiding more than one or two regiments of its mobile missiles in the field. The remaining forty or so regiments, each controlling nine single-warhead missiles, keep their truck launchers parked in garages, where they are highly vulnerable.

Russia also has thirty-six ten-warhead nuclear missiles carried on railway cars that were designed to be hidden along Russia's vast rail network. But these railcars have been confined to fixed vulnerable garrisons in keeping with a pledge made by President Gorbachev to President Bush in 1991.

These vulnerabilities have led Russia to ready some of its submarines in port and mobile missiles in garages to launch on warning, along with its silo-based missiles. The time available for deciding to launch these weapons is shortened by the presence of American, British, and French submarines cruising in the North Atlantic only 2,000 miles from Moscow. This proximity means that the nuclear-release procedures require a response time of

17. For detailed discussions of U.S. and Russian reliance on launch on warning, see Blair, *Logic of Accidental Nuclear War*; and Blair, *Global Zero Alert* . For a succinct and authoritative confirmation that the U.S. command system is geared to this option, and indeed that it not only "powerfully biased the president's decision process toward launch *before* the arrival of the first enemy warhead," (p. 194) but also would "drive the president inevitably toward [such] a decision," (p. 191), see the interview with General George Lee Butler, former commander of the U.S. Strategic Command, in Jonathan Schell, *The Gift of Time: The Case for Abolishing Nuclear Weapons Now* (Henry Holt, 1998), esp. pp. 191–94.

less than fifteen minutes from the time of enemy missile detection to the liftoff of friendly missile forces. The Russian command system is geared to operate within this time frame, and the procedures are regularly exercised with drills. The crews on board docked submarines, for example, have demonstrated the ability to fire while surfaced at pierside within nine to fifteen minutes after receiving the order.[18]

The Russian General Staff, after receiving permission from the president through his nuclear suitcase (Cheget), would attempt to exercise launch on warning in either of two ways. One is to send unlock and launch authorization codes held by the General Staff in war rooms directly to individual weapons commanders, who then would perform the launch procedures. (This is how the United States would exercise its launch-on-warning option.) Or members of the General Staff could personally push launch buttons from war rooms at Chekhov near Moscow or from alternative facilities at Penza. This scheme would bypass the subordinate commanders and missile launch crews down the chain of command.

To cope with the perceived threat of decapitation posed by Pershing II missiles slated for deployment in Western Europe during the early 1980s, the Soviets developed and tested a command link meant to give the top political leadership push-button launch control over a portion of their land-based rocket force, bypassing even the General Staff, to shave off a few minutes of launch reaction time.[19]

It is obvious that the rushed nature of launch, from warning to decision to action, risks causing a catastrophic mistake. The danger is compounded by the erosion of Russia's ability to reliably distinguish natural phenomena or the launch of peaceful sounding rockets into space from a true missile attack. That a quick launch decision today would draw on less reliable information than would have been available during the cold war is not lost on Russian planners. They well recognize the increasing difficulty of launching on true warning as well as the danger of launching on false warning.

A serious incident that demonstrated the acute pressure on Russia's command system under the short time constraints allowed by its launch-on-warning posture and the system's susceptibility to false warning occurred in January 1995. Russian radars detected and began tracking one or more rockets fired from a spot near the coast of Norway.[20] Interpreting the radar blips

18. Blair, *Logic of Accidental Nuclear War*; and Blair, *Global Zero Alert*.

19. Personal communications with former Russian command system designer, August 1997.

20. This incident is discussed in Blair, Feiveson, and von Hippel, "Taking Nuclear Weapons Off Hair-Trigger Alert"; Blair, *Global Zero Alert*; and Peter Pry, "War Scare," unpublished manuscript.

as a possible attack by a Western missile submarine, the nuclear command system started the countdown to a launch decision for the first time in its history. The event activated President Yeltsin's nuclear suitcase and triggered an emergency teleconference between him and his nuclear advisors. About eight minutes elapsed—only a couple of minutes short of the procedural deadline for reaching a decision on whether to launch on warning—before it was determined that the rocket posed no threat to Russia. As it turned out, it was a U.S. scientific rocket launched from Andoy Island off the Norwegian coast to study the northern lights.

The end of the cold war undoubtedly helped moderate the Russian response to this false alarm and more generally alleviated the danger of mistaken launch caused by the decline in Russian technical capabilities. Given the milder political climate, decisionmakers on both sides will be more inclined to doubt the validity of any reports they receive of an impending missile strike. Nevertheless, the close coupling of two arsenals geared for rapid response carries the inherent danger of producing a mistaken launch and escalating volleys of missiles in return. The possibility of such an apocalyptic accident cannot be ruled out even under normal conditions. And if the Russian command system comes under stress from an internal or international crisis, the danger could suddenly become much more acute.

Beyond the danger of launching on false warning, keeping thousands of warheads poised for immediate launch increases the susceptibility of nuclear weapons to other types of accidents or unauthorized acts.

During the cold war such risks were subordinated to the overriding requirement to deter an enemy believed to be willing to mount a cold-blooded nuclear strike. This rationalization is no longer defensible, if ever it was. Today, when both countries seek normal economic relations and cooperative security arrangements, perpetuating the readiness to launch nuclear weapons on the mere warning of an attack defies reason. Yet cold war planning against first strikes is so entrenched in the nuclear weapon bureaucracies that it will yield only to directives from presidents to substitute a safer policy.

De-alerting Strategic Forces

Remedies of varying effectiveness are available to improve the operational safety of the nuclear postures. In principle, both countries could spend more to upgrade their command and early warning networks and increase their resilience to attack. This would allow them to reduce their reliance on prompt launch and strengthen their capability to retaliate after riding out an attack. To this end Russia is, in fact, investing scarce resources to excavate deep underground command posts and upgrade an unusual second-strike command instrument formally called Perimeter and colloquially known as the "dead hand."[21] This remedy is expensive, as is the alternative of repairing Russia's early warning network.

A third, less expensive remedy that increases the operational safety of the nuclear arsenals is through traditional arms control: the START nuclear weapons reductions. Under the START III framework endorsed at Helsinki in 1998 by Presidents Clinton and Yeltsin, the strategic arsenals would shrink to 2,000–2,500 on each side by 2008. These reductions will promote safety, but only over decades as START III is succeeded by follow-on START agreements. If current alert practices are not changed, ten years from now many hundreds of warheads on each side would still remain ready to launch on a few minutes' notice.

The near-term remedy proposed in this book is to de-alert the missile forces, an action that promises rapid and large improvements in operational safety by increasing the amount of time needed to prepare nuclear missiles for launch. The United States and Russia could move independently down this path, but could move more quickly in parallel.

President Bush set a notable precedent for de-alerting nuclear weapons at the end of September 1991 when the Soviet Union began to split apart in the wake of the August coup attempt and as the Soviet nuclear weapons establishment threatened to disintegrate with it. On the advice of General George L. Butler, commander of the Strategic Air Command, Bush ordered an immediate stand-down of that part of the U.S. strategic bomber force that for decades had stood ready for takeoff within fifteen minutes. Nuclear weapons on bombers were unloaded and put in storage. In addition, Bush took off alert the large number of land- and sea-based strategic missiles slated for elimination under START I—450 Minuteman II missiles along with the missiles in ten Poseidon submarines—even though this treaty had not yet

21. If top Russian leaders do not get a clear picture of an apparent missile attack, or if for any reason they fail to give timely authorization to retaliate, the General Staff can activate this system to ensure quasi-automatic retaliation in the event of the decapitation of the Russian nuclear control system. Once activated, computers tied into special radio nodes, underground radio antennae, and command rockets would form and disseminate launch signals to the strategic forces if the sensors register nuclear detonations on Russian territory and the radio nodes lose contact with the General Staff. The launch signals sent by command rockets can fire missiles out of silos and off mobile launchers without any participation on the part of launch crews in the field.

been ratified by either party. These measures were completed in a matter of days and encouraged comparable actions by Russia.

President Gorbachev reciprocated a week later by ordering the deactivation of more than 500 land-based rockets and 6 strategic submarines, by promising to keep his strategic bombers at a low level of readiness, and by putting the rail-based missiles in garrison. The timing for carrying out these reciprocal steps remains uncertain.[22] Both countries also commited to withdraw to central storage and destroy a large part of the thousands of shorter-range tactical nuclear weapons deployed with their armies and surface navies.

Presidents Clinton and Yeltsin took a further symbolic step together in 1994 when they pledged to stop aiming strategic missiles at each other's country. This change, though a welcome gesture, has little military significance.[23] Preprogrammed wartime target coordinates remain in the missiles' memories, and missile commanders can activate these target files within seconds. Selecting targets in this fashion is in fact a standard U.S. procedure for launching missiles in wartime, and thus the accord did not extend the launch preparation times by even a single second. Similarly the Russian General Staff can use a computer network called Signal A to override the agreement and retarget all Russia's silo-based missiles at the United States in ten seconds.[24]

Moreover, the pact had no significant effect on the risk or consequences of an accidental or unauthorized Russian launch. Although, to fulfill their obligations, the Russian military set their intercontinental missiles on what they call a "zero flight plan," this setting does not reduce the danger of illicit launch, and an unprogrammed missile launched illicitly or accidentally automatically would switch back to its primary wartime target. This target might be a Minuteman silo in Montana or a command center in Washington, London, Paris, or Beijing.

Having taken these real and symbolic steps during the past six years, the United States and Russia reached the present situation described earlier: 5,000 strategic warheads, the equivalent of 100,000 Hiroshima bombs, still remaining poised for launch at a moment's notice. The de-alerting process has stalled.

22. General Habiger contends that Gorbachev's de-alerting pledges were not fulfilled. Personal communications with Blair, Feiveson, and von Hippel.

23. See note 1.

24. Bruce Blair, "Russian Nuclear Policy and the Status of Detargeting," Testimony before the House Committee on National Security, March 13, 1997. In fact, if the General Staff transmits a launch order directly to the missiles over Signal A in the mode called "automatic regime," the missiles automatically switch over to their primary wartime target.

A Prescription for Change

It is time to revive de-alerting with another large step toward a stand-down of U.S. and Russian strategic missiles. Possessing the most robust forces and cohesive command system, the United States should take the lead by announcing that it will withdraw from active deployment the U.S weapons that most menace Russia's missile silos and underground command posts. These are the 50 MX silo-based missiles, which are armed with 10 warheads each, and the 400 high-yield W88 warheads fitted atop some of the missiles on Trident submarines. We also recommend immobilizing all 500 Minuteman III land-based missiles, which are armed with 3 warheads apiece; halving the number of submarines deployed at sea in peacetime; and cutting the number of warheads on each submarine-borne missile from 8 to 4. The operations of ballistic missile submarines should also be altered so that their crews would require about a day to ready missiles for launching.[25]

De-alerting through Reciprocal Initiatives

To reduce the concerns that have driven Russia to maintain its missiles ready to launch on warning, the U.S. president should order the following.

—Immediately download to storage the 500 warheads on the 50 MX missiles (which will, in any event, be retired under START II).

—Disable all 500 Minuteman III missiles by pinning open safety switches in their silos (as was done for the Minuteman IIs in 1991). If Russia reciprocates, these missiles should be immobilized in a manner that would take considerably longer and more visible actions to reverse.

—Remove to storage the warheads on the four Trident submarines that are to be retired under START III and reduce the number of warheads on each remaining submarine missile from eight to four.

—Take the high-yield (500 kiloton) W88 warheads off the Trident II missiles, place the warheads in storage, and replace them with 150 kiloton W76 warheads.

—Allow Russia to verify these actions by using some of the ten annual reentry vehicle and ten data update inspections permitted by START I. Accept a greater number of inspections if Russia will also do so.

25. The de-alerting recommendations herein draw largely upon Blair, Feiveson, and von Hippel, "Taking Nuclear Forces Off Hair-Trigger Alert"; and Bruce Blair, Harold Feiveson, and Frank von Hippel, "De-alerting Russian and American Nuclear Missiles," United Nations Institute for Disarmament Research *NewsLetter*, no. 38 (1998).

—Put all U.S. ballistic missile submarines at sea on a low level of alert, so that it would take at least twenty-four hours to prepare their missiles for launch, and keep most or all U.S. submarines out of range of Russian targets. (This would follow the British example, discussed later). Consider ways to make these changes verifiable in the future and discuss possible reciprocal arrangements with Russian officials.

Even after these actions are taken, six U.S. submarines carrying up to 576 warheads would remain undetectable at sea, and the immobilized Minuteman IIIs could be destroyed only by a massive Russian attack on 500 silos.

In response to the U.S. initiative the Russian president could order the following.

—Remove the warheads from all of Russia's forty-six SS-24 rail- and silo-based missiles (which will, in any event, be retired under START II).

—Immobilize all other silo-based missiles (most are slated for retirement under START II).

—Remove the warheads from the fifteen or so ballistic missile submarines likely to be retired under the START II and III agreements.

—Place all ballistic missile submarines (in port and at sea) in a condition such that their missiles could not be launched for at least twenty-four hours

—Disable the launchers of all truck-mobile ballistic missiles so that they cannot be activated for at least a few hours.

After these actions are taken, 128 to 400 warheads on two Russian submarines would remain untargetable at sea and 9 to 18 SS-25 warheads on truck-mobile launchers would remain hidden in the field. About 2,700 Russian warheads immobilized on silo-based ICBMs could be destroyed only by attacks on some 340 missile silos.

De-alerting Submarine-Launched Missiles

To achieve START II limits, the United States plans to retire four of its eighteen ballistic missile submarines and to reduce the number of warheads on each submarine-launched missile from eight to five or fewer. Later, to meet the START III goals, the United States would most likely eliminate an additional four submarines and reduce the number of warheads on each missile to four. All these actions should be taken at once. Russia could then immediately remove the warheads from the submarines it plans to scrap under the START agreements.

Without elaborate verification arrangements neither country could determine the alert status of the other's submarines at sea. Both nations, however, should lower launch readiness. Because the submarines are untargetable at sea, delaying a retaliatory launch would not increase their vulnerability to attack. Approximately two-thirds of the U.S. SSBN fleet (twelve out of eighteen) is normally at sea, and most (eight out of twelve) at sea are traveling to or from their launch stations in a state of modified alert: the crew needs about eighteen hours from the time it departs home port to perform procedures, such as installing code devices (called "inverters") on the launch tubes that bring a submarine to full alert. U.S. submarines at sea should simply stay on modified alert throughout their patrols.

Their patrol areas could also be changed from the Northern to the Southern Hemisphere, putting them days to weeks of transit time from launch stations. Their readiness could be reduced further by removing their missile guidance sets and storing them onboard. It would take about three hours per missile to install the sets, or about three days per submarine to re-alert all twenty-four missiles if the guidance systems were reloaded one at a time. Russian submarines lack this option; their missiles are not accessible from inside the vessel. However, equivalent measures could be taken.

Russia should also pledge to keep its missiles on submarines in port off launch-ready alert in a manner that could be verified by the United States and would take a day or more to reverse. The United States does not maintain submarines in port on alert and has never launched a ballistic missile from a nonsubmerged submarine.

De-alerting Silo-Based Missiles

The START II ban on multiple-warhead, land-based missiles does not go into effect until 2007, and their deactivation under the Helsinki agreement is not required until 2003, but the parties could act earlier to take most silo-based warheads off alert. The easiest method, although one not readily verified on a continuous basis, would be to physically pin open switches in the missile silos in the circuits that would carry the signals to the first stage rocket engines to ignite. Maintenance crews would then have to enter each silo, manually remove the pins, and close the switches before the missiles could be fired remotely.

Negotiators at the Helsinki Summit envisioned actions that would take even longer to reverse. They agreed that Russia and the United States would have five extra years to dismantle the multiple-warhead missiles slated for elimination under START II, as long as these missiles were "deactivated by removing their nuclear warheads or taking other jointly agreed steps." The United States prefers that Russia deactivate missiles by removing warheads, an act that would take weeks to reverse. The absence of the warheads on the missiles could be checked during the inspections permitted under START, and efforts to remount the warheads would be apparent to surveillance satellites.

Russian experts argue, however, that their country does not have adequate facilities to store such a large number of warheads taken from missiles and maintain them in good condition. They are therefore now considering other options, including immobilizing the massive silo lids so that heavy equiment would be required to open them, or removing the battery that operates the missile-guidance system during flight. (Russian experts claim that the reinstallation of a battery into a missile would actually take 20 percent longer to complete than the reinstallation of a warhead.) A third possibility would be to replace the aerodynamic missile nose cones with flat-faced covers, which would shelter the warheads but not allow the missiles to fly a normal trajectory.

De-alerting Land-Mobile Missiles

De-alerting Russia's mobile land-based missiles (the United States has none) could begin by removing the ten warheads from each of the thirty-six rail-mobile missiles to be eliminated under START II. Russian sources indicate that there is enough storage capacity for this number of warheads.

For the truck-mobile missiles, one possibility for de-alerting while in garrison might be to alter the garages. Currently, the roofs of these shelters are designed to slide open, allowing the launcher inside to be erected and the missile fired. Additional measures might incapacitate the launcher itself in ways that would take a long time to reverse.

De-alerting Strategic Bombers

Neither Russia nor the United States maintains bombers on daily alert. Probably no more than half of Russia's dubious arsenal of 80 bombers and 800 warheads could return to alert within a few days to a week.

The U.S. bomber force ended its daily alert operations in 1991. This entailed removing the weapons from the bombers and placing them in storage depots at their three home bases (Whiteman in Missouri for 14 B-2s; Barksdale in Louisiana and Minot in North Dakota for a total of 44 operational B-52Hs). Re-alerting bombers in a crisis would take twelve hours for the first several planes, and thereafter could be accomplished at a rate of 1 bomber, carrying 16 or 20 warheads, an hour. At this constant rate of re-alerting, the maximum warhead loading of 1,088 weapons on 58 bombers in total would be achieved in about three days.[26]

Strategic bombers should be further de-alerted by transferring their weapons to off-base locations. The arsenals could be distributed to depots at former bomber bases, achieving greater dispersion of warheads and improving their survivability. During a crisis the weapons could be transported back to the three primary bomber bases or the bombers could fly to the depots. In either case the initial re-alerting of U.S. bombers to launch-ready status would require at least several extra hours compared with the current arrangements. Thus the first several American bombers, each with sixteen or twenty warheads, would achieve full alert perhaps sixteen hours or so after the decision to re-alert was made.

This adjustment is especially recommended for the B-2 bomber force and its 320 warheads because of its potential for penetrating Russian territory undetected and delivering new B-61 earth-penetrating bombs, which are designed to destroy underground command posts. Russian bombers should also conform to the same principle of removing their weapons to off-base locations.

Security Implications

This blueprint for a U.S. initiative on de-alerting would dramatically establish the country's intention not to pose a first-strike threat to Russia while preserving ample capacity to satisfy reasonable requirements of deterrence. With almost 600 U.S. warheads remaining invulnerable at sea, each capable of destroying the heart of a large city, the United States would preserve ample capacity to deter any nuclear aggressor. At the same time, the U.S. daily alert force would relinquish enough of its counterforce threat to Russia to induce a reciprocal relaxation of the Russian nuclear posture. We believe this U.S. change would persuade Russia to follow suit and take most of its missiles off hair-trigger alert. The changes would accelerate the implementation of agreements for disarmament already negotiated under START II and to be negotiated under START III. We estimate that most of the job could be completed within a year or two.

26. These re-alerting estimates may overstate the speed of force generation during a crisis, although quarterly exercises in which the bombers are uploaded with weapons and taxied down the runway provide considerable practice for the air and ground crews.

Capabilities already exist to confirm that nuclear weapons have been taken off alert. For instance, the number of ballistic missile submarines in port can be monitored using satellites, and most other measures could be checked during the random on-site inspections permitted by START I. Over the longer term, additional technical means could be engineered to provide more frequent checks that nuclear missiles posed no immediate threat. For example, electronic seals could be used to ensure that a component, such as a guidence jet or inverter removed from a missile had not been replaced. The integrity of such seals could be verified remotely through satellite relay using encrypted communications.

Global Zero Alert

U.S. and Russian military leaders might insist on maintaining small portions of their current arsenals on high alert, perhaps hundreds of warheads each, until U.S.-Russian relations improve further or until Britain, France, and China joined in adopting similar measures to reduce the readiness of their nuclear arsenals. If so, they should choose their most survivable forces so there will be less incentive for launch on warning.

By all indications Britain, France, and China have already assumed a de facto de- alerted posture. Britain recently announced that its strategic monad of SSBNs are now "routinely at a 'notice to fire' measured in days rather than the few minutes' quick reaction alert sustained throughout the Cold War."[27] France has kept its ballistic missile submarines at sea on lower alert than has the United States. And China has traditionally maintained a very low state of nuclear readiness.

The United States and Russia should aspire to establish the highest possible standards of safety for their own nuclear armaments, move as rapidly as possible to take their missiles off alert, then take further steps to increase the time required to reactivate these weapons.

The ultimate goal would be to deactivate most if not all ballistic missiles and then eventually eliminate most warheads and missiles in a manner con-

27. The quotation is from the British Ministry of Defense, *Strategic Defense Review, Supporting Essay Five: Deterrence, Arms Control, and Proliferation* (London: Stationery Office, June 1998), found on http://www.mod.uk/policy/sdr/essay05.htm on July 11, 1998. The information on the French SSBN modified alert posture is based on personal communications with a French military official. The Chinese nuclear posture is discussed in Walter Pincus, "U.S., China May Retarget Nuclear Weapons: 'Confidence-Building Symbol' Would Have Little Military Significance, Official Says," *Washington Post*, June 16, 1998, p. A10.

sistent with the START III arrangements as outlined at the Helsinki Summit. The desired effect is to ensure that weapons could not be employed unless lengthy and detectable preparations are undertaken. To carry out such an extensive program, the means for verification would have to be strengthened to ensure that every nuclear state would know whether another country was making nuclear missiles ready to launch. Mechanisms for providing such forewarning are technically feasible.

Moving toward a global stand-down of nuclear arms will undoubtedly encounter strong resistance from those whose dominant fear remains a secretly prepared surprise attack. The design of our de-alerting proposal takes into account this already remote possibility.

Common Arguments against De-alerting

Many of the common objections to de-alerting are contained in a recent report issued by the National Defense University and Lawrence Livermore National Laboratory. A section titled "The Dangers of De-Alerting" reads in part,

> de-alerting measures that have been proposed in the name of safety and stability concerns would not solve any of the alleged problems for which they are advocated and, in fact, would make many of them far worse, including in the area of basic security of nuclear weapons.
>
> Most fundamentally, the majority of recent de-alerting proposals are unverifiable and some would lead to crisis instability. De-alerting undermines a basic principle of deterrence; namely, the ability to retaliate promptly so as to prevent any aggressor from assuming it can achieve a "fait accompli." In this context, assertions that de-alerting of U.S. strategic forces would eliminate fear of surprise attack have not been demonstrated, and substantial evidence suggests de-alerting would make such an attack more attractive by making an effective first strike possible at very low attack levels. This possibility would only increase tensions on both sides and provide incentives to strike first. Any moves to place nuclear forces back on alert in a crisis (if needed for deterrence or survivability) would be seen as escalatory if taken, and would be destabilizing if not. Finally, de-alerting major portions of the U.S. deterrent force would undermine alliance security guarantees and further exacerbate the disparity in U.S. and Russian theater nuclear forces levels.

For these reasons, the United States should not make significant changes to its current alert posture. De-alerting should not be allowed to become a back door to unilateral disarmament.[28]

These criticisms and others deserve a careful dissection and response.

—"De-alerting would make . . . an effective first strike possible at very low attack levels."

This criticism assumes that a country would remove the warheads from all its missiles and concentrate them at a small number of depots that could be targeted by an adversary. Our proposal assumes no such thing. By contrast, it seeks to de-alert strategic forces in a manner that hedges against a possible sudden deterioration of U.S.-Russian relations. Both sides would maintain a sufficient number of nuclear weapons in survivable deployments and capable of reconstitution for retaliation in the event of a surprise enemy nuclear attack regardless of the attack's magnitude.

For the United States the core secure reconstitutable force would probably be on deployed missile submarines. Furthermore, nuclear warheads or vital components for land-based missiles could also be protected by dispersed and hardened storage sites. For example, land-missile warheads could eventually be stored individually in empty missile silos, partially filled with concrete so that they were no longer deep enough to hold an ICBM, or in newly constructed bunkers near the missile silos. Such storage of Minuteman warheads in dispersed, secure, hardened silos would provide strong protection against even a large attack, facilitate the re-alerting of Minuteman forces during a nuclear crisis, and support reconstitution of the forces in the remote event of a surprise nuclear strike against them.[29]

Further protection against a large-scale surprise attack would derive from the de-alerting measures themselves. Insofar as these constraints are verifiable and slow to reverse, the fear of attack would be minimized.

—"Any moves to place nuclear forces back on alert in a crisis . . . would be seen as escalating if taken and would be destabilizing if not."

28. Robert Joseph and Ronald Lehman, "Executive Report," *U.S. Nuclear Policy in the 21st Century* (National Defense University and Lawrence Livermore National Laboratory, 1998), p. 18.

29. Warheads might be interspersed among silos in the same flight as their parent Minuteman missile. That is, for example, each flight of ten silos under the control of a local launch center could have five missiles without warheads sitting in silos and five warheads without missiles sitting in the other silos. Their close proximity would increase the chances of remating them during a crisis or conflict.

As already noted, the parties would always retain a formidable and secure reconstitutable force. These survivable deployments would greatly dampen the pressures and incentives on either side to realert their forces during a crisis because they would provide ample and stable deterrence in any imaginable circumstances.

The logical, and not a little ironic, conclusion of the argument that de-alerting would make re-alerting dangerously unstable is that the world is safer if large numbers of nuclear weapons remain on hair-trigger alert. This view grossly inflates the requirements of deterrence and understates the importance of safety.

—"A basic principle of deterrence [is] the ability to retaliate promptly."

Says who? The certainty of retaliation is arguably far more important than the timing of retaliation. The core requirement of deterrence is to project a credible threat to inflict immense devastation on a nuclear aggressor; deterrence does not hinge on whether retaliatory forces are unleashed one hour, one day, or one week later.

—"The majority of recent de-alerting proposals are unverifiable."

Verification is not essential to ensure the invulnerability of a de-alerted deterrent force, but it is probably essential to make de-alerting politically acceptable. Adequate verification of locatable systems (ICBMs in missile silos or garrison, SLBMs on submarines in port, and bombers in their home bases) can be achieved through careful design, national technical means, and adaptations of already existing START verification provisions. The downloading of the number and type of warheads that SLBMs carry at sea could be readily verified before submarines go on patrol.

Other promising dealerting possibilities, such as keeping boats at sea on modified alert or out of range of putative targets, would doubtless require more novel methods of verification as well as new forms of U.S.-Russian cooperation. But these monitoring arrangements are technically and politically feasible.

—"De-alerting would undermine alliance security guarantees and further exacerbate a disparity in U.S. and Russian theater nuclear force levels."

If a disparity in theater nuclear force levels would have undermined extended nuclear deterrence to U.S. allies, the wholesale unilateral withdrawal of U.S. tactical and theater nuclear forces in 1991 and 1992 would have done so. The United States chose to return many thousands of tactical nuclear warheads to storage sites on U.S. soil, leaving only 150 bombs for NATO aircraft still deployed overseas. And the NATO strike aircraft were taken off quick-reaction alert; their nuclear payloads were placed in storage at the bases. In short, the vast majority of U.S. tactical and theater nuclear weapons around the world were brought home, and the few that remained overseas were de-alerted.

If U.S. strategic forces are de-alerted, the nuclear security of our allies would still be under the same umbrella as that held over the United States itself. Moreover, it should be noted that two of America's nuclear allies, Britain and France, have themselves unilaterally adopted a de-alerted posture for their nuclear forces.

—"De-alerting Russian forces is superfluous because Russia already imposes strict safeguards against the unauthorized launch of its strategic forces."

In many respects the Russian nuclear command system was designed to provide for much more centralized and stringent control than the U.S. system. For instance, two-way feedback loops connect the General Staff with unmanned silos to enable continuous monitoring of missile launch status and any improper actions by subordinate echelons. The General Staff can electronically override unauthorized commands issued by lower command posts and can electronically isolate the deviant centers from their missiles.

Impressive as the architecture of Russia's nuclear command and control system is, however, it was not designed to cope with the strains that now burden it. The dangers of mistaken or unauthorized launch appear to be growing as the system deteriorates in physical, organizational, and human terms. Given the possible consequences of command failure in Russia, the burden of proof falls on the shoulders of those who assert that such failure is too remote to justify serious concern. Abundant evidence suggests the opposite.

De-alerting does not solve the age-old conundrum of designing a foolproof method of "guarding the guardians." But at least it buys time for responsible leaders to gain decisive influence over nuclear decisionmaking. The delays imposed on any re-alerting decisions might also limit the magnitude of a misguided nuclear strike.

—"The political climate is not conducive to de-alerting, and Russia's growing reliance on nuclear weapons diminishes the chances that its military establishment will accept the policy."

De-alerting is a cause as well as an effect of the political climate. The

United States can improve the climate by de-alerting in a manner that demonstrates its positive nuclear intentions and reduces its nuclear threat to Russia. Russian military planners can appreciate the advantage to Russian security that a de-alerting regime can provide. From a narrow military standpoint Russia would be better off with mutual de-alerting than without it.

Russian military planners no doubt worry that U.S. and NATO conventional aircraft could not only severely disrupt Russian attempts at re-alerting during wartime, but could also destroy a large portion of the Russian strategic arsenal using precision-guided conventional weapons.[30] But this concern should not be exaggerated. Russian analysts appreciate the implausibility of NATO's mounting a large bolt-from-the-blue conventional assault. They assume several months advance warning of such an attack, time enough to fully re-alert their strategic forces. Moreover, Russian planners realize that the loss estimates given earlier would be sustained over two or three months, and they would therefore have ample time to decide whether to resort to nuclear weapons.

—"U.S. de-alerting, even if fully reciprocated by Russia, could be exploited by China or unfriendly nations, particularly the so-called rogue states, that might brandish weapons of mass destruction. By the same token, Russia needs to maintain strategic forces on high alert to deter China."

The United States does not require many nuclear weapons to project a deterrent threat to any rogue state, and a large de-alerted U.S. nuclear arsenal could not be prudently discounted by a potential adversary. If U.S. national security required a more overt nuclear threat, ample time would be available under plausible scenarios to re-alert a small number of strategic weapons systems. In any case, U.S. planners would probably prefer nuclear-armed aircraft and sea-launched cruise missiles to carry out such missions, and these delivery systems are not alert today.

Similar considerations apply to Russia's nuclear posture. Russia does not need thousands of nuclear weapons on high alert in peacetime to deter China's small, de-alerted nuclear forces (its theater nuclear weapons are also believed to be de-alerted) nor to deter a Chinese conventional attack. In the event of a confrontation with China, a de-alerted Russian arsenal would suffice to deter Chinese attack. If Russia's national survival became seriously

30. Russian assessments show, for example, that such conventional aircraft strikes could destroy 60 percent of Russian strategic missile silos, 15 percent of mobile strategic forces, and almost 100 percent of strategic submarines in port, not to mention the considerable damage that could be inflicted on strategic early warning sites and command posts. See. for example, Alexei Arbatov's appendix in this book.

threatened—either because China put its nuclear arsenal on alert or invaded with conventional forces—Russia could re-alert an adequate number of nuclear forces in response.

—"De-alerting would prevent nuclear personnel from receiving proper training; they would lose proficiency in operating forces at high states of readiness and their morale would decline."

The proficient performance of alert and launch procedures already largely depends on exercises and training in simulators. It is worth recalling that no country has any actual experience in conducting strategic nuclear operations in wartime. Morale might suffer somewhat from a perceived loss of mission priority, but other ways to address this concern must be found. After all, the cold war ended, and pretending otherwise to keep up the morale of nuclear warriors is a dubious rationale.

—"De-alerting puts the cart before the horse. The horse is new presidential nuclear guidance that revises the requirements of deterrence to allow for a sharp reduction in alert levels and the number and type of targets that must be covered."

Systematic de-alerting presupposes a dramatic change in nuclear policy and bold direction from the president. Such guidance needs to downgrade the importance of prompt attack on opposing nuclear forces and command systems and acknowledge the paramount importance of safety and safeguards.

Prospects for the De-alerting Agenda

Despite presidential inaction on the de-alerting agenda, some headway has been made toward its adoption. A crucial boost occurred when former Senator Sam Nunn publicly endorsed the basic concept in 1997.[31] His caution and credibility in defense affairs prompted the Joint Chiefs of Staff to undertake a thorough analysis of Nunn's specific de-alerting proposals as well as his general argument and led to a more comprehensive study of possible de-alerting options. Senator Nunn and Bruce Blair met General Joseph Ralston, vice-chairman of the Joint Chiefs of Staff, to exchange views on de-alerting possibilities. Simultaneously, an interagency working group

31. Sam Nunn and Bruce Blair, "From Nuclear Deterrence to Mutual Safety," *Washington Post*, June 22, 1997, p. C1.

within the executive branch was formed to consider this agenda and make appropriate recommendations to the secretary of defense and other senior national security officials.[32]

Congressional interest in de-alerting also gained strength during this period as Senators Tom Daschle and Jeff Bingaman embraced the concept and called on the Clinton administration to give it serious consideration. Other Senators, notably Pete Domenici, also expressed some support for the idea.[33] And Bingaman managed to overcome Republican resistance to holding hearings on the issue, which convened in March 1998. In late 1998, Senator Bob Kerrey advocated a bold step down this road. He called for the unilateral de-alerting of the U.S. forces down to START III levels and serious examination of a total U.S. and Russian stand down.

Popularization of the de-alerting idea has resulted from its visibility in the general media, ranging from segments aired on *60 Minutes* and *Frontline* to coverage by the *New York Times*.[34] The issue achieved a sufficiently high profile to draw both support and criticism from major editorial writers.[35] Grassroots awareness of the agenda also grew because of the media, and many nongovernmental organizations concerned with nuclear security endorsed de-alerting. De-alerting also formed the centerpiece of a recent nonaligned initiative of eight nations led by Ireland and Sweden (calling for global zero alert of nuclear forces); their UN resolution was passed in late 1998.

The U.S. government has not yet embraced de-alerting, however, although it has actively studied the possibilities. One possible scenario for more attention to de-alerting would be if the Russian Duma fails to ratify START II and negotiations on START III remain stalled. In this case de-alerting may by default become the dominant alternative agenda for reviving a dialogue with Russia on strategic nuclear arms.

Alternatively, if START II is ratified, weapons systems slated for elimination under this and subsequent START agreements could become candi-

32. Bill Gertz, "Pentagon Panel Weighs Lower Nuclear Alert Status," *Washington Times*, December 12, 1997, p. 1.

33. Ian Hoffman, "Domenici Leans toward 'De-Alerting,'" *Albuquerque Journal*, November 14, 1997.

34. See Brian Hall, "Overkill Is Not Dead," *New York Times Magazine*, March 15, 1998. Also, Tim Zimmerman, "Take Nuclear Weapons Off Hair-Trigger Alert," *U.S. News and World Report*, December 29, 1998; and James Kitfield, "Don't Get MAD, Get De-Alerted," *National Journal*, January 3, 1998.

35. Endorsing de-alerting was the editorial page of the *New York Times*, "Russia's Nuclear Temptation," January 12, 1998. Opposing the idea was the *Wall Street Journal*, "Stay on Alert," January 20, 1998.

dates for early deactivation, and the more survivable systems that remain could be moved to lower alert as the current launch-on-warning postures are increasingly recognized to be anachronistic.

Conclusion

The continuing risks of mistaken or illicit nuclear attack associated with the hair-trigger postures are vestiges of the cold war that defy justification in today's world. These risks, run in the name of deterrence, stem from a misplaced emphasis on deliberate bolt-out-of-the-blue surprise attacks, but the more serious dangers today consist of accidental, unauthorized, or inadvertent attack. The progressive deterioration of Russia's command system only heightens these concerns.

By removing their nuclear missiles from launch-ready alert, the United States and Russia could establish a far higher standard of operational safety without eroding nuclear deterrence. De-alerting unilaterally and in parallel should be undertaken to slow the reaction times of most missiles from minutes to hours or days. Weapons taken off alert cannot be fired on false warning, and they are far less susceptible to other forms of accidental or unauthorized use.

This agenda of operational arms control warrants urgent consideration. The former adversaries no longer have reason to fear a deliberate surprise nuclear attack and can no longer justify operating their nuclear forces as though this threat still exists. Their hair-trigger postures are vestiges of an era that has passed.

CHAPTER SEVEN

Nuclear Forces under
Staged Reductions

This chapter describes how U.S. and Russian nuclear weapons, and eventually those of the other charter nuclear weapon states, could be reduced through a series of reductions to a level of 200 warheads per country. We propose that the reductions be done in three stages. The first (START III) would reduce the number of operational strategic warheads in the U.S. and Russian arsenals to 2,000 warheads each. Stage two (START IV) would reduce them to 1,000 operational warheads of all types. Stage three (START V) would reduce them to 200 total warheads. Such reductions could be carried out in many different ways, and the future force structures presented here are primarily intended to illustrate how deep reductions could be implemented in a stabilizing manner.

U.S. and Russian Nuclear Forces at the Beginning of 1998

U.S. and Russian nuclear forces will be derived largely from their existing forces for at least the next ten years. Table 7-1 gives an overview of these forces at the beginning of 1998. The United States and Russia have somewhat more than 7,000 and 6,000 *operational strategic* warheads, respectively. The United States also has about 1,000 and Russia perhaps 4,000 *operational tactical* nuclear warheads, all of which are currently in storage.

In this book the word *operational* refers to warheads that are associated with delivery vehicles allowed by treaties and have not been designated for elimination. Operational warheads can be either *deployed*, that is mated to their delivery systems, or demated and *stored* for possible future deployment on permitted delivery systems. Aside from operational warheads, there can also be *reserve* or *hedge* warheads that cannot be legally deployed under current treaties but are nevertheless kept in storage for possible future rede-

Table 7-1. U.S. and Russian Operational Nuclear Forces
at the Beginning of 1998

Country and weapon	Launchers	Warheads
United States		
ICBMs in silos	550	2,000
SLBMs on submarines	432	3,456
Bombers	92	1,800
Tactical weapons	0	970
Total		~8,200
Russia		
ICBMs in silos	355	2,890
Mobile ICBMs	396	720
SLBMs in submarines	384	1,824
Bombers	70	806
Tactical weapons	0	3,900
Strategic ballistic missile defense	100	100[a]
Total		~10,200

Source: William M. Arkin, Robert S. Norris, and Joshua Handler, *Taking Stock: Worldwide Nuclear Deployments 1998* (Washington: Natural Resources Defense Council, March 1998), pp. 14, 27.

a. These nuclear missile defense warheads may have recently been replaced by conventional warheads.

ployment. There are also spare warheads for routine stockpile maintenance and warheads in storage pending dismantlement.

Relatively few additions to the U.S. and Russian strategic nuclear forces are expected in the near future. The United States has no current plans to develop or deploy new types of strategic delivery systems. However, several test model B-2 bombers are being refurbished to fully operational configurations, and four of the eight Trident I armed ballistic missile submarines are being retrofitted with Trident II missiles, bringing the total to fourteen Trident II armed submarines. In addition, Minuteman III ICBMs are undergoing a program to extend their lives to 2020 and improve their accuracy.

On the Russian side the SS-25 mobile ICBM may still be in production at a low rate. A new version of the SS-25, the all-Russian-built SS-27 (known in Russia as the SS-25M or the Topol-M), which is to be built in both road-mobile and silo-based versions, was first deployed in early 1998. Several new Russian systems, including the SS-NX-28 SLBM, a new ballistic missile submarine, and a new air-launched cruise missile (ALCM) are also reportedly being developed, but at a very slow pace.[1] At the same time, as discussed in Alexi Arbatov's appendix to this book, Russia's strategic forces

1. The list of Russian systems under development is based on comments by General Eugene Habiger, commander in chief of the U.S. Strategic Command. He further stated that the only new Russian system undergoing a normal development was the SS-27. Barbara Starr, "Russian Nuclear Modernization in Slow-down," *Jane's Defence Weekly*, August 28, 1996, p. 5.

Table 7-2. U.S. and Russian Strategic Nuclear Forces
at the Beginning of 1998

Country and weapon	Launchers	Warheads
United States		
Silo-based ICBMs		
Minuteman III	500 (× 3 warheads)	1,500
MX	50 (× 10 warheads)	500
SLBMs		
Trident I	192 (× 8 warheads)	1,536
Trident II	240 (× 8 warheads)	1,920
Bombers		
B-2	21 (× 16 bombs) ⎫	
B-52H	71 (× 20 ALCMs, ACMs, or bombs) ⎬	1,800
Total		7,250
Russia		
Silo-based ICBMs		
SS-18	180 (× 10 warheads)	1,800
SS-19	165 (× 6 warheads)	990
SS-24	10 (× 10 warheads)	100
Mobile ICBMs		
SS-24	36 (× 10 warheads)	360
SS-25	360 (× 1 warhead)	360
SLBMs		
SS-N-18	192 (12 Delta III × 16 × 3 warheads)	576
SS-N-20	80 (4 Typhoon × 20 × 10 warheads)	800
SS-N-23	112 (7 Delta IV × 16 × 4 warheads)	448
Bombers		
Bear H6	29 (× 6 ALCMs or bombs)	174
Bear H16	35 (× 16 ALCMs or bombs)	560
Blackjack	6 (× 12 ALCMs, SRAMs, or bombs)	72
Total		6,240

Source: Arkin, Norris, and Handler, *Taking Stock*, pp. 14, 27.

are facing widespread obsolescence that will make it difficult and perhaps impossible to deploy as many warheads as permitted under START II.

U.S. and Russian Strategic Forces under START I and II

Table 7-2 presents a more detailed breakdown of U.S. and Russian strategic nuclear forces. These already reflect many of the constraints mandated by START I. START II will require far deeper reductions. (The central provisions of the two START treaties are described in chapter 1).

For the United States, reductions to the START II level are straightfor-

Table 7-3. Notional START II Forces at the End of 2007

Country and weapon	Launchers	Warheads
United States		
Silo-based ICBMs		
Minuteman III	500 (× 1 warhead)	500
SLBMs		
Trident II	336 (× 5 warheads)	1,680
Bombers		
B-2	20 (× 16 bombs)	320
B-52H	16 (× 20 ALCMs or ACMs)	360
B-52H	53 (× 12 ALCMs or ACMs)	636
Total		3,496
Russia		
Silo-based ICBMs		
SS-19	105 (× 1 warhead)	105
SS-27	40 (× 1 warhead)	40
Mobile ICBMs		
SS-25	45 (× 1 warhead)	45
SS-27	70 (× 1 warhead)	70
SLBMs		
SS-N-20	60 (3 Typhoon × 20 × 10 warheads)	600
SS-N-23	80 (5 Delta IV × 16 × 4 warheads)	320
New SSBNs	24 (2 SSBNs × 12 × 4 warheads)	96
Bombers		
Bear H16	35 (× 16 ALCMs)	560
Bear H6	28 (× 6 ALCMs)	168
Blackjack	6 (× 12 ALCMs)	72
Total		2,076

Source: Russian numbers based on Paul Podvig, "The Russian Strategic Forces: Uncertain Future," *Breakthroughs*, M.I.T. Securities Studies Program, vol. 7 (Spring 1998), pp. 11–21. Podvig's figure for the current number of Bear H6 bomber is one lower than those Arkin, Norris, and Handler used for table 8-2, thus the change in that number between these two tables represents different starting assumptions rather than the elimination of one bomber.

ward and were set by the 1994 Nuclear Posture Review (see table 7-3). Each leg of the triad will simply be scaled back. The 50 ten-warhead MX ICBMs will be eliminated as required by the treaty, and 450 to 500 Minuteman III ICBMs will be kept but downloaded from three warheads to one. Fourteen Trident submarines will be deployed, each with twenty-four Trident II missiles; these missiles will be downloaded from eight to five warheads, for a total of 1,680. The strategic nuclear bomber force will consist of 21 B-2s, each capable of carrying 16 bombs, and 71 B-52Hs,[2] each equipped to carry

2. The Nuclear Posture Review called for 66 B-52Hs to be retained, but this was later increased to 71. Of these, 44 will be operational, 12 will be used as trainers, and the remaining 15 will be assigned to attrition reserve–depot maintenance status. See Robert S. Norris and William M. Arkin, "NRDC Nuclear Notebook: U.S. Strategic Forces, End of 1996," *Bulletin of the Atomic Scientists*, vol. 53 (January-February 1997), pp. 70–71.

either 12 or 20 cruise missiles.[3] All B-1B bombers will remain as conventional bombers.

The possible structure of Russian strategic forces under START II is much less clear, given the great uncertainty about Russia's ability to maintain its existing forces, much less build new ones. The number and structure of Russian forces over the START II time frame will likely be determined more by Russia's ability to fund adequate maintenance and life extension programs than by its ability to deploy new strategic forces. The one thing that does seem clear is that Russia will not be able to deploy enough deliverable warheads to reach the START II limit of 3,500 warheads. The notional Russian START II force structure presented in table 7-3 and discussed later is based on analysis by Paul Podvig.[4]

START II will require Russia to eliminate all its 10-warhead SS-18 and SS-24 ICBMs, although allowing up to 90 SS-18 silos to be retained to house new single-warhead missiles. However, up to 105 of the 6-warhead SS-19 ICBMs can be downloaded to a single warhead each and retained. Russia currently deploys about 360 single-warhead mobile SS-25 missiles. However, even if, as seems likely, the lifetime of this missile is extended to fifteen years, only 45 would remain by the end of 2007. Thus, leaving aside new production, the Russian ICBM force would be reduced from its current total of nearly 3,500 warheads to about 105 on silo-based SS-19s and 45 on mobile SS-25s.

Assuming that production of the SS-27 essentially supplants that of the SS-25 (they are built at the same factory) and that it is built at the same rate of about ten a year that the SS-25 was built during the 1990s, by the end of 2007 Russia would have about 110 SS-27s. Podvig estimates that the first 40 would be silo based and the next 70 would be the road-mobile version. Thus the total Russian START II ICBM force at the end of 2007 would consist of about 260 single-warhead missiles.

Aging and obsolescence, coupled with a severe shortage of funds for both routine maintenance and new construction, will almost certainly prevent

3. B-52H bombers can be equipped with an internal rotary launcher capable of carrying eight cruise missiles, and are also able to carry up to 12 cruise missiles on external pylons and thus can carry up to 20 cruise missiles. Under START II, B-52Hs could be configured to carry 20 weapons (rotary launcher plus external pylons), 12 weapons (external pylons only), or 8 weapons (rotary launcher only). B-2 bombers are able to carry up to two rotary launchers, each able to carry 8 bombs or cruise missiles, although at present only bombs are carried. Mark Lambert, ed., *Jane's All the World's Aircraft, 1991–92* (Surrey, U.K.: Jane's Information Group, 1991), p. 371; and Paul Jackson, ed., *Jane's All the World's Aircraft, 1998–99* (Surrey, U.K.: Jane's Information Group, 1998), p. 662.

4. Paul Podvig, "The Russian Strategic Forces: Uncertain Future," *Breakthroughs*, M.I.T. Securities Studies Program, vol. 7 (Spring 1998), pp. 11–21.

Russia from deploying all 1,750 SLBM warheads it is allowed under START II. Podvig estimates that only eight Russian ballistic missile submarines will still be operational by the end of 2007, five Delta IV submarines (each armed with 16 four-warhead missiles) and three Typhoons (each armed with 20 ten-warhead missiles). In late 1996, construction began on the first of a new class of ballistic missile submarine, which is expected to enter service in 2004. The precise nature and number of the missiles that this new submarine will carry is not publicly known, but is likely to be either 12 or 16 relatively small missiles per submarine. Assuming 12 four-warhead missiles and that 2 of these new ballistic missile submarines can be deployed by the end of 2007, the START II Russian force could include 10 submarines carrying 1,016 warheads.

Russia's strategic bomber force has suffered from such a severe lack of financing that its future viability is in question. However, Podvig notes that Russia's remaining TU-95MS Bear and TU-160 Blackjack bombers are all of relatively recent construction. The Bears were built in the late 1980s and the Blackjacks in 1991–92, and both could stay in service beyond 2010. Podvig projects a Russian START II bomber force composed of the current 63 Bears and 6 Blackjacks, carrying 800 nuclear cruise missiles. Although we use these figures in table 7-3, other projections for the future Russian bomber force are much lower. In an appendix to this book, Alexei Arbatov projects that Russia will have no more than 20 strategic bombers remaining by 2010.

The overall Russian force structure under START II shown in table 7-3 therefore contains 2,076 nuclear warheads, well below the START II limit of 3,500. However, unlike the U.S. numbers, these numbers are highly speculative. The actual number of bomber weapons may be much lower. But greater emphasis on maintenance and life extension for the SS-25s could lead to 100 or more additional SS-25s remaining in service at the end of 2007.

The most dramatic deviation from this projection might occur if severe Russian economic difficulties prevent significant maintenance and life extension efforts. This could lead to strategic forces falling to or even well under 1,000 nuclear weapons by the end of 2007. An improved Russian economy, however, could enable a greater number of weapons to be deployed, particularly if Russia sees its security environment as evolving in an unfavorable direction. But at the Helsinki Summit in March 1997 Presidents Clinton and Yeltsin agreed to a START III goal of reductions to a level of 2,000–2,500 strategic weapons by the end of 2007, contingent on the ratification of START II by the Russian Duma. Thus, assuming it ratifies START II, Russia would appear to have little incentive to build up its forces much beyond the 2,000 or so warheads shown in table 7-3.

Criteria for Force Reductions

Many different, although interrelated, considerations must be taken into account if the large existing nuclear forces are to be reduced in a stabilizing manner. These include:

—Survivability. As discussed in chapter 3 the only realistic role for nuclear weapons is to deter the use of nuclear weapons by other countries. This requires that an adequate portion of the force must be able to ride out and survive any plausible attack by a nuclear aggressor.

—Crisis stability. No country should perceive an advantage in striking first, even if war seems likely.

—Low launch readiness. As discussed in chapter 6, to the greatest extent possible, nuclear forces should be incapable of surprise attack because measures taken by other states to guard against the possibility of a surprise attack often increase the risk of accidental or unauthorized use.

—Arms race stability. No country should see advantage in developing new weapons or increasing its number of deployed weapons.

—Safety and security. Nuclear forces should be as immune as possible to accident, theft, or unauthorized use.

—Transparency. Nuclear forces should be deployed in ways that allow other parties to adequately verify their number and operational status.

—Cost. The cost of deploying and operating nuclear forces may constrain options for future force structures. In general, cost considerations will lead to the use of existing delivery vehicles rather than new systems optimized for a new strategic environment.

There are numerous synergies and trade-offs between these criteria. For example, survivability is the key to crisis stability and arms race stability. However, survivability usually is obtained by hiding missiles, which makes it difficult to verify their launch readiness, although it may be easier to verify whether they are within range of targets. The various advantages and disadvantages of particular force configurations must be weighed carefully when designing future nuclear forces.

The discussion in this chapter focuses on technical issues and the criteria above. However, it must be recognized that national traditions, military service rivalries and biases, and other factors could be crucial in shaping the ultimate structure of the nuclear forces.

Tactical, Reserve, and Ballistic Missile Defense Warheads

In addition to strategic weapons, the United States and Russia have operational tactical nuclear weapons such as long-range nuclear SLCMs and nuclear bombs for tactical bombers.[5] Russia also has, among other types, nuclear antiship, antiaircraft, and antisubmarine weapons.[6] After START II is implemented the United States plans to retain several thousand reserve strategic warheads that could be redeployed onto its partially downloaded Trident and Minuteman III missiles and onto its B-1 bombers. Russia's plans, if any, for reserve strategic warheads are not known. Finally, Russia has one hundred missile interceptors, deployed as part of its strategic ABM system near Moscow, which have historically been equipped with nuclear warheads. These other nuclear weapons cannot be ignored in carrying out the deep cuts proposed in this book.[7]

The illustrative force structures for START IV and START V advanced in the remainder of this chapter and reflected in the tables take into consideration these nonstrategic and reserve warheads. But the detailed discussion of how they should be treated is put off until chapter 8.

British, French, and Chinese Forces

The staged reductions by the United States and Russia to 2,000 warheads (START III), and certainly the reductions to 1,000 warheads (START IV),

5. Long-range SLCMs have enough range to play strategic roles, and are similar in many respects to strategic ALCMs. Russia regards these weapons as strategic, not tactical, weapons. Thus the Helsinki agreement spoke of exploring measures on "nuclear long-range sea-launched cruise missiles and tactical nuclear systems." As part of the START I Treaty, both the United States and Soviet Union made politically binding declarations not to deploy more than 880 long-range (greater than 600 km) nuclear SLCMs. However, for simplicity and because the 1991 unilateral initiatives on tactical weapons included SLCMs, we will refer to them here as tactical weapons.

6. Land-based nuclear air defense weapons are sometimes categorized together with nuclear missile defense weapons as nuclear strategic defense weapons. These weapons could take a strategic defensive role against U.S. strategic bombers. However, as a result of the 1991 mutual unilateral initiatives (see chapter 9), all the warheads for these weapons are in storage. Moreover, these weapons could have tactical uses as well, and nonnuclear versions probably exist. Given this situation, and that we are calling for the elimination of these weapons, nuclear air defense weapons should be treated as tactical weapons rather than complicate matters by creating a separate category of weapons for which the United States has no equivalent. This approach too would be consistent with the fact that these weapons have already been treated as tactical weapons in the unilateral initiatives.

7. Robert S. Norris and William M. Arkin, "Nuclear Notebook: U.S. Nuclear Weapons Stockpile, July 1996," *Bulletin of the Atomic Scientists*, vol. 52 (July-August 1996), pp. 61–63.

assume that France, Britain, and China will at least agree to limit the sizes of their nuclear forces to near current levels. Reductions to 200 warheads will require direct involvement by these countries.[8]

Britain

Britain has recently deployed three new Vanguard-class SSBNs, with a fourth under construction, each able to carry 16 U.S.-built Trident II missiles. Until recently, it also had about 100 nuclear bombs for tactical aircraft, but the bombs were withdrawn from service on March 31, 1998, and are likely to be dismantled.[9] Thus the British nuclear arsenal now consists only of SLBMs deployed on four submarines. It appears that Britain intends for individual submarines to carry SLBMs with differing numbers of warheads, with some SLBMs being armed with only one or two warheads to allow options for limited strikes. As part of its Strategic Defence Review, the results of which were announced in July 1998, the British Defence Ministry announced that only one submarine would be kept on patrol at any time, and that it would carry only 48 warheads.[10] This corresponds to an average of three warheads per missile and is reduced from the previously announced ceiling of 96 warheads per submarine. Moreover, the missiles will not be targeted and will be at a reduced state of alert, a "notice to fire" of several days. In the past, Britain has leased from the United States only enough Trident II missiles to equip three of its four submarines, on the assumption that one submarine will always be undergoing a refit. This practice will apparently continue. According to the Strategic Defence Review, the British stockpile will be less than 200 operationally available nuclear warheads.

France

The French nuclear arsenal contains warheads for delivery both by SLBMs and by the ASMP, an air-to-ground missile carried by tactical aircraft. All

8. These descriptions and projections are based on information from Robert S. Norris and William M. Arkin, "NRDC Nuclear Notebook: British, French and Chinese Nuclear Forces," *Bulletin of the Atomic Scientists*, vol. 52 (November-December 1996), pp. 64–67; Robert S. Norris, Andrew S. Burrows, and Richard Fieldhouse, *Nuclear Weapons Databook*, vol. 5: *British, French, and Chinese Nuclear Weapons* (Boulder, Colo.: Westview Press, 1994); and William M. Arkin, Robert S. Norris, and Joshua Handler, *Taking Stock: Worldwide Nuclear Deployments, 1998* (Washington: Natural Resources Defense Council, 1998), pp. 13, 39–46.

9. "News Briefs: UK Withdraws Tactical Nukes From Service," *Arms Control Today* (March 1998), p. 28.

10. The *Strategic Defence Review* is available online at: http://www.mod.uk/policy/sdr/index.htm.

of France's nuclear bombs and nuclear-armed short- and intermediate-range ballistic missiles have now been retired. France's SLBM force now consists of one new Triomphant-class submarine armed with 16 M45 SLBMs capable of carrying six warheads each, and 48 six-warhead M4 SLBMs deployed on three older SSBNs, for a total of 384 warheads. France intends to move to an all Triomphant force of four submarines by about 2005. At that point the French force would consist of four SSBNs and enough missiles to fully equip three—48 SLBMs carrying as many as 288 warheads (with one submarine assumed to be undergoing a refit). A new SLBM, the M51, is planned for deployment on these submarines sometime after 2010.

Approximately 65 nuclear ASMP air-to-ground missiles with a range of 300 km are deployed on land-based Mirage 2000N and aircraft carrier—based Super Etendard attack aircraft. The ASMP will also be deployed on the Rafale fighter-bomber when the land-based and naval nuclear-capable variants of this plane become operational around 2005. A version of this missile, the "ASMP plus," with a range of 500 km may also be deployed sometime after 2005.

China

Much less is known about current Chinese nuclear forces and future plans for these forces than for the other charter nuclear weapons states. China is believed to possess 250–300 nuclear warheads deliverable by ballistic missiles or aircraft, although the ranges of almost all are far less than what would be considered strategic by the United States or Russia. It may also possess battlefield nuclear weapons—artillery shells, short-range rockets, or demolition munitions.

China apparently has a small number of silo-based, single-warhead DF-5A ICBMs, perhaps as few as seven or as many as twenty. It is reportedly developing a new ICBM, the DF-31, that could be deployed by the end of the century. The DF-31 will likely have a single warhead and a relatively short range for an ICBM, about 8,000 km, and apparently will be based in caves. China is also believed to be developing a new full-range ICBM, the DF-41, which will be mobile and may be MIRVed. The country has not yet tested or deployed a MIRVed missile, although the deployment of multiple satellites from space launch rockets indicates that it has most of the technology needed to do so. China is also currently believed to deploy about 100 single-warhead, intermediate-range ballistic missiles (the DF-3, DF-4, and DF-21), with ranges varying between 1,800 and 4,750 km. The DF-3 and DF-21 are both road-mobile, while the DF-4 is based in silos and tunnels and caves.

China is believed to operate one Xia-class SSBN armed with 12 single-warhead Julang-1 SLBMs. The 1,700 km range of the Julang-1 greatly limits its potential target coverage and deployment areas. China is developing a longer-range single-warhead SLBM, the Julang-2, which is expected to be deployed on a new class of SSBN.

China currently deploys two types of nuclear-capable aircraft. It has 120 B-6 bombers (based on the Russian TU-16 Badger) with a combat radius of about 3,100 km and about 30 shorter-range nuclear-capable A-5 attack aircraft (a modification of the Russian MiG-19), with a combat radius of 400 km. It also has many other types of aircraft that could potentially be given the capability to deliver nuclear weapons.

Nuclear Force Structures at Low Force Levels

In the process of reducing national nuclear forces to 200 warheads at low alert levels, new issues will be raised regarding the structure of the forces. Survivability will be even more important than today. When each country has only a small number of warheads deployed, their survivability must be beyond question. In addition, the triad concept as traditionally practiced by the United States and Russia may not make sense (if for no other reason than cost) when a country has only a few tens of warheads deployed in the field.[11] Each country is likely to concentrate its efforts on those force components it believes are most survivable and effective. This choice could be very different for different countries.

---

11. A key argument underlying the triad was that the different basing modes synergistically improved each other's survivability. For example, to have a significant chance of destroying U.S bombers, Russia would have had to attack them from close-in submarines with short-flight-time SLBMs, which were not accurate enough to destroy U.S. ICBM silos. Assuming the Russian ICBMS and SLBMs were launched at the same time, U.S. ICBMs could then be launched, based on the unambiguous evidence of the SLBM warhead explosions, in the roughly fifteen minutes before the more accurate Russian ICBM warheads arrived. But if the Russian ICBMs were launched first, so as to arrive at the same time as the SLBM warheads, the U.S. bombers could be dispersed as soon as the ICBM launches were detected and would have enough time to have a high probability of escaping. However, with the small forces proposed here, in which all forces are either deactivated or deployed unlocatably in the field, this synergism no longer applies.

Single-Warhead Silo-based ICBMs

Silo-based, single-warhead ICBMs have a number of significant advantages. They are controllable and secure, relatively easy to de-alert and verify, and their single warhead allows targeting flexibility, particularly in scenarios involving the use of only a few nuclear weapons.[12] They are the only delivery system for which multiple warheads are *never* vulnerable to destruction by a single attacking warhead: destroying a silo-based ICBM force requires a relatively large-scale attack using accurate missiles. This has potentially significant implications for the de-alerting and deactivation advocated in this book: a small silo-based ICBM force that was deactivated by removing its warheads and placing each warhead in an otherwise empty missile silo could not be totally destroyed by an attacking force of equal size unless the entire attacking force was expended (and even so, some of the deactivated ICBMs would be likely to survive). Other force elements that are not deployed out of their bases are vulnerable to destruction by only a few warheads—in the U.S. case perhaps only four or five: two B-52H bases, one B-2 base, and one or two Trident submarine bases.

Nevertheless, because their locations cannot be concealed, silo-based ICBMs will remain vulnerable to attack by accurate missiles (and perhaps even by conventionally armed cruise missiles). Put another way, silo-based ICBMs are the only basing mode considered here in which a given weapon *cannot* be made survivable, at least as long as accurate missiles exist, even though some portion of an ICBM force would be expected to survive an attack by a force of equal size. Verifiably deactivating silo-based ICBMs would prevent them from being rapidly launched, but they could remain vulnerable to any deployed SLBMs or to reactivated ICBMs. As long as vulnerable, silo-based missiles exist, there could be pressures to be ready to launch them on warning of an attack. Their vulnerability could thus be an obstacle to the nearly complete de-alerting that is a central objective of the program laid out in this book.

The United States, Russia, and China currently deploy silo-based missiles; France recently retired its silo-based missiles, and Britain has never deployed any. Given the highly secure SSBN force of the United States, elimination of silo-based ICBMs as part of reductions to small nuclear forces would seem to be a possibility it could at least consider. However, even though

---

12. However, to the extent that it is necessary to deliver a single warhead, it would also be possible to deploy a small number of otherwise MIRVed SLBMs with a single warhead. A single warhead could also be delivered via a cruise missile from a bomber.

after START II the Russian silo-based ICBM force will be highly vulnerable to U.S. Trident II SLBMs, silo-based missiles have always been the central component of Russia's strategic forces and for this reason, as well as economic ones, Russia may be more reluctant to give up such missiles. China may also choose to retain silo-based missiles.

Ballistic Missile Submarines

The great strength of ballistic missile submarines is their survivability. Properly operated, quiet SSBNs are essentially unlocatable and thus invulnerable once at sea. Submarines in port are highly vulnerable, however, and the United States, Britain, and France have therefore kept a large part of their SSBNs at sea at all times, although as a result of its Strategic Defence Review Britain will now routinely keep only one SSBN at sea. The same characteristics that make SSBNs so survivable, however, may also make it more difficult to be confident that those at sea are not on a launch-ready status.

The greatest concern with SSBNs as a component of very small nuclear forces is likely to be the possibility of tracking by hostile attack submarines, given that the absolute numbers of deployable SSBNs will be small. For example, the future number of deployable British or French SSBNs is likely to be at most two or three each, and an accident involving one could reduce either force to no more than one or two that are deployable. The possibility of trailing by Russian attack submarines, while perhaps technically implausible, could be a concern for such a small force. As we suggest in this book, combining British and French forces into a single nuclear force containing perhaps six to eight submarines (comparable in size to the SSBN force the United States might maintain) could considerably ameliorate this concern.

The United States, Britain, and France appear to have enough confidence in the survivability of their SSBNs to make them a central component of a small nuclear force. Britain has already gone to a nuclear force based only on SSBNs. The situation with Russia is less certain. Russian submarines historically have been noisier, and thus less survivable, than U.S. submarines. But they have become successively quieter and are probably survivable in their current operating areas.[13] In recent years, however, Russia has maintained only a small part of its SSBNs at sea at any one time.[14]

13. Eugene Miasnikov, "Can Russian Submarines Survive at Sea? The Fundamental Limits of Passive Acoustics," *Science and Global Security*, vol. 4, no. 2. (1994), pp. 213–51.

14. The total annual number of Russian SSBN patrols declined from 37 in 1991 to 13 in 1997. The annual number of Russian SSBN patrols were 1991: 37; 1992: 28; 1993: 19; 1994:

Although from a purely technical point of view Russia could probably operate its SSBNs survivably, Russian decisionmakers may not feel confident about this, and Russian-Soviet tradition, which has always favored land-based missiles, may also weigh against relying heavily on SSBNs as the core of a small force. The retention of an SSBN force could be counterproductive to the objectives laid out in this book if Russia was either unable or unwilling (perhaps because of a lack of confidence in their survivability) to keep a significant force at sea. To compensate for its currently small number of deployed SSBNs, Russia apparently maintains several submarines in a dockside launch-on-warning posture at all times, and continuation of such a practice would be contrary to the de-alerting goals laid out here. Given the slow rate at which new weapons have been developed and deployed by China, it is far from clear that in the time scale considered here, China could produce a ballistic missile submarine force that would be survivable against U.S. or Russian antisubmarine warfare forces.

Bombers

Bombers have a number of advantages. They can be readily and verifiably de-alerted, and their long flight times to targets may make them less suited to surprise attack.[15] They are the only strategic delivery system capable of recall once launched. They can, in principle, search out and attack a target whose location is only approximately known, and they can be dispersed to many different airfields so that they cannot themselves be easily targeted.[16]

19; 1995: 14; 1996: 12; and 1997: 13. (U.S. Navy, Office of Naval Intelligence, "Russian Strategic and General Purpose Nuclear Submarine Patrols, 1991–1996," letter, March 26, 1997, and "Russian Strategic and General Purpose Nuclear Submarine Patrols, 1997," letter, March 11, 1998, both released under the Freedom of Information Act to Joshua Handler at the Center for Energy and Environmental Studies at Princeton University.) Thirteen patrols a year at an average of 72 days a patrol gives an average of 2.6 ballistic missile submarines at sea at any one time. (The 72-day patrol length figure is from General John J. Sheehan, commander in chief, U.S. Atlantic Command, in testimony before the House Appropriations Committee, *Department of Defense Appropriations for 1996*, pt. 3, March 7, 1995, p. 335). Although this number of submarines at sea is small compared with the number of U.S. ballistic missile submarines, it is still greater than that of either France or Britain.

15. However, an attack by a small number of stealth bombers or cruise missiles might not be detected until they actually reach their targets, raising a threat of an attack with no warning. George N. Lewis and Theodore A. Postol, "Long-range Nuclear Cruise Missiles and Stability," *Science and Global Security*, vol. 3 (1993), pp. 49–99.

16. Although searching out a target may be an advantage for conventional bombing missions, nuclear attacks are generally launched against fixed geographic points. Moreover, most strategic bombers are now cruise missile carriers rather than bomb droppers.

Bombers can also be launched on warning, either to carry out a retaliatory attack or to seek out a safe place to wait out an attack.[17] In addition, they can provide a hedge against future deployments of strategic ballistic missile defenses.

However, bombers and the cruise missiles they carry are potentially vulnerable to air defenses. Although dispersal to achieve survivability would probably become more effective as nuclear arsenals are reduced, a political decision to disperse would be required. Because bombers assigned to conventional duties could be adapted for nuclear use relatively easily and because nuclear bombers deployed with only a small number of weapons could be adapted to carry more, bombers could pose a breakout threat unless nuclear bombs themselves are rigidly controlled (but such a breakout threat might be viewed as less threatening than a breakout based on ballistic missiles).

Only the United States and Russia operate intercontinental strategic bombers. The strong strategic bomber tradition and the desire to retain conventional heavy bombers make the retention of strategic bombers in a small U.S. nuclear arsenal relatively more likely, while the lack of such factors makes the elimination of Russian strategic bombers a real possibility. All the charter nuclear weapons states except Britain retain shorter-range nuclear-armed aircraft, and such aircraft are likely to be retained in at least some small nuclear forces.

Mobile ICBMs

Mobile ICBMs can be deployed on roads, railroads, or ships sailing on rivers (as is reportedly under consideration for future missiles in China). Their greatest advantage is that when deployed out of garrison they are generally regarded as highly survivable. Barrage attacks against deployment areas could be successful only if the attacker had a large number of warheads, and deep cuts would make this tactic unworkable. Verification of the number of deployed mobile ICBMs is already provided for in START I, but procedures to prevent out-of-garrison mobile missiles from being made launch ready without notice would still need to be worked out.

In garrison, mobile missiles are vulnerable to attack, and Russia has thus given its missiles in garrison the ability to be rapidly launched under attack.

17. However, successfully launching bombers under missile attack, particularly against SLBMs, imposes extremely demanding timelines. At a minimum, airbases distant from any coast, an effective and rapid early warning system, and a highly trained bomber force would be required.

Thus mobile ICBMs could contribute to rapid-launch pressures unless most or all are dispersed out of their garrisons. There is also some concern that out-of-garrison mobile missiles could be located by future space-based or other sensors quickly and accurately enough for them to be attacked, perhaps even by conventionally armed cruise missiles or fighter-bombers. Mobile missiles in the field may also be more vulnerable to accidents or unauthorized use than silo-based missiles.

Only Russia and China now deploy long-range mobile missiles, although current Chinese versions have intermediate rather than intercontinental range. Mobile missiles could be an important part of a small Russian force and could also be important for China. The United States, France, and Britain have no plans to develop or deploy them.

Long-Range Sea-Launched Cruise Missiles

Although U.S. and Russian nuclear arms agreements have generally excluded them (their number was limited by an agreed statement attached to START I), long-range, nuclear-armed SLCMs (sea-launched cruise missiles), such as the Russian SS-N-21 and the U.S. nuclear Tomahawk, have sufficient range to play a strategic nuclear role. The primary advantage of nuclear SLCMs deployed on quiet submarines would be their high survivability at sea. Because the number of potential SLCM-carrying submarines could be several times larger than the number of SSBNs, nuclear SLCMs could be dispersed over more submarines, with each submarine carrying only a small number of nuclear warheads. As with bombers, nuclear SLCMS might also be seen as a useful hedge against the deployment of strategic ballistic missile defenses. Verification of deployments would likely be complex and intrusive, both because SLCMs are small, and because conventional variants exist. Nevertheless, verifying the number of deployed SLCMs and the status of nondeployed SLCMs on shore should be a manageable problem.[18] As with SLBMs, it could prove more difficult to verify the launch readiness of SLCMs deployed at sea without compromising their survivability.

SLCMs are potentially vulnerable to air defenses, although one would expect most to get through current national air defenses. They have the poten-

18. George N. Lewis, Sally K. Ride, and John S. Townsend, "Dispelling Myths about Verification of Sea-launched Cruise Missiles," *Science*, vol. 246 (November 10, 1989), pp. 765–70; Valerie Thomas, "Verification of Limits on Long-range Nuclear SLCMs," *Science and Global Security*, vol. 1, nos. 1–2 (1989), pp. 27–57; and John Parmentola, "Using Shipboard Inspections to Monitor Limits on SLCMs," *Science and Global Security*, vol. 1, nos. 3–4 (1990), pp. 335–38.

tial to be used in zero-warning surprise attacks, and if several countries were to have them, they might not leave a clear return address for retaliation. In addition, deploying nuclear SLCMs on attack submarines, which have conventional military roles, may risk entangling nuclear weapons in a conventional conflict.

As a result of the U.S.-Russian mutual unilateral initiatives in 1991, all long-range nuclear SLCMs were withdrawn from deployment and placed in storage depots.

Force Structures at Low Levels

In principle, stable small forces could likely be constructed using any of the five types of force elements discussed here, either singly or in combination. The choice of which force elements to include will be different for different countries, and we have not carried out a detailed analysis of the relative merits of each element for each country considered here. Thus the compositions of the 1,000 and 2,000 warhead force structures presented in this chapter are based on somewhat arbitrary choices.

In constructing the 1,000 and 2,000 warhead forces, we have been guided by several general concepts. First, that SLBMs will remain a central component of the small U.S., British, and French nuclear forces. Second, that the status of silo-based ICBMs as the only force that must be irreversibly launched on warning to survive argues strongly for their elimination as rapidly as practicable. Third, that Russia is unlikely to retain strategic bombers over the long run. And fourth, to avoid undoing the progress that has already been made in limiting them, long-range nuclear SLCMs should be treated as tactical weapons and left in storage until an agreement is reached on their elimination. None of these concepts is beyond debate (particularly the second), nor is it certain that they would yield the most sensible and stable small forces: this is a question deserving considerable further study. But these concepts provide a self-consistent basis for illustrating one way in which future stable small forces might be constructed.

START III: Reductions to 2,000 Operational Warheads

The START III reductions proposed here would reduce the forces of the United States and Russia to a total of 2,000 operational strategic warheads by the end of 2007. This is similar to the level of 2,000–2,500 warheads

Table 7-4. Notional U.S. and Russian 2000-Warhead (START III) Strategic Nuclear Forces at the End of 2007

Country and weapon	Launchers	Warheads (survivably deployed)
United States		
ICBMs in silos		
Minuteman III	300	300
Submarines	240 on 10 SSBNs ($\times$ 4)	960 (480)
Strategic bombers	35 B-52Hs + 20 B-2s	420 + 320
Totals		2,000 (480)
Russia		
ICBMs in silos		
SS-19	105	105
SS-27	40	40
Land-mobile		
SS-25/SS-27	115	115 (23)
Submarines		
SS-N-20	60 in 3 submarines ($\times$ 10)	600
SS-N-23	80 in 5 submarines ($\times$ 4)	320
New SLBMs	24 in 2 submarines ($\times$ 4)	96
	(2 subs survivably deployed)	(96–400)
Bombers		
Bear H6	15	90
Bear H16	35	560
Blackjack	6	72
Totals		1,998 (202–394)

agreed on for START III by Presidents Clinton and Yeltsin in Helsinki and identical to the number recently proposed by the Committee on International Security and Arms Control of the U.S. National Academy of Sciences.[19]

It seems likely that the United States, for bureaucratic if not other reasons, would reduce its force to 2,000 warheads in the same way that it plans to do so for START II—by spreading the cuts among all three legs of its nuclear triad. This approach is reflected in the 2,000-warhead force shown in table 7-4, which assumes that 300 single-warhead Minuteman III missiles in silos would be retained. Half the B-52Hs and 1 B-2 are assumed to be retired, leaving a bomber force consisting of 35 B-52Hs and 20 B-2s.

The United States would retain SLBMs as a central element of its strategic nuclear forces, although a reduction in the number of SLBM warheads would probably be required. Depending on how many bomber and ICBM

19. Committee on International Security and Arms Control, U.S. National Academy of Sciences, *The Future of U.S. Nuclear Weapons Policy* (Washington: National Academy Press, 1997).

warheads are retained, 900 to 1,300 warheads might be deployed on SLBMs. One option for reducing the number of SLBM warheads would be to further download each Trident II missile from 5 to 4 warheads, which might allow all 14 ballistic missile submarines to be retained. However, allowing downloading below 4 warheads may place more burden than is desirable on arms control measures for limiting (and verifying) numbers of warheads.

Alternatively, 5 warheads could be retained per SLBM, but the number of SLBMs per submarine reduced from 24 to 16.[20] This would also allow fourteen submarines to be retained, and an early decision to pursue this option would produce significant cost savings by reducing the number of Trident II missiles purchased.[21] As a final alternative the number of submarines could be reduced to perhaps ten. This would probably produce the greatest cost savings by reducing both the number of submarines operated and the number of SLBMs purchased (because the United States now has ten Trident II–equipped SLBMs, there would be no need to buy any more for deployment).[22] We have adopted this approach, along with reducing to 4 warheads per missile, in table 7-4..

The Russian 2,000-warhead force structure is likely to be shaped by obsolescence and cost issues and thus seems likely to include both silo-based

20. The number of missiles per SSBN could be reduced by removing the missiles and then removing equipment from the launch tubes necessary to launch missiles (or otherwise modifying the launch tubes so that they could not be used to launch SLBMs). Following an inspection to confirm that the launch tubes were no longer usable, the hatches on the launch tubes could be welded shut (and possibly tagged and sealed for future inspection).

21. Robert S. Norris and William M. Arkin, "NRDC Nuclear Notebook: U.S. Strategic Nuclear Forces, End of 1997," *Bulletin of the Atomic Scientists*, vol. 54 (January-February 1998), pp. 70–72. Another possible way of saving money would be to not buy additional Trident IIs and retain some Trident Is in service. However, it is unclear if the cost of extending the service lives of the Trident Is (which would require new booster stages) and maintaining two types of SLBMs rather than one would be less than buying and maintaining the new Trident IIs.

22. The savings associated with this approach would be greatest if the number of ballistic missile submarine bases could be reduced from two to one (presumably the one in Kings Bay, Georgia, since the base in Bangor, Washington, is at present not configured to support Trident II missiles). A key argument for keeping two bases was that the need to provide full coverage of Russian targets required submarines in both oceans. Downloading the Trident IIs could substantially increase their range and make coverage of all of Russia (and China) from a single ocean possible, provided that the range increase is not prevented by warhead reentry overheating or other reentry problems. However, such a step would conflict with our proposal (in chapter 6) that the range of Trident II be fixed at its current value by replacing off-loaded warheads with weights so as to allow the submarines to patrol in southern seas out of range of Russia.

ICBMs and strategic bombers.[23] The Russian START III force shown in table 7-4 is based on these conditions.

We estimate that under START II Russia would be able to field only slightly more than 2,000 strategic warheads by the end of 2007 (see table 7-3). Under this projection Russia would need to eliminate only 76 warheads to meet the START III limit of 2,000. The force structure shown in table 7-4 assumes that this is done by eliminating 13 Bear H6 bombers, giving a 1,998-warhead START III force. Should our START II estimate prove optimistic in terms of the number of warheads Russia could deploy (for example in the number of bombers it could maintain), Russia might not need to eliminate any warheads from its START II force to meet the START III limits.

As discussed in chapter 12, both countries would be required to begin verifiably dismantling all or a fixed portion of the warheads withdrawn from deployment, with the pits and other fissile components placed in monitored storage. Each country would be limited to about 500 nondeployed reserve warheads. All other strategic nuclear warheads would be subject to dismantling as quickly as feasible. In addition, to reduce breakout concerns, all or a specified portion of ballistic missiles removed from operational status should be eliminated (or verifiably converted to use as space launchers). Except for a small number of missiles retained for testing, no ICBMs or SLBMs beyond those directly associated with accountable warheads would be permitted (maintenance of missiles could be carried out when missiles are de-alerted, since at the 2,000-warhead level and below, only a small number of all missiles will be armed with warheads and kept ready to launch).

In addition to the reductions, it is critical that at this stage both countries be required to take most of their forces off alert and deactivate them. As discussed in detail in chapter 6, the deactivated forces should be configured in such a way as to require a lengthy and observable process to ready them for use. All bombers and silo-based ICBMs would probably be fully deactivated, while some of the mobile ICBMs and SLBMs would be deployed survivably in the field. Table 7-4 assumes that both countries are limited to keeping no more than 25 percent of their operational strategic warheads deployed in the field. Because they are survivable, these weapons need not be ready to launch on short notice.

23. For example, the mobile version of the SS-25 requires five to six times as many personnel to operate and is much more expensive to operate than the silo-based version. Steven J. Zaloga, "RVSN Revival Rests w/ theTopol-M," *Jane's Intelligence Review*, April 1, 1998, p. 5.

Table 7-5. Notional U.S. and Russian 1000-Warhead (START IV) Nuclear Forces in 2012

Country and weapon	Launchers	Warheads (survivably deployed)
United States		
Bombers	20 B-2s	320
Submarines	160 on 10 SSBNs ($\times$ 4)	640 (256)
Totals		960 (256)
Russia		
Silo-based ICBMs	65	65
Land-mobile ICBMs	95	95 (19)
Submarines		
Delta-4 SS-N-23	48 on 3 SSBNs ($\times$ 4)	192
New SSBNs	60 on 5 SSBNs ($\times$ 4)	240
	(2 subs survivably deployed)	(96–128)
Bombers		
Bear H16	17 bombers $\times$ 16	272
Tactical bombs	132	132
Totals		1,000 (115–147)

START IV: Reductions to 1,000 Operational Warheads

Under the staged reductions proposed here, the United States and Russia would have to reduce to 1,000 operational warheads each by the end of 2012. A small number of reserve warheads outside this limit might be permitted, but they would be subject to full verification. All tactical weapons would be eliminated; as discussed in chapter 8, an exception might be made for tactical bombs, which would be counted against the 1,000 limits.

At this point it would be feasible for the United States to eliminate its ICBM force, and such action is reflected in the force structure presented in table 7-5. (However, as discussed earlier, retention of silo-based ICBMs has some benefits, and certainly alternative force structures to the one we propose could be justified.) The strategic bomber force would comprise 20 B-2s, with the B-52Hs either eliminated or converted to conventional roles. The submarine-based force could consist of ten submarines, each carrying sixteen 4-warhead Trident II missiles, for a total of 640 warheads.

Russia might find it difficult to deploy as many as the 1,000 warheads it would be permitted. It is likely that all SS-19 and SS-25 ICBMs would have been retired by this time. Assuming SS-27 production continues at a modest rate of 10 a year (and that these are evenly divided between silo and road-mobile versions), Russia's ICBM force would consist of 65 silo-based SS-27s and 95 road-mobile ones, for a total of 160 ICBM warheads.

By 2012 Russia will almost certainly have retired all of its Typhoons and at least some additional Delta-IVs.[24] We assume that three Delta-IVs, carrying 192 warheads, will remain in service. Assuming it will be able to deploy its new ballistic missile submarine at a rate of one every two years, it could have two or three additional new SSBNs by the end of 2012. We assume three, giving a total of five new SSBNs carrying 240 warheads. This gives a total SLBM force consisting of eight submarines carrying 108 missiles with a total of 432 warheads.

All of Russia's Bear and Blackjack bombers would be approaching their planned service lifetimes by 2012, and no new strategic bomber is believed to be under development. Thus the state of its strategic bomber force is problematic, and Russia could choose to abandon it at or before this point. However, we assume that Russia is able to maintain in service half of its current Bear H16 bombers, while retiring all its Bear H6 and Blackjack bombers. This would leave seventeen Bear H16 bombers, capable of carrying up to 272 long-range cruise missiles.

This strategic force structure would contain 864 warheads. As discussed in chapter 8, all tactical nuclear weapons were to be eliminated by the end of the START IV implementation period with the possible exception of bombs for short-range aircraft, which would be counted against the overall ceiling of 1,000 warheads. We assume that Russia retains 136 such weapons to bring its total to 1,000 warheads. This Russian START IV force is shown in table 7-5.

These projections for Russian forces involve significant uncertainties. If, for example, Russia could not retain any strategic bombers in service, it could not come close to the 1,000 warhead limit, unless it retained a large number of bombs for shorter-range aircraft. But should the new class of ballistic missile submarine carry more warheads than we assume (for example, carrying 16 ten-warhead missiles instead of 12 four-warhead missiles), Russia might even be capable of deploying more than the 1,000 warheads permitted.

---

24. Podvig notes that the Delta-IVs entered service in 1985–90 and could thus potentially remain in service until 2015. This assumes that they are provided with new SS-N-23 ballistic missiles, which have lifetimes shorter than the submarines. The plant at which the SS-N-23s were produced appears to have the necessary production capability to fulfill this requirement. Podvig, "Russian Strategic Forces," p. 17.

START V: Reductions to 200 Warheads

In the final stage of the reductions we propose, the United States and Russia would be joined by Britain, France, and China in reducing warheads to 200 for each country, including reserve weapons, by 2020. Notional 200 warhead forces are laid out in table 7-6. Even more than in the other tables, these force structures are only illustrative.

The United States is assumed to divide its warheads more or less evenly between SLBMs and bombers. The Trident II SLBMs are assumed to carry 4 warheads, with three missiles per submarine, for a total of 96 warheads on eight submarines. The bomber force is assumed to consist of twenty B-2s with 100 associated warheads. Assuming that the reductions to this level use counting rules similar to those used in START II, in which delivery systems are counted as carrying the number of weapons for which they are equipped, the rotary launchers on the B-2s would have to be replaced or modified so that each plane could carry only five bombs or cruise missiles.

Russia's nuclear warheads would likely be primarily divided between land-based missiles and SLBMs, with possibly some short- or medium-range aircraft. In the notional force shown in table 7-6, Russia deploys eight ballistic missile submarines each carrying three SLBMs downloaded to (or designed to carry) 4 warheads, for a total of 96 warheads. Eighty warheads are deployed on mobile SS-27s or a follow-on road-mobile ICBM, and the remaining 24 warheads permitted are assumed to be bombs assigned to a small force of tactical nuclear bombers.

The force structure shown in table 7-6 assumes that Britain and France will agree to an overall limit of 200 warheads on their combined forces, resulting in a western European nuclear force equal to that of the United States, Russia, or China. Such an agreement may be necessary to ease Russian concerns about the possibility of a combined attack by the United States, Britain, and France. If by 2020 a combined attack is not a concern, Britain and France could each retain 200 warheads. (Following the implementation of its 1998 Strategic Defence Review, Britain will already be below 200 warheads.)

Assuming that Britain and France continue to operate four ballistic missile submarines each, deploying 4 SLBMs per submarine and downloading each SLBM to 4 warheads each would give 64 warheads per country, for a total of 128. If necessary, both Britain and France should be able to keep two of these submarines at sea at all times, which would provide them with a highly survivable deterrent. The remaining 72 permitted warheads could

Table 7-6. Notional 200-Warhead Forces in 2020

Country and weapon	Launchers	Warheads (survivably deployed)
United States		
Submarines	24 on 8 submarines (× 4)	96 (24)
Bombers	20 B-2s	100
Russia		
Land-mobile ICBMs	80 SS-27 or follow-on	80 (8)
Submarines	24 on 8 submarines (× 4)	96 (12)
Bombers		24
Western Europe		
Submarines	32 on 8 submarines (× 4)	128 (16)
Air-delivered	Air-delivered weapons (ASMP or follow-on)	72
China		
Mobile ICBMs	130 mobile IRBMs and ICBMs	130 (4)
Submarines	48 on 4 submarines (× 1)	48 (12)
Bombers		20

be deployed on air-delivered ASMP-type weapons, operated by France or also partially deployed on British aircraft. Alternatively they could deploy fewer air-delivered weapons or none and deploy additional SLBM warheads.

It is difficult to predict the development of China's nuclear forces or how China might choose to structure its forces under a 200-warhead limit. Table 7-6 reflects the assumption that China would most likely preserve a diverse force based on mobile or cave-based missiles, SLBMs, and air-delivered weapons. It might be necessary to allow it to retain intermediate-range nuclear missiles, although it should be pressed to eliminate its shorter-range nuclear ballistic missiles.

Excessive downloading of SLBMs could put unnecessary burdens on arms control measures for nuclear warheads. Thus SLBMs designed to carry eight or more warheads would not be allowed to be downloaded to fewer than four.[25] Such SLBMs could be deployed with, for example, a single warhead, as part of a program to de-alert most of the nuclear forces, but would still be counted as 4 warheads (with 3 of them in storage on-shore) against

25. Under START I, ICBMs and SLBMs cannot be downloaded by more than four warheads. START II modified this to allow 105 missiles of one kind of ICBM to be downloaded by up to five warheads (in practice this applies only to the Russian six-warhead SS-19). "START II Executive Summary," *Arms Control Today*, vol. 23 (January-February 1993), START II supplement, pp. 3-4.

the 200 permitted total warheads. If any country desires to deploy more SLBMs than would be possible with a lower limit of four warheads per SLBM, it could of course build new single-warhead SLBMs.[26]

Almost all the permitted warheads would be demated from delivery systems and placed in secure storage. Table 7-6 assumes each country keeps about 25 warheads survivably deployed in the field. These should not be ready to launch on short notice, but this status might or might not be required to be verifiable. Again, some SLBMs might be downloaded to only a single warhead as part of this de-alerting program: the number of warheads survivably deployed would be counted and verified.

Crisis Stability

The deep reductions and de-alerting envisioned in this book are based on the assumption that relations between the nuclear weapons states will improve as the reductions proceed. Nevertheless, it is essential to consider questions of stability because relations could worsen and, in particular, a crisis severe enough to make the use of nuclear weapons plausible could arise. Moreover, the stability of forces casts a long shadow, carrying implications that go far beyond the actual occurrence of a crisis. Military and political planners will necessarily have to consider scenarios in which nuclear attacks occur, and nuclear balances that are not stable will lead to mutual concern and mistrust, possibly even harming relations and impeding reductions.

Under the nuclear reductions plan described in this book, the bulk of the nuclear forces will be deactivated so that lengthy procedures, such as remating of warheads, would be required to make the weapons operational. Depending on how this deactivation is carried out, deactivated warheads and their delivery systems could be vulnerable, raising stability questions that must be considered. It is likely that any crisis in which nuclear use became imaginable would be preceded by a period of deteriorating relations, during which the forces of potential adversaries could be reactivated. However, a crisis could develop so quickly that forces could not be fully reactivated (or to avoid deepening the crisis are not reactivated), raising the possibility that one country might be able to launch an attack on the deactivated forces of another. We consider each of these possibilities.

26. It might also be possible to allow previously MIRVed SLBMs to be deployed with a single warhead if they are equipped with a new bus or final stage that is capable of deploying only a single warhead, and the old buses are verifiably destroyed.

Forces Fully Reactivated

Today's strategic forces are far from completely survivable. Large parts, such as ICBMs in silos or garrisons and SLBMs on submarines in port, are vulnerable. As long as both sides have hundreds of warheads that could survive a surprise attack, the vulnerability of the remainder should not be so important. Nevertheless, the vulnerability of silo-based ICBMs in particular has led both Russia and the United States to develop and maintain very dangerous launch-on-warning policies. In addition, a rapid-launch requirement demands rapid decisionmaking and communication of orders, highlighting the vulnerability of command and control and raising the prospect of a decapitating strike on national commanders.

START II will improve this situation by eliminating MIRVed ICBMs. This contributes to stability by rendering the ICBMs less attractive targets: an attacker would have to expend on average more than one warhead to destroy one warhead. However, the vulnerable silo-based forces, even though reduced in size, could still drive both sides to continue to maintain launch-on-warning policies. Perhaps even more important, unless Russia's financial situation improves so that it can operate submarines out of port and mobile ICBMs out of garrison in much higher numbers than it does today, the vulnerability of these forces combined with their ability to launch from their ports or garrisons will provide pressure to continue to rely on launch-on-warning policies.

The notional START III forces laid out here would not significantly change the crisis stability of the forces when the forces were fully activated, except in the sense that if the forces had been de-alerted in the manner we advocate, the United States and Russia would have opportunity to become comfortable operating their nuclear forces without relying on launch on warning.

The 1,000-warhead START IV forces outlined here should further improve stability by greatly reducing the number of silo-based ICBMs. Russia's forces, however, may still provide rapid-launch incentives unless the country can increase at-sea and in-field deployment rates. For economic and other reasons it may retain silo-based ICBMs. But assuming these 1,000-warhead forces are deployed and operated in ways consistent with maintaining stability (which may not be the case in practice), they could be highly stable.

This conclusion applies even more strongly to fully activated U.S. and Russian 200-warhead forces (table 7-6). The relatively small sizes of these forces could allow increased attention and funding to be devoted to maintaining their ability to operate survivably in the field. In addition, the high survivability of the individual force elements would allow a delayed retaliation decision, thereby easing pressures on command and control systems. The combined forces of Britain and France, based primarily or exclusively on submarines at sea at all times, should similarly be highly stable. The future (and even current) structure of China's forces is very unclear, but it is likely that they would raise the greatest crisis stability concerns. The survivability of China's nuclear deterrent would likely depend on its ability to develop quiet, survivable submarines and on the survivability of its mobile land-based missiles, the prospects of which are difficult to assess.

Forces Not Fully Reactivated

If a crisis arose quickly and unexpectedly, on a time scale shorter than that required to reactivate nuclear forces, an attack could be launched against forces that were not yet fully activated, possibly destroying a large part of them. And the race to reactivate forces in a rapidly developing crisis could itself make the crisis even more dangerous.

We next consider the implications of a rapidly developing crisis for three ways in which deactivation and de-alerting could be carried out:

—In the first way, *all* of the strategic weapons on each side are verifiably deactivated so that observable and time-consuming activities, such as remating warheads, would be required to make them operational. These deactivated forces might not be survivable against an opponent's reconstituted forces.

—In the second arrangement most of the forces would be deactivated, but some portion would be deployed so that they were both fully survivable and carried with them everything needed to deliver their warheads. Ideally, such forces would be de-alerted and unable to launch rapidly. For example, submarines could deploy to sea with the guidance sets for their SLBMs removed from the missiles and stored elsewhere on the submarine. However, in the absence of verification of alert status, an adversary would likely assume that they were on alert.

—In the third arrangement all forces would be deactivated, that is, physically incapable of launching, but some would be survivably deployed in the field. For example, submarines could deploy to sea without the nosecones (which would be hidden on land) for their missiles. These forces would not be continuously monitored in a manner that would reveal their locations, but other technical means might be applied to provide confidence that they are unable to launch their weapons.

The stability of the first option, in which all forces are deactivated, would depend on whether it is possible to make them survivable. The simplest model of deactivated forces, in which all the warheads and delivery systems were gathered in a few locations and were subject to monitoring, would obviously result in highly vulnerable forces. There are ways to increase the survivability of a deactivated force, at least in terms of the number of warheads required to destroy it. Each deactivated warhead could be stored separately, perhaps even in a hardened site, so that no more than one could be destroyed by any attacking warhead, as would also be the case for any deactivated silo-based ICBMs. Similarly, mobile missiles and bombers could be stored at many separate locations, although there may be no way to ensure the survivability of deactivated SSBNs without deploying them to sea (which is essentially the third option). And other, more complex schemes could be devised to further increase the survivability of deactivated forces.

However, the complexity and probably the cost of such approaches are inconsistent with a world in which nuclear weapons play a relatively minor role (the major exception to this might be deactivated ICBMs with their warheads dispersed among empty former missile silos). If a country judged that this level of effort was needed for making an entirely deactivated force survivable, it would be very unlikely to entirely deactivate the force in the first place.

A completely deactivated force in which either the warheads or delivery systems or both were vulnerable could be highly destabilizing in a crisis because of the concern that one country could rapidly make a small portion of its forces operational and use them to destroy the entire strategic force of another country. Such de-alerted forces might also be vulnerable to an attack using a small number of hidden nuclear weapons (for example submarines could be vulnerable to a bomb hidden in a harbor) or even to conventional weapons.

It may be that technical measures could be developed to deal with the vulnerability of de-alerted forces. It might be possible to lengthen the time needed to reactivate forces compared with the time required to make them survivable but not yet ready to launch. For example, if a monitoring system indicated to the United States that Russia was taking steps to reactivate its forces, the United States could disperse its nuclear warheads from their storage areas and send its submarines to sea and disperse or put on strip alert most of its bombers. But it is unclear if a practical system could be devised that would allow weapons to be deployed survivably before an adversary's weapons could become operational when the adversary has a head start; nor does this approach solve the problem of attacks using hidden nuclear or conventional weapons. During a crisis it could also result in a great deal of rapid strategic nuclear activity that could obstruct efforts to resolve the crisis.

Another possible technical response to the stability problems raised by this arrangement would be to deploy defenses against both air and missile attacks at nuclear warhead storage sites and at bases of delivery systems. If such defenses were capable of protecting only a very limited area, they could be deployed without raising the kind of concerns that make defenses capable of covering wider areas such an obstacle to achieving deep nuclear reductions. However, the problem of building defenses that would be effective enough in the face of the adversary's countermeasures to provide high confidence that the strategic forces are truly survivable, particularly without using nuclear warheads on the interceptors, remains unsolved.

In the second option above, most of the forces would be verifiably deactivated, but some portion would be survivably deployed in the field and carry with them everything needed to launch, although they would not be maintained in a rapid-launch status. This arrangement would ensure that some survivable forces would always be available. Countries would have experience with operating deployed forces, and in a reactivation scenario there could be a gradual increasing of deployment levels with no abrupt break from having no forces deployed to having some deployed.

However, at the same time that this approach provides assured survivability for some of the forces, their de-alerted status might not be clearly observable to other countries. These countries would therefore assume that other countries' forces could be used in a first strike against their own deactivated forces. All countries would still have some survivable forces, but this is not an ideal situation because the partial vulnerability of forces will erode confidence and in a crisis encourage countries to begin to reactivate forces.

At least in the near term the third option appears the most attractive and is what the United States, Russia, and the other nuclear weapon states should strive for. Under this option, the forces would be fully deactivated and some portion survivably deployed in the field, but unlike option two, the deactivated status of the forces would be verifiable. The primary problem with this arrangement is how to verify that the forces are deactivated without compromising their survivability. As discussed in chapters 6 and 11, however, there are ways to do this.

These three alternatives will appear as stark choices only in the third stage of reductions. In the first and second stages, reductions to 2,000 and 1,000 warheads respectively, the United States and Russia will undoubtedly insist that some warheads remain survivably deployed in the field at all times, whether or not the survivable component could be de-alerted in a verifiable manner.

CHAPTER EIGHT

Tactical and Reserve
Nuclear Warheads

The force reductions discussed in chapter 7 are focused on operational strategic nuclear weapons. However, both the United States and Russia have other types of nuclear weapons, such as tactical nuclear weapons or nondeployed strategic warheads (often referred to as reserve or hedge nuclear weapons). Russia may also have a number of nuclear warheads for its strategic ballistic missile defense system around Moscow. These additional weapons cannot be neglected in carrying out the deep reductions proposed in this book.

Operational Tactical Nuclear Weapons

Both the United States and Russia have a significant number of tactical nuclear weapons. These weapons are not currently limited by arms control agreements, with the exception of a politically binding commitment in START I on ceilings for deployments of long-range nuclear sea-launched cruise missiles (SLCMs).

Tactical Weapons after the Cold War

The United States currently has only two types of tactical nuclear weapons: about 650 B61 tactical bombs (of which perhaps 150 are based in Europe and Turkey) for dual-capable aircraft and 320 nuclear warheads for SLCMs, which are stored in depots in the United States for possible deployment on attack submarines (table 8-1).[1] There is considerable uncertainty about the

---

1. William M. Arkin, Robert S. Norris, and Joshua Handler, *Taking Stock: Worldwide Nuclear Deployments, 1998* (Washington: Natural Resources Defense Council, 1998), p. 14.

Table 8-1. U.S. and Russian Tactical Nuclear Weapons at the Beginning of 1998

Country and weapon		
United States		
B61 tactical bomb	650	
Nuclear sea-launched cruise missile	320	
Total	970	
Russia	Arbatov	NRDC
Atomic demolition munitions	200	0
Air defense warheads	600	1,100
Land-based tactical aviation weapons	1,000	1,600
Naval anti-ship, anti-submarine, and land-attack weapons	2,000	1,200
Total	3,800	3,900

Sources: U.S. numbers and Russian numbers labeled NRDC from Arkin, Norris, and Handler, *Taking Stock*, pp. 14, 27. Russian numbers labeled "Arbatov" are from Alexei Arbatov's appendix to this book.

current state of Russian operational tactical weapons. Two recent estimates conclude that Russia has just under 4,000 tactical weapons (table 8-1); however, these estimates differ significantly in every subcategory.[2] Russia may also have additional large numbers of tactical weapons in reserve or awaiting dismantlement.[3]

Although at present Russia has several times more operational tactical weapons than the United States, according to Alexei Arbatov's appendix to this book, virtually all will reach the end of their service lives by 2003, and the assembly of new tactical weapons is proceeding at a very low rate. He estimates that, even in the absence of further agreements to reduce tactical weapons, Russia will have at most a thousand by 2003 and possibly no more than a few hundred. U.S. and Russian tactical weapons in storage are not mated to launchers. As far as is known, all are in storage depots, including storage sites at tactical aviation and naval bases.

Do U.S. and Russian tactical weapons still have a meaningful purpose? The rapid decline in the number of tactical weapons in the last decade reflects in large part the perceived lack of missions for them.[4]

2. These estimates are from Alexei Arbatov's appendix to this book; and from Arkin, Norris, and Handler, *Taking Stock*, p. 27.

3. The Natural Resources Defense Council estimates that Russia may have as many as 12,000 tactical weapons in reserve or awaiting dismantlement. Arkin, Norris, and Handler, *Taking Stock*, p. 27. In his appendix to this book Arbatov notes that Russian estimates are that the United States has several thousand tactical warheads in storage.

4. As of 1991 the United States had just under 7,000 tactical nuclear weapons and the Soviet Union had about 21,700. Robert S. Norris and William M. Arkin, "Nuclear Notebook: U.S. Nuclear Weapons Stockpile (June 1991)," *Bulletin of the Atomic Scientists*, vol. 47 (June 1991), p. 49; and Arbatov's appendix in this book.

The remaining U.S. tactical weapons provide no unique capabilities. A strategic bomber such as the B-2 is just as capable of delivering nuclear bombs as a tactical bomber, and essentially anything a nuclear sea-launched cruise missile (SLCM) can do, a nuclear air-launched cruise missile (ALCM) can do as well.[5] Tactical weapons are sometimes cited as having low yields that make them more suitable for tactical use. However, the lowest warhead yields for strategic and tactical bombs and cruise missiles are similar.[6]

U.S. tactical weapons are no longer needed to deter conventional attacks on western Europe. With the breakups of the Warsaw Pact and the Soviet Union, the United States and its NATO allies have unquestioned conventional superiority. Tactical weapons have no advantage over strategic weapons in deterring or responding to nuclear attacks by China or any other country that might acquire nuclear weapons.

Military considerations aside, many European leaders view U.S. nuclear weapons as a stabilizing element and favor their presence in Europe in at least small numbers in the midterm.[7] Therefore, although there appears no military or technical justification for the continued deployment of U.S. nuclear weapons in Europe, a withdrawal of U.S. tactical weapons should not be done unilaterally and abruptly.[8] It needs to be preceded by consultations with the NATO allies and almost certainly should be conducted in conjunction with a withdrawal of Russian tactical nuclear weapons from most or all of European Russia. The withdrawal of U.S. and Russian tacti-

5. The argument is sometimes made that nuclear Tomahawks have a unique capability in that they can be covertly launched from submarines just off the coast of the target nation. However, the strategic Advanced Cruise Missile is not only stealthier than a Tomahawk, but because of its much greater range can be launched from an undetected strategic bomber a thousand or more kilometers away from the target country.

6. The warheads for the strategic ALCM and the nuclear SLCM have selectable yields with the same lowest-yield selection. Although the tactical B61 bombs may have a lower minimum yield (0.3 kt) than the strategic variant of the B61 (reported to be less than a kiloton and by some accounts the same 0.3 kt), this difference is at worst not large, and a number of these tactical B61 variants could simply be incorporated into the strategic bomb stocks. Bomb yields from Robert S. Norris and William Arkin, "NRDC Nuclear Notebook: U.S. Nuclear Stockpile, July 1997," *Bulletin of the Atomic Scientists*, vol. 53 (July-August 1997), pp. 62–63; and Greg Mello, "New Bomb, No Mission," *Bulletin of the Atomic Scientists*, vol. 53 (May-June 1997), pp. 28–32.

7. Andrew J. Goodpaster, C. Richard Nelson, and Steven Philip Kramer, "Nuclear Weapons and European Security," policy paper, Atlantic Council of the United States, April 1996.

8. A 1997 National Academy of Sciences study reaches the same conclusion, arguing that although their withdrawal should involve extensive high-level consultations, U.S. tactical weapons are no longer needed in Europe. Committee on International Security and Arms Control, U.S. National Academy of Sciences, *The Future of U.S. Nuclear Weapons Policy* (Washington: National Academy Press, 1997).

cal weapons from Europe might occur as part of a phased process in which these weapons are eliminated.

From a Russian perspective, tactical weapons are widely viewed as becoming more important as Russian conventional forces weaken. In particular, nuclear weapons are increasingly considered important for deterring a conventional attack by NATO or China and deterring chemical or biological attacks. As Alexei Arbatov notes in his appendix in this book, this consideration influenced the development of the new Russian military doctrine of 1993, which, contrary to the announced Soviet doctrine, reserved the right to use nuclear weapons first. The Russians' perceived need for such tactical weapons may be the greatest barrier to significantly reducing or eliminating these weapons. At the same time, however, Russia is also concerned about threats posed by U.S. tactical weapons deployed in Europe and U.S. nuclear SLCMs and faces substantial economic and technical obstacles in rebuilding its now largely obsolescent tactical force.

Reducing or Eliminating Tactical Weapons

The deep reductions proposed in this book must include tactical as well as strategic weapons.[9] The March 1997 Helsinki Summit statement raised the possibility of bringing these weapons into the nuclear arms control process, saying that in the context of the START III negotiations, the United States and Russia "will explore, as separate issues, possible measures relating to nuclear long-range sea-launched cruise missiles and tactical nuclear systems, to include appropriate confidence-building and transparency measures."[10]

Reductions in tactical weapons are more than just a necessity for deep cuts; they are a matter deserving to be pursued with some urgency. The collapsing state of the Russian tactical forces presents a unique opportunity to obtain significant reductions in these weapons. Limits that captured these obsolescence-driven reductions could forestall a large-scale deployment of a new generation of Russian tactical weapons. Tactical weapons, particu-

---

9. Recent discussions of arms control for tactical weapons include William C. Potter, "Unsafe at Any Size," *Bulletin of the Atomic Scientists*, vol. 53 (May-June 1997), pp. 11–14; Nikolai Sokov, "Tactical Nuclear Weapons Elimination: Next Step for Arms Control," *Nonproliferation Review*, vol. 4 (Winter 1997), pp. 17–27; and Stephen P. Lambert and David A. Miller, "Russia's Crumbling Tactical Nuclear Weapons Complex: An Opportunity for Arms Control," INSS occasional paper 12, Institute for National Security Studies, U.S. Air Force Academy, April 1997.

10. "Joint Statement on Parameters on Future Reductions in Nuclear Forces," reprinted in *Arms Control Today*, vol. 27 (March 1997), pp. 19–20.

larly some Russian ones, may also be more vulnerable than strategic weapons to theft or unauthorized use. Although this concern may often be overstated, to the extent that is valid, the sooner actions are taken to reduce such dangers, the better.[11]

There are a number of preliminary steps that would be very useful, and are perhaps necessary, as prerequisites to actual reductions in tactical weapons, and should be pursued immediately. These include:

—Data exchanges. The uncertainty about current holdings of both operational and nonoperational (but not yet eliminated) tactical weapons is a major barrier to limiting them. Unlike strategic weapons, on which the U.S. and Russia regularly exchange detailed data, there have been essentially no data exchanges on tactical weapons. Beginning such exchanges is an important and necessary step in reducing tactical weapons and should be a top priority.[12]

—Withdrawal to storage. An agreement to withdraw all tactical weapons to secure storage would be a modest step because all of them are already believed to be in storage. Nevertheless, a formal agreement to place all tactical weapons in storage would still facilitate carrying out verification measures and would help address concerns about the safety and security of the weapons.

—Formalization of the Bush-Gorbachev-Yeltsin unilateral initiatives on tactical weapons (see chapter 9). This would clarify the initiatives and make them legally binding.

—Verification measures. The difficult problem of verifying limits on tactical weapons is a major obstacle to negotiated reductions of them. The weapons are more difficult to verify because their delivery systems are generally smaller than strategic delivery systems and tactical nuclear weapons often either have conventional variants or are delivered by systems that are also used to deliver conventional weapons. Cooperative verification measures associated with any of the above steps would not only increase the value of the steps but would also provide useful experience in designing future verification regimes and increase confidence that such verification will be effective.

11. In particular, it is believed that all tactical weapons are already in storage and Russia is eliminating them as rapidly as its infrastructure can manage.

12. At an April 1998 meeting of the Permanent Joint Council set up under the Russia-NATO Founding Act, Russia did provide summary data on its progress in dismantling tactical nuclear weapons that it committed to eliminate as part of the 1991 mutual unilateral initiatives. British American Security Information Council, BASIC report 64, June 4, 1998, p. 4.

A package consisting of some or all of the above steps could establish a basis for significant negotiated reductions in tactical weapons. Once this foundation was in place, there would be several ways in which the weapons could be dealt with in conjunction with the phased nuclear reductions advocated in this book.

First, tactical weapons could simply be merged with strategic weapons under one overall limit on nuclear weapons. For example, a START III limit of 2,000 warheads could apply to *all* the operational nuclear warheads of each country. Each country could choose to retain tactical warheads at the price of retaining fewer strategic warheads. This arrangement would allow the greatest flexibility in structuring forces while beginning the necessary process of reducing tactical weapons. It also recognizes the convergence between tactical weapons and strategic weapons that has been occurring as the shortest-range tactical weapons are retired.

The approach also avoids the need to set up a separate accounting and verification system for tactical warheads. However, this may not be an advantage. It is almost certain that more rigorous verification measures will be needed for tactical weapons relative to strategic weapons if they are be to verified with equal confidence. Thus merging tactical weapons in with strategic weapons could risk complicating and delaying the conclusion of a START III agreement on strategic weapons.

A second approach would be to reach companion agreements on tactical weapons. This separate approach would be consistent with the Helsinki Summit statement. The United States and Russia could agree to reduce their stocks of tactical warheads to, for example, 500 each as part of the START III reduction to 2,000 strategic warheads, with this number being decreased, possibly to zero, in subsequent stages. These reductions could take place as a result of a formal negotiated agreement or via a more informal process such as an extension of the unilateral initiatives of 1991. In the near term this approach might help reassure Russia as well as U.S. allies that tactical weapons will be available if actually needed. As with a merger with strategic weapons, rigorous verification of such a separate limit would likely require intrusive and complex measures, which could be difficult to achieve agreement on in the near future.

Either approach could be coupled with geographic restrictions on deployments. One possible restriction would be a ban on foreign basing.[13]

13. President Yeltsin proposed that nuclear weapons be restricted to the territory of their home countries at the April 1996 Nuclear Safety Summit in Moscow (although this announcement was apparently aimed primarily at the Russian public). Michael R. Gordon, "Summit in Moscow Urges A-Test Ban," *New York Times*, April 21, 1996, p. 1.

This would force the withdrawal of all U.S. nuclear weapons from Europe, together with a Russian agreement to withdraw all of its tactical weapons from areas west of the Urals.[14] However, such a mutual withdrawal from Europe, if not directly connected with significant reductions in tactical weapons, could be counterproductive because obtaining a withdrawal of U.S. tactical weapons from Europe may be the greatest incentive Russia has for agreeing to tactical weapons reductions.

Withdrawing weapons from Europe might proceed in phases, perhaps beginning with a freeze on tactical deployments there, such as has been suggested by Jonathan Dean, then moving on to the creation of a nuclear-free zone in central and eastern Europe (not including Russia), and finally achieving complete withdrawal of tactical weapons from the Atlantic to the Urals. Alternatively, the number of tactical weapons in the Atlantic-to-Urals zone could be limited to 100 or 200 on each side. This could be combined with a ban on the deployment of nuclear weapons in central European states, including deployment in any new NATO members, the former Soviet republics west of Russia (and the Kalingrad Oblast), and possibly in western Russia.

A third way of proceeding would be to agree to eliminate all tactical weapons, perhaps in conjunction with the START III reductions to 2,000 warheads. This would have the advantage of being a dramatic step, eliminating all U.S. and Russian nuclear weapons primarily intended for battlefield use, leaving only strategic weapons intended primarily to deter nuclear attacks. It would also eliminate Russia's concerns about U.S. forward-deployed tactical weapons.

Rapid elimination has a number of disadvantages, however. As noted earlier, it may cause serious concern among U.S. allies as well as within Russia. In particular, although there is speculation that Russia may eventually abandon its poorly maintained strategic bomber force, there is no indication that it would want to abandon its ability to deliver nuclear weapons by shorter-range aircraft, particularly given its security concerns with regard to China and NATO.

A more realistic plan thus might be a phased approach aimed at eliminating these weapons as part of the START IV reductions to 1,000 operational weapons. Our START III and IV force structures shown in tables 7-4 and 7-5 are based on such a phased plan, which might involve:

14. Such a removal of Russian tactical weapons from western Russia may be politically necessary so that countries within range of these weapons would not press for matching U.S. deployments. An exception might possibly be made for Russian tactical naval weapons at northern fleet naval bases on the Kola Peninsula, which are primarily directed at countering the U.S. Navy.

—Preliminary steps such as data exchanges, withdrawals to storage, and formalization of the 1991 unilateral initiatives that would facilitate further reductions and would be taken as soon as possible. These might be combined with some geographic limitations, such as a freeze on deployments.

—Whether by an extension of the 1991 unilateral reductions or through negotiations, the number of operational tactical weapons on each side would be reduced significantly. This could occur by applying an equal ratio (for example, each side could reduce by a factor of two) or by reductions to equal low levels, for example to 500 each. Such a reduction could be put into practice quickly, particularly once the preparatory steps have been taken, so that a goal of no later than the end of 2003 should be set for this step. We recognize that rigorous verification of such a limit may be unattainable on this time scale.[15] However, given the lesser importance of tactical weapons relative to strategic ones and that each side will still have several thousand strategic weapons, a more relaxed verification scheme could be temporarily accepted for tactical weapons.[16] Such verification may be more consistent with the relatively informal approach to limiting tactical weapons taken in the 1991 unilateral initiatives.

—Following these reductions, tactical weapons would be subject to increasingly rigorous verification. Measures could include tagging and possibly "fingerprinting" individual warheads, making challenge inspections for nondeclared warheads, and establishing a chain of custody from storage sites to dismantling sites (see the discussion of verification measures in chapter 11). The application of these measures would prepare the way for the elimination of tactical weapons. Elimination should occur as soon as possible, but no later than the START IV cuts to 1,000 weapons in 2012.

—At some point, perhaps in conjunction with the START III date of 2007, all tactical weapons would be withdrawn from Europe, including the western parts of Russia.

Still another way of proceeding would be to distinguish tactical bombs from other tactical weapons. The rationale for such an approach is discussed briefly in box 8-1.

---

15. The verification discussed here applies only to operational warheads. Verification of the destruction of eliminated tactical warheads is discussed in chapter 9.

16. For example, each side could be required to declare the number, type, and location of its operational tactical weapons. Because these weapons would be in storage facilities and not deployed with operational forces, random inspections of the facilities could confirm the general validity of the declarations. However, no systematic effort to locate nondeclared weapons would be put into effect at this point.

Box 8-1. Tactical Bombs

In seeking to eliminate tactical weapons, it may be useful to treat tactical bombs differently from other tactical weapons. Russia may decide to phase out its strategic bomber force, but is likely to want to retain some shorter-range nuclear bombers. Similarly, China, which has only shorter-range nuclear bombers, will likely seek to retain some bombs. Allowing nuclear bombs for such shorter-range aircraft could greatly ease the concern of countries such as Russia about eliminating all their other tactical weapons, and thus make reaching an agreement much easier. Such an approach would also recognize that tactical bombs are essentially indistinguishable from strategic bombs.

Under such an approach, tactical bombs would be declared and treated as any other tactical weapon through the suggested reductions to about 500 tactical weapons in the intermediate step toward eliminating tactical weapons discussed in this chapter. However, at the point that all tactical weapons were to be eliminated (possibly as part of the START IV reductions in 2012), each country would have two choices of what do with its nuclear tactical bombs: either to eliminate them or to retain some and count them against its numerical limit on strategic warheads. In effect, all bombs would now be counted as strategic weapons, with all other tactical weapons being eliminated. Shorter-range bombers intended or equipped for nuclear delivery should be declared and their numbers limited to a level compatible with the overall number of nuclear bombs.

A similar approach with regard to intermediate-range missiles may also need to be taken when China, whose nuclear missile force is composed primarily of such missiles, is brought into the reduction process, as well as with France if it insists on retaining its nuclear ASMP air-to-ground missiles.

Reserve Warheads

Reserve warheads should ultimately be included in an overall limit on the number of warheads, and all warheads in excess of this limit, including the large hedge and inactive stockpiles now planned by the United States, should be verifiably destroyed.

Following the implementation of START II, the United States apparently intends to maintain about 4,000 warheads in the operational stockpile: 3,500 deployed warheads and about 500 spares for routine maintenance.[17] In addition, 2,500 other strategic warheads will be held in reserve and assigned to a hedge stockpile. These include about 1,000 ICBM warheads that could be used to increase Minuteman warhead loadings from one to three per missile; up to 1,000 SLBM warheads that could be used to increase Trident warhead loadings from five to eight per missile; and several hundred bombs and cruise missile warheads.

An additional reserve category, the inactive stockpile, will contain strategic warheads that are placed in storage with their tritium removed. After START II is implemented, it is expected that 2,500 to 3,000 U.S. warheads, mostly strategic ICBM, SLBM, and bomber warheads, would be in the inactive stockpile. There are no plans to dismantle these warheads; they could be returned to service if supplied with tritium. The principal justification for this reserve is to provide replacement warheads in case a warhead type were to develop reliability concerns. They could also be used to replace weapons withdrawn for destructive testing and to provide spare parts.[18]

No information is available publicly about Russia's plans for its stockpile of reserve warheads. However, it could load only 525 additional warheads onto the ballistic missiles it would be allowed to retain under START II (by uploading the 105 SS-19 ICBMs permitted under the treaty from one to six warheads). To expand its force further, Russia would need to deploy more delivery vehicles (unless it were possible to convert the single-warhead SS-27 into a multiple-warhead missile).

A small reserve stockpile would be sufficient for providing spares to substitute for warheads that are withdrawn for maintenance or remanufacture, or for replacing warheads or warhead components that are subjected to destructive testing during normal stockpile maintenance. A reserve stockpile about one-tenth the size of the deployed stockpile should be enough. A larger reserve stockpile might be needed if it also had to serve as a backup in case a deployed warhead type developed serious safety or reliability problems. For example, W78 warheads might be retained as a backup to the W87 warheads that will be deployed on the Minuteman III. We advocate in chapter 6 replacing the 400 W88 warheads deployed on Trident missiles with lower-yield W76 warheads. The withdrawn W88s could be retained

17. Robert S. Norris and William M. Arkin, "NRDC Nuclear Notebook: U.S. Nuclear Weapons Stockpile, July 1995," *Bulletin of the Atomic Scientists*, vol. 51 (July-August 1995), pp. 77–79; and Norris and Arkin, "NRDC Nuclear Notebook: U.S. Nuclear Weapons Stockpile, July 1996," *Bulletin of the Atomic Scientists*, vol. 52 (July- August 1996), pp. 61–62.

18. Norris and Arkin, "NRDC Nuclear Notebook: U.S. Nuclear Stockpile, July 1997," *Bulletin of the Atomic Scientists*, vol. 53 (July-August 1997), pp. 62–63.

to replace some of the W76 warheads should these develop problems. With additional missile flight testing, spare ICBM warheads might be used on SLBMs, and vice-versa. Thus, after implementation of START II, the United States might be justified in maintaining at most 1,000 reserve strategic warheads, but not the 5,000 or more that are now planned for the hedge and inactive reserve stockpiles.

For the START III reductions to 2,000 strategic operational warheads, the stockpile of U.S. and Russian reserve warheads should be limited to no more than 500 each. These would be subject to verification measures similar to those for deployed weapons, and all warheads in excess of the limits on deployed and reserve warheads would be verifiably dismantled and the recovered fissile material placed under bilateral or international safeguards. As the total number of warheads is reduced from 2,000 to 1,000 in the START IV reductions, the allowed number of reserve warheads should be decreased at least proportionately.

At very low force levels, concerns about the possible failure of a type of warhead are best addressed by deploying a mix of warhead types so that the failure of one type would affect only a small fraction of the force. The disabled warheads could be replaced, if desired, by remanufactured versions of the same warhead or by newly built warheads of another type. A requirement to maintain reserve warheads to replace each deployed warhead is unnecessary and would needlessly inflate stockpiles.

If, as we also recommend, the launch readiness of nuclear forces is reduced substantially, the requirement for reserve warheads could and should be eliminated entirely. As discussed in chapter 6, at 2,000 warheads and less, most operational warheads would be stored in monitored bunkers or on immobilized ICBMs, with a small part of the total stockpile deployed on submarines or mobile missiles on patrol. In this case the warheads in monitored storage could act as the reserve force, and all routine maintenance needs could be met by rotating warheads between deployed and stored status. At the START V stage proposed here, the forces of all nations would be limited to 200 warheads each, including reserve and tactical warheads.

Ballistic Missile Defense Warheads

A final category of nuclear weapons encompasses the warheads deployed on interceptors of strategic ballistic missile defense systems. Russia has long operated an antiballistic missile (ABM) defense system with 100 nuclear-armed interceptors deployed near Moscow. However, recent reports indicate that the nuclear warheads on the system's interceptors have been removed and the interceptors converted to conventionally armed interceptors.[19] The United States has no comparable system, and its plans for possible future ballistic missile defense systems rely exclusively on nonnuclear interceptors.

We do not believe that the benefits obtained from the use of nuclear-armed interceptors are great enough to justify their continued use, given that their retention is contrary to objectives of greatly reducing numbers of and reliance on nuclear weapons. In the START III reductions the United States and Russia should agree to ban all nuclear-armed ballistic missile defenses, and Russia should be required to either denuclearize or deactivate the Moscow ABM system if it has not already done so.

19. "Newsbreaks," *Aviation Week and Space Technology* (March 2, 1998), p. 21.

CHAPTER NINE

Transparency and Irreversibility in Nuclear Warhead Dismantlement

The START III parameters accepted by Presidents Clinton and Yeltsin at their summit meeting on March 21, 1997 in Helsinki could open a new chapter in arms control. All previous U.S.-Russian strategic nuclear arms control negotiations used delivery systems as the measure of merit to account for limitations. START III, in contrast, would focus on nuclear warheads as an independent parameter, not just as a function of their means of delivery. Collaboration between the United States and Russia to dismantle and eliminate nuclear warheads will be the crucial test of whether the two countries can effect deep reductions in nuclear weapons together.

A second dramatic change flows from developments that neither the U.S. government nor the Russian government control. Russia's declining capacity to build and maintain a large strategic nuclear force suggests that reductions in deployed warheads below the Helsinki parameters of 2,000–2,500 are almost inevitable. This could result in unilateral Russian reductions, or these reductions could be matched by U.S. reductions.

Devising a Framework for Warhead Dismantlement

The first parameter accepted at Helsinki by Presidents Clinton and Yeltsin was "establishment by December 31, 2007, of lower aggregate levels of 2,000–2,500 strategic nuclear warheads for each of the parties."[1] The obsolescence of Russian strategic systems combined with Russia's economic straits may mean that by 2007, or shortly thereafter, Russia will have fewer than

---

1. "Joint Statement on Parameters on Future Reductions in Nuclear Forces," White House Press Release, March 21, 1997, in Hans Binnendijk and James Goodby, *Transforming Nuclear Deterrence* (Washington: National Defense University Press, 1997), appendix A.

the permitted 2,000 deployed warheads, perhaps many fewer. Reductions to 1,500, 1,000 or even fewer deployed warheads have been mentioned informally by Russian specialists. Thus the Helsinki parameters in respect to deployed warheads may be irrelevant to how many Russia will actually have.

The second Helsinki parameter called for "measures relating to the transparency of strategic nuclear warhead inventories and the destruction of strategic nuclear warheads ... to promote the irreversibility of deep reductions including prevention of a rapid increase in the number of warheads."[2] An understanding that the two sides will seek to achieve transparency and irreversibility in warhead dismantlement is new to the SALT–START process. Critics of START II in Russia have complained that the United States would have a very considerable advantage in a breakout scenario by uploading Trident and Minuteman III, and this is probably one reason why Clinton and Yeltsin were able to agree in Helsinki that warheads should be directly addressed in START III. But a more fundamental reason is that as deeper reductions in delivery vehicles are implemented, monitored warhead dismantlement becomes nearly essential to avoid a rapid reconstitution of nuclear forces. In anticipation of deep cuts in deployed forces, monitored warhead dismantlement and measures to make that process irreversible deserve top priority on the nuclear reductions agenda.

Thanks to legislation sponsored in 1991 by Senators Sam Nunn and Richard Lugar, the U.S. Congress acknowledged the financial difficulties Russia would have with obligations to reduce nuclear weapons delivery systems and decided to provide assistance. The Clinton administration assumed the executive responsibilities with gusto. Although direct support for warhead dismantlement has not been provided under the Nunn-Lugar program, U.S. assistance did have an impact on the safety and security of Russian warheads. U.S. support was supplied in the form of assistance for Russian rail transport, including protective blankets, and storage containers and a major storage facility for the fissile material from dismantled warheads. But the task is huge and much remains to be done. Congressional support in the future for warhead dismantlement activities in Russia will be a crucial element in determining the success or failure of efforts to inject this issue into the mainstream of arms control.

An idea of the magnitude of the problem can be gained by considering that approximately 4,500 strategic warheads are being removed from deployed status by Russia, including those formerly deployed in Ukraine

2. "Joint Statement on Parameters."

and Kazakstan, just as a result of START I. Probably thousands of other nondeployed nuclear warheads have become or will become excess to military needs. This is in addition to the elimination of several thousand tactical nuclear warheads. Under the latter program the Russians, in the Bush-Gorbachev and Bush-Yeltsin statements, agreed to eliminate nuclear warheads for missiles and artillery before 2000 and nuclear mines before 1998. One-third of the short-range nuclear warheads from surface ships and multipurpose submarines, as well as from land-based naval aircraft, were to be eliminated before 1996. One-half of the tactical nuclear ammunition stocks of the air force were to be eliminated before the end of 1997. One-half of Russia's antiaircraft nuclear warheads were to be eliminated before the end of 1996. This is a formidable task, complicated by the 1994 agreement among Ukraine, Russia, and the United States to move Ukrainian warheads to the head of the dismantling queue.[3]

Based on Russian statements and other information, in recent years Russia may have been dismantling 2,000 nuclear warheads a year. Probably many of those were tactical, although strategic warheads removed from Ukraine were given top dismantling priority. For its part, the United States was dismantling 1,500–1,800 warheads a year, although that rate seems to have slowed recently. The result, according to the U.S. National Academy of Sciences, is that "50 or more metric tons of plutonium on each side are expected to become surplus to military needs, along with hundreds of tons of highly enriched uranium (HEU)."[4]

Mainly because monitoring by national technical means was impossible, the disposition of nondeployed warheads has not been a prime concern of arms control negotiations in the past. The problem of monitoring has eased somewhat with the end of the cold war, but sensitivities about design information still remain: what to do with excess warheads and the fissile mate-

---

3. In *Basic Reports*, no. 64 (June 4, 1998), p. 4, the British American Security Information Council reported the following from a source that described an April 29, 1998, meeting of the NATO-Russia Permanent Joint Council: "the Russians outlined their progress on implementing an informal agreement on reducing tactical nuclear weapons reached by Presidents Bush and Gorbachev in 1991. They reported that 80 percent of Russia's warheads had been destroyed and that destruction would be complete by 2000. They also provided a breakdown of weaponry already destroyed: 80 percent of artillery shells, tactical missiles and landmines, half of anti-air missiles, one-third of tactical sea-based missiles, and all antiballistic missile warheads. Other sources at the meeting stressed that Russia did not offer a base number for these reductions. Unofficial Russian sources indicate that the elimination program covers only 13,700 of Russia's 21,700 tactical nuclear weapons."

4. National Academy of Sciences, Committee on International Security and Arms Control, "Executive Summary" (Washington: National Academy Press, 1994), p 1.

rial they contain also is an important unresolved issue, particularly with respect to plutonium. Russia and other countries would like to use plutonium for fuel in civilian nuclear reactors. The United States has opposed a plutonium economy since President Carter's time because it poses huge control problems for a nonproliferation regime and low-enriched uranium fuel is readily available. However, in its fiscal year 2000–05 program priorities, the U.S. Department of Energy proposes to design, equip, and construct a plutonium conversion facility with capacity to process two metric tons of plutonium per year. DOE also proposes to design, procure equipment for, and begin construction of a mixed oxide fuel fabrication facility.[5]

The job of securing all this weapons-useable material and ensuring that it can never again become the core of a nuclear explosive has only just begun. The program of deep reductions described in this book will add significantly to the task. The ultimate objective of the U.S.-Russian nuclear reductions program we envisage is to bring total warheads—nondeployed as well as deployed—down to a level of a few hundred for each country. In this program there is no way to avoid negotiated obligatory reductions in nuclear warheads.

Large numbers of nondeployed warheads present a serious potential for reconstitution of nuclear forces, especially if means of delivery are readily available. A deep reductions program, therefore, requires Russia and the United States to find an agreed method of reducing warheads under verifiable conditions, to make the eliminations irreversible, and to find a way to confirm how many nondeployed warheads exist. These measures can only be achieved incrementally because they push the envelope of monitoring capabilities and political acceptability.

Warheads brought within a system designed to monitor dismantlement can be subjected to accounting techniques and procedures similar to those that Clinton and Yeltsin accepted in principle in their joint statement of May 10, 1995 (see appendix 9A). Many variations could be devised; which mix of techniques and procedures are used depends on how the commitment to dismantle nuclear warheads is framed.

—The most basic requirement, and the easiest to achieve, would be to monitor how many warheads have been dismantled over a given period.

—Much more complex would be an obligation to dismantle all or an agreed portion of warheads removed from deployment as a result of START II and START III.

—A middle ground would be an agreement to dismantle a number of

5. Department of State, "Expanded Threat Reduction Initiative," briefing presented at the Carnegie Endowment for International Peace, Washington, D.C., March 6, 1999.

warheads equivalent to the number taken out of deployment as a result of START II and START III.

The most basic objective of monitoring provisions would be to confirm that an object brought to a dismantling facility is a warhead and that what emerges from the dismantling facility is fissile material from the same warhead. We will know how many warheads have been removed from deployed status, but associating the dismantling with a particular type of warhead will require either a rigorous tagging and tracking system or a system of comparing warheads in the dismantlement queue to a known template for a specific warhead type or both. The sensitivities about compromising design information, as might be required by this procedure, present major obstacles.

In view of the importance of templating in identifying types of warheads that are being dismantled, we recommend that an independent commission be established under the auspices of the U.S. National Security Council to review current classification guidelines for the specific case of U.S.–Russian nuclear arms reductions. A similar commission should be established by the Russian authorities. The two countries should have joint meetings to facilitate a mutual understanding on the key issues.

Accounting for the total number of warheads possessed by a country is still more demanding because of the possibility that some could remain outside the accepted system of accountability. This is why exchanges of data covering production rates over several previous years are so important to build confidence in the declarations of warhead and fissile material inventories. Even then, something like an "anywhere, anytime" monitoring system ultimately may be needed as numbers of warheads dip below several hundred apiece. Experience with monitoring the simpler process of a commitment to warhead dismantlement will be the first step that could lead ultimately to a requirement that each country limit itself to some verified number of total warheads, including reserves. This experience should be gained in connection with START III reductions. In the program proposed in this book, ceilings on total warhead numbers would not be imposed until reductions to the 1,000-warhead level.

Irreversibility Options

Irreversibility of nuclear warhead dismantlement is an indispensable feature of a warhead-centered arms control regime and has its own peculiar monitoring requirements. Monitoring the inventory of fissile material from dismantled warheads held in long-term, secure storage is a minimum requirement to ensure irreversibility of the reductions process. An agreement that there will be no new production of fissile material for warheads that would vitiate the entire commitment to irreversibility is another basic building block. The U.S.-Russian agreement to monitor production of plutonium at dual-purpose reactors in Tomsk and Krasnoyarsk is a useful precedent because it provides a method for confirming that this plutonium will not be used for weapons.

The U.S.-Russian joint project to build a storage facility in Russia to hold dismantled Russian warheads includes a joint understanding that fissile material placed in storage there will never again be used for weapons. U.S.-Russian and International Atomic Energy Agency (IAEA) monitors would confirm that the fissile material was not being removed to fabricate new weapons.

Further steps toward irreversibility deserve very serious attention. These would involve difficult-to-reverse changes to the characteristics of the nuclear components of dismantled warheads. This is being done in the most decisive manner possible in connection with the U.S. purchase of 500 metric tons of Russian highly enriched uranium from dismantled warheads. Russia provides low-enriched material to the United States by blending highly enriched material from nuclear warheads with low-enriched material. Intermediate steps are also available. Changing the shape of the nuclear components, for example, would encourage irreversibility.

Implications for Missile Limitations

One of the main verification problems in a program of deep cuts is whether a nuclear weapon state could conceal warheads or fissile material from the disarmament process. When this possibility is combined with the "legal" possession by the weapon state of a large number of missiles set aside for space launch activities (the START Treaties do not require destruction of all missiles withdrawn from deployment) the threat of possible concealed weapons becomes even more serious. Even when bombers, submarines, and missile silos have been destroyed to comply with reduction agreements, extra missiles could in theory be used as reloads for permitted launchers or in some instances erected on surface launch pads using cranes.

The concerns arising from these potentialities could become a serious obstacle to deep cuts. For these reasons, our group believes Russia and the United States should agree in START III to destroy all intercontinental-range ballistic missiles withdrawn from deployment to comply with the START treaties and subsequent reduction agreements, or at least a large specified part of these missiles. The two governments would also agree to destroy reserve missiles that are surplus to the needs of the permitted level of forces. Future production of these missiles would be restricted, applying the perimeter-portal verification procedures developed in implementing the Treaty on Intermediate Range Nuclear Forces. In both cases—existing missiles and future production—there would be agreed, verified exceptions for replacement of permitted missiles, reliability testing, and space exploration and satellite launch. This action by the United States and Russia would also give greater authority to the efforts of the Missile Technology Control Regime to control exports of missile components.

Implications for Tactical Nuclear Weapons

Presidents Clinton and Yeltsin agreed at their March 1997 Helsinki meeting "that in the context of START III negotiations their experts will explore, as separate issues, possible measures relating to nuclear long-range sea-launched cruise missiles and tactical nuclear systems, to include appropriate confidence-building and transparency measures."[6] Tactical nuclear warheads have not yet been included in verified limitations or reductions. Two "shorter-range" Soviet missile systems, the SS-12 and the SS-23, were included in the U.S.-Soviet treaty on intermediate-range and shorter-range missiles. These missiles and their support systems were eliminated in accordance with procedures laid down in the treaty, but nothing was said in the treaty about eliminating warheads. In September and October 1991 Presidents Bush and Gorbachev announced in separate declarations that they would address tactical or substrategic warheads directly without a formal agreement and with no agreed monitoring procedures. Their actions can be summarized as follows.

The United States would withdraw all its nuclear artillery shells and all nuclear warheads for short-range ballistic missiles to the United States. These and any similar warheads currently stored in the United States would be dismantled and destroyed. All tactical nuclear weapons, including nuclear-armed cruise missiles, would be withdrawn from U.S. surface ships and attack submarines. Nuclear weapons associated with land-based naval air-

6. "Joint Statement on Parameters."

craft also would be removed. Many of these weapons would be dismantled and destroyed and the remainder placed in secure central storage areas. All strategic bombers would be removed from day-to-day alert status and their weapons returned to storage areas. President Bush called on the Soviet Union to take comparable, although not identical measures.[7]

On October 5, 1991, President Gorbachev announced that the Soviet Union would take reciprocal actions. The most important were the following. All nuclear artillery ammunition and nuclear warheads for tactical missiles would be destroyed. Nuclear warheads of antiaircraft missiles would be removed from the army and stored in central bases; part of them would be destroyed. All nuclear mines would be eliminated. All tactical nuclear weapons would be removed from surface ships and multipurpose submarines. These weapons, as well as weapons from ground-based naval aviation would be stored, with part being destroyed.[8]

In the context of START III the United States and Russia will have to decide what to do about operational tactical warheads, that is, those in storage as a result of the Bush-Gorbachev-Yeltsin actions but that could be readily mated with compatible delivery systems. Chapter 8 discusses this issue. There we pointed out that in addressing tactical nuclear warheads an important question is whether, for purposes of accounting for deployed, operational warheads, these weapons should be combined with strategic weapons under a single warhead ceiling, with freedom to mix. We recommended against that option, favoring instead a separate track for tactical weapons, leading ultimately to elimination. We recognized that monitoring the levels of operational tactical nuclear warheads will be subject to many shortcomings, even though they may all be in storage.

In any case the unilateral declarations by Bush and Gorbachev should be supplemented by data exchanges and random inspections of storage facilities as confidence-building measures. Thus as soon as the objection that design information would be compromised by identifying specific warhead types is overcome, tactical warheads slated for dismantling should be identified. The original Bush-Gorbachev-Yeltsin understandings also might be strengthened by tighter controls over nuclear-capable sea-launched cruise missiles in storage. (The problem of accounting for nondeclared warheads,

7. This description is drawn from a White House fact sheet dated September 27, 1991, published in the *NATO Review*, no. 5 (October 1991), p. 11.

8. This summary is drawn from a Novosti report of President Gorbachev's televised address of October 5, 1991, published in *Survival*, vol. 33 (November-December 1991), pp. 569–70.

of course, would remain.)

For the longer term, however, these extensions of the Bush-Gorbachev initiatives are not sufficient either from the perspective of verification or from the standpoint of breakout. The initial reductions of tactical nuclear warheads should be followed by increasingly rigorous monitoring measures, as described in chapter 11. In reductions beyond START III, tactical warheads should be identified as such for dismantling purposes. Tactical warhead inventories should be used as a test bed to experiment with monitoring requirements for accounting for nondeployed warheads not yet in the queue for dismantling. Challenge inspections, for example, and certainly chain of custody would be examples of such monitoring techniques.

A comprehensive and fully fleshed out monitoring system to deal with the possibility of nondeclared tactical warheads should be deferred, however, until arrangements for verification of total holdings of strategic weapons are put in place, when very intrusive measures will be necessary. Exchanging detailed data on production and dismantling rates of tactical weapons over a period of years will be helpful in providing limited assurance that all such weapons have been brought within the system of accountability. And locating storage facilities for tactical weapons at remote distances from potential delivery systems also would be a useful measure.

Some Russian estimates indicate that most Russian tactical nuclear weapons made before 1991 will be beyond their certified life within the next several years. As noted in chapter 8, elements within the Russian military attach great importance to tactical nuclear weapons, which they see as offsetting Russia's weakness in conventional military forces. There is no doubt that these views are deeply and sincerely felt, but we doubt that missions exist for either Russian or U.S. tactical nuclear weapons that are essential to the basic security needs of the two countries. Occasionally mentioned as a possible Russian defensive measure in Asia, some types of tactical nuclear weapons would require predelegation for use to relatively low-level commanders. Nuclear weapons used defensively by Russia probably would be detonated on Russian soil. For these reasons, and because of the portability of tactical nuclear warheads, our group recommends that the two governments set elimination of such warheads as a priority goal while recognizing that this may not be easy for the Russian government and that monitoring problems will almost certainly require that the goal be achieved in phases.

Cooperative and Negotiated Warhead Dismantlement

The distinction between coordinated, cooperative measures and negotiated, treaty-based measures is well illustrated by the case of nuclear warhead dismantlement. The distinction is based on the purpose to be achieved. The purpose of cooperative strategic warhead dismantlement is to provide increasing levels of confidence that dismantling is taking place, increase mutual understanding concerning the size and nature of each other's stocks of weapons and fissile material, and improve the security of fissile materials against theft. These goals should involve data exchanges, some level of confidence that what is in a container is likely to be a warhead, and that what goes into secure storage is likely to have come from the same warhead. It requires something beyond joint material protection, control, and accountability, probably spot checks at storage facilities.

The purpose of negotiated, treaty-based strategic warhead dismantlement is to prevent nuclear breakout and to deal with hedge policy. This means rigorous verification, clearly a necessary step to deep cuts. Such verification requires a formula for mandatory dismantlement, plus stringent methods of accountability, plus, at the least, jointly monitored storage of dismantled nuclear components to ensure irreversibility. Verification may require templating and maintaining a chain of custody (tags and seals). It will require a method of ascertaining that what went into a dismantling facility was a nuclear warhead and that what came out was fissile material from the same warhead.

Cooperative reduction of tactical nuclear weapons is meant to build confidence that tactical warheads are in safe and secure storage and increase transparency regarding numbers and locations of tactical nuclear weapons. Data exchange would be absolutely required, and an understanding that all tactical warheads would be placed in storage facilities would be almost certainly necessary. A method of spot checks to confirm numbers of operational tactical warheads in storage would be very desirable, although this would border on a treaty-based requirement.

A negotiated, legally binding arrangement for tactical nuclear warheads, as noted above, would be necessary to deal with the break-out potential. Deep cuts in strategic weapons could not omit tactical warheads. Rigorous monitoring systems, including counting numbers of warheads in operational storage, and probably verified elimination of tactical warheads identified as to type, will have to be based on a legally binding treaty.

Experience Gained in the 1994–95 Talks on Nuclear Warhead Dismantlement

Although the focus of top-level interest was elsewhere, many discussions and negotiations between Russian and American officials took place in 1994–95 on warhead dismantlement issues. These may shed some light on process and substantive questions in future transparency and irreversibility discussions. The 1994–95 talks were more like the pre-Gorbachev Soviet style than the 1986–92 style. By 1994 the Gorbachev and early Yeltsin days of radical thinking and quick agreements had been replaced by caution and long silences, by unclear lines of authority and unexplained reversals of position. The sources of Russian conduct in nuclear negotiations in the mid-1990s stemmed from traditional Russian attitudes—the penchant for secrecy, especially—overlain with the inevitable confusion of a governing apparatus still adapting to a new social system. Russia's desperate need for financial resources also influenced the course of negotiations and helped define the limits of the possible. All of this produced a Russian negotiating style that was more transparent and much less influenced by propaganda needs but less consistent and purposeful than the Soviet style.

Despite this background noise a surprising amount of progress was made in talks at various levels, ranging from the summit to technical-level analyses, in defining the nature of the problems and finding solutions. After all, the two sides were dealing with issues that were almost completely new to negotiations between them. Not since the days of the first American disarmament proposal of the nuclear age—the Baruch plan of the 1940s—had the United States suggested that the dismantling and elimination of nondeployed nuclear warheads become a matter for negotiation between Moscow and Washington. Deployed warheads were counted in START I and START II but there were no mutual obligations concerning the destruction of nondeployed warheads.

This began to change when President Bush and President Gorbachev decided that part of their holdings of tactical nuclear weapons should be eliminated. It also changed when the United States, during the Bush administration, offered to purchase 500 metric tons of highly enriched uranium (HEU) from dismantled Soviet nuclear warheads. This offer was put into effect as part of a revenue-sharing arrangement between Russia, Ukraine, and the United States during the Clinton administration in 1994. Ukrainian observers who had worked in the Soviet nuclear weapons establishment were permitted to oversee the dismantling of the warheads removed from Ukraine to Russia. Americans are permitted to monitor the facility where Russian technicians blend down the HEU to create low-enriched uranium (LEU) for commercial nuclear fuel.

Beginning in 1994 the Clinton administration began to urge Russia to join with the United States in addressing the dismantling of U.S. and Russian nuclear warheads. "Transparency and irreversibility" became the stated objectives of the United States with regard to converting nuclear warheads to nonmilitary purposes. The administration was strongly supported in this by the U.S. Senate. A condition to the ratification of START I, offered by Senator Joseph Biden, requested the administration to seek "an appropriate arrangement" to monitor "numbers of nuclear stockpile weapons" inter alia.[9]

On January 14, 1994, Presidents Clinton and Yeltsin agreed to establish a joint working group to consider steps to ensure the transparency and irreversibility of reducing nuclear weapons. The working group (Ambassador Goodby was the U.S. chair; a senior official of MINATOM initially chaired the Russian side) readily reached agreement at a meeting in May 1994 that it would examine options for reciprocal inspections of storage facilities containing plutonium and HEU removed from nuclear weapons, examine options for declaring all stocks and locations of HEU and plutonium, civil and military, and define options to make transfers of fissile materials from weapons to nonweapons purposes irreversible. These terms of reference were reinforced by a September 1994 summit meeting where the United States and Russian presidents agreed to:

—Exchange detailed information at the next meeting of the Gore-Chernomyrdin Commission on aggregate stockpiles of nuclear warheads, on stocks of fissile materials, and on their safety and security. The sides will develop a process for exchanging this information on a regular basis.
—Direct their joint working group on nuclear safeguards, transparency, and irreversibility to pursue by March 1995 further measures to improve confidence in and increase the transparency and irreversibility of the process of reducing nuclear weapons.[10]

Before this September 1994 Yeltsin-Clinton meeting, Under Secretary of State Lynn Davis and Russian Deputy Foreign Minister Georgi Mamedov had

9. "Senate Foreign Relations Committee Report on START I," 103 Cong. 2 sess., September 8, 1992.
10. White House Office of the Press Secretary, "Joint Statement on Strategic Stability and Nuclear Security by the Presidents of the United States of America and the Russian Federation," September 20, 1994," p. 3.

met and instructed the joint working group, beginning by March 1995, to

—define options to make transfers of fissile materials from weapons to nonweapons purposes irreversible;

—consider options for an exchange of data on inventories of fissile materials removed from dismantled warheads;

—examine options for reciprocal inspections of storage facilities containing plutonium and highly enriched uranium removed from nuclear weapons; and

—address special safeguards problems related to the cutoff of production of fissile materials for weapons and the feasibility and specific methods for placing fissile materials released as a result of the disarmament process under IAEA safeguards.[11]

The joint working group was to report on its progress at the next summit meeting. These instructions were consistent with the previously agreed terms of reference of the working group (the cutoff also had been a part of the terms of reference), and deadlines had been set for reporting progress. The exchange of data called for by the two presidents in their joint statement was even more urgent, however, since the next meeting of the Gore-Chernomyrdin Commission would be held in Moscow in December 1994.

On the margins of that commission meeting (where no data were exchanged), Ambassador Goodby handed copies of a "nonpaper" on transparency and irreversibility to the Russian Foreign Ministry, Defense Ministry, and Ministry of Atomic Energy. The objectives the U.S. government had in mind were to

—build confidence in each side's understanding of the size of the other's stockpiles of nuclear weapons and fissile materials and the rate of reduction in these stockpiles;

—build confidence on each side that the nuclear arms reductions being undertaken are irreversible and, in particular, that fissile materials declared excess to military needs are not being used to make new nuclear weapons; and

—build each side's confidence that nuclear weapons and fissile materials are secure and provide the information and openness needed to strengthen our mutual cooperation toward that end; and build public, legislative, and international confidence in the nuclear arms reduction process, support mutual efforts to extend and strengthen the nonproliferation regime, ratify and implement the START Treaties, and consider further arms control measures.

11. White House Office of the Press Secretary, "Report of September 1994 Presummit Meetings on US-Russian Security Issues," September 28, 1994, p. 2.

To accomplish these ends, the United States envisaged a transparency and irreversibility regime that would include exchanges of detailed information on aggregate stockpiles of nuclear warheads and stocks of fissile materials and mutual reciprocal inspections to confirm the stockpiles of HEU and plutonium removed from nuclear weapons. The regime would also include a cooperative arrangement to monitor warheads declared excess and awaiting dismantlement; cooperative measures to confirm and clarify reciprocal declarations of fissile material stockpiles, including limited spot checks at fissile material sites, not including fissile material in weapons or naval fuel or within naval fuel fabrication facilities; and exchanges of fissile material production records and visits to production sites.

Meanwhile, technical talks were being held between U.S. and Russian experts to work out a method of confirming that fissile components from dismantled nuclear warheads were inside containers destined for storage. On March 16, 1994, U.S. Secretary of Energy Hazel O'Leary and Russian Minister of Atomic Energy Viktor Mikhailov agreed to start work on conducting reciprocal inspections of plutonium removed from dismantled nuclear weapons.

At a meeting held in Moscow in May 1994 to define the terms of reference for this study, the two sides agreed on a two-step procedure: familiarization visits to Rocky Flats and Tomsk-7 to review each side's monitoring equipment and methods and development of coordinated methods for conducting inspection measurements for plutonium removed from dismantled nuclear weapons and placed inside storage containers, recognizing that procedures and equipment used must not reveal sensitive data on each other's nuclear weapons designs or weapons components.

The United States also proposed a third step: to negotiate an agreement regarding an overall regime for confirming the inventories of fissile materials from nuclear weapons dismantlement. In addition, the United States suggested that highly enriched uranium from dismantled nuclear weapons be included in a subsequent study. The Russians replied that these proposals should be presented to their Ministry of Foreign Affairs.

In a familiarization meeting at the Rocky Flats facility in July 1994 the United States demonstrated, using its own equipment, measurement techniques to confirm (yes or no) the presence of plutonium inside a storage container based on gamma-ray spectrum analysis, confirm (yes or no) the presence of a threshold mass of plutonium based on neutron count rate, estimate the mass of plutonium based on neutron count rate inside a storage container declared by the United States to contain an ingot of plutonium; and confirm the rough size and shape of an inert sphere, based on a radiograph, inside a storage container.

A subsequent visit to Tomsk-7 was to be followed by the negotiation of a comprehensive monitoring regime, in the U.S. view, but implementing the regime would almost certainly require a U.S.-Russian agreement making it legally possible to proceed with an exchange of certain classified or sensitive information. The Russians believed that a U.S.-Russian agreement to protect any sensitive information exchanged between the two countries was essential, and so stated at a meeting of the joint working group in Moscow in April 1995. Their emphasis from the outset was on protection of information, while the United States, basing its position on the U.S. Atomic Energy Act, emphasized that a generic description of what information might be exchanged also should be included in an agreement for cooperation. This difference in emphasis persisted throughout the negotiations.

The other remaining issue involving the agreement for cooperation concerned the scope of the information that might be exchanged. The U.S. side proposed several categories for potential exchanges, believing that this was preferable to amending the agreement each time the sides agreed on a new area for cooperation. The Russian side favored a more cautious, step-by-step approach. Russian experts on information security visited the United States in September 1995 for on-site briefings on how the United States would protect sensitive information furnished by Russia, and a reciprocal visit to Russia by U.S. security experts took place in January 1996. Both sides were satisfied with what they saw.

As is apparent from this brief history, the U.S. and Russian teams made considerable progress in 1994–95 in working out an agreement to protect sensitive information that might be exchanged pursuant to a transparency and irreversibility regime. They also were far along in designing a system for monitoring plutonium from dismantled warheads destined for long-term storage. Some of the main techniques were agreed to as early as October 1994, following the reciprocal visits to Rocky Flats and Tomsk. An agreement to begin a demonstration of a reciprocal inspection system had been drafted by the United States and handed to the Russians. Some progress had been made in exploring how highly enriched uranium warhead components destined for storage might be monitored. Of course, a major U.S.-Russian project, nearing completion, was the construction of a large facility in the Urals for long-term storage of the fissile components of more than 10,000 dismantled Russian nuclear warheads. And, as stated earlier, the understanding with Russia was that dismantled warheads stored in this facility would never again be used for weapons purposes. A joint U.S.-Russian monitoring arrangement would oversee this arrangement, supplemented by the International Atomic Energy Agency.[12] Monitoring the blending down of highly enriched uranium from Russian warheads, as required in the context of the HEU purchase, also was under way.

There were, however, two important missing links in the transparency and irreversibility regime discussed between the Americans and the Russians in 1994–95. One was an agreement to share data on nuclear warhead and fissile material inventories. The United States gave the Russians a draft text of such an agreement in the summer of 1995, but a U.S.-Russian discussion of the text never occurred. Informally, some Russians gave the impression that the scope of the data exchange went well beyond what they were prepared to consider. The categories of data that the United States was ready to discuss included the number of nuclear weapons produced each year over a period of time, together with the type of associated weapon system and production location. For fissile material the United States suggested sharing data on annual production by type, enrichment or grade, and production site. There were other categories as well. The United States proposed spot checks as a device for confirming the accuracy of declarations of fissile material stockpiles. The only monitoring affecting nuclear warheads would relate to dismantled warheads. The United States had made clear that a reciprocal and evolutionary approach to transparency and irreversibility should be adopted and, in that spirit, there was a possibility of taking some experimental first steps. The absence of a dialogue on data exchange precluded that, however, throughout 1995.

The other missing element in a transparency and irreversibility regime was chain of custody, that is, tagging and monitoring warheads declared excess before their dismantlement and arrival at the storage site. In their joint statement of May 10, 1995, Presidents Clinton and Yeltsin agreed to investigate this part of a transparency and irreversibility regime. At the level of experts, both sides understood that this was what was meant by their agreement to seek to define "intergovernmental arrangements to extend cooperation to further phases of the process of eliminating nuclear weapons."[13] The United States had pointed to the necessity of some additional measures to confirm that materials arriving at storage sites came from nuclear warheads. The United States was not proposing to monitor the actual

---

12. James E. Goodby, "Loose Nukes: Security Issues on the U.S.-Russian Agenda," Institute for International Studies, Stanford University, April 1997, pp. 5–6.

13. See the appendix to this chapter.

dismantlement procedure. There was, however, no official discussion of this subject in 1995.

In the fall of 1995 the Russian government decided to change its negotiating team to place the Ministry of Foreign Affairs in charge of implementing the May 10 decisions of the two presidents. Ambassador Poulat Abdulaev was named the head of the Russian delegation. He was supported by two deputies, one from the Ministry of Defense, the other from MINATOM. In addition, the Russians suggested that the site of the U.S.-Russian meetings be shifted from Moscow to either Geneva or Helsinki and that regularly scheduled meetings be held a few times a year. The idea apparently was to place the talks on a more formal footing, rather like the strategic arms talks of previous years. Washington readily agreed to these suggestions, while preferring a more intense work schedule, and the first meeting under the new arrangements was set for late November 1995 in Geneva. The Russians noted that their instructions for this important meeting and the formal confirmation of their appointments to the delegation would be matters for the Russian president and his staff to decide.

Not long before the scheduled meeting the State Department received a telephone call from the Russians saying that they were not ready for the Geneva meeting. After some weeks of delay a senior Russian embassy diplomat visited the State Department on January 4, 1996. His message, from Moscow, was that the Russian government was reviewing its policies on transparency and irreversibility. No meetings could be scheduled until the policy review had been completed. There was no information as to when that time might come.

This was the end of the first attempt to work out a transparency and irreversibility regime for the dismantlement of nuclear warheads. Ambassador Goodby's contemporary assessment was that the Russian ministries lacked incentives to engage in this new and sensitive area for U.S.-Russian cooperation, that there were political risks for those Russians who did advocate it, and that the Russian government at the time was nearly dysfunctional.[14] As far as has been informally ascertained since from Russian sources, this characterization of the Russian situation in 1995 was pretty much on mark. The Russian Ministry of Atomic Energy (MINATOM) and Ministry of Defense were never enthusiastic about the transparency and irreversibility talks and along with other agencies recommended in the summer of 1995 that negotiations be stopped. The decision to stop was then evidently made

14. Memorandum from James E. Goodby to Under Secretary of State Lynn Davis, September 19, 1995.

in the office of the Russian president, Prime Minister Viktor Chernomyrdin having passed the issue to Boris Yeltsin. Among the reasons given by Russian sources for this reluctance to pursue the negotiations were that there existed no legislative basis to support transparency agreements, the 1995 law on international agreements would force the administration to submit any agreement to the Duma for ratification, and the upcoming elections were diverting the attention of the leadership.

However, Goodby's assessment also noted that in the United States transparency and irreversibility had been given a lower priority than other security issues on the U.S.-Russian agenda and that the complexity of the subject matter discouraged high-level attention. He called for a higher priority and urged more public outreach on the issues involved. Referring to the cancellation by the Russian government of what could have been a decisive U.S.-Russian meeting in Geneva in late November 1995, he wrote in a December 29, 1995, memorandum that the transparency and irreversibility regime that Russia and the United States were trying to establish "would make it possible to move into the next phase of nuclear arms control: negotiated reductions of nuclear warheads for the first time in the history of strategic nuclear arms control. This should be and could be the Clinton Administration's unique contribution to nuclear constraints. All this is now at risk."[15]

After a delay of more than a year, the Clinton-Yeltsin agreement at Helsinki in March 1997 placed this issue squarely in the context of START III. The question of dismantling warheads is no longer a free-standing proposition disconnected from other key elements of the U.S.-Russian relationship, as had been the case in 1994–95. Because of this policy shift on the part of both Moscow and Washington, there is an improved outlook for an agreement between the two that would achieve transparency and irreversibility in the process of transferring fissile material from military to nonmilitary purposes. Furthermore, joint U.S.-Russian technical workshops starting in 1996 have provided some technical support for transparency measures. Several technologies were examined at these meetings, including radiation fingerprinting and tags and seals for chain-of-custody measures. Participants believe that once there is a political decision on transparency, effective implementation measures could be developed within one to two years.

15. Memorandum from James E. Goodby to Assistant Secretary of State Thomas E. McNamara, December 29, 1995.

Reflections on Russian Government Policymaking

Russian foreign policymaking at top levels during the mid-1990s was erratic and dominated by short-run political needs, reflecting Yeltsin's illness and his preoccupation with juggling political forces in Russia. Collegial decisionmaking of the type that occurred in the Soviet Politburo from time to time had apparently given way to a more autocratic manner, as practiced by Yeltsin. A system of checks and balances hemmed him in, however, since he had to take into account actions and opinions of the Duma, regional officials, ministers, and the possessors of new wealth. Follow-on actions after important decisions were haphazard. Yeltsin seemed unable to prevent his government from reversing earlier presidential decisions or ignoring them.

In nuclear matters several statements of intent were issued jointly by Presidents Clinton and Yeltsin that Russian officialdom chose to disregard. The most egregious example was their joint statement of May 10, 1995, in which the two presidents in very precise terms endorsed early action on several important measures of transparency and irreversibility of nuclear weapons dismantlement only to see the negotiations broken off at the urging of Russian officials six months later. In this particular instance there were detailed U.S.-Russian discussions at senior levels in the Ministry of Foreign Affairs and the Ministry of Atomic Energy about how to frame the two presidents' intent, and about its urgency, before and after the May 10, 1995, statement was issued. According to the Russians, interagency discussions had been held in Moscow that resulted in instructions to implement the May 10, 1995, statement. Still, neither the Russian president nor the prime minister was able or willing to enforce the decision when some officials in the bureaucracy (probably inspired by the "security organs") concluded that transparency did not suit Russia.

For a time Prime Minister Chernomyrdin became one of the major discussion partners with the United States through the mechanism of the Gore-Chernomyrdin Commission. He was a competent and businesslike manager, but his authority over the "power ministries" in Moscow was limited. Only on September 10, 1996, as part of a temporary transfer of authority occasioned by his impending surgery, did President Yeltsin decree that these ministries should report to Chernomyrdin. His authority over the power ministries seemed to be limited even after that period.

Overall, U.S.-Russian cooperation has tended to proceed well when only one ministry was involved but poorly when several had to be consulted. As an example of at least a partial success, the Ministry of Atomic Energy, motivated by a desire to sustain its huge industrial and technological base, blessed the U.S.-funded cooperative laboratory-to-laboratory efforts aimed at improving fissile material protection, control, and accountability (MPC&A). Also, Viktor Mikhailov, the minister of atomic energy, sought U.S. help in constructing a major secure storage facility for a significant part of the plutonium and highly enriched uranium derived from dismantled nuclear warheads. After some delays the project proceeded and became one of the largest of the Nunn-Lugar cooperative programs.

In addition, the Ministry of Defense was very cooperative in certain limited but important areas. The protection and the safety of nuclear warheads in the hands of the military was the responsibility of this ministry. The United States offered equipment and methodologies; U.S.-Russian cooperation proceeded smoothly and received the praise of senior Russian military officials.

The Russian government, lacking other options, has positioned its nuclear forces squarely in the center of the defensive image it presents to the world. A case in point was the announcement, during the Kosovo conflict, that President Yeltsin had endorsed "a blueprint for the development and use of non-strategic nuclear weapons."[16] This situation inevitably affects other aspects of the relationship, usually negatively. U.S.-Russian cooperative arrangements have dealt, fairly successfully, with the reductions of nuclear weapons required by START I and the problems created by the collapse of the Soviet Union. Attempts have even been made to put U.S.-Russian strategic relations on a firmer institutional basis through military-to-military contacts and a strategic stability working group. But these have not been sufficient to change the basic equation. Nuclear plans and deployments on both sides continue to influence U.S.-Russian relations nearly ten years after the end of the cold war. U.S.-Russian cooperation in a variety of areas that need not, and probably should not, be the subjects of formal U.S.-Russian arms control negotiations is badly needed. A properly constituted, high-level forum for addressing such possibilities would encourage a more rapid transition to a post–cold war relationship in strategic nuclear arrangements.

16. David Hoffman, "Kremlin to Bolster Nuclear Stockpile," *Washington Post*, April 30, 1999, p. A19.

Appendix 9A: Joint Statement on the Transparency and Irreversibility of the Process of Reducing Nuclear Weapons, May 10, 1995

The President of the United States of America and the President of the Russian Federation, after examining the exchange of views which took place during the December 1994 meeting of the Gore-Chernomyrdin Commission in regard to the aggregate stockpiles of nuclear warheads, stocks of fissile materials, and their safety and security, as well as a discussion of the Joint Working Group on Nuclear Safeguards, Transparency and Irreversibility of further measures to improve confidence in and increase the transparency and irreversibility of the process of reducing nuclear weapons,

—Reaffirm the commitment of the United States of America and the Russian Federation to the goal of nuclear disarmament and their desire to pursue further measures to improve confidence in and increase the transparency and irreversibility of the process of nuclear arms reduction, as they agreed in January and September 1994;

—Reaffirm the desire of the United States of America and the Russian Federation to exchange detailed information on aggregate stockpiles of nuclear warheads, on stocks of fissile materials and on their safety and security and to develop a process for exchange of this information on a regular basis; and

—Express the desire of the United States of America and the Russian Federation to establish as soon as possible concrete arrangements for enhancing transparency and irreversibility of the process of nuclear arms reduction.

Taking into account the proposal by President B. N. Yeltsin for a treaty on nuclear safety and strategic stability among the five nuclear powers, they declare that:

—Fissile materials removed from nuclear weapons being eliminated and excess to national security requirements will not be used to manufacture nuclear weapons;

—No newly produced fissile materials will be used in nuclear weapons; and

—Fissile materials from or within civil nuclear programs will not be used to manufacture nuclear weapons.

The United States of America and the Russian Federation will negotiate agreements to increase the transparency and irreversibility of nuclear arms reduction that, *inter alia*, establish:

—An exchange on a regular basis of detailed information on aggregate stockpiles of nuclear warheads, on stocks of fissile materials and on their safety and security;

—A cooperative arrangement for reciprocal monitoring at storage facilities of fissile materials removed from nuclear warheads and declared to be excess to national security requirements to help confirm the irreversibility of the process of reducing nuclear weapons, recognizing that progress in this area is linked to progress in implementing the joint U.S.-Russian program for the fissile material storage facility at Mayak; and

—Other cooperative measures, as necessary to enhance confidence in the reciprocal declarations on fissile material stockpiles.

The United States of America and the Russian Federation will strive to conclude as soon as possible agreements which are based on these principles.

The United States of America and the Russian Federation will also examine and seek to define further measures to increase the transparency and irreversibility of the process of reducing nuclear weapons, including intergovernmental arrangements to extend cooperation to further phases of the process of eliminating nuclear weapons declared excess to national security requirements as a result of nuclear arms reduction.

The Presidents urged progress in implementing current agreements affecting the irreversibility of the process of reducing nuclear weapons such as the June 23, 1994, agreement concerning the shutdown of plutonium production reactors and the cessation of use of newly produced plutonium for nuclear weapons, in all its interrelated provisions, including, *inter alia*, cooperation in creation of alternative energy sources, shutdown of plutonium production reactors mentioned above, and development of respective compliance procedures.

The United States of America and the Russian Federation will seek to conclude in the shortest possible time an agreement for cooperation between their governments enabling the exchange of information as necessary to implement the arrangements called for above, by providing for the protection of that information. No information will be exchanged until the respective arrangements enter into force.

CHAPTER TEN

Completing the Deep Cuts Regime

This chapter discusses how Britain, France, and China could be engaged in an irreversible process of nuclear disarmament, and how the arsenals of the three de facto nuclear weapon states—Israel, India, and Pakistan—could be controlled.

In the final stage of the deep cuts program, all five Non-Proliferation Treaty (NPT) nuclear weapon states—the United States, Russia, France, the United Kingdom, and China—would reduce their nuclear weapons to an equal level of 200 warheads each, perhaps 200 warheads for Britain and France together, under a stringently verified scheme that destroys all but the permitted warheads and delivery systems.[1] With a few exceptions the remaining warheads would be separated from their delivery systems. Warheads and delivery systems would be kept in internationally monitored, dispersed, and perhaps defended storage sites on the territory of the owner states. The weapons could be withdrawn in situations of national emergency, but not without giving warning. India, Pakistan, and Israel would store their nuclear weapons materials and delivery systems on their own territories under similar monitored conditions.[2] We propose that the United States break from the tradition of incremental reductions without a stated long-term perspective that has characterized its policy on nuclear weapons and nuclear reductions and take the initiative in promoting a deep cuts program. Russia should be invited to join in taking the lead on the program and in mak-

1. According to Article IX of the Non-Proliferation Treaty, the five are those that had manufactured and exploded nuclear weapons before January 1, 1967.

2. This approach is outlined in Jonathan Dean, "The Final Stage of Nuclear Arms Control," *Washington Quarterly*, vol. 17 (Autumn 1994); and *Ending Europe's Wars:The Continuing Search for Peace and Security* (Twentieth Century Fund Press, 1994), chap. 14. A 100–300 warhead force has also been suggested by the Committee on International Security and Arms Control, National Academy of Sciences, *The Future of U.S. Nuclear Weapons Policy* (Washington: National Academy Press, 1997), pp. 79–83. Admiral Stansfield Turner, *Caging the Nuclear Genie: An American Challenge for Global Security* (Boulder, Colo.: Westview Press, 1997), advocates a similar program.

ing a well-publicized announcement of its aims. Early announcement would also allow future participants to be informed in advance of the role it is hoped they would play. Governments and publics throughout the world would be encouraged to give the program maximum support.

All five NPT weapon states will almost certainly consider some actions, such as entry into force of the Comprehensive Test Ban Treaty, adoption of a fissile cutoff treaty, inclusion of the de facto nuclear weapon states in the program, and radical improvement of the nonproliferation regime, to be essential requirements for safe implementation of the deep cuts program.[3] Consequently, they will probably make the completion of their own reductions to the 200-warhead level in this third stage explicitly depend on achieving these steps. We believe that for their part India and Pakistan will ultimately consider the deep cuts program an important move toward fulfillment of their own demands that the five NPT weapon states make time-bound commitments for eliminating their nuclear weapons. Given the potential benefits for their own security and the pressure of public opinion that would fall on nuclear weapon states that block the program by holding back, it is probable that all of the states will ultimately decide to participate.

Engaging Britain, France, and China

The previous chapters described how, at the START IV stage of the deep cuts program, the United States and Russia would offer to reduce their arsenals to 1,000 warheads each, provided that Britain, France, and China agree to join in negotiating reductions in their own forces when the 1,000- warhead level is reached, pledge to carry out a comprehensive exchange of data on their nuclear forces modeled on the earlier U.S.-Russian exchange, and commit themselves not to increase the overall level of their deployed weapons in the interim. In the final phase of the deep cuts program, these three governments would be invited to join in reducing their nuclear arsenals under the same conditions the United States and Russia have applied to their reductions.

Reductions and controls on the Chinese, French, and British arsenals are a necessary precondition for really deep cuts by the United States and Russia. Russia, more inclined than the United States to consider the other three

3. The fissile cutoff treaty and inclusion of the threshold states in the program are discussed in this chapter and chapter 11. Improvements in the nonproliferation regime are also covered in chapter 11.

NPT weapon states, especially China, as potential threats, has repeatedly called for their participation in negotiations on reducing nuclear forces. When he signed START II in January 1993, President Boris Yeltsin called on Britain, France, and China to pledge cuts or limits on their nuclear weapon arsenals, and he has proposed this on numerous occasions since.[4] At the same time, it is highly unlikely that the United States would seriously consider reductions to a minimum arsenal in the absence of parallel action by China, or that either the United States or Russia would be willing to move to minimum arsenals without commensurate action by India, Pakistan, and Israel.

This approach should be generally acceptable to the British, French, and Chinese governments. Britain, France, and China have all declared their willingness in principle to negotiate reductions of their nuclear weapons but only after the arsenals of the United States and Russia, now tens of times larger, have come much closer to their level.

Officials in Britain and France have indicated that the appropriate stage for their countries to join disarmament negotiations is after the United States and Russia have reduced to a level of about 1,000 nuclear weapons each.[5] At the Non-Proliferation Treaty Extension Conference in April 1995, Britain's Foreign Secretary Douglas Hurd formally stated that the United Kingdom would join in reductions once the "U.S. and Russian stockpiles were in the hundreds."[6] France probably would be willing to join the United Kingdom at that stage.[7] In recent years, China has been less specific regarding its nuclear force planning, stating merely that the United States and Russia "should take the lead in drastically reducing their stockpiles of all types of nuclear weapons and means of delivery."[8]

China's conditions for joining in negotiated reductions are likely to be

4. Yeltsin had already made this same request during a visit to London at the beginning of his presidency in January 1992. Alexei Arbatov, "Mutilateral Nuclear Weapons Reductions and Limitations," in *Strategic Views from the Second Tier: The Nuclear Weapons Policies of France, Britain, and China*, edited by John Hopkins and Weixing Hu (New Brunswick, N.J.: Transaction Publishers, 1995), p. 213.

5. Atlantic Council, "Nuclear Weapons and European Security," *Bulletin*, vol. 6 (October 31, 1995).

6. Michael Littlejohns and Bernard Gray, "UK 'has halted the buildup of N-material,'" *Financial Times*, April 19, 1995.

7. Craig Whitney, "Cold War over, France Plans a Slim, Volunteer Military," *New York Times*, February 23, 1996, p A3. Background on recent French thinking on nuclear weapons is given in David Yost, "France's Nuclear Dilemmas," *Foreign Affairs* (January-February 1996), pp. 108–18.

8. *China White Paper on Arms Control and Disarmament* (Beijing: Xinhua News Agency, November 16, 1995), section 6.

threefold. First, Beijing will insist that the other four declared nuclear weapon states join in its proposed no-first-use commitment. Second, it will insist that the United States and Russia reduce their nuclear stockpiles to a level comparable to those of China, Britain, and France. Third, China may insist that the United States provide assurances that it will continue to observe the Antiballistic Missile (ABM) Treaty and also accept some limitations on the capability of theater missile defense systems. These are all actions that we propose be undertaken in any case. China may also add some political conditions, including a new understanding on Taiwan.

Beijing fears that U.S. proposals to collaborate with Russia, Japan, and South Korea on theater missile defense systems are aimed at China.[9] Because Russia also holds negative views about ballistic missile defenses and because the United Kingdom and France, with their small nuclear arsenals, are likely to be uneasy about deployment of nationwide missile defenses in the United States and probably ultimately in Russia, the willingness of the United States to provide credible long-term assurances on limiting its ABM program may be a crucial factor in gaining the agreement of the other four nuclear weapon states to move to a low force level.

Five-Power Reductions

In the course of their negotiations, the five NPT weapon states would work out a program of step-by-step reductions down to the level of 200 warheads each, this limit to include both strategic and tactical weapons, using procedures pioneered in earlier U.S.-Russian reductions: continuing data exchange with spot-check verification; dismantling of all reduced warheads; transfer of fissile material from dismantled warheads to monitored storage and disposition of fissile material to preclude its reuse for weapons. All five governments would destroy the missiles withdrawn from deployment and end production for military purposes of ballistic missiles with ranges greater than 300 kilometers, with limited, verified exceptions for replacement of missiles under the permitted limit and for satellite launch and space exploration.

As the reductions continue, reserve warheads too would be dismantled

9. See Liu Huaqiu, "Evaluation and Analysis of China's Nuclear and Control Policy," *Beijing Xiandai Junshi*, November 11, 1995, in Foreign Broadcast Information Service, *Daily Report: China*, December 22, 1995, pp 6–11; and Sha Zukang, "Some Thoughts on Non-Proliferation," Seventh Carnegie International Non-Proliferation Conference, January 1999, Washington. Sha Zukang is director-general, Department of Arms Control and Disarmament, Ministry of Foreign Affairs of China.

in phases, and their plutonium and highly enriched uranium components removed. This fissile material, together with all remaining stocks of unweaponized fissile material of all five states, would be transferred to monitored storage and disposition.

In the initial stage, monitoring stored fissile material still in the form of weapons components and monitoring delivery systems would be carried out by an agency established by the five powers and using their personnel. Later, the International Atomic Enery Agency (IAEA) could undertake monitoring of storage of fissile material from dismantled weapons, assuming that measures would have been developed to prevent dissemination of knowledge about warhead construction to IAEA personnel from nonweapon states. Agreed measures would also be needed to dispose of materials recovered from dismantled weapons.

To the extent that a de-alerting program had already been agreed on and implemented among the five nuclear weapon states, this fact would much simplify the reduction process. Among the possible steps in de-alerting would be exchange of data on warheads and fissile material and separation of most warheads from delivery systems, placing both in monitored storage.

Composition of the Residual Force

Each of the five governments would determine the composition of its own residual force under the 200-warhead ceiling. The United States, France, and Britain might decide to have most of their 200-warhead quotas on missile-equipped submarines, with the United States retaining some bombers. Russia and China might give greatest emphasis to land-based mobile launchers with some submarines and bombers. Most of the warheads of these residual arsenals would be separated from delivery systems and placed in dispersed and hardened storage on the territory of the owner state under monitoring by mixed teams from the five states.[10]

It is difficult to forecast all the decisions of the five powers in a situation distant from the present. However, if there is agreement to do so, and as a transitional stage of protection against concealed weapons, each weapon state could also be permitted to deploy, in addition to its stored weapons, a small, survivable force large enough to retaliate against a sneak attack and to create severe damage, but not large enough to destroy other weapon states

10. There might also be some early agency participation in monitoring to reassure governments of nonweapon states and their publics that this system was operating as claimed. Later, if the system worked well, it could be further internationalized.

or their residual arsenals in a surprise attack of its own. The size of these forces would be agreed by the five. To illustrate, a force might comprise two or three missile-equipped submarines at sea with a total of ten single-warhead missiles or the equivalent in mobile land-based missiles. These missiles, although highly survivable, should not be on high alert if practical measures to prevent this can be worked out, as discussed in chapter 6.

Multiple storage sites would be allowed each government. In the United States and Russia, for example, for protection the warheads might be placed singly in former missile silos partially filled with concrete so that they were no longer deep enough to hold a missile. With the exceptions described above, remaining delivery systems, including all long-range bombers, whether or not configured for nuclear delivery, would also be placed under international monitoring. This step is essential to forestall cheating, given that warheads could be more easily concealed than delivery systems.

The nuclear weapon states would have to agree on the conditions under which weapons could be withdrawn from storage. Agreement would be needed on a specified, limited number of preannounced and monitored exercises to withdraw delivery systems from storage.[11] With these exceptions both warheads and delivery systems could be withdrawn from storage and assembly sites by owner governments only in situations that threaten their national survival or that of their allies. If it desired them, each weapon state would be permitted limited ground-based endoatmospheric point defenses against aircraft and missiles at the storage sites of warheads and launchers. Such limited optional deployments would not create the obstacles for deep cuts, which, as noted earlier in this chapter and as detailed in chapter 5, would arise from efforts to establish nationwide missile defenses. A global missile warning system operated jointly by the five weapon states might also be considered.

Weapon states could withdraw their stored arsenals from monitored storage after notification to other weapon states and description of the circumstances. For example, unexplained loss of a deployed submarine or several mobile launchers might be grounds for withdrawal of the residual force

11. To ensure the stability of the system, it is desirable to keep removal of warheads from storage to a minimum to prevent a situation in which a weapon state could create alarm and uncertainty by frequently pulling its weapons out of storage and exercising their dispersal. Consequently, under monitoring, owner countries might agree to withdraw delivery systems but not weapons from storage at prescribed intervals to exercise their dispersal. Mating exercises would use dummy warheads. Warheads could be inspected for reliability by their owner states in their storage sites and one-for-one replacement would be possible from a single, monitored production plant.

from storage after notification. Monitors would not resist withdrawal but would inform other countries immediately that withdrawal was taking place.

Later, if the program worked over a considerable period and there was full confidence that the verification system was working effectively, deployed delivery systems could be reduced in number and possibly eliminated. Indeed, if participants had enough confidence in the system, an alternative to the deployed small force would be to deactivate the entire residual force from the outset, as Bruce Blair, Michael Mazarr, and Roger Molander have suggested.[12] At a still further stage, it might be possible to dismantle the remaining warheads and keep their components in monitored storage.

Each of these steps would add further periods of time and additional warning between a decision to use nuclear weapons and the earliest possible time of their use. Indeed, the final backup for a dismantled deep cuts force, or even for a situation of complete elimination of nuclear weapons, is the capability of the weapon states using materials from the civilian nuclear power fuel cycle to reassemble a nuclear force within six months or so. Non-weapon states with civilian nuclear energy facilities could produce an atomic weapon in a somewhat longer time, but not the developed arsenals of which the weapon states would be capable.

Until the point of total elimination of nuclear forces is reached, deep cuts participants would have to agree to forgo nationwide missile defense systems. A jointly operated global missile warning system might be established. However, possession of a nationwide missile defense system would put into question the deterrent effects of the residual arsenals, especially the small deployed force permitted each nation, and could give the state with a missile defense system an important military advantage over the other states, theoretically (although perhaps not realistically) placing it in a position to use its small deployed force to attack another weapon state and to protect itself against retaliation with its defenses while it mobilized its stored force. Once deployed, even limited nationwide missile defenses could be expanded rapidly. For that reason the January 1999 decision of the Clinton adminis-

12. Michael Mazarr and Roger Molander have proposed that the warhead holdings of the five weapon states be reduced to a low level and then disassembled and placed in monitored storage. However, their proposals do not provide for a small deployed deterrent force like that suggested here. Michael Mazarr, "Virtual Nuclear Arsenals," *Survival*, vol. 37 (Autumn 1995), pp. 7–26; and Roger Molander and Peter Wilson, "The Nuclear Asymptote: On Containing Nuclear Proliferation," Rand report MR 214-CC (1993). See also Robert A. Manning, "Back to the Future: Toward a New Post-Nuclear Ethic" (Washington: Progressive Foundation, 1994); and Bruce Blair, *Global Zero Alert for Nuclear Forces* (Brookings, 1995).

tration to proceed with a "thin" nationwide missile defense could decisively block warhead reductions to the low levels proposed here.

Why 200 Warheads?

The 200-warhead figure illustrates one possible outcome of negotiations among the five states. It could nearly as easily be 400 or 100. But the number is not arbitrary and several important factors were involved in its selection.

We are talking here of a residual force that might exist for some time. Its size should be small enough to mark a clear break from past nuclear strategy and to provide a transition to possible elimination of nuclear weapons. At the same time, the residual force should be large enough so that it would be substantial in the unlikely event that it ever had to be withdrawn from storage and mobilized. It should also be large enough that, given dispersed and possibly defended storage sites, reliably destroying the entire immobilized force at the same time would be a very stiff challenge for an attacker, whether a weapon state or a proliferator. (Beyond that, the small deployed force permitted each country could not be destroyed and could retaliate.)[13]

Moreover, as discussed in the next chapter, no matter how rigorous the verification system established, residual uncertainties in the fissile material stockpiles of at least the United States and Russia are likely to be equivalent to several hundred warheads at a minimum. Under these circumstances, cuts below 200 warheads might not be feasible for a long time.

As a final factor the warhead level for each state should be set low enough not to allow a significant increase by any of the NPT nuclear weapon states. In fact, the 200-warhead level is comparable to that of the smallest declared

---

13. Further as regards survivability of the stored warheads and delivery vehicles, a large simultaneous attack would be needed to eliminate all the defended storage sites for weapons and delivery systems. It is very unlikely that a proliferant could secretly amass so large an arsenal of warheads and accurate long-range delivery systems. It would be easier for a weapon state. Even so, the remaining deployed mobile missiles or submarines at sea would be available for retaliation, and the attacker would probably face the combined opposition of other remaining weapon states–their forces would not have been attacked and would remain intact.

In case of breakout from the system by one of the nuclear weapon states using its stored weapons, the odds against success would increase still further because the warning given through withdrawal of the weapons from monitored storage and the time required for mating warheads and delivery systems would permit other weapon states to at least disperse some of their stored systems. Moreover, breakout is unlikely to occur without political warning. If breakout by one weapon state does occur, the remaining weapon states would have important security interests of their own for cooperating in common action against the breakout state and would already be formally committed to do so through a Security Council decision to take common action against those who violated the regime.

weapon state, the United Kingdom, which has announced that it will uni-laterally reduce its nuclear stockpile to less than 200 warheads. It is also close to some estimates of the size of the Israeli nuclear force.

Why the Same Warhead Level for Each Weapon State?

We believe that by the time the five weapon states have gone through the many steps needed to reach the 200-warhead force—very deep cuts by the United States and Russia, full data exchange among the five, agreed proce-dures for verifying warhead dismantlement, transfer of fissile material to monitored storage, and destruction of surplus launchers and missiles—they will realize that they are operating within a very different framework of rela-tionships than in the past. If this is the case, it may be relatively easy to come to agreement on equal warhead levels for all.

An equal 200-warhead level for all five states might be the simplest and most straightforward approach. The Chinese government will probably be the most difficult of the weapon state governments to win to participation in this program. Beijing will be especially alert as to whether it is being given equal status as a world power. Proposals that the United States or the United States and Russia should have larger arsenals than China's would trigger long debates as to why this should be so in a regime that seeks to neutral-ize nuclear weapons and questions about what broader uses the U.S. and Russian governments are planning. However, with regard to assigning 200 warheads each to Britain and France, a strong argument can be made that these two countries are allied to one another and also to the United States, and that it might be more equitable to Russia and China to give Britain and France together a quota of 200 warheads for the European Union. It may be harder to negotiate this outcome than individual limits of 200 warheads each, but our tables of residual forces in chapter 7 assume that it will be possible to do.

There have been some imaginative allocations of warhead levels on a basis other than an equal number for each weapon state. Alexei Arbatov has proposed overall equality between Russia and the United States in total warheads, equality in SLBM warheads between Russia on one side and France and Britain on the other, and equality between Russia and China in deployed Intercontinental Ballistic Missile (ICBM) warheads.[14] Perhaps this

---

14. See Arbatov, Appendix A, p. 318.

is what will actually happen. Perhaps agreement on respective levels would take months or years to achieve, as it did at the outset of nuclear arms control negotiations, with negotiators struggling for even the smallest perceived advantage. But we would hope they would not have to spend so much time on this issue, which would be a secondary one under the proposed program.

Impact on Extended Deterrence

The U.S. policy of extended nuclear deterrence, protecting its NATO allies and Japan against nuclear or overwhelming conventional attack through the threat of retaliation with its own nuclear weapons, has often been justified by U.S. nuclear planners as a means of neutralizing possible motivation in the protected states to develop nuclear weapons of their own. Whether or not this view remains founded in post–cold war circumstances, it is clear that the extended deterrence policy has been reassuring to those allies in the past and that they will want to examine closely the deep cuts regime for its effects on their own security.[15]

As regards commitments for extended deterrence by other weapon states, the United Kingdom has joined in commitments to defend members of NATO, and France has suggested that it might ultimately commit its nuclear weapons to the defense of the European Union. On paper, at least, Russia has similar commitments to those members of the Commonwealth of Independent States that have entered mutual defense agreements with it, among them Belarus and Kazakhstan. China may once have had an understanding on this subject with North Korea, but it is doubtful whether it now has any nuclear defense commitments with other states.

We believe the security of the NATO allies and Japan would materially improve under the deep cuts program. With almost all of the small remaining nuclear arsenals of the weapon states immobilized in monitored storage and a policy of no first use, any risk of large-scale surprise nuclear attack on a nonnuclear weapon state would be eliminated and the risk of any nuclear attack would be very small. There is little doubt that western Europe and Japan would be more secure and would also feel more secure with smaller, more controlled Russian and Chinese arsenals.

15. In a hotly contested UN General Assembly vote in December 1998, Japan, Canada, and all nonnuclear weapon European NATO member states except Turkey withstood strong U.S. pressure to vote no and abstained in the "New Agenda" resolution calling for convening an international convention on nuclear disarmament and nonproliferation. This important vote appears to indicate that Japan, Canada, and the NATO allies now attach greater importance to the continuation of moves toward nuclear disarmament than to continued American nuclear protection.

To be sure, the no-first-use pledge we propose in chapter 5 would rule out first use of nuclear weapons for any purpose, including defense of allies. But allies would share in its benefit of reduced possibility of any use of nuclear weapons. Moreover, the no-first-use commitment would not preclude retaliatory use of nuclear weapons against an attacker using nuclear weapons. The stored residual arsenals of the three western states foreseen under the deep cuts program would be available for this purpose and could still provide deterrent protection to their allies against nuclear attack. In particular, the small operational force permitted all NPT weapon states would be immediately available for retaliation against possible nuclear attack. A no-first-use commitment would also not affect continuation of support to allies by conventional forces.

The deep cuts program should improve the security of allied states in other ways. The program predicates beneficial relations among the nuclear weapon states and should strengthen those relations considerably because carrying out the program would require the nuclear weapon states to repeatedly share some of their most sensitive military secrets with one another.

Russia no longer has conventional preponderance over NATO, so NATO conventional forces, plus further conventional disarmament in Europe, can together prevent armed conflict with Russia and defend NATO countries if conflict occurs. While conventional arms limitation agreements in Asia are being sought, U.S. conventional naval and air forces could give decisive assistance to Japan in coping with possible conventional attack by China and to South Korea if North Korea remains a problem.

Controlling the Arsenals of the De Facto Nuclear Weapon States

The Indian and Pakistani nuclear tests of May 1998 dealt an even more serious blow to the nonproliferation regime than India's first test of nuclear weapons in 1974. They are also an urgent warning about the dangers of nuclear weapons as such. Consequently, the tests reinforce both the necessity to bring India, Pakistan, and Israel into a deep cuts regime and the necessity for the NPT weapon states themselves to adopt an approach like the deep cuts program.

The international community has been seeking to dissuade India and Pakistan from weaponizing and deploying nuclear weapons. We assume the United States will intensify its satellite coverage of India and Pakistan, and it should develop a means of passing on to both India and Pakistan, on a regular basis, satellite imagery of the armed forces of the other country, especially of the systems capable of delivering nuclear weapons. This would reassure them that alarming developments are not taking place. Russia could cooperate by providing its own satellite imagery. Such an exchange could have a deterrent effect on readying delivery systems for use.

Agreement should also be sought between India and Pakistan to immobilize their systems capable of delivering nuclear weapons, both aircraft and missiles. One way of doing this would be for the two countries to agree on a bilateral commitment not to increase the number of their delivery systems or to change their location. They could create a system of multilateral monitoring to verify this commitment. Verification could be by mixed Indian-Pakistani teams with neutrals as an additional team element, or by some group more acceptable to India and Pakistan. The United States, Russia, and China could guarantee this arrangement.

The five weapon states have appealed to India and Pakistan not to test further, to sign and ratify the Comprehensive Test Ban Treaty (CTBT), and to enter negotiation on a fissile cutoff treaty. Both governments have in general terms indicated willingness to do so. But before a cutoff treaty is implemented and before India ratifies the CTBT, New Delhi will probably require that the five NPT weapon states themselves undertake significant action toward fulfilling their NPT commitments to eliminate their nuclear weapons.

This is a further compelling reason for the NPT states to undertake a program of deep cuts in their own nuclear arsenals. Their willingness to make these cuts could cause India and Pakistan to feel their demands for total elimination of nuclear weapons have been answered by substantial moves and to be more willing to sign and ratify the CTBT and negotiate a fissile cutoff treaty.

The five weapon states should also invite India, Pakistan, and Israel to participate in negotiations on the deep cuts program. The five NPT weapon states would first negotiate among themselves the deep cuts program as discussed in the previous section. As these negotiations moved toward conclusion and before the NPT weapon states signed a final agreement, they would call on the three de facto weapon states to make specific commitments of their own to the program.

The ideal outcome would be for India, Pakistan, and Israel to follow the example of South Africa: dismantle all their warheads and place the recovered fissile material in internationally monitored storage. However, the response from all three is likely to be that they will be willing to do this only when the five NPT states themselves are prepared to do the same.

Because that point is still far off, the most practical arrangement at this stage would be for India, Pakistan, and Israel to place their nuclear materials and their nuclear-capable delivery systems in monitored storage on their own territory with the same right of withdrawal as the five weapon states. As with the five NPT weapon states, the storage sites of the nuclear material of India, Pakistan, and Israel and of their potential delivery systems for nuclear weapons would be internationally monitored. The sites could be dispersed and defended. Although unlike the weapon states they would not have a few delivery systems still deployed, all three states could withdraw weapons or weapons materials from storage on the same stringent conditions as those for the NPT weapon states: in situations threatening national existence. As with the five NPT states, Israel, India, and Pakistan would be called on to end their production of long-range missiles except for verified replacements, space exploration, and satellite launch.

In placing their materials in storage, India, Pakistan, and Israel could be given the option of specifying the nature and number of their nuclear weapons and the nature and amount of their fissile material. Data exchange and transparency could have clear benefits for all. But it is unlikely that Israel would want to state the exact amount of its holdings because this could elicit demands from Arab states for Israel either to eliminate all of its weapons or for the Arab states to be entitled to have an equal number. It is also doubtful that it would be advantageous for India and Pakistan to give specific figures on their holdings. The five weapon states would not wish to propose that India and Pakistan increase their arsenals to the two hundred warhead level to match those of the weapon states. Making Indian and Pakistani holdings public is likely to bolster Pakistani demands for numerical equality with India that will be difficult to negotiate. Publication of the holdings of India and Pakistan would also support their claims for status as nuclear weapon states under the NPT. But it is not desirable to consolidate the weapon status of India and Pakistan by amending the NPT. Opening the NPT to amendment could also open the way for unproductive amendment proposals and undermine the validity of the treaty. Deliberate silence seems the best course.

Would the three de facto weapon states be likely to accept this proposed regime? We believe so. As noted, deep cuts by the five NPT states would move toward fulfillment of India's and Pakistan's calls on the weapon states to eliminate their weapons. Under the deep cuts program, the five weapon states would transfer to internationally monitored storage both the fissile content of all warheads that exceed the permitted level and their entire stocks of unweaponized fissile material. This action would meet the desire of India and Pakistan for the weapon states to relinquish their reserves of fissile materials in connection with a fissile cutoff agreement.

There would be many security gains for all three states from the proposed system. Placing most warheads and delivery vehicles in monitored storage would make impossible a large-scale nuclear attack without warning. India's fear of preemptive Chinese nuclear attack and Pakistan's fear of preemptive Indian attack should be greatly reduced. A Security Council decision, proposed in the next section, to take joint action against any country or group initiating or threatening use of weapons of mass destruction would offer these three states increased protection against many potential threats. In addition, Israel might request further guarantees of conventional assistance from the United States to meet specified threats. The United States, Russia, and China might also extend security guarantees to both Pakistan and India. We believe that these inducements, combined with the reluctance of the NPT weapon states to act without the remaining three and with the support of world public opinion for having all the known nuclear weapon states reduce and immobilize their nuclear arsenals under international monitoring will be effective in bringing action.

Parallel Actions

Along with the actions of the nuclear weapon states themselves, completion of the deep cuts program will require other actions by both nuclear and nonnuclear states. These include, in addition to the ratification and entry into force of the Comprehensive Nuclear Test Ban Treaty, negotiation, ratification, and implementation of a fissile cutoff treaty, implementation of the Chemical Weapons Convention, agreement on and entry into force of a verification protocol for the Convention on Biological Weapons, strengthened safeguards under the Non-Proliferation Treaty, measures to limit both ballistic missile proliferation and conventional forces, and security assurances and no-first-use commitments by the nuclear weapon states. These steps will all require detailed attention by governments as the deep cuts program proceeds.

Comprehensive Nuclear Test Ban Treaty and Fissile Cutoff

The Comprehensive Test Ban Treaty and a fissile cutoff are indispensable to a deep cuts program. The CTBT would provide additional assurance that the weapon states are not developing new types of nuclear weapons and that potential proliferants are not developing nuclear arsenals of their own. The treaty has now been signed by all the important countries with the exception of India and Pakistan, but it has not yet been ratified by the United States, Russia, or China. Even if ratified, the treaty will not come into force until India and Pakistan join.

A fully verified global treaty ending the production of fissile material for weapons is essential to any process of nuclear disarmament. The treaty will place an upper limit on the size of the arsenals of all of the nuclear weapon states and make irreversible the disarmament for the NPT weapon states through dismantling warheads and transfer of their fissile material to monitored storage.[16] Negotiations on such a treaty were urged by President Clinton in 1993, and the fissile cutoff issue was referred to the Geneva-based Conference on Disarmament in late 1993 after a positive vote in the General Assembly. The negotiations were not launched, in large part because Pakistan was insisting that a cutoff should address fissile material already produced, and India was insisting that the charter nuclear weapon states commit to a timebound disarmament process. Following the May 1998 nuclear tests, however, both India and Pakistan have agreed to let the negotiations begin. Further details of the fissile cutoff are in chapter 11.

Improved Safeguards

Along with the deep reductions by the nuclear weapon states, nonnuclear states, too, would be expected to undertake new commitments. The most important of these, in addition to successful implementation of the Comprehensive Test Ban and a compliance protocol to the Biological Weapons Convention, would be to cooperate fully with more stringent verification procedures proposed by the International Atomic Energy Agency following the discovery of Iraq's clandestine nuclear weapons program. These measures encompass various kinds of environmental monitoring, anytime-anywhere challenge inspections, and aerial overflight rights that would allow the agency to look for undeclared weapons-related activities.

---

16. Steve Fetter and Frank von Hippel, "A Step-by-Step Approach to a Global Fissile Materials Cutoff," *Arms Control Today*, vol. 25 (October 1995), pp. 3–8; Frans Berkhout and others, "A Cutoff in the Production of Fissile Material," *International Security*, vol. 19 (Winter 1994), pp. 167–202; and Lisbeth Gronlund and David Wright, *Beyond Safeguards: A Program for More Comprehensive Control of Weapon-Usable Fissile Material* (Union of Concerned Scientists, 1994).

Box 10-1. Proposed Treaty Restricting Missile Production

A missile treaty might be along the following lines. The five nuclear weapon states would propose a global treaty restricting production to long-range ballistic, surface-to-surface missiles of over 300 km range on the model of the Non-Proliferation Treaty. In distinction to the NPT, however, the five weapon states would from the outset offer to commit themselves to reduce their own holdings of long-range ballistic missiles to an internationally monitored level of no more than 200 each and pledge not to produce further ballistic missiles for military purposes, other than for replacements.

The weapon states could also announce their readiness, in the event that a worldwide missile treaty is achieved, to support establishment of an international agency for low-cost space and satellite launch open to all states and to contribute surplus launching systems and missiles for this purpose. As further inducements, they might offer to share technology for defense against short-range ballistic missiles and also to undertake the major share of costs of establishing a worldwide warning system to observe missile firing and testing open to all treaty parties.

The treaty would not preclude production of missiles for nonmilitary uses—satellite and other space launches—by states other than the five weapon states, but nonweapon states would have to agree to use both new production and existing missiles only for space exploration and satellite launches and to place production and storage of stocks under international monitoring.

Because each of the weapon states would retain up to 200 ballistic missiles under the deep cuts program, although most would be in monitored storage, and other countries would not be permitted missiles for military purposes,

Restricting Ballistic Missiles

Under the deep cuts program the nuclear weapon states would undertake to destroy both missiles and launchers withdrawn from deployment and end production of long-range ballistic missiles for military purposes, with limited, verified exceptions for replacement, testing, satellite launch, and space exploration. India, Pakistan, and Israel would undertake a similar commitment to freeze production and deployment of long-range ballistic missiles. This regime could be inaugurated in START III by agreement between Russia and the United States to exchange complete information on missile holdings and destroy surplus missiles or place them in monitored storage for potential satellite launch.

there would, as in the Non-Proliferation Treaty, be an element of inequity in this proposed treaty to restrict production of long-range ballistic missiles for weapons. However, the United States and Russia would be making very deep cuts in their missile holdings under the deep cuts program and the other inducements described here would be important.

It would be highly desirable to ban long-range cruise missiles as well as ballistic missiles, and this possibility should be seriously explored. However, because they are seen as alternatives to piloted fighter-bombers for conventional missions, resistance to a cruise missile ban would probably be far greater than to restrictions on production of ballistic missiles. This issue might therefore be postponed to a second stage of the suggested treaty.

Verification of a treaty restricting production of long-range ballistic missiles would mean continuous portal-perimeter monitoring at the facilities at which rocket motors are made. (At present, this monitoring is the most costly part of the Intermediate-Range Nuclear Forces [INF] Treaty verification arrangements. Remote monitoring of the portals and perimeters and tagging of the missile stages during visits, when a certain number were ready to be delivered, might be less costly.) The regime for space launch vehicles could include a "just in time" rule, that is, missiles would be produced or delivered only for an immediate launch. The number of missiles including spares that would be at a site at a given time would thus be held to a minimum (the last suggestion is from Harald Müller).

Field tests of such missiles would be without reentry vehicles. Missiles produced for space exploration and satellite launches would be limited in number, and both storage sites and actual launches would be checked. Verification would also include the worldwide missile warning system.

Such undertakings could be used by the weapon states to launch negotiations on a worldwide treaty restricting production for military purposes of ballistic missiles with a range of more than 300 kilometers, the range now used by the Missile Technology Control Regime. It is certainly in the interest of the nuclear weapon states to seek such an agreement because uncontrolled long-range missile capabilities could transform the covert acquisition of nuclear weapons by a potential proliferant into a strategic threat. Indeed, the five weapon states may be reluctant to move to deep cuts unless there is also some prospect of a worldwide restriction on missile production by other states.

Conventional Disarmament

Deep cuts in nuclear forces could in some cases intensify the destabilizing effects of existing numerical superiorities in conventional forces. This issue does not affect the United States, which is not threatened by conventional forces. This is also the case for Britain and France, which are protected by membership in NATO and by the limits on Russian conventional forces contained in the Conventional Forces in Europe (CFE) Treaty as well as by the general deterioration of Russian forces. China also does not appear to need nuclear weapons to deter conventional attack. However, some of the other participants in the deep cuts program could feel the need for additional assurances with regard to conventional forces.

Israel has long made it a condition of its agreement to a Mideast nuclear free zone and the elimination of its nuclear weapons that there be agreement by the Arab states to far-reaching reductions in their conventional forces. But the deep cuts program does not call on Israel to eliminate its nuclear weapons. Instead, it would place them in monitored storage. Doing this would impose a delay in their use and give others advance warning of possible use, but would not categorically prevent their use in an emergency. In these circumstances Israel may not feel compelled to require the full conventional cuts it would demand as a price for completely eliminating its nuclear weapons. However, as mentioned earlier in this chapter, it might ask the United States to provide it with additional conventional assurances as a condition of entering the deep cuts program.

The deep cuts program would not change the overall force balance between India and Pakistan. It would only impose requirements for monitored storage and notification of withdrawal and thus a limited delay in possible use. Settlement of the Kashmir issue would be a political desideratum but perhaps not a requirement. Confidence-building measures, including cutting back force projection weapons such as combat aircraft, attack helicopters, tanks, mobile artillery, mobile antiaircraft, and combat bridging, along the India-Pakistan border would be useful. In addition, there may be a need for outside guarantees for the security of India and Pakistan.

Russia, with its conventional forces in disarray, may feel the need for some type of limitation on NATO and Chinese conventional forces before it agrees to a deep cuts program. This might take the form of negotiated reductions or it might lead to establishing broader keep-out zones for heavy armaments at the borders (especially at the border with China). Alternatively, Russia and China could agree on a common limit on the number of

CFE-type armaments (combat aircraft, attack helicopters, heavy tanks, armored combat vehicles, and self-propelled heavy artillery) and also sur-face-to-surface missiles that Russia could deploy in eastern Russia (Russian forces west of the Urals are already regulated by the CFE Treaty) and that China could deploy in the northern half of its country. A similar but less far-reaching restriction was in fact agreed upon by China, Russia, and the Central Asian states in April 1996.

Security Council Action

The UN Security Council could also back a deep cuts program with an advance decision to take joint action, including both sanctions and poten-tial military action—under conditions of advance one-time suspension of the veto right for this purpose by the five permanent members—against states or groups that initiate the use of nuclear weapons or threaten their use, non-weapon NPT signatories that seek to develop nuclear weapons, or coun-tries that seek to remain outside the international system of safeguards and controls over their nuclear installations. Given the grave dangers that uncon-trolled nuclear weapons could pose to international security in a situation of minimum arsenals, no one can be outside this regime. It should also be known in advance that covertly prepared breakout will be met with the for-midable military forces of a large coalition.

Today, potential use of the veto right by permanent members of the Secu-rity Council decreases the value of their security assurances. Prospects for permanent relinquishment of the veto are negligible at this time. But for the important purpose described here, the five permanent Security Council members may be willing to restrict their veto right as a one-time action, the more so because doing this would provide additional assurance of common action and a legal basis for such action by remaining permanent members if one of them breaks out of the agreement.

If they had not already done so, the nuclear weapon states would under-take a no-first-use pledge in participating in this Security Council decision. In addition, they could pledge not to use their nuclear weapons against non-weapon states unless the latter had used nuclear weapons.[17]

With these decisions the weapon states would be providing nonnuclear states broader security assurances than they have been willing to extend in

17. This simpler and more direct version of negative security assurances was suggested by Morton Halperin in his 1996 report proposing a new nuclear policy review (Council on For-eign Relations).

the context of the Non-Proliferation Treaty: many nonnuclear states consider the security guarantees extended by the weapon states at the NPT extension conference in April and May 1995 inadequate compensation for permanent relinquishment of the possibility to possess nuclear weapons.[18] At the same time, given the proposed voluntary suspension of the veto by the weapon states, this Security Council decision would be an obstacle against breakout from the deep cuts regime by any of them.[19]

As an alternative to a Security Council pledge of joint action against states or groups initiating or threatening the use of nuclear weapons, the pledge of joint council action could be broadened to cover action against those initiating or threatening the use of all weapons of mass destruction. This approach to security assurances might help in deterring use of chemical and biological weapons and might also make it easier for weapon states, as urged in chapter 5, to relinquish the use of nuclear weapons as a possible response to attack by chemical and biological weapons.

Both versions of a Security Council pledge discussed here would exclude use of nuclear weapons as a last resort against overwhelming conventional attack. According to the terms of the proposed agreement establishing monitored storage for remaining warheads permitted under the deep cuts program, each nuclear weapon state would have to make the decision on its own as to whether it was faced by a situation, including conventional attack, that threatened its national survival. Presumably, a state that believed itself to be in this situation could withdraw the weapons, use them, and then face the international consequences.

Significance of the Deep Cuts Program

Taken together, the steps foreseen for this final stage of the deep cuts program would largely neutralize nuclear weapons. The steps would eliminate the possibility of a large surprise attack and greatly reduce the possibility

18. Their positive assurances are contained in UN Security Council resolution 984, April 11, 1995, which states that "the Security Council and above all its nuclear weapon State permanent members, will act immediately in accordance with the relevant provisions of the Charter of the United Nations, in the event that [nonnuclear weapon states] are the victim of an act of, or object of a threat of, aggression in which nuclear weapons are used . . . the nuclear weapon State permanent members of the Security Council will bring the matter immediately to the attention of the Council and seek Council action to provide, in accordance with the Charter, the necessary assistance to the State victim."

19. Jonathan Dean, "Expanding the Security Council Role in Blocking the Spread of Nuclear Weapons," *Transnational Law and Contemporary Problems,* vol. 2 (Fall 1992).

of rogue or accidental launch from a nuclear weapon state or threshold state, as well as nuclear threats by nuclear weapon states. They would materially reduce the risk of theft or illegal sale of warheads or fissile materials and cut the motivation for proliferation that arises from existing arsenals. And they would insulate against pressures for competitive expansion of nuclear arsenals that could come from deterioration of political relations between weapon states. Consequently, these steps would greatly decrease the salience and political importance of nuclear weapons in international affairs, reducing them from a primary to a secondary role.

CHAPTER ELEVEN

Verifying Deep Reductions in Nuclear Forces

Countries will not agree to deep reductions in their nuclear forces if they believe their security could be undermined by undetected violations. Such concerns should be dealt with by designing the residual forces so the stability of deterrence would not be sensitive to undetected cheating and by establishing a verification system that would detect cheating or preparations for a breakout on a scale that would be judged significant. Achieving the second goal will require an unprecedented degree of transparency and cooperation among the nuclear weapon states.

A comprehensive verification system would have three components:

—measures to monitor restrictions on allowed numbers of nuclear warheads and fissile material production and stockpiles, and to improve safeguards on peaceful nuclear activities;

—measures, patterned after those established by the START treaties, to monitor allowed numbers and types of nuclear delivery vehicles and launchers; and

—measures to monitor restrictions on the deployment and alert status of nuclear forces.

Some of these measures, particularly those that involve monitoring nuclear materials and related facilities, could be carried out by the International Atomic Energy Agency (IAEA). Other verification tasks, especially those that involve monitoring nuclear warheads and missiles, could be performed by a new verification authority established by the parties to the deep cuts agreements. Such an authority might evolve from the bilateral arrangements already created by the START agreements and other arrangements that are being discussed by the United States and Russia for monitoring storage and dismantling of excess nuclear warheads.[1]

1. Frank von Hippel, "Fissile Material Security in the Post-Cold-War World," *Physics Today*, vol. 48 (June 1995), p. 26.

Nuclear Weapons and Fissile Materials

Nuclear arms control agreements in the past have not sought to control nuclear warheads directly. They have concentrated instead on large delivery systems that can be far more readily monitored through national intelligence capabilities. For the deep reductions in nuclear forces advocated in this book, however, it is absolutely essential that nuclear warheads and the fissile materials necessary for their construction come under direct control. Although national intelligence will remain important in an expanded verification system, monitoring limits on nuclear warhead and fissile material stockpiles will require cooperative verification measures, including

—declarations of the location and status of all nuclear warheads and fissile material stockpiles;

—verification of these declarations through on-site inspections and exchanges of data on the design and operating history of the facilities used to produce warheads and fissile materials;

—verification of the dismantling of nuclear warheads and of the storage and disposition of the fissile materials contained in them;

—verification of a ban on the production of additional fissile materials for weapons; and

—improved IAEA safeguards on peaceful nuclear activities.

Declarations of Warheads and Fissile Materials

COMPREHENSIVE DECLARATIONS. At the outset the United States and Russia, followed later by the other declared nuclear weapon states, would produce a comprehensive declaration of the location, type, status, and unique identifier for all nuclear explosive devices and all canisters containing pits or other forms of fissile material. The declarations, which would be updated at agreed intervals, would include information on all deployed and stored nuclear warheads in the active stocks, warheads awaiting dismantlement, and fissile components and materials. For stored warheads and components the location would be a certain declared facility and a position within that facility. For sea-based or mobile land-based systems the warhead location might be given as the corresponding ship hull number or mobile missile base and launcher.

The idea of a declaration of nuclear warheads, although unprecedented in scope and ambition, has been advanced in various forums. For example, the establishment of a comprehensive register for nuclear weapons was a principal recommendation in the report of the National Academy of Sciences, *Management and Disposition of Excess Weapons Plutonium.*[2] Such a register was also suggested by Germany in 1993, although the suggestion was dropped at the request of the United States and other nuclear weapon states.[3]

However, the United States and Russia have been discussing the possibility of bilateral declarations. At the January 1994 and succeeding summits they agreed to exchange data on warhead and fissile material stockpiles and to arrange reciprocal inspections to confirm declarations of excess warheads and fissile materials.

The most complete description of what the U.S. and Russian governments agreed to do is found in the joint statement issued by Presidents Clinton and Yeltsin after their meeting in Moscow on May 10, 1995 (reprinted in chapter 9).[4] As a first step in putting the transparency procedures in place, the joint statement called for a U.S.–Russian agreement allowing the two governments to exchange sensitive information needed to confirm that declared objects were real warheads or warhead components and providing that this information would be fully protected. The U.S. Congress has twice waived certain provisions of law so that such an agreement could enter into force soon after the president had certified that it met U.S. national security needs. Unfortunately, as described in more detail in chapter 9, Russia broke off the transparency negotiations in fall 1995 and they have not been resumed. But because much of the technical groundwork for implementing transparency measures has now been laid, it should be possible to put the measures in place relatively quickly once Russia decides to move forward.[5]

In addition, the U.S. Department of Energy has taken a valuable step toward increased transparency by publishing a report that summarizes U.S. plutonium production and use from 1944 through 1994.[6] The report, *Plutonium: The First 50 Years*, provides a comprehensive accounting of pluto-

2. Committee on International Security and Arms Control, National Academy of Sciences, *Management and Disposition of Excess Weapons Plutonium* (Washington: National Academy Press, 1994), pp. 7–8 and throughout.

3. Harald Müller, "Transparency in Nuclear Arms: Toward a Nuclear Weapons Register," *Arms Control Today*, vol. 24 (October 1994), pp. 3–7.

4. "Joint Statement on the Transparency and Irreversibility of the Process of Reducing Nuclear Weapons," Moscow, May 10, 1995.

5. See also Frank von Hippel and Oleg Bukharin, "U.S.-Russian Cooperation on Fissile Material Security and Disposition," Proceedings, Summer Course of the International School on Disarmament and Research on Conflicts, Sienna, Italy, July 29–August 8, 1996.

6. U.S. Department of Energy, *Plutonium: The First 50 Years*, DOE/DP-0137 (February 1996).

nium inventories at each DOE facility, including the sum of the quantities of plutonium in the U.S. nuclear weapons stockpile and in pits at the Pantex warhead assembly and disassembly facility. It also provides a summary of the production of plutonium at DOE sites, small acquisitions of foreign plutonium, and removals of plutonium from the stockpile. A similar report on the production and use of U.S. highly enriched uranium is in preparation. As discussed later, however, these reports point to several difficulties that will bedevil verification of declarations of fissile material stockpiles.

TAGS. Verification would be improved if all declared nuclear warheads and canisters containing pits or fissile materials were equipped with a unique identification number or tag that was specified in the declaration. These tags, sealed so that they could not be altered, removed, or replaced without alerting inspectors, would have two advantages. First, they would allow a "chain of custody" in which individual warheads could be tracked from deployment sites to storage bunkers to dismantlement facilities. Similarly, canisters containing pits or other fissile warhead components could be tracked from dismantling facilities to storage sites to facilities for the civil use or disposal of the material. Second, it would not be necessary to inspect or count each controlled item to gain confidence in the accuracy of the declaration. Inspectors could authenticate the tags in a randomly selected sample of items, thereby reducing the inspection effort and its intrusiveness.[7] Tags would simplify verification in another way as well because the discovery of an untagged warhead or canister would constitute a violation.

A tagging scheme could rely on existing serial numbers or surface features, or it could use several different kinds of applied tags, such as barcoded labels or plastic holographic images overlaid by a tamper-proof tape.[8]

7. Without sampling, inspectors would have to count every warhead or container of fissile material at every site in a reasonably short amount of time for comparison with the declaration, and possibly verify the authenticity of each warhead and the contents of each canister of material. Sampling could greatly reduce the number of warheads and canisters that would be examined. For example, a detailed inspection of only 28 randomly selected warheads would provide at least 95 percent confidence that no more than 10 percent of the warheads are bogus and that the number of warheads at declared sites does not exceed the declared number by more than 10 percent. In addition, there would be at most a 25 percent chance that a 5 percent violation would escape detection (that is, 50 of 1,000 warheads were phony or undeclared), and a 1 percent chance that a 15 percent violation would go undetected. Even a 1 percent violation would have a 25 percent chance of detection. These calculations are valid for a large but unspecified number of declared warheads; the confidence level would be higher (but the inspection savings due to sampling proportionately lower) if the number were less than 100.

8. Annex 6 of the Inspection Protocol of START I defines a unique identifier as "a non-repeating alpha-numeric production number, or a copy thereof, that has been applied by the inspected Party, using its own technology."

Tags are used by the United Nations in Iraq to log and track items that could be used both for civilian and military purposes, by the IAEA to safeguard civilian nuclear materials, and by the U.S. military to track weapons (including nuclear warheads).[9] These tags require that inspectors have physical access to the tag, but it is possible to imagine a tag that could be authenticated outside a container or at a distance. For example, electronic tags could be used that would emit a coded signal containing the unique identifier of the weapon component when interrogated by a radio transmission.[10] The use of tags for verification, while not yet applied to warheads, is provided for in the START Treaty.[11] Although certain technical issues would have to be worked out, there should be no problem in instituting an effective tagging system for warheads and sealed canisters containing warheads, components, or fissile materials.

Verifying the Declarations

NUCLEAR WARHEADS. Data on warheads (or canisters containing pits) would be verified primarily by regular and short-notice inspections at declared facilities, combined with challenge or suspect-site inspections to verify the absence of warheads at other locations. Inspectors could, for example, count the number of warheads in a particular declared storage bunker and compare this to the number listed in the data exchange. The use of tags would allow inspectors to select a random sample of warheads and to verify that each had a valid tag corresponding to a warhead listed in the declaration.

It would be necessary for inspectors to make certain that tagged objects contain authentic nuclear warheads or fissile components. Gamma ray detectors could confirm the presence of plutonium or highly enriched uranium, but could not confirm so easily that the object inside the canister was an authentic nuclear warhead or pit without revealing sensitive design information. One possibility is to use a combination of radiation and other distinctive signatures to "fingerprint" types of nuclear warheads or pits, which

9. A specific tamper-tape system used in Iraq and in the United States is the CONFIRM seal. This is a tape placed over a unique identifier. The tape is an adhesive, imbedded with microscopic beads of colored glass in several strata forming a specific design (such as the UN logo). It is see-through and is read through reflected light. On-site Inspection Agency, private communication, July 25–26, 1996.

10. Steve Fetter and Thomas Garwin, "Using Tags to Monitor Numerical Limits in Arms Control Agreements," in *Technology and the Limitation of International Conflict*, edited by Barry M. Blechman (Washington: Johns Hopkins Foreign Policy Institute, 1989), pp. 33–54.

11. Annex 6 to the Inspection Protocol of START I, which describes procedures for associating unique identifiers with mobile missiles or their launch canisters.

could then be used as a template to ensure that warheads or pits in tagged canisters are authentic.[12] A detailed signature would be extremely difficult to counterfeit but would have to be formed in a way that did not reveal important design information.

It also would be necessary to ensure that other, untagged objects do not contain warheads or pits. If the object is not too large, gamma ray and neutron detectors could confirm the absence of plutonium or highly enriched uranium. Large objects could contain enough shielding to prevent such detection in a reasonable amount of time, however, in which case the inspected party should be required to use other methods to demonstrate that no warheads or pits are contained within.

Confidence in verification at declared facilities could be substantially increased by installing portal-perimeter systems. Objects entering and exiting the facility would be monitored as they passed through the portal; declared warheads or pits would have their tags authenticated, while other objects would be inspected to ensure that they do not contain warheads or pits. (Once again, sampling could be used to minimize disruption of the normal operation of the facility.) In this way, portal-perimeter systems would foreclose the possibility that undeclared warheads or pits could make use of declared facilities, forcing a cheater to develop a parallel, clandestine system to store, maintain, repair, or deploy illegal warheads. Because portal-perimeter monitoring is expensive, its use would likely be limited to a small number of sites.

To further increase confidence in the accuracy and completeness of the declaration, detailed information could be provided on the history of each nuclear device (date and place of assembly, deployment, disassembly, test explosion, and so forth) and the operation of facilities at which nuclear explosives had been designed, tested, assembled, stored, deployed, maintained, modified, repaired, and dismantled, as well as facilities that produced crucial weapon components and materials. These records could be checked for internal consistency and for consistency with declarations of production and other records, and with archived intelligence data. Allowing extensive interviews with former and current officials responsible for nuclear weapons would also improve confidence in the declarations.

FISSILE MATERIAL. In general, verification of fissile material declarations would be more difficult than verification of warheads. This is principally

12. Theodore B. Taylor, "Verified Elimination of Nuclear Warheads," *Science & Global Security*, vol. 1 (1989), pp. 18–19. See also Theodore B. Taylor, "Dismantlement and Fissile Material Disposal," in Frank von Hippel and Roald Sagdeev, eds., *Reversing the Arms Race: How to Achieve and Verify Deep Reductions* (Gordon and Breach Science Publishers, 1990).

Table 11-1. Estimated Military Fissile Material by Country, 1994, and Potential Number of Nuclear Explosives

Country	Plutonium (tons)	Weapons-grade HEU (tons)	Warhead equivalents[a]
Russia	130	1,000	100,000
United States	85	650	75,000
France	5	24	3,000
China	4	20	2,500
United Kingdom	3.5	8	1,500
Israel	0.4	–	100
India	0.4	–	100
Pakistan	–	0.2	20
Total	230	1,700	180,000

Source: David Albright, Frans Berkout, and William Walker, *Plutonium and Highly Enriched Uranium, 1996*, SIPRI (Oxford University Press, 1997), pp. 399–402.

a. Assumes 4 kilograms of plutonium or 12 kilograms of U-235 for each fission explosive.

because warheads are subject to simple item accounting, while fissile materials are not. In general also, record keeping is better and more accurate for warheads than for fissile materials. Although it is likely that the nuclear weapon states know, with very little uncertainty, how much plutonium and highly enriched uranium (HEU) they have in nuclear weapons and in discrete storage forms such as pits, metal "buttons," and canisters filled with plutonium oxide, they will know less precisely how much plutonium and HEU is in spent fuel, in metal scraps, in deposits inside pipes and glove boxes, and in various liquid solutions and wastes. Indeed, the best estimates of national inventories even by the owners of the fissile materials will contain uncertainties of at least a few percent. A few percent corresponds to a lot of weapons, as shown in table 11-1, which gives estimates of military fissile material accumulations by the declared and undeclared nuclear weapon states.

It would be fairly straightforward, if time consuming, to verify the accuracy of some categories of information provided in a fissile material data exchange. For example, using standard assay and sampling techniques, inspectors could verify that selected canisters contained material of the amount and isotopic composition specified in the declaration. However, other information, such as the amount and composition of fissile materials in a particular type of warhead, would likely remain unverified, at least until that warhead type was slated for dismantling. Indeed, some such data might not even be exchanged, much less verified. The amount of sensitive information would grow smaller as the number of allowed warheads decreased, however, and the prospect that such data eventually would be subject to verification would be a powerful incentive to give accurate declarations at earlier stages.

More difficult than verifying the accuracy of a fissile material declaration, however, would be verifying its completeness. Even if inspectors could verify the amount of plutonium in every declared warhead or canister, how could they be sure that every container or kilogram of plutonium was declared? The obvious approach is to verify the total size of the stockpile by verifying estimates of the total amount of material produced. Although production estimates inevitably contain uncertainties, they provide a useful cross-check of stockpile declarations and limit the size of possible undeclared stocks.

Verifying plutonium production would involve examining records of the fabrication of uranium fuel and target rods for plutonium-production reactors; design of the fuel and the reactors and typical fuel loadings in the core; dates of fuel loading and discharge and monthly production of thermal energy; design and operating records of the reprocessing plants; and volume, isotopic concentrations, and disposition of the various waste streams. Verifying HEU production would involve reconstructing, from records of facility design and operation, the daily flow rates and uranium-235 concentrations of uranium feed, enriched uranium product, and depleted uranium tails flowing through the enrichment cascades, as well as the amount of uranium of various enrichments in wastes or released into the environment.

The value of this method of verifying production declarations would depend almost entirely on the accuracy, completeness, and authenticity of the records that are provided. One can check that operating records are consistent with the declaration and that the records are internally consistent, but this should not be confused with confirming their accuracy. It may, however, be possible for inspectors to find physical evidence to corroborate the records. For example, ratios of neutron transmutation products in permanent components of plutonium-production reactors would provide an estimate of the total amount of heat and plutonium produced during the life of the reactor.[13] Estimates derived in this way would be uncertain by perhaps 10 percent, but would be largely independent of record keeping by the host country. In the case of uranium enrichment, ages determined by accumulated products of uranium radioactive decay and isotope ratios in depleted

13. Steve Fetter, "Nuclear Archaeology: Verifying Declarations of Fissile Material Production," *Science and Global Security*, vol. 3, nos. 3 and 4 (1993), pp. 237–59; and T. W. Wood and others, "Fiasibility of Isotopic Measurements: Graphite Isotopic Ratio Method," Pacific Northwest National Laboratory, Richland, Washington, April 1994.

uranium tails stored at the facilities could confirm records of product and tails assays over a particular time period.[14]

Because of the inevitable uncertainties in verifying past production, it might be possible for the United States and Russia to conceal the existence of a large number of undeclared warheads (or enough material to build them), although to do so might require withholding or doctoring records. Without detailed study it is difficult to say how much these uncertainties could be narrowed. One benchmark is provided by *Plutonium: The First 50 Years*. According to this report, out of slightly more than 100 tons of plutonium produced in the United States for weapons, 2.8 tons are designated as "inventory difference," which is defined as the difference between the quantity of nuclear material held according to records of production and disposition and the quantity measured by a physical inventory.[15] This does not mean that uncertainties in the U.S. stockpile of plutonium cannot be reduced to less than 2.8 tons, but it does suggest how difficult it may be to do so. To put this uncertainty in perspective, 2.8 tons of plutonium is enough to build at least several hundred nuclear weapons, and it is almost as large as the entire estimated stockpile of weapons plutonium in the United Kingdom. Uncertainties in HEU production are likely to be even larger because the United States did not measure how much HEU went into waste streams and did not keep precise records of the enrichment even of various product streams.[16] Soviet record keeping may have been still more imprecise.

Challenge inspections could be used to search for hidden stockpiles of warheads or fissile materials at undeclared facilities. Although concealed warheads and fissile materials would be almost impossible to detect in the absence of information indicating where to look, a country would always face the risk that such locations would be revealed as a result of leaks or whistleblowing. Indeed, citizen reporting of treaty violations by governments should be encouraged and protected under national and international law.[17]

14. Fetter, "Nuclear Archeology."

15. This does not mean that 2.8 tons of plutonium is missing or was stolen or diverted. It is believed that much, if not all, of the inventory difference can be attributed to systematic overestimates of plutonium production in reactors, together with systematic underestimates of plutonium retained in equipment and discharged in wastes. Less plutonium probably was produced and more probably exists in the stockpile in difficult-to-measure forms than appears in the accounting records. The inventory difference might be reduced substantially as facilities are decontaminated and the resulting plutonium wastes analyzed.

16. U.S. Department of Energy, private communication, 1996.

17. Joseph Rotblat, "A Nuclear Weapon-Free World Leading to a War-Free World," paper prepared for "1996: Disarmament at a Critical Juncture," a conference at the United Nations, April 23, 1996.

Nevertheless, in assessing the stability of a regime of deep reductions, it would be prudent to assume that the United States or Russia could, if it chose, conceal several hundred warheads or enough fissile material to build several hundred warheads. Given equal degrees of transparency and assuming proportional uncertainties, China, France, and Britain, and India, Pakistan, and Israel could conceal a few tens of warheads or an equivalent amount of fissile material.

The recent experiences of verifying the nuclear disarmament of South Africa and Iraq also suggest caution in this regard. These countries produced far less fissile material than any of the nuclear weapon states. In both cases inspectors had unusually wide access to facilities, records, and people, and yet it was difficult for them to verify with high confidence that they had identified all significant inventories.

South Africa announced in March 1993 that it had secretly built and later dismantled six nuclear bombs. The decision to disarm was made in July 1990, and within one year the bombs were dismantled, documents were destroyed, production and assembly facilities were decommissioned, and HEU weapon components were cast into nonweapon shapes for storage and international inspection.[18] The South African government then decided that a full disclosure of its nuclear program would be required to secure international confidence in its nonnuclear status and gave the IAEA a complete history of the program and permission to conduct inspections at any relevant locations and to interview former managers and workers.

IAEA inspectors easily verified that declared weapons and facilities had been respectively dismantled and decommissioned and that the declared amount of HEU had been placed in monitored storage. But providing assurance that South Africa did not have any undeclared weapons or HEU was more difficult, a matter of concern because South Africa claimed that the Valindaba enrichment plant had produced considerably less HEU than its design capacity would have allowed. A materials balance of the plant revealed very large uncertainties because plant operators kept poor records of the enrichment of the depleted uranium tails.[19] In the end, however, the IAEA concluded that "the amounts of HEU which could have been produced by the pilot enrichment plant are consistent with the amounts declared." This conclusion was based largely on an analysis of the original operating records of the plant, which the IAEA judged to be authentic.

18. David Albright, "South Africa and the Affordable Bomb," *Bulletin of the Atomic Scientists*, vol. 50 (July 1994), p. 37.

19. Thomas Cochran, "Highly Enriched Uranium Production for South African Nuclear Weapons," *Science and Global Security*, vol. 4, no. 2 (1994), pp. 161–76.

The Iraqi case, of course, featured a much more adversarial relationship between the inspectors and the host country. In the aftermath of the Gulf War the Security Council established the United Nations Special Commission on Iraq (UNSCOM) to uncover and destroy the country's chemical, biological, and long-range missile capabilities and to assist the IAEA in eliminating Iraq's nuclear weapons program. An "anytime, anywhere" inspection system was imposed on Iraq, in which UNSCOM and IAEA inspectors had the right "to conduct no-notice inspections of declared and undeclared facilities throughout Iraq with full access and no right of refusal."[20] Despite this, Iraq was able to conceal for some time several significant undertakings to produce fissile material. It made incomplete and misleading declarations, impeded inspections, destroyed documents, and disguised certain activities. Eventually, UNSCOM and the IAEA gained confidence that they had located all significant nuclear weapon activities, but the process to gain this confidence took time and, in some instances, threats of force.[21]

The South African and Iraqi experiences show that verifying warhead and fissile material declarations will not be quick or easy. However, these cases also show that it is possible to gain adequate and widespread confidence if verification comprises a comprehensive set of measures, including routine and challenge on-site inspections, examination and analysis of facility records, interviews with key personnel, remote sensing, and environmental monitoring.

Verifying the warhead and fissile material declarations of the United States and Russia will be an enormous endeavor. Because it will take many years for states to gain confidence in the accuracy and completeness of the declarations, verification should begin as far in advance of deep reductions as possible. In the first stage of reductions, uncertainties in the nuclear weapon stockpiles would not be of much concern; but as the two countries achieve greater reductions, they must gain confidence in the initial stockpile declarations. As the number of allowed nuclear weapons falls into the hundreds, states are far more likely to have confidence in a declaration whose accuracy had been verified for several years and for tens of thousands of nuclear warheads than one whose verification had begun recently and only after thousands of warheads had already been dismantled.

20. Jonathan B. Tucker, "Monitoring and Verification in a Non-Cooperative Environment: Lessons from the UN Experience in Iraq," *Nonproliferation Review*, vol. 3 (Spring-Summer 1996), p. 2.
21. Ibid., pp. 3–14.

Dismantling Warheads and Disposition of Fissile Material

Once warheads destined for dismantling are declared, tagged, and authenticated, their destruction could be monitored with confidence by tracking them from deployment or storage sites to dismantlement facilities and finally to the storage and ultimate disposition of the recovered fissile materials.

In the first step the tagged warheads would be checked periodically at locations from the initial declared deployment or storage site to the dismantlement facility. All the steps of actually dismantling the warheads probably could not be monitored directly without revealing sensitive information, so an indirect method will be necessary, although as suggested later, monitoring of measures to disable pits irreversibly might be possible. One indirect method of monitoring would be to install a portal-perimeter system around the dismantlement facility and monitor the inflow of nuclear weapons and the outflow of canisters containing plutonium pits and HEU components, with periodic checks that no warheads or fissile components remained inside.

A particular nuclear warhead would be counted as dismantled when the corresponding component is placed in monitored storage. If desired, the components could be fingerprinted according to their emissions of neutrons and gamma rays in response to a neutron source and associated with particular warhead types.

A possible complication is added if dismantling and stockpile maintenance activities are done at the same facility. In such circumstances, it would simplify monitoring if dismantling and maintenance could be segregated by using different perimeters and portals within the same facility. It would be necessary, however, to verify that maintenance facilities were being used solely to repair or replace existing warheads, not to build additional warheads.

Along with portal monitoring there also may be direct methods to verify dismantling, particularly to verify that the dismantling is made irreversible. For example, the pits could be "stuffed" with steel wire, an idea suggested by Matthew Bunn and Richard Garwin, based on a technology developed by Los Alamos National Laboratory. In this scheme a wire is inserted into the hollow plutonium sphere of a pit through the tube in which tritium is inserted. A pit so stuffed with tangled wire could not be compressed to a critical geometry that would allow an explosion, and the wire could almost certainly be frayed in a manner to make it impossible to retract. Such stuffing could be readily verified by inspectors observing the insertion of the wire into the pit. Inspectors could also use gamma ray pictures of the canisters in which the pits are put to confirm that they are hollow pluto-nium spheres with tangled wire inside.[22]

After emerging from the dismantling facility, the tagged and sealed con-tainers of pits and other fissile material components would be stored at mon-itored sites. Later the irreversibility of disarmament could be strengthened by converting the fissile materials to unclassified forms and then disposing of them, for example, by blending HEU with natural uranium or mixing plutonium recovered from weapons with high-level radioactive wastes. Such operations could be readily verified by existing materials measurement and accounting procedures.

Banning Production of Fissile Material for Weapons

An essential element of a deep cuts regime would be an agreement by all declared and undeclared nuclear weapon states not to produce any addi-tional fissile material for weapons. Four of the nuclear weapon states have announced that they have permanently ended their production of fissile mate-rial for weapons and the fifth, China, has indicated privately since the early 1990s that it is not producing material for this purpose. India, Pakistan, and Israel may be producing fissile material for weapons, but if so, at a rel-atively low rate.[23] A universal and verified ban on the production of fissile material for weapons or production outside international safeguards has been under consideration by the Conference on Disarmament in Geneva since 1994. But progress was blocked until recently by the insistence of India and Pakistan, supported by a number of nonweapon states, that any ban be linked to negotiations on global nuclear disarmament, which the NPT weapon states refused to accept. However, since the May 1998 nuclear tests by India and Pakistan, both countries have agreed to enter negotiations on a cutoff.

The starting point for verifying a production ban would be declarations by the nuclear weapon states of the status and location of all facilities at which plutonium had been produced and separated and where uranium had been enriched. Verification of the cutoff would then involve

—monitoring all declared facilities that are shut down;

22. Matthew Bunn, "'Pit Stuffing': How to Disable Thousands of Warheads and Easily Verify Their Dismantlement," and Richard L. Garwin, "Comment on Matt Bunn's 'Pit Stuff-ing' Proposal," in *Public Interest Report*, vol. 51 (March-April 1998).

23. Before its recent nuclear tests, Pakistan claimed it had not produced HEU since 1990. However, it was producing LEU, and LEU can be enriched to HEU very quickly. Pakistan may be doing so now.

—monitoring all declared operating facilities to confirm that any HEU or separated plutonium produced after the treaty comes into force is used only for nonweapon purposes under international safeguards; and

—verifying the absence of clandestine, undeclared production facilities.

Each of these tasks has been investigated by the IAEA. The most comprehensive verification system examined with respect to declared facilities would apply full safeguards to all nuclear material in a state or under its control, except those military stocks of fissile material that would exist at the date of entry into force of a cutoff treaty. In such a system, safeguards would be applied to all uranium enrichment plants, nuclear reactors, stores of spent fuel, reprocessing plants, and facilities for the storage, conversion, or fabrication of nuclear materials (except for existing military stocks). A less comprehensive system would exempt power and research reactors fueled with natural or low-enriched uranium, facilities for fabricating fresh fuel for these reactors, and their spent fuel stores. We prefer the more comprehensive approach.[24]

MONITORING SHUT-DOWN FACILITIES. Several facilities in the declared and undeclared nuclear weapon states have produced weapons-usable materials, including many plutonium-production reactors, reprocessing lines, and enrichment facilities that are no longer operating. Verifying that these facilities remain shut down should be straightforward. Remote visual observation from satellites would be able to detect renewed activity at a closed facility, and detection of heat with infrared sensors and vapor plumes from cooling towers would reveal the operation of reactors or gaseous-diffusion enrichment facilities. In addition, inspectors could apply seals on critical plant equipment and install cameras and other devices that could record any forbidden activities. Periodic on-site inspections would check the seals and surveillance equipment and also verify that there was no unexplained activity at the site.

MONITORING OPERATING FACILITIES. Some nuclear weapon states will continue to operate civilian reprocessing and uranium enrichment facilities after a ban on the production of fissile materials for weapons takes effect. In addition, some military reactors and reprocessing lines might be operated for nonmilitary purposes. For example, Russia continues to operate three plutonium production reactors to produce heat and electricity for neigh-

24. Thomas Shea, "Safeguarding Reprocessing and Enrichment Plants: Current and Future Practices," Seminar on Safeguards and Non-Proliferation, IAEA headquarters, November 16–17, 1995; and Frans Berkhout and others, "A Cutoff in the Production of Fissile Material," *International Security*, vol. 19 (Winter 1994), pp. 167–202.

boring communities, and it continues to separate plutonium from the spent fuel discharged by these reactors because it is not suitable for long-term storage. Russia also operates two tritium production reactors. Similarly, the United States is operating a military reprocessing line at Savannah River to stabilize certain radioactive wastes and plans to resume tritium production in the future.

Such activities could be safeguarded using measures now employed by the IAEA to safeguard similar activities in non–nuclear weapon states. These include establishing and reviewing material accountancy and control systems, independent measurements of inventories and inventory changes, and application of containment and surveillance measures. Facilities that handle fissile material in bulk form—reprocessing plants, enrichment facilities, and certain chemical conversion and fuel-fabrication facilities—would demand the most attention and resources. In these cases various special procedures have been developed for the IAEA. For example, at enrichment plants designed for LEU production, the enrichment of uranium fluoride in cascade header pipes can be measured either continuously or intermittently to verify the absence of HEU production.[25]

A special problem arises in monitoring facilities that are collocated with allowed activities related to nuclear weapons. For example, sites with operating or shutdown reprocessing and enrichment plants may also contain facilities for the storage or processing of allowed military stocks of plutonium and HEU, tritium production, or nuclear weapons research and development. In these instances verification would be complicated by the desire of the inspected country to protect classified information.

A 1993 study prepared for the U.S. Department of Energy analyzed this problem for many U.S. facilities.[26] The study examined verification measures of varying degrees of intrusiveness, including remote sensing, environmental monitoring, IAEA-type safeguards, and challenge inspections. It noted that sensitive weapon-related operations generally could be cordoned off from operations essential to verifying a production cutoff. When it would be essential for inspectors to have access to areas with classified activities, shrouding and masking measures could be employed to protect sensitive information. Protecting sensitive information would probably lose impor-

25. Shea, "Safeguarding Reprocessing."

26. "Transparency Measures for DOE SNM Production Facilities," prepared for the U.S. Department of Energy by Brookhaven National Laboratory, Oak Ridge National Laboratory, Oak Ridge Y-12 Plant, Pacific Northwest Laboratory, and Savannah River Technology Center, Washington, 1993.

tance as the number and intensity of weapon-related activities shrank and the degree of transparency of nuclear operations increased.

DETECTING UNDECLARED FACILITIES. As important as verifying that material for weapons is no longer produced at declared facilities is providing assurance that no undeclared facilities for this purpose exist. The IAEA study lists the measures that would be required to provide such an assurance: systematic analysis of open literature and expanded state declarations, expanded access for routine inspections, provisions for challenge inspections to investigate suspect sites, and wide-area environmental measurements of radionuclides that might be emitted in conjunction with undeclared reprocessing and enrichment operations. These last measures could include airborne radiation mapping and sampling of soil, water, and sediments. The eighty to one hundred radionuclide monitoring stations currently envisioned as a monitoring network under the Comprehensive Test Ban Treaty might be used to complement other environmental sampling measures. Analysis of these measures is now under way in the IAEA, partly in regard to a cutoff but more directly under its 93+2 Programme to strengthen the present safeguards regime.

HEU FOR NONWEAPONS PURPOSES. The verification of a cutoff is complicated by the use of HEU for nonweapons purposes. At present all U.S. and British nuclear-powered ships and submarines are fueled with weapon-grade HEU, and many Russian submarines also use HEU. HEU-fueled naval reactors typically require an initial charge of 200–400 kilograms of uranium-235, with refueling every five to twenty years or more. The total HEU requirements for the United States and Russia are 1–2 tonnes a year for each country, and for Britain, 0.1–0.2 tonnes a year. These requirements are small compared with the quantities of HEU being extracted from excess weapons and available in buffer stocks. Such sources, therefore, would be more than sufficient to supply all existing naval reactors over their remaining lifetime, obviating any need for new production. Nevertheless, this material will somehow have to be accounted for and some assurance given that it is not being diverted to weapons.

One means could be that taken under paragraph 14 of the INFCIRC/153 model safeguards agreement, which provides that nuclear material, including HEU, may be released from IAEA safeguards for "non-proscribed military activity" (naval reactors, for example). The agency must be kept informed of the total quantity and composition of the unsafeguarded nuclear material, and safeguards must be applied when the material is discharged from the reactor and returned to the civilian inventory. Under this procedure, which has never been invoked, a country would declare that a certain quantity of HEU would be used in naval reactors, allow the IAEA to verify that this amount of HEU had been fabricated into naval reactor fuel, and later invite the IAEA to assay and safeguard the spent HEU fuel after it had been removed from the reactor. This approach, while straightforward in theory, would have to be tailored in practice to accomodate sensitivities of the U.S. Navy, and perhaps the navies of other countries, regarding the detailed design of their nuclear fuels.

However, the time during which the HEU in naval reactor fuel would be outside of safeguards could be from five to more than twenty years. This is not significant for the nuclear weapon states today, given their large stockpiles of unsafeguarded HEU, but it could raise serious questions in the later stages of disarmament, or if the states without nuclear weapons or India, Pakistan, or Israel developed nuclear-powered submarines. For this reason, we advocate that all future naval reactors be fueled with LEU. Although current LEU-fueled naval reactors are refueled more frequently than the most modern U.S. naval reactors, a twenty-year refueling period could be achieved by reactors using uranium enriched to only 20 percent or less. The LEU cores for the same core life would be larger, however, than those employing HEU.[27]

COSTS OF VERIFICATION. In 1995 the IAEA Secretariat estimated that a comprehensive verification effort that applied "safeguards-type measures to all nuclear material in a State or under its control, except those military stocks of fissile material which would exist at the date of entry into force of a cutoff treaty," would require 25,000 person-days of inspection effort (PDI) a year at an annual cost of $140 million to monitor 995 facilities in the eight declared and undeclared nuclear-weapon countries. This can be compared to the 8,200 PDI and $67.5 million expended by the IAEA Department of Safeguards in 1993.[28] The costs of such a comprehensive verification sys-

27. Thomas Dominic Ippolita Jr., "Effects of Variation of Uranium Enrichment on Nuclear Submarine Reactor Design," M.S. thesis, Massachusetts Institute of Technology, 1990.

28. The IAEA also estimated the costs of less comprehensive monitoring systems. For example, a system that covered all stores of separated fissile materials (except exempted stocks), mixed-oxide, HEU, and U-233 conversion and fuel fabrication plants, uranium enrichment plants capable of producing HEU, plutonium-fueled power reactors, and fast power and test reactors, but did not cover thermal power reactors, R&D facilities for uranium enrichment, or spent fuel stores, would require 5,000 PDI a year and should cost $40 million. George MacLean and James F. Keeley, "Calculating Costs: A Critical Assessment of Verification Costs for a Fissile Material Cutoff Treaty," in Peter Gizewski, ed., *Non-Proliferation, Arms Control and Disarmament: Enhancing Existing Regimes and Exploring New Dimensions* (Toronto: Centre for International and Security Studies, York University, 1998), pp. 107–28.

tem would represent a substantial increase in the IAEA safeguards budget, but compared with the costs of maintaining nuclear forces in their current scale, they are very modest and comparable with the costs of verifying other arms control agreements such as INF, START, and CWC.

Improving Safeguards on Peaceful Nuclear Activities

Certain types of facilities and activities in the civilian fuel cycle are very difficult to safeguard using current technology, and the possibility that significant diversions of fissile materials might not be detected in a timely manner could undermine confidence in a deep cuts regime. Particularly worrisome are facilities that handle or produce (or are capable of producing) weapon-usable materials in bulk form: uranium enrichment, reprocessing, and mixed-oxide fuel fabrication facilities. Such concerns could be ameliorated by improving safeguards to provide better assurance of nondiversion or by modifying, restricting, or prohibiting these activities.

First is the danger that uranium enrichment facilities that produce low-enriched uranium for reactor fuel could be reconfigured to produce weapons-grade uranium. For a sense of the magnitude of this problem, consider that an enrichment plant producing LEU for ten large power reactors would have a total separative capacity of about one million separative work units (SWU) a year. If this one plant, which represents only 2 to 3 percent of current world separative capacity, were reconfigured to produce weapons-grade uranium, it could produce 5 tons of HEU a year, enough to build at least 250 warheads.[29] This can be compared with a total allowed stockpile for the United States and Russia of 200 warheads in our proposed third stage of reductions.

The safeguards problem is particularly acute for civilian reprocessing and plutonium recycling programs. A typical large power reactor discharges 200 kilograms of plutonium annually in its spent fuel, enough for more than twenty nuclear weapons. The plutonium discharged from power reactors contains a higher fraction of certain undesirable isotopes (plutonium-240 and plutonium-241) than the weapon-grade plutonium produced in dedicated military production reactors. The radioactive decay of these undesirable isotopes produces neutrons and heat, complicating bomb design and

29. At a tails assay of 0.3 percent U-235 in the depleted uranium, it requires about 200 SWU to produce 1 kilogram of HEU from natural uranium. A 1-million SWU plant then could produce 5,000 kilograms of HEU, or enough for 250 to 400 warheads, assuming that 12 to 20 kilograms of HEU would be needed to build an implosion-type weapon.

leading some observers to argue that reactor-grade plutonium is unsuitable for weapons. Unfortunately, it has been established that a state or group that could make a nuclear explosive with weapon-grade plutonium could make an effective device with reactor-grade plutonium.[30]

The plutonium produced by power reactors is inaccessible for use in weapons as long as it remains locked in the highly radioactive spent fuel, but increasingly it is being separated in civilian reprocessing facilities. Indeed, the large civilian reprocessing plants now operating in France, the United Kingdom, and Russia together produce more than 20 tonnes of plutonium each year, enough plutonium to make several thousand nuclear weapons a year. Undetected diversions of even 1 percent a year from such plants could, over several years, equal the allowed military stockpiles of plutonium in the third stage of the deep cuts program. Opportunities for diversion also exist in mixed-oxide fuel fabrication plants, where a mixture of separated plutonium and natural uranium is used as a substitute for low-enriched uranium in the manufacture of fresh reactor fuel.

Concerned about small diversions by states without nuclear weapons and the possibility of a large breakout by any state with enrichment or reprocessing facilities, the nuclear weapon states are likely to require that barriers to the acquisition of nuclear weapons by current nonweapon states be increased as one condition for agreeing to deep cuts in their own arsenals. In addition, the weapon states will be concerned about the possibility that another weapon state might use large stocks of separated civilian plutonium to rapidly expand its nuclear arsenal. For this reason restrictions on civilian uranium enrichment and plutonium separation and use should be considered under a deep cuts regime.

Several types of restrictions could be considered. First, only economically justified production and use of separated weapons-usable fissile material should go forward. By this standard all current separation of plutonium should end, at least until plutonium fuels become economically competitive with LEU fuels. And even if plutonium fuels become economical several decades from now, the separation of plutonium should not exceed the demand for plutonium fuels. Second, new institutional arrangements should be explored that would provide better assurance against diversion and

30. U.S. Department of Energy, "Nonproliferation and Arms Control Assessment of Weapons-Usable Fissile Material Storage and Excess Plutonium Disposition Alternatives," DOE/NN-0007 (January 1997), pp. 37–39; National Academy of Sciences, *Management and Disposition of Excess Weapons Plutonium*, chap. 1; and J. Carson Mark, "Explosive Properties of Reactor-Grade Plutonium," *Science & Global Security*, vol. 4, no. 1 (1993), pp. 111–28.

breakout. For example, enrichment, reprocessing, and mixed-oxide fuel fabrication plants could be owned and operated by international consortia, with the IAEA acting as custodian for all separated plutonium and highly enriched uranium. In addition, such facilities could be located only on the territory of countries judged proliferation safe by the international community. Third, technical innovations in nuclear fuel cycles should be pursued that could make diversion and breakout significantly more difficult. For example, fuel cycles could be developed that produce reduced quantities of plutonium with high percentages of the heat-producing Pu-238 isotope, which would make the design of plutonium weapons more difficult.[31]

These restrictions could decrease substantially the risk that civilian nuclear facilities will be used for weapons purposes. One should bear in mind, however, that even the complete elimination of the civilian nuclear power industry would not eliminate the possibility of proliferation or breakout. As long as the scientific and engineering knowledge of how to build nuclear weapons and related facilities exists, so too will the possibility that clandestine facilities might be built or that countries might withdraw from the deep cuts agreement and embark on a massive bomb-building program, perhaps using the huge stocks of plutonium in buried spent fuel.

Delivery Vehicles and Launchers

At each stage of disarmament, limitations would be placed on the numbers and characteristics of nuclear delivery vehicles and associated launchers. Verification of these limitations would include monitoring

—the elimination or conversion of all delivery vehicles of a specified type and associated launchers beyond those allowed;

—limitations on the production of nuclear-capable delivery vehicles and associated launchers;

—limitations on the maximum number of warheads allowed on delivery vehicles of a specified type; and

—limitations on the number of delivery vehicles of a specified type and associated launchers.

The INF and START Treaties provide valuable precedents and experience on how each of these verification tasks could be accomplished. The

---

31. See, for example, Alex Galperin, Paul Reichert, and Alvin Radkowsky, "Thorium Fuel for Light Water Reactors: Reducing Proliferation Potential of Nuclear Power Fuel Cycle," *Science & Global Security*, vol. 6, no. 3 (1997), pp. 265–90.

INF Treaty eliminated all U.S. and Soviet ground-launched missiles with ranges between 500 and 5,500 kilometers. The START Treaties limit the number of categories of strategic delivery vehicles—ICBMs, SLBMs, and bombers—and the number of nuclear weapons that each type may carry.[32] Many of the verification arrangements established by these treaties could simply be extended, with minor modifications, to a multilateral deep cuts agreement among all the nuclear weapon states.

In each of these treaties the initial step is a comprehensive exchange of data, followed by baseline inspections to verify the accuracy of the data. For ICBM silos, ballistic missile submarines, and strategic bombers, these declarations can be verified with high confidence. Verification of treaty provisions is achieved through a combination of national technical means (NTM—satellite observations, monitoring of telemetry, and other intelligence information), and "cooperative measures" to improve NTM, and on-site inspections. A multilateral deep cuts agreement might rely less on NTM if the second-tier nuclear weapon states (particularly China) believe that it puts them at a disadvantage vis-à-vis the United States and Russia.

Elimination and Conversion

START I specifies procedures for eliminating ICBM silos, mobile ICBMs and their launchers, SLBM launchers, and heavy bombers.[33] Mobile ICBMs and their launchers and launch canisters must be eliminated according to certain procedures at specified facilities that are subject to on-site inspection. The elimination of heavy bombers is handled in a similar manner. ICBM silos are to be destroyed in situ, and SLBM launchers must be eliminated in designated facilities by removing the missile section or the launch tubes from the submarine. The elimination of silos and SLBM launchers is verified by NTM, aided by prior notification and other measures to facilitate monitoring.

Except for mobile ICBMs and heavy ICBMs, START does not include provisions for eliminating missiles, nor does it limit the number of missiles that may remain outside launchers. A deep cuts agreement should, however, require the elimination of all missiles above the permitted level, except

32. The verification procedures and protocols under these treaties are explained in detail in the treaties themselves and in documents prepared by the U.S. Department of Defense's On-Site Inspection Agency: "START," October 1994; "Article by Article Analysis of START," undated; and Joseph Harahan, "A History of the On-Site Inspection Agency and INF Treaty Implementation, 1988–91," March 1993.

33. See "Protocol on Procedures Governing Conversion or Elimination of the Items Subject to START I, July 31, 1991."

for a specified number for replacement, testing, and space launch. This could be accomplished according to the procedures specified for mobile and heavy ICBMs in START or for missiles destroyed under the INF Treaty.

START allows the conversion of nuclear bombers to conventional roles, subject to specified requirements designed to allow verification. These include requirements that the converted bombers be based separately from nuclear bombers, that the bombers be used only for nonnuclear missions and that neither they nor their crews be used in exercises for nuclear missions, and that the bombers have observable differences from bombers with nuclear roles. In addition, storage areas for heavy-bomber nuclear weapons must be located at least 100 kilometers from air bases where converted bombers are based. These provisions are subject to on-site verification.

Monitoring Production Facilities

A small number of facilities in the nuclear weapon states have been used to produce nuclear delivery vehicles. It is likely that these have already been identified by intelligence agencies, if not already made public by the producing countries. Most of these facilities would be shut down under a deep cuts regime. The few that would remain open to produce replacement missiles could be monitored using portal-perimeter systems, as is done under the START and INF Treaties.

For example, START provides for continuous monitoring of production facilities for mobile ICBMs. In Russia this is the facility that produces SS-25 missiles and launch canisters. Items leaving the facility must go through a monitored portal, at which point U.S. inspectors have the right to determine, typically through visual inspection, that the items are as declared. Each of the accountable items is given a unique identifier. In addition, the United States and Russia are allowed "suspect-site" inspections of other facilities on an agreed list that in the past produced components (such as rocket engines) that could be used for the covert assembly of mobile missiles.[34] Such arrangements could be extended to facilities that produce silo-based ICBMs and SLBMs, which, in theory at least, might be launched from platforms other than silos and submarine tubes.

It will be necessary, especially in the latter stages of a deep cuts agreement, to monitor and limit the production of nuclear-capable delivery vehi-

34. See article XVI of the "Protocol on Inspections and Continuous Monitoring Activities of the START I Treaty," and annex 5 ("Procedures for Continuous Monitoring") to the "Inspection Protocol, July 31, 1991."

cles, even if that type of vehicle had never been used in a nuclear role. For example, it will be desirable to limit the production of space-launch vehicles to the number needed for planned space launches (including a reasonable buffer stock). Similarly, the total number of long-range bombers (conventional and well as nuclear) and air-launched cruise missiles (ALCMs) should also be limited. Such restrictions would build additional barriers to breakout and help to build confidence in the stability of the deep cuts regime.

Monitoring Warhead Loadings

Verifying the number of nuclear weapons that a delivery vehicle carries or is equipped to carry could be done according to START procedures. To verify SLBM warhead loadings, a short-notice inspection of a submarine base would be requested, and activities at the base would be curtailed until the inspectors arrived. The inspectors would select a limited sample of missiles to be checked, the nose cones would be removed, and the inspectors would count the number of warheads.[35] START I permits the inspected party to shroud warheads and other devices on the bus to protect sensitive information. Similarly, START II provides for on-site inspections of heavy bombers to confirm that they are equipped to carry no more than the declared number of nuclear bombs or nuclear-armed air-launched cruise missiles.

Under START I, if the number of permitted missile warheads is reduced by more than two below the warhead loadings specified in the initial declaration, the old bus must be destroyed and a new one deployed. START II relaxes this last condition on the grounds of economy. To speed reductions, it would be best to adopt the START II procedures for the initial stages of a deep cuts agreement. The requirement that excess warheads be placed in monitored storage and be verifiably dismantled would give further assurance that the downloading was not easily reversible. In the third stage the agreement might prescribe that all SLBMs be equipped with new buses, either a single-warhead bus or one allowing the launch of an agreed upon small number of warheads. In this case the old buses could be destroyed, and random inspections of SLBMs allowed to ensure that the missiles were not equipped with more heavily MIRVed buses.

Confidence in warhead loadings would also be strengthened by limi-

35. Under START I, counting rules were established to assign specified numbers of warheads to specific weapon systems. The United States and Russia, however, are allowed to get treaty credit for downloading the weapon systems if the downloading can be properly verified. The on-site inspections under START I have been visual; in principle they could be done using radiation measurements, but so far such inspections have not been agreed to or done.

tations on flight testing and exchanges of telemetry data. For example, START prohibits flight tests of MIRVed ICBMs after 2003, and tapes containing all telemetric information broadcast during a flight test must be provided to the other party.[36] A deep cuts agreement should contain similar provisions.

Monitoring Numbers of Delivery Vehicles

Total numbers of bombers, SLBMs, and fixed and mobile ICBMs also could be monitored using START procedures. Under START, Russian mobile ICBMs are given unique identifiers, and each missile and launcher is attached to a particular base. The United States can then request that all the missiles associated with a specified base be returned to the base and that the roofs of the missile shelters be opened so that the number of missiles can be counted with NTM. The United States would also be able to perform an on-site inspection to make certain that the specific numbered missiles associated with the base are, in fact, the ones that have been recalled. Similarly, Russia can request that the United States display in the open all the bombers of a specified bomber base to allow counting.[37] The number of SLBM launchers is readily monitored with NTM.

In most cases it should be straightforward to apply START procedures to a multilateral deep cuts agreement. In a few instances, however, special procedures will have to be worked out. For example, China evidently wishes to hide its mobile missiles in caves in a kind of shell game.[38] Special verification arrangements will be necessary to allow these missiles to be counted without compromising their survivability. One possibility would be to tag each missile and declare all deployment caves and allow the inspecting party to request a short-notice inspection of a particular missile or cave. In this way one could verify that declared caves did not contain untagged, undeclared missiles and that declared missiles were present only in declared caves. Challenge inspections of undeclared sites, together with NTM and

36. "Protocol on Telemetric Information of START I, July 31, 1991."

37. See article X of "Inspection Protocol of START I." Under START I, Russian mobile ICBMs and the U.S. MX missile are given unique identifiers. For the Russian ICBMs the identifiers are spray-painted numbers; for the MX a metal plate is bolted or riveted on the first stage of the missile. Jonathan Bowers, On-Site Inspection Agency, private communication, July 23, 1996.

38. For a discussion of cave basing see Litai Xue, "Evolution of China's Nuclear Strategy," in John Hopkins and Weixing Hu, eds., *Strategic Views from the Second Tier: The Nuclear Weapons Policies of France, Britain, and China* (New Brunswick, N.J.: Transaction Publishers, 1995).

monitoring of missile production facilities, would provide assurance that undeclared missiles did not exist.

Deployments and Operations

The final task for a deep cuts verification system would be to monitor agreed upon restrictions on the launch readiness or alert status of nuclear forces, such as the removal of warheads or other key components from delivery vehicles. In general this could be done with procedures similar to those used to monitor warhead loadings. Random, short-notice inspections of bomber and naval bases could verify the launch readiness of the force. For example, an inspection of submarines at pier side could confirm that the warheads or some other agreed upon component such as shrouds or guidance systems needed to support a launch had been removed from the submarine. Continuous or random inspections at declared storage sites could confirm that the warheads or other components remained separated from the delivery vehicles.

It would be desirable to work toward a regime in which the launch readiness of all weapon systems could be verified continuously without impairing the survivability of at least a portion of the force. Such a regime would allow all parties to receive constant reassurance the forces of other countries were not being readied for attack. If the warheads were removed and stored at fixed sites, video cameras or on-site inspectors could verify that the warheads remained in storage and that no preparations were being made to remove them. For silo-based ICBMs or pier-side SLBMs, video cameras or special seals could verify that the silo doors or launch tube hatches had not been opened and that no preparations had been made to reinstall warheads, shrouds, or guidance systems.

As discussed in chapter 6, more complex arrangements would be necessary to verify the launch readiness of systems such as SLBMs at sea and mobile ICBMs. One possibility would be to equip these systems with tags that could be interrogated remotely and would verify that an agreed upon component necessary for launch was missing. For example, the monitoring agency could query a randomly selected mobile missile or submarine at sea, which would signal back that it had not been readied for launch. An agreement that ballistic missile submarines would patrol out of range of specified targets could be verified by equipping each submarine with a tamper-proof box that would continuously record its location using an inertial measurement unit. The box could be queried remotely at regular intervals to determine in a simple yes or no answer whether the submarine had remained within the allowed boundaries.[39]

Various measures could be adopted to ensure that such interrogation would not make submarines at sea or mobile missiles out of garrisons vulnerable to attack. The signal could be relayed through a transmitter owned by the country being interrogated so as to conceal the origin of the signal, or a time delay of a few hours could be incorporated into the response to allow the submarine or missile to move to a different location before the location during interrogation was revealed. In addition, the queried side could limit the number of queries to an agreed upon level so that there would be no opportunity to locate more than a single submarine or mobile missile at one time.

Conclusion

A new and vital component of the deep cuts verification system is the comprehensive and verified declaration of all nuclear weapons and stocks of fissile material in the nuclear weapon states. Confidence in the accuracy of the declarations will have to be built up gradually as the parties allow increasing transparency and as the amount of information considered sensitive decreases. In the final analysis, however, no verification regime could provide absolute assurance that the United States or Russia had not concealed a few hundred warheads (or enough material to build a few hundred) or that the other nuclear weapon states had not concealed a few tens of warheads. It is important that residual nuclear forces, together with other political and security arrangements, be designed to deal with the inherent uncertainties that will accompany the very deep cuts we propose.

Another new element of the verification system proposed here is measures to verify the alert status of nuclear forces to confirm that delivery vehicles are not capable of being launched and are not being readied for attack. These verification measures will, of course, be closely tied to the specific actions or procedures adopted by the parties to reduce the launch readiness of their forces. The main challenge will be to design the de-alerting procedures and corresponding verification measures in ways that would not decrease the survivability of a core retaliatory force or otherwise lead to an

39. Lieutenant Colonel Guy Martelle, On-Site Inspection Agency, private communication, July 25, 1996.

unstable situation during a crisis. Although we have suggested ways in which this might be done, finding the best solution will require detailed analysis by the military establishments of each party and extensive cooperation between the parties.

Finally, it is interesting to compare the verification regime for our deep cuts proposal with that of the START treaties. In any arms control treaty, two types of threats must be considered: cheating, in which a party violates treaty provisions clandestinely, and breakout, in which a party openly abrogates the treaty. For START, analysts have concluded with virtual unanimity that any militarily significant violation would be detected. However, they have pointed to the possibility that either party could break out of the treaties by uploading missiles or bombers. The U.S. Senate Committee on Foreign Relations noted that Russia could upload each of the 105 SS-19 ICBMs allowed under the treaty from one to six warheads or could equip heavy bombers with more nuclear weapons than specified. The committee noted that because the testing and training required to maintain the augmented capability on a day-to-day operational basis would likely be detected, "such scenarios would appear to be more suited to breakout than cheating."[40] The capability of the United States to rapidly increase warhead loadings is much greater under START II than it is for Russia, generating serious concerns about U.S. breakout potential in the Russian legislature.

With the comprehensive verification system that we advocate, breakout would be much more difficult. Although a country could legally store thousands of warheads and hundreds of nondeployed missiles under START, it could not do so under the deep cuts program. Any significant preparation for breakout would be detected and would itself constitute a violation of the treaty. Any party intending to cheat or break out of the treaty would have to evade verified restrictions along several fronts: on fissile materials or nuclear warheads or both, on delivery vehicles, and on operational practices. Thus, although the reductions we advocate are far deeper than those required by the START Treaties, the comprehensiveness of the verification system should provide a comparable level of assurance against militarily significant cheating and breakout.

---

40. Senate Committee on Foreign Relations, "START II Treaty," 104th Congress, executive report 104-10, December 15, 1995, p. 35.

CHAPTER TWELVE

The Next Nuclear Posture Review?

Carrying out plans for deep reductions in nuclear forces will depend not just on the emerging international environment but on domestic politics: will decisionmakers be prepared to take on political opposition to such initiatives in their own countries? Assuming no major deterioration in international politics in the coming years, reducing reliance on nuclear weapons ultimately will depend on effective domestic leadership that can elicit a consensus in support. As was apparent after the conclusion of the 1993–94 Nuclear Posture Review (NPR), an international climate that seemed propitious for disarmament measures was not sufficient to counter entrenched U.S. domestic perceptions of the continued importance of large and activated nuclear forces. Domestic politics has been decisive in determining the nuclear priorities of other states as well—not least Russia, where the future of START II remains hostage to the ideological divisions among members of the Russian parliament.

This chapter explores the political opportunities for and potential constraints on a future U.S. administration that attempts to carry out the agenda proposed in this study. Based on the experiences of the first term of the Clinton administration, the analysis examines the political and bureaucratic dynamics that influenced two recent initiatives: the 1993–94 Nuclear Posture Review and the 1996 decision by the United States to sign the African Nuclear Weapons Free Zone Treaty (ANWFZ). Both are instances of a post–cold war administration attempting to define and articulate the purpose of nuclear forces absent a Soviet adversary. Are there lessons to be learned from these policy struggles that could inform future efforts at nuclear policy innovation? If so, what domestic conditions would have to be altered to permit more ambitious proposals to succeed?

The Nuclear Posture Review

The election of Bill Clinton in 1992 coincided with continuing dramatic change in the international climate prompted by the collapse of the Soviet Union and the dissolution of the Warsaw Pact. For the first time in decades the United States faced no plausible threat of deliberate strategic attack nor a credible conventional adversary in Europe. The overarching threat of a concerted attack from Russian strategic forces had diminished. A fundamental rationale for the nuclear posture—to deter massive conventional defeat by the Warsaw Pact—had diminished or disappeared. Former adversaries were being converted into recipients of American aid to help ease their transition into democracy, dismantle nuclear weapons rendered obsolete by international agreements, and protect nuclear assets from unlawful seizure or accidental use. Finally, the successes of the Bush administration in reaching sweeping arms control agreements with Russia, including strategic force reduction agreements and measures to withdraw most tactical nuclear weapons deployed overseas, provided the new president with an ambitious and promising agenda based on bipartisan support.

In addition to overseeing the implementation of START I and II, the new administration pledged to strengthen the partnership with Russia; to enfranchise states in the former Soviet republics in furtherance of additional arms control and nuclear safety agreements; and to seek limits on nuclear testing as well as negotiate new agreements to preserve the Anti-Ballistic Missile Treaty. An agreement reached between the two governments in January 1994 to detarget missiles away from each other's territories, though symbolic, was seen as a vital step in building mutual confidence.

The fragility of political conditions called for bold American initiatives to help counter divisive forces in Russian society. There was pervasive and profound economic dislocation after the dissolution of the Soviet Union, growing pressures on the Russian government to provide alternative means of occupation for salient sectors of the Russian economy—not least members of the Russian military elite encountering the threat of economic dispossession—and an increasingly vocal and fractious parliament, many of whose members perceived American intentions with deep skepticism. In addition to economic and technical support to help Russia in meeting its obligations to dismantle nuclear forces under START I, the administration embraced an ambitious agenda of cooperative ventures to advance common objectives of denuclearization and threat reduction.

The Clinton administration also accorded unprecedented priority to stemming the proliferation of nuclear and other nonconventional technology to the third world. The continued viability of the Nuclear Non-Proliferation Treaty (NPT), in particular, scheduled for a final review and a vote on its extension in April 1995, required that the administration be able to demonstrate that the United States and other nuclear powers had made progress toward nuclear disarmament, including a comprehensive ban on nuclear testing. The necessity of preserving and strengthening the NPT was made all the more urgent by revelations that Iraq and North Korea, both NPT signatories, had covertly acquired nuclear technologies.

With the changing character of nuclear risks in Russia and the former Soviet republics—shifting from the dominant threat of central nuclear exchange to the growing risks of failure of authority over nuclear weapons—and the demands of smaller states for greater reciprocity in the NPT, policies guiding U.S. nuclear forces, arms control, and nonproliferation became conceptually and politically linked. Although formally acknowledged under article VI of the NPT, the linkage between the nuclear policies of the five nuclear powers and the credibility of the nonproliferation regime became a more influential consideration.[1] Efforts to remove nuclear weapons from Ukraine, Kazakhstan, and Belarus required that they be persuaded of the benefits of supporting the NPT and other nonproliferation arrangements, including the Lisbon Protocol. Negative perceptions among third world states of the legitimacy of the NPT in turn held out the possibility that the knot holding the nonproliferation regime together could unravel without greater inducements for states to remain in or join the agreement. In addition to demonstrating progress in reducing U.S. and Russian arsenals, there was renewed interest in security assurances for NPT adherents, including formal adoption of the policy not to target nonnuclear countries (unless they were allied in aggression with a nuclear power.)[2]

The administration also faced severe fiscal challenges as it tried to harmonize the goals of reducing the defense budget with the need to support

1. As summarized by Director of the US. Arms Control and Disarmament Agency John Holum, under article VI "the nuclear weapon states promise measures to reduce and eliminate their nuclear arsenals." Testimony before the Senate Foreign Relations Committee on the Second Strategic Arms Reduction Treaty, 104 Cong. 1 sess., January 31, 1995.

2. The policy was articulated in June 1978 by then Secretary of State Cyrus Vance: "The United States will not use nuclear weapons against any non-nuclear-weapons state party to the NPT or any comparable internationally binding commitment not to acquire nuclear explosive devices, except in the case of an attack on the United States, its territories or armed forces, or its allies, by such a state allied to a nuclear weapon state, or associated with a nuclear weapon state in carrying out or sustaining the attack" U.S. Arms Control and Disarmament Agency, *Documents on Disarmament, 1978* (Washington: 1979), p. 384.

missions vital to U.S. security interests. In the aftermath of Desert Storm, the primacy of superior conventional technologies and the "reconnaissance strike complex," as William Perry, former secretary of defense, termed the array of advanced conventional forces and technologies demonstrated during the war, dominated conceptions of U.S. global military strategy. In a climate of austerity the costs of maintaining strategic forces competed directly with new requirements for conventional capabilities. The professional military, especially the surface navy and the army, seemed increasingly uninterested in nuclear weapons in any case, especially when it came to triage decisions over resources.

Taken together, these trends suggested to many that an overall deemphasis, if not fundamental redefinition, of existing U.S. nuclear doctrine was virtually inevitable. Emerging security challenges seemed unrelated to a strategy of deterrence based on the threat of preplanned, prompt, and massive counterforce operations, especially against targets that had been vastly diminished in importance or had disappeared. Russian willingness to sustain a course of weapon reduction and dismantlement required a more conciliatory doctrine, including the possibility of further progress on the de-alerting of U.S. strategic forces to reassure Russian leaders and achieve commensurate measures needed to improve operational safety in Russia.

The ability of the United States to persuade other states not to acquire or retain nuclear forces also depended on the credibility of arguments about the risks—not the benefits—of nuclear arsenals. The effectiveness of efforts to devalue the currency of nuclear weapons internationally, many argued, would be limited as long as the United States and other nuclear powers continued to emphasize the critical importance of nuclear security in their own countries. As for deterrence, the United States could respond to any conceivable regional military threat with a small fraction of its nuclear arsenal.

The appointment of Les Aspin, former chairman of the House Armed Services Committee, as Clinton's first secretary of defense, along with several civilian defense experts in key subordinate positions in the Pentagon, added to the perception that the administration was poised for ambitious changes. The first post–cold war Pentagon was to be guided by people who had helped pioneer programs to reduce nuclear dangers in the crumbling Soviet Empire, convinced that nuclear security was increasingly a matter of cooperative efforts to prevent the loss of control over nuclear weapons and materials. As a member of Congress, Aspin had emphasized the urgency of such measures—a program that came to be known as Cooperative Threat Reduction—and had articulated doubts about the relevance of nuclear deterrence for redressing modern security threats. In addition to emphasizing the dissolution of authority in Russia, Aspin stressed the rise of aggressive third world states seeking weapons of mass destruction, states whose ambitions were unlikely to be tamed by traditional superpower strategy.[3]

Was this the prevailing logic within the new administration? In truth, it was never clear where the administration was headed, largely because the president had so rarely addressed nuclear issues. The rhetoric of the campaign and the administration's earliest statements nevertheless indicated a commitment to a demanding arms control agenda that would require policy innovations, even if only to implement the many agreements undertaken by President Bush. The highly publicized call for a fundamental review of the role and purpose of nuclear weapons, in particular, seemed to presage significant change. With both houses of Congress under Democratic control and the heightened stature accorded new administrations, this seemed a moment of maximum opportunity for the president to establish a lasting nuclear legacy.

The Process

Even without the pressures of external change, shrinking resources, or a shift in political parties, it is the common impulse of new administrations to review the priorities of their predecessors. In the Clinton administration the call was for fundamental reevaluation of the basic premises and objectives of all national security programs. Aptly named the Bottom Up Review, the first initiative, beginning in the summer of 1993, focused on conventional forces, an attempt to rationalize and win consensus for a post–cold war strategy that fulfilled vital missions with drastically reduced resources.

The decision to postpone a review of nuclear forces until after the Bottom Up Review was completed was a reflection of the greater urgency given to budgetary imperatives, dominated by conventional force requirements. The formal conduct of the NPR did not begin until the fall of 1993. The administration encountered both service and congressional criticism early on, however, for its failure to consider fully the interrelationships among conventional and nuclear requirements. Key decisions affecting future force structure, basing, and infrastructure (including the requirements for dual-capable bomber force levels) were being raised in the Bottom Up Review before the results of the Nuclear Posture Review.[4]

3. See, for example, "Three Propositions for a New Era Nuclear Policy," speech delivered by Representative Les Aspin, Massachusetts Institute of Technology, June 1, 1992.

4. For further discussion, see for instance *Briefing on Results of the Nuclear Posture Review*, Hearings before the Senate Committee on Armed Services, 103 Cong. 2 sess. (Government Printing Office, 1994), pp. 1–60.

The NPR began as a White House–sanctioned Pentagon study to be carried out under the direction of civilian appointees in cooperation with military officers and career officials. According to several participants, it was a microcosm of Aspin's zeal to systematically reorganize national security policy and implement the ambitious structural reforms in the Pentagon that he had long considered as a "defense intellectual" and a member of the moderate wing of the military reform movement.

As described by Aspin, the NPR was to be an exercise in political-military analysis, an effort to match the design of forces with the political objectives that nuclear deterrence is meant to uphold. It would differ from other Pentagon initiatives especially in its emphasis on the fundamentally political character of nuclear policy and the ever diminishing importance of nuclear warfighting for deterring future threats. Requirements would derive from policy, looking to, as Aspin put it, "where . . . you go after START II."[5] And it would be comprehensive. As stated in Aspin's announcement in fall 1993, the study would "incorporate reviews of policy, doctrine, force structure, operations, safety and security, and arms control in one look."[6]

Despite this broad mandate, the NPR's distribution to or approval by other concerned agencies was apparently never widely debated. Although many assumed that the study would be subject to further review—"not a Defense Department fait accompli," as one State Department official put it—Pentagon officials apparently never considered outside involvement seriously. "It was the Aspin-Clinton show," said one participant, to be conducted in the free-wheeling way Aspin was accustomed to and reinforced by the full delegation of authority to him by the president, "We certainly weren't about to invite any weirdos from ACDA [Arms Control and Disarmament Agency]," he added.[7] The terms of reference, drafted from guidance given by Secretary Aspin, had called for an outside panel of experts to critique the product. Despite the importance of political considerations in the review, however, including the link between U.S. nuclear force plans and nonproliferation policy, no interagency or outside review ever occurred.

Even for those familiar with the defense planning bureaucracy and the history of failed efforts by civilians to achieve innovations in nuclear operations, there were reasons to hope that the NPR could produce results, at least as long as Aspin was at the helm. It was portrayed as a genuine effort to create a nuclear tabula rasa, a baseline from which creative thinking and

5. Quoted in *Briefing on Results of the Nuclear Posture Review,* p. 31.
6. Quoted in Bruce Carey, "U.S. Reviewing Entire Nuclear Weapons Policy," U.S. Information Agency, Washington, October 29, 1993.
7. Interview with Navy participant in the NPR, August 1996.

ambitious reform proposals would emerge. Why not? The mandate was wide open and had the backing of the secretary of defense who had the confidence of the president. Seemingly like-minded people were in charge and, they thought, there was no compelling substantive reason for opposition.

The resignation of Les Aspin in January 1994 gave leadership responsibility for the NPR to John Deutch, who replaced Deputy Secretary of Defense William Perry after Perry was appointed to succeed Aspin. As quickly became evident, this shift left the NPR without a senior-level champion—Deutch was not interested in the NPR. Joint stewardship for the effort had already been delegated to the vice chairman of the Joint Chiefs of Staff, Admiral William Owens, assisted by the Commander in Chief of Strategic Forces Command Henry Chiles. Operational responsibility was shared by Ashton Carter, assistant secretary of defense for nuclear security and counterproliferation (later renamed assistant secretary of defense for international security policy) and Carter's military assistant, Lieutenant General Barry McCaffrey, who was shortly thereafter replaced by Lieutenant General Wesley Clark. To carry out the directives and conduct analysis, six working groups were established, each to examine specific aspects of the role of nuclear weapons in U.S. security, from force structure to deterrence strategy to plans and operations.[8]

According to numerous participants and observers, the initial enthusiasm of Ashton Carter, who was closely allied with both Secretary Aspin and William Perry, suggested a sincere belief in the power of analysis to change thinking and overthrow orthodoxy. As one report described the NPR, "[Carter] appointed six working groups staffed by uniformed officers and civilians to hold closed door hearings at the Pentagon. . . . He urged them to free themselves from Cold War thinking and consider the issues creatively. . . . Everything was up for grabs."[9] His statements to colleagues at the time emphasized his determination to implement changes in the nuclear posture in a way that would fundamentally transform its cold war preoccupations, "especially . . . the hair-trigger alert status and 24-hour operations required of nuclear forces by the SIOP [Single Integrated Operation Plan]," according to one account.[10]

8. In addition, the principal deputy assistant secretary, Frank Miller, a veteran of several administrations' nuclear policy formulation, chaired the working group on strategy and deterrence and the Executive Committee, which was to oversee the overall study. For an elaboration of the structure of the review, see *Briefing on Results of the Nuclear Posture Review*, p. 6.

9. David B. Ottaway and Steve Coll, "Trying to Unplug the War Machine," *Washington Post*, April 12, 1995, p. A1.

10. Ottaway and Coll, "Trying to Unplug the War Machine," refer to Carter as "a minor cult figure in Washington's small but intense community of nuclear weapons specialists," especially "those who favor rapid reduction and elimination of nuclear weapons."

From its inception the rhetoric of the NPR as articulated by Aspin and Carter struck some Pentagon professionals as implying a zealous assault on existing procedures and lines of authority. Changes in the target plans and the structure of the nuclear command undertaken by the Bush administration, including the consolidation of the Strategic Air Command into the Strategic Command in 1992, had already stressed the system, albeit with no publicized signs of discord, and were still being implemented. Plans for the targeting and deployment of forces, in any case, were and would remain the purview of experienced professionals. "We know how to produce nuclear war plans. We have the methodology, we can analyze damage expectancies," said one mid-level operations officer, who was infuriated by what he perceived to be excessive intrusion by recently appointed and inexperienced Clinton officials.[11]

According to some accounts, there were at least two important exceptions to this point of view among senior military officers. Owens, for one, is widely reported to have been a harsh critic of nuclear weapons and apparently expressed strong views in this regard over the course of the NPR. In addition, Commander of the Strategic Air Command (later Strategic Command) General Lee Butler, who was present for the early planning phases of the NPR until his retirement in 1994, recently revealed that he had argued for major operational reforms and deep reductions in nuclear forces—down to 2,000 warheads, according to his own account. Neither Owens nor Butler is credited with successfully changing the prevailing views of military colleagues over the course of the NPR.

There was skepticism about the NPR among career bureaucrats as well, including some who had witnessed these kinds of bold initiatives before, usually early in new administrations before appointees have the chance to become seasoned by the realities of government service. Frank Miller, in particular, the respected Pentagon authority on nuclear issues who became Carter's principal deputy after serving in four previous administrations, had been part of many policy struggles between appointees and the established bureaucracy, not least in his effort to temper the assault on deterrence policy launched by enthusiasts of the Strategic Defense Initiative in the early years of the Reagan administration.

Miller saw himself as the new appointees' link to the institutional memory—and institutional minefields—that had to be considered before launching a challenge to the nuclear establishment. Miller bore the scars of past clashes between appointees and careerists and had learned how to be a "samurai

11. Interview with former Pentagon official, June 1994.

bureaucrat" according to a colleague. As he saw it, he would help educate and protect his boss, tempering Carter's more brash tendencies while interpreting Carter's tasking orders in terms that the bureaucracy could understand.

Miller was more deeply skeptical of Soviet, now Russian, intentions than some members of the new administration seemed and was particularly concerned about unilateral U.S. concessions to Russia until the evidence for Russian conversion to democracy was more compelling. He had one basic metric for nuclear deterrence: simply put, U.S. nuclear forces were needed in quantities sufficient to destroy enemy nuclear launch sites. As long as Russian forces capable of attacking the United States were deployed and operational, there was no question that the United States needed alert and highly capable forces for full target coverage. Russian rhetoric about peace and partnership or the demands of third world states for greater political equity were simply not a sufficient basis for deactivating or reducing U.S. capabilities below a critical level.

Miller also had most recently spearheaded the Bush administration's targeting review, including what he calls "a quiet revolution" in nuclear planning that had resulted in scaling back the Single Integrated Operational Plan, the centralized plan for U.S. strategic nuclear war operations, and provisions for more "adaptive" targeting that in theory could provide the president with a greater range of nuclear options in a crisis. The perception among some officials involved in the Bush review was that this exercise had answered the question of how much is enough (although the number of needed warheads has continued to change, from 4,700 in 1992 to 3,500 in 1995 to 2,000–2,500 currently.) Consolidating the nuclear commands into a single entity under the Strategic Command, Miller believed, had finally created a coherent system to integrate doctrine, targeting, and force requirements. Not least among the factors driving his judgment was the degree to which he had earned a place at the table in the inner sanctum of the nuclear planning community, a hard-won victory that depended on amicable working relationships.

Miller was thus not seized with the urgency that Carter and some of his subordinates came to express about operational risks of the nuclear posture or the supposed pressures imposed on decisionmakers by a policy requiring forces to be launched promptly to have any assurance of survival. He disagreed with Carter and others who argued that a president would be faced with a stark use or lose choice in crisis, precluding alternative options. He was convinced that many of these problems had been tackled in 1991 and were already being resolved.[12]

12. Interview with Pentagon official, September 1996.

Miller's conception of a revolution in nuclear operations achieved in the Bush administration, however, did not track with the more radical ambitions of some of his new colleagues, one of whom caustically dismissed Miller's previous reforms as "an amelioration of evil."[13] What changes may have been made earlier were cosmetic, at best, according to critics. "These plans were just the old SIOP, doing everything we were doing before, but just smaller only because the Russian target base had shrunk," said one.[14] The criteria for targeting had not changed significantly since the height of the cold war, based on the planning staff's sense of what was needed to destroy what adversaries most valued, from nuclear weapons to leadership to "other military targets." Target criteria allowed for great latitude in interpretation, allowing multiple weapons to be targeted against not just nuclear forces but nuclear storage sites, petroleum facilities, and the manufacturing base, for example, notwithstanding the claim that the category of "war-supporting" industry (which had allowed for such miscellaneous targets as shoe factories in previous plans) had been deemphasized. As one participant summed it up, "Opponents of change defined deterrence as 'what has to be held at risk' in the target base, going after what the adversary values. If he values his grandma, we have to target grandmas."[15]

Miller and Carter in fact had different conceptions of the purpose of the NPR, according to several accounts. For Miller this was an opportunity to analyze who the "bad guys and potential bad guys" were, identify what they valued, and determine accordingly what, if anything, needed to be changed in the existing plans to sustain a credible deterrent. The purpose was to identify a deterrent strategy for a new threat environment, not a new targeting strategy.

For Carter and others the basic premise of maintaining a centralized nuclear attack plan, a model for redundant targeting of a vast array of Russian and other military assets that was poised for massive and prompt launch, was a dangerous atavism of the cold war. The commitment to initiate the prompt use of nuclear weapons at the strategic or theater level was not consistent with post–cold war imperatives, where the risk of deliberate attack was far less urgent than inadvertent or accidental launch prompted by miscalculation.[16] At its core the problem was that the United States and Russia maintained target coverage requirements that could not be satisfied after

13. Interview with former Pentagon official, August 1996.
14. Interview with Pentagon official, June 1996.
15. Interview with former Pentagon official, August 1996.
16. The logic underlying the need to shift doctrinal and targeting assumptions after the cold war is discussed in detail in chapter 4.

an attack. Therefore, both sides were operating a hair-trigger plan, a strategy rendered even more high risk by the fragile and worsening conditions in Russia.

The Pentagon was thus about to launch a review of nuclear policy that involved fundamental theological differences about nuclear weapons between appointees and career officials, and even in some cases among appointees, according to several accounts.[17] The basic character of deterrence was in dispute, a metaphor for broader disagreements over the utility of nuclear weapons after the cold war and even the extent to which the Russian threat had changed. At least two conceptual frameworks were represented and bound to collide: a vision of nuclear security that deemphasized reliance on preplanned targeting and prompt operations in favor of "mutual assured safety" and cooperative nuclear risk reduction, and the opposing view that the uncertain nature of changes in Russia and that state's predilection for aggression compelled adherence to classic deterrence as well as new nuclear options for emerging threats.

Questions drafted under Carter's direction were added to the agreed terms of reference to set the agenda for the individual working groups, each of which was assigned specific areas of inquiry: force structure and infrastructure; plans, operations, and command and control; and counterproliferation policy. Carter asked the groups to consider issues well outside the norm: to develop options that eliminated all prompt counterforce weapons, consider ways the alert level of U.S. and Russian forces could be significantly reduced, explore the linkage between the U.S. nuclear force posture and third world incentives for proliferation, and consider whether the United States should formally renounce the right to initiate the use of nuclear weapons as part of its nonproliferation strategy. Carter was most preoccupied with promoting safety over promptness of response, pushing for the elimination of the hair-trigger alert status of the two sides' forces and the de facto doctrine of launch on warning.

The working groups were provided with briefing materials to inform discussion and help answer the questions posed to them. A stream of outside experts, some, such as Brookings Institution analysts Bruce Blair and John Steinbruner, known for their less than orthodox views, were also invited to give briefings. Several put forward arguments in favor of major innovations— why the United States should take its strategic forces off alert, for example, or why prompt counterforce response was a high-risk strategy that was no longer needed. Officials "gave a polite reception" to the outsiders, accord-

17. Interviews with several participants in the review conducted in 1996–97.

ing to one account, or "looked puzzled beyond redemption," according to another.[18] Members of the working groups tended to treat experts' articles and papers as obscure academic treatises, remote from the realities of operational planning. According to one participant, some were actually counterproductive. A briefing book provided by one private expert presenting the case for policies for no first use, negative security assurances, and other steps for reducing nuclear dangers, for example, "just provided people with a concise list of what to argue against."[19]

The most important divisions in the NPR were sparked by Carter's attempt to force the bureaucracy to develop options that, in his view, would devise a new targeting strategy that could harmonize U.S. operational policy and the criteria for force requirements in support of a stated declaratory doctrine of strict retaliation. If U.S. policy is to deter adversaries by maintaining forces capable of surviving and responding to an attack, it follows that forces be made sufficiently survivable to ride out an attack and still be able to launch a devastating retaliatory blow that would preclude any perceived advantage to the aggressor. A policy of riding out an attack eliminated the need for (and reduced the risk of) forces configured for rapid reaction.

Force requirements should be planned accordingly, eliminating vulnerable systems that require prompt launch to survive (such as fixed, multiple-warhead ICBMs) and getting rid of outmoded operational notions at odds with a policy of retaliation. This would allow for radical restructuring and reduction of forces and alert levels while still maintaining a credible deterrent against any conceivable adversary.

Most of the career military and civilian officials involved in the review, however, overwhelmingly opposed the idea that a policy of ride-out or proposals to de-alert forces be allowed to replace or preclude existing options, including launch on warning, whatever the perceived political logic. For some, any deviation from a posture that allowed for a variety of launch options, up to massive and early launch if the situation warranted it, by definition weakened deterrence. Reserving a variety of launch options accepted the tension between the implied message imparted by the configuration of forces and how a decision to launch would actually take place. As a former air force chief of staff explained, this is essential given "the concern over giving the attacker, no matter how remote the potential, the comfort of a formal U.S. ride-out policy." As in several other instances, the logic hinges

18. Interview with former Pentagon official, December 1996.
19. Interview with former Pentagon official, June 1996.

on the need to heighten the uncertainty of potential enemies about U.S. plans, a direct contradiction of the view that deliberately reducing Russia's uncertainty was an urgent imperative to increase stability and prospects for cooperative nuclear reductions.

A central question raised in this discussion was what constituted a "requirement." Carter's view was that requirements should reflect what was needed to maintain a survivable force poised for retaliation. Opponents argued that nuclear force requirements had to be driven by what would best destroy particular target sets, particularly high-priority targets such as an enemy's forces. Many senior officers had long acknowledged that a successful, disarming strike against Russian forces was implausible, but the preparation for such operations still remained vital to the strategy of deterrence. As one participant summarized it, "This leads to the paradox of force requirements being driven by the scenario of prompt response," even if such a contingency is understood to be unlikely.[20] Other proposals to change the character of targeting as such—deemphasizing plans to hold nuclear forces at risk, for example, in favor of countermilitary (conventional) forces—also met with skepticism.

Nuclear forces were diminished in numbers, but their configuration was believed by many, consciously or not, to require essential conformity with previous arrangements. Each leg of the nuclear triad had to be preserved and options for continued modernization carefully protected. Any move to vastly reduce or eliminate the ICBM force was particularly resisted at Strategic Command. "That is something we at STRATCOM feel strongly about," said air force Lieutenant General Arlen D. Jamison, the Strategic Command's deputy commander in chief, emphasizing the already diminished status of nuclear forces and cuts in the stockpile.[21] As the NPR ensued, the Strategic Command relied on its own analysis of the capabilities required under any conceivable level of negotiated force reductions, plans that placed heavy emphasis on flexibility, readiness, and prompt response as the precondition for fewer weapons.

In addition to strategic policy, some of the questions concerned one of the most sensitive issues facing the administration: whether and how nuclear weapons could be used against not only nuclear but nonnuclear regional threats. The subject had been debated among officials in the previous admin-

20. Interview with former Pentagon official, December 1996.
21. Cited in Bill Gertz, "The New Nuclear Policy: Lead But Hedge," *Air Force Magazine*, vol. 78 (January 1995), p. 6. As Gertz emphasizes, "The real news of (the NPR) is what it did not change. . . . The NPR made no apparent shift in the underlying concept of deterrence" (p. 35).

istration, including as part of a nuclear targeting review initiated by Secretary of Defense Richard Cheney. Quasi-official reports stressing the need to devise nuclear plans for third world contingencies were released publicly, prompting media and public criticism.[22] The Clinton administration distanced itself from these conclusions, deferring to the political sensitivities of the upcoming NPT review conference by reiterating the standing policy that the United States does not target nonnuclear countries. But the debate intensified internally, especially in light of the discovery in January 1992 of a nuclear program in North Korea that precipitated a flurry of diplomatic and military threats against Pyongyang.[23] The issue was to reemerge several times after 1994 and prompted a revision of formal U.S. policy, as is discussed later.

The Outcome

The bureaucratic arrangements set up to conduct the NPR were an early indication that the endeavor would fall short of Aspin's ambitions. The NPR was organized to delegate work to the Pentagon bureaucracy, particularly mid- to lower-level officials, many of whom had little background in nuclear issues and for whom the political dimensions of nuclear deterrence were not particularly compelling. Like the Bottom Up Review and the Quadrennial Defense Review that followed it, the NPR was organized in a way that inhibited discussions of broad dimensions of policy, with individual groups disaggregated by subject area in an elaborate staffing scheme that operated without benefit of sustained senior leadership.

Some more senior military officers and career officials appointed to over-

22. A study group commissioned by then Commander of the Strategic Air Command Lee Butler and chaired by former Secretary of the Air Force Thomas Reed released a report in late 1991 that highlighted the risks of failing to prepare nuclear responses against nuclear, chemical, and biological threats from regional adversaries. As Reed testified before Congress in January 1992, "It is not difficult to entertain nightmarish visions in which a future Saddam Hussein threatens American forces abroad, U.S. allies or friends, and perhaps even the United States itself with nuclear, biological, or chemical weapons. If that were to happen, U.S. nuclear weapons may well be a resource for seeking to deter execution of the threat." Cited in William M. Arkin, "Agnosticism When Real Values Are Needed: Nuclear Policy in the Clinton Administration," F.A.S. Public Interest Report, *Journal of the Federation of American Scientists*, vol. 47 (September-October 1994), p. 7.

23. Although North Korea had long been included in targeting scenarios as a hostile state allied with China, until recently considered a nuclear-armed enemy, the discovery of a clandestine program in North Korea itself reinvigorated discussions about the limitations of conventional forces in deterring motivations for or actually destroying countries' nuclear capabilities.

see the effort not only were opposed to the radical departures being put forward by political appointees, but, as they became increasingly obvious, not supportive of the overall review process. Generals Barry McCaffrey and Wesley Clark, in particular, "hopelessly outmatched Carter in the art of bureaucracy," according to a participant.[24]

The situation worsened when it became clear that few senior officials inside or outside the Pentagon wanted to be associated with the review after its inception, especially on occasions when a controversy threatened to or did erupt publicly. John Deutch and Admiral Owens were exceptions. Deutch, however, was widely perceived to be interested mainly in finding savings from nuclear cuts; he lost interest in force restructuring when it was demonstrated that the savings would be offset by higher initial costs for dismantling and related activities. Admiral Owens, for his part, is said to have been vocal in his criticism of existing nuclear policies and even to have proposed some radical reforms of his own, but he was never willing to fight for his views when he encountered opposition. And the president and his close White House advisers never indicated clearly that they had a stake in the outcome.

The enduring problem was that the working groups were simply ignoring Carter's assignments to come up with wide-ranging options. The groups continued instead to generate graphs and analysis in support of a steadily growing consensus emphasizing the need to maintain the structure, doctrine, and force levels of the current posture, to go no lower than the limits set for START II, and to oppose consideration of other, even minor, innovations.

Whether they had clear guidance and directives is open to question. As Carter became involved in competing policy priorities, operational control for the working groups fell increasingly to Frank Miller and the senior military officials. According to several accounts, Miller had consistently set about to help deflect some of the more radical ideas being put forward by Carter, either by trying to persuade him of the inevitable backlash of moving too ambitiously or by recasting directives to blunt their predictably abrasive impact.

By January 1994 the working group that had been asked to answer "why we need nuclear weapons" presented its results to Deutch. The conclusions not only championed the cold war status quo but were so pedestrian that Carter declared the session "a disaster."[25]

Carter took action, appointing two people on temporary assignment to

24. Interview with former Pentagon official, August 1996.
25. Interview with former Pentagon official, June 1996.

the Pentagon to try to rescue the review: Steve Fetter, a University of Maryland professor trained in physics who was active in arms control debates, and Lieutenant Commander Leo Mackay, a naval officer who had written his Harvard doctoral dissertation on nuclear strategy under Carter's direction and was serving as Carter's military assistant. It was an unconventional solution, to say the least. Carter arranged for the two to receive high-level clearances needed for full access to the relevant planning documents, in itself a bureaucratic precedent. According to Fetter, Carter then declared Fetter "in charge of organizing the next NPR briefings . . . but without ever telling any one else that they should cooperate with or support me."[26] Miller, for example, found out about the unorthodox arrangements by accident.

Fetter and Mackay set about to construct alternative targeting strategies and force postures, conducting independent analyses of the assumptions being used to evaluate plans and requirements, from the calculation of force exchange ratios to the cost of alternative force configurations. They analyzed proposals for radical changes in detail, including postures operating with much smaller strategic forces, different targeting doctrines, a dyad with no land-based missiles, and the removal of remaining nuclear weapons from Europe.

These proposals were then taken to the staff in Miller's office (Nuclear Forces Policy) who were in charge of preparing the official briefing materials, the approved view graphs that would be used to present the arguments to Deutch and Owens. Fetter and Mackay encountered immediate resistance but were able to overcome initial objections by pulling rank. After each draft was produced, however, a small group convened in Miller's office to "haggle over the wording," as one put it. Although no proposed options were actually deleted at this point, "this was an opportunity for Frank to improve the 'pros' for his preferred (status quo) option, and the 'cons' for the new options."[27]

Even as the official working groups were continuing to meet, Carter arranged to present some of the findings of his counterreview to Deutch and Owens in two briefings between March and April 1994. The briefings to Deutch included analysis of six options, which ranged from the perfunctory discussion of the status quo to eliminating the land-based leg of the triad to a minimum deterrent force at very low levels. The analysis presented detailed plans for the forces needed to fulfill deterrence requirements under different operational assumptions, including different ways to calculate damage

26. Interview with Steve Fetter, December 1996.
27. Correspondence with former Pentagon official, February 1997.

expectancies and other planning criteria. The original mandate of the review was to explore these kinds of options, answering the basic question of how the nuclear force posture could fulfill strategic and political objectives with less risk, lower costs, and greater compatibility with the changes in the threat environment.

Although there was brief discussion of the status quo option in these sessions, the core of the analysis tried to demonstrate empirically how a policy of prompt launch under alert conditions distorted the level of requirements well beyond what was needed for post–cold war deterrence. Even if unstated as a matter of policy, the emphasis on the ability to launch promptly, the briefers argued, had created conditions that undermined the credibility of U.S. assurances to Russia that it would use nuclear weapons only in retaliation. The ambiguity of U.S. intentions reflected in the difference between stated policy and the operational posture, they asserted, could prompt an adversary to strike first in a crisis for fear of having no retaliatory capability left after a U.S. strike.

The arguments in favor of a fully operational ride-out force were consistent with Carter's concerns about operational safety and supported a U.S. policy of retaliation. The core of the arguments emphasized the risks imposed by the disjuncture between a stated policy of retaliation and operational practices that were biased against riding out an attack. The long-standing mismatch between political assumptions about the utility of nuclear weapons and actual plans, to say nothing of the resulting inflation in force requirements, had lost any justification after the demise of the Soviet Union, the briefers argued. More important, the discord increasingly interfered with efforts to achieve agreements for greater force reductions and operational safety with Russia, measures needed to hedge against the more credible threat of a nuclear crisis precipitated by the collapse of the Russian government's tenuous political control.

The idea that ambiguity is a virtue for deterrence was presented in these briefings as anathema for achieving greater stability with Russia. The arguments also assaulted the logic that was dominating the analysis of the working groups, which argued that deterrence was best served by keeping a variety of launch options and a triad of forces that definitely included land-based missiles. The debate, in short, was a microcosm of the divergent perceptions of how to manage U.S.-Russian relations after the cold war.

It was the second briefing to Deutch, scheduled for April 22, 1994, that ultimately "triggered a revolt" in the Pentagon, according to Mackay.[28] Prior

28. Interview with Leo Mackay, August 1996.

dissemination of Carter's briefing charts among the Chiefs and the Joint Staff set off alarm bells when it was discovered that Carter would be presenting Deutch with proposals to drastically reduce or eliminate the ICBM force, consider taking the force off alert, and even more radical proposals. Reacting to a leaked copy of the briefing (or, in actuality a copy of one of the several drafts circulating around the Pentagon), four deputy chiefs for operations and plans from each of the services sent a letter to Joint Staff Director Vice Admiral Richard Macke objecting to Carter's freelance operation and insisting that the briefing be canceled.[29]

Only two of the options to be presented to Deutch had been vetted by the working groups, the officers complained, while any decision to eliminate ICBMs or otherwise modify the triad had been vehemently opposed in the working groups. The office of the Secretary of Defense, they charged, had violated the terms of the review by ignoring the duly appointed representatives of the Joint Chiefs of Staff, who were still meeting in the official process, and by putting forward its own options without consultation. The Office of the Secretary of Defense, moreover, was not authorized to do targeting analysis. Just the idea of "off-line" briefings were heresy for the military officers and career professionals, particularly based on analysis from subordinates who had been given access to planning documents and targeting data in violation of accepted protocol.

The letter, intended to prevent Carter from briefing Deutch and to force the review back into the working groups, was leaked to Congress. It surfaced on April 20 during a Senate Armed Services Committee hearing receiving testimony from Commander of the U.S. Strategic Command Admiral Henry Chiles. Asked by ranking minority member Strom Thurmond if he supported the elimination of land-based missiles, Chiles hastened to reassure the senator that no such proposal had been seriously entertained in the NPR working groups. To the contrary, "ICBMs are necessary in our force of the future and I believe we have argued that point within the Nuclear Posture Review." In the same hearing Chiles also cautioned against a policy of riding out nuclear attacks, linking the danger of this posture to the threat of "rogue leaders in the world" who would no longer be deterred.[30]

29. The letter was signed by Air Force Acting Deputy Chief of Staff for Plans and Operations Major General Larry Henry, Army Operations Deputy Lieutenant General John Tilelli, Navy Assistant Deputy Chief of Naval Operations for Plans, Policy and Operations Rear Admiral John Redd, and Marine Corps Acting Operations Deputy to the Joint Chiefs of Staff Brigadier General Thomas Wilkerson. See Elaine Grossman, "Four Services Sign Letter to Block Carter's Nuclear Posture Briefing," *Inside the Air Force*, vol. 5, April 29, 1994, pp. 1, 8–9.

30. *Department of Defense Authorization for Appropriations for FY95 and the Future Years Defense Program*, Hearings before the Senate Committee on Armed Services, 103 Cong. 2 sess., pt. 1, p. 995.

The hearing thus put the head of the Strategic Command on record as opposing substantive changes in the force posture before the conclusion of the review.

These incidents escalated into opportunities for partisan attack against the Clinton administration. Four Republican senators sent a letter to the president objecting to Carter's attempts to make an end run on the NPR, for example: "it is our understanding that (despite the conclusion of the working group supporting START II force levels), a force structure that eliminates the land-based leg of the Triad is still being considered, and may be the preferred option of the NPR's chairman." The letter went on to emphasize the hazards of such a proposal, including the sudden vulnerability of the United States to a first strike. "Using only a handful of weapons, any nation with ICBM capability could mortally wound the U.S.'s ability to defend itself simply by attacking our bomber bases, submarine bases, and Command, Control and Communications centers." The letter notes that this threat would emerge not only from Russia but "China and other nations."[31]

Carter's second briefing to Deutch went forward despite objections. One participant claims that Deutch found the case for eliminating ICBMs compelling during this session. Concerns about operational safety aside, Deutch was reportedly attracted by the savings that would result from not having to rebuild the Minuteman III force over the next ten to fifteen years, which otherwise would need investment for new motors and guidance packages.

Any moves in this direction, however, were apparently distracted by a further uprising of internal opposition directed against Carter. The most dramatic showdown occurred in a meeting of regional commanders, initiated to "call Ash on the carpet," according to one report. The generals stated many of the same objections that had been expressed in the letter to Macke, but in a much more pointed and, some say, brutal way. The final argument was that Carter had no authority to present options to the secretary of defense or any other political appointee unless these proposals had been considered and approved by the working groups.

Carter was said to be visibly shaken and tried to reason with the officers, arguing that it is not appropriate for colonels and lower-level military personnel to craft U.S. national policy. The briefings with Deutch were exploratory: "They were just options," he was said to argue in his defense. He had presented the full range of possibilities, including retaining the sta-

---

31. The letter was signed by Senators Conrad Burns (Mont.), Malcolm Wallop (Wyo.), Alan Simpson (Wyo.), and Dirk Kempthorne (Idaho). The full text is cited in Grossman, "Four Services," p. 9.

tus quo, and had no intention of subverting the Joint Chiefs. His pleas fell on deaf ears. For the disaffected officers who hovered outside the door and gloated while the meeting was under way, Carter had finally been properly chastised.[32]

Watching Carter get his head handed to him may have given his critics cheap thrills, but it was not a good precedent for civil-military relations. Even if the political repercussions of conducting a counter-review were predictable, the incident raised serious issues about civilian authority. No one at senior political levels, however, defended Carter's right to carry out his study, even if it could be argued that it was the only way to carry out directives from the secretary of defense in the face of determined bureaucratic roadblocks. In retrospect, one senior civilian official who was centrally involved even questions whether there was any significance to these events. "We had to do this by consensus," he argued; "there's a difference between a breakdown of authority and abiding by the rules of consensus."[33] That said, it is not clear why civilian appointees were given a mandate to oversee a policy review if they were not going to be granted the authority to carry it out. President Bush had given full support to his deputies (including Secretary of Defense Richard Cheney, Chairman of the Joint Chiefs Colin Powell, and National Security Adviser Brent Scowcroft) to override bureaucratic obstacles and implement directives known to have his full commitment. The outcome of a study of reforms of the nuclear posture conducted by consensus among mid-level officers and career officials was a preemptive fait accompli, a way to ensure ratification of the status quo.

From that point the NPR became an exercise in face-saving or "slapping a happy face" on what was left of this disastrous initiative, as another participant put it.[34] The remaining discussion was highly circumscribed, focusing mostly on modest cuts unrelated to doctrine, such as reductions in Minuteman III missiles, from 500 to 300–350, and limits on the number of B-52s and B-2 bombers. A proposal to store nuclear warheads separately from ICBMs, supported by Carter and considered briefly as a possible initiative to be presented to President Boris Yeltsin when he came to Washington for a summit in September, was opposed by the air force and languished.[35]

32. Interviews with NPR participants, conducted 1996–97.

33. Interview with former Deputy Secretary of Defense John Deutch, February 1997.

34. Interview with Steve Fetter, June 1996.

35. See Elaine Grossman, "At Last Minute, Nuclear Posture Review Supports 450–500 ICBMs—for Now," *Inside the Air Force*, September 23, 1994, p 10. The public accounts of conflicts between Carter and military officers, however, are disputed by one key participant. Referring in particular to the meeting between Carter and the three star generals, this person claimed that it was entirely about process. "The services didn't feel adequately involved but

Most of the NPR's final deliberations were promptly leaked to congressional critics and thus were adjudicated in a highly charged political environment. A letter from Chiles to Perry that was leaked to Congress in September saying Chiles could not support anything less than 500 ICBMs, for example, added to the pressure on Deutch and Perry to avoid further congressional controversies. Intense maneuvering and backpedaling continued until the day before the results of the NPR were to be presented to the president.[36]

In the end Carter's office produced thirty-seven pages of charts and diagrams for public release (along with classified materials provided to brief the president), recommending that there be no significant changes in the nuclear weapons policies of Clinton's predecessor. Forces would go no lower than START II levels, nuclear weapons would be retained in Europe at current levels, and there would be no serious alterations in U.S. operational policies. Secretary Perry was provided with several rationales for the decision to avoid major departures from the past, including the disparity in the pace of dismantling U.S. and Russian forces mandated by START (which could lead to U.S. "numerical inferiority") and the uncertainty in Russia and the danger of a resurgence of an adversary "still armed with 25,000 nuclear weapons." For all its travails, the new policy approved by the president ended up trimming the numbers of Trident submarines and B-52 bombers and proclaiming a firm commitment to a "lead and hedge" strategy with options to upload and reconstitute U.S. forces should the cold war return.[37]

The review reaffirmed the central importance of retaining a triad of strategic forces based on "the leading edge of technology" and in sufficient numbers to "hedge against a reversal of reforms and the nuclear reductions process and a return to an authoritarian military regime in Russia hostile to the United States," as well as to provide for a reserve force in the event of nuclear aggression by a third party.[38] The NPR also imposed requirements on the Department of Energy to maintain the viability of nuclear weapons without testing, including the ability to design and produce new warheads, maintain a robust science and technology infrastructure, and ensure adequate supplies of tritium.

---

that was no big deal," he explained. To the degree there was any friction, it occurred outside the Pentagon: "[Robert] Bell at the NSC or [Undersecretary of State Lynn] Davis at State were resentful that DOD had control," but the military, especially Lieutenant Generals Clark and McCaffrey, were always "good collaborators." Telephone interview, January 1997.

36. Grossman, "At Last Minute," p 10.

37. Speech delivered by William J. Perry, Henry L. Stimson Center's 1994 Award for Public Service Ceremony, Decatur House, Washington, September 20, 1994.

38. William J. Perry, *Annual Report to the President and the Congress*, Defense Department, February 1995, p. 10.

Finally, the effort to force consideration of reforms proved remarkable only in the extent to which it ratified a nuclear order that even helped to slow the momentum of the Bush administration's arms control initiatives. The NPR's outcome also directly contradicted Aspin's original mandate, moving from "where do we go after START II," as he had put it, to what to do under the constraints of START I and II. The NPR formalized the administration's commitment to a strategy of hedging, a concept that came to define other aspects of policy as well—from commitment to a robust program of "stockpile safety" to preserve vital aspects of the nuclear infrastucture to the reasons given for opposing de-alerting schemes that could undercut the U.S. ability to "reconstitute a nuclear fighting force" in crisis, in the words of a senior White House official.

Eventually, a shifting political climate, including the conservative shift in congressional opinion after the 1994 election and growing tensions with Russia over NATO expansion and the Duma's reluctance to ratify START II, gave those who had argued against any significant deemphasis of nuclear forces a sense of vindication. It was right to temper the excesses of reformers, they agreed, a conclusion that the administration has never seen fit to challenge.

Paradoxically, one senior appointee with central authority for the NPR has since disclaimed that there was ever any serious intent to change the U.S. force posture or overall policy. According to this person's recollection, there was consensus among top officials as early as late 1993 that the international climate precluded consideration of any significant changes in the nuclear force posture. "It would have been idiotic to take unilateral reductions beyond START II before getting START I implemented and START II ratified," he stressed, claiming that only "self-absorbed arms controllers and unilateral disarmers" ever argued to the contrary. "We always knew it was not the right time to change the force posture," he continued, not for reasons of domestic politics but because of "historical realities," including the confused conditions in Russia and the more immediate need to move forward with other initiatives, such as eliciting Ukrainian agreement for removing nuclear weapons from its soil.[39] The real issue was not the U.S. force posture, but "how to deal with the breakup of the Soviet Union, get START I implemented, and START II ratified."[40]

39. As for changes in operational practices, such as de-alerting, "we went into the review thinking de-alerting was a good way to go, but there was nothing there," he explained. "We even invited Bruce Blair to give a briefing [about de-alerting options]," but according to this account, Blair's proposals "just didn't pass the laugh test." Telephone interview, February 1997.

40. This person is remembered by others as extremely active in efforts to get the bureau-

It is not clear exactly why or exactly when progress in START beyond a hedged START II posture came to be seen as politically or substantively incompatible with U.S. nuclear objectives, at least as a concern prompted by international developments. The severe technical and political constraints in Russia that delayed START I implementation and continue to impede START II ratification were problems recognized in 1994. Could the United States have helped alleviate the pressures on Russia and have achieved its own arms control objectives by moving more quickly toward START III or by other measures to reassure the Russian government, as are now being considered?[41] Although the answer for many would be obviously yes, it was simply "out of the question," according to a former official who was instrumental in the conduct of the NPR. Despite repeatedly emphasizing that international realities precluded such actions, his core concern seems to better reflect domestic politics: "Do you really think Clinton would have been reelected if he had moved, without START I or START II, to go unilaterally to START III?"[42]

The political climate for Russian supporters of START was noticeably (and predictably) damaged by the rhetoric in the NPR, which questioned the motives of Russia in being slow to dismantle weapons in compliance with START I or stressed the importance of U.S. nuclear weapons to hedge against a resurgent Russian adversary. Ironically, the hedge strategy proved to be a self-fulfilling prophesy, adding an irritant in U.S.-Russian relations and lending credibility to the anti-Western hawks in the Duma who were resisting nuclear reductions as part of their strategy to discredit U.S. motives. When the new study was presented to Russian leaders and military officers in New York and subsequently in Moscow, it met with overt hostility. Instead of helping pro-Western politicians who had hoped the review would provide them with ammunition to prove that the United States was now a partner, it instead "provoked a sigh of relief on the part of those people who

---

cracy to develop options for significant departures from existing policy. In his recollection such initiatives actually came from "good young people" at the special assistant level who had no authority—the "Fetter types." Driven by personal convictions about the need for "minimum deterrence" and "unilateral arms control," they were never in synchronization with the objectives and beliefs of senior officials like Deutch or Perry: "these guys did good, quality work, but there was never any use for it," he concluded. Telephone interview, February 1997.

41. Efforts were made at the March 1997 Helsinki Summit to consider ways to overcome the continued reluctance of the Russian Duma to ratify START II, by agreeing to a "framework" agreement for START III allowing Russia and the United States to move toward a level of 2,000–2,500 weapons. The Duma has still not ratified the agreement.

42. Interview with Pentagon official, February 1997.

didn't believe our relations were changing," according to Duma member Alexei Arbatov.[43]

Belatedly, the Duma's hostile reception of William Perry when he traveled to Moscow in 1997 to present the case for START II persuaded him that the United States had to offer inducements as part of the ratification bargain. This led to a framework agreement to allow the two sides to move to a level of 2,000–2,500 deployed weapons, the baseline for START III. The Joint Chiefs supported Perry in proposing such a move, partly out of concern about the costs of the hedge strategy (for which funds had not been programmed beyond 1998) and as part of a larger bargain to modify operational plans. Perry was not so lucky with Congress, for whom the threat to return to START I is seen as an important bargaining chip to induce the Russians to ratify START II—a view shared by many administration officials—and who continue to legislate against unilateral reductions in U.S. forces.

Reverting to the practice of its predecessors, the administration conducted a closely guarded analysis in 1997 of the presidential guidance for U.S. nuclear policy, a review that included only a handful of people from the White House and the Pentagon. The study resulted in a new presidential decision directive (PDD-60) that revises the formal guidance adopted during the Reagan administration calling for the ability of U. S. nuclear forces to "prevail even under the condition of a prolonged war."[44] The notion of prevailing in a nuclear war was widely considered a chimerical mission even with massive nuclear forces. But the formal recognition of this reality after sixteen years was reportedly prompted by Commander of the Strategic Command General Eugene Habiger and Chairman of the Joint Chiefs General John Shalikashvili, who had informed the president in February 1996 that existing directives for nuclear strategy "could not be met if the U.S. arsenal was reduced much below the ceiling of 3,000 to 3,500 weapons set by the 1993 START II Treaty with Russia."[45]

43. Quoted in Ottaway and Coll, "Trying to Unplug the War Machine," *Washington Post*, April 12, 1995, p. A1. According to their account, a briefing presented by Carter and Perry to Russian Defense Minister Pavel Grachev provoked unintended antagonism when an interpreter translated "lead" in the "lead and hedge" strategy as "dominate" and "hedge" as either "shrubbery" or the "ability to break out from treaty commitments." The more substantive reasons for opposition included Russian concerns about the renewed American commitment to "hard-target kill" targeting options and preparations for prompt operations, including alert levels for missile forces.

44. See chapter 4 for further discussion; and R. Jeffrey Smith, "Clinton Directive Changes Strategy on Nuclear Arms; Centering on Deterrence, Officials Drop Terms for Long Atomic War," *Washington Post*, December 7, 1997, p. A1.

45. See chapter 4 for further discussion; and Smith, "Clinton Directive," p. A1.

As articulated by Robert Bell, the National Security Council senior director for defense policy and arms control who spearheaded the study (along with Frank Miller in the Pentagon), the directive has shifted from prevailing in or winning a nuclear conflict to a greater emphasis on deterrence. It does not alter existing requirements to be prepared to launch large or small nuclear strikes promptly in response to a nuclear attack, and it reaffirms the central importance of a triad of strategic forces. The directive also retains the option to initiate the use of nuclear weapons against aggressors, now modified to include nonnuclear nations who have "prospective access" to nuclear capabilities.

The Pentagon also initiated a study in 1998 of possible measures to reduce the alert status of U.S. and Russian forces. The study is still not completed, and its potential recommendations have not been discussed publicly. Several senior administration officials have expressed serious doubts about the feasibility and even the wisdom of de-alerting schemes, however. The fundamental basis for skepticism about constraints on operational readiness is in part based on doubts about whether the risk of inadvertent Russian nuclear attack is actually serious and whether any U.S.-proposed de-alerting measures would be seen by the Russians as anything but an effort to further compromise Russian security. For those who believe Russia is and will remain an aggressor, de-alerting schemes that seriously intrude on operational readiness are perceived as potentially compromising deterrence if they deny the ability of the United States to regenerate forces in crisis and impinge upon the training and planning infrastructure needed for prompt nuclear response. Even as the public debate about de-alerting seized the mainstream media and gained advocates such as former Senator Sam Nunn, administration advisers have resisted these ideas and implied that the bargain struck in gaining support of the Strategic Command for a 2,000–2,500 START III weapon level involved at least the tacit understanding that the readiness of forces not be changed markedly.[46]

Failure to move forward with START III, which may be an increasingly plausible outcome, could have a chilling effect on all aspects of U.S.-Russian cooperation and likely preclude any further progress toward reducing nuclear dangers. The reaffirmation of nuclear weapons by both sides could in turn presage a change in the politics of proliferation, undercutting the viability of cooperative denuclearization agreements and rendering meaningless the pledges made by the nuclear powers to reduce reliance on nuclear weapons as part of the global nonproliferation bargain. In the aftermath of

46. Interviews with NSC and Pentagon officials, 1997–98.

the Indian and Pakistani nuclear tests, moreover, serious concerns about the Non-Proliferation Treaty have eclipsed much of the optimism of the early 1990s. According to one commentator, "The clay of history is beginning to harden again."[47]

Targeting the Third World and the African Nuclear Weapons Free Zone

A critical part of the Nuclear Posture Review's mandate was to examine the role of nuclear weapons in deterring new regional adversaries. The NPR working group examining new missions for nuclear forces after the cold war focused on the adequacy of U.S. military responses to the threat of chemical and biological weapons proliferation, given the absence of commensurate U.S. chemical and biological weapon capabilities. The main question was whether conventional forces were "good enough" to deter unconventional threats, according to an official, and if not, how nuclear weapons could best be configured to fill the gap.[48]

The utility of nuclear weapons to deter use of third world nuclear weapons and other weapons of mass destruction had been a subject of growing debate among officials and experts since the late 1980s. Analysis of nuclear options against third world aggressors emerged from targeting reviews conducted by the air force and the Strategic Air Command even before the war against Iraq. The Nuclear Weapons Employment Policy (NUWEP) formulated in early 1991 and issued in 1992 under Secretary of Defense Dick Cheney, for example, initiated formal directives to plan for nuclear operations against countries with the potential to develop weapons of mass destruction.[49] The consolidation of strategic nuclear forces under the Strategic Command in

47. Quoted in R Jeffrey Smith, "Clinton Decides to Retain Bush Nuclear Arms Policy," *Washington Post*, September 22, 1994.

48. Interview with NSC official, May 1996.

49. For further discussion see, for example, Hans M. Kristensen and Joshua Handler, *Changing Targets: Nuclear Doctrine from the Cold War to the Third World* (Greenpeace Foundation, 1995), pp. 3–6. The NUWEP prompted studies commissioned by the Strategic Air Command to analyze nuclear weapons after the cold war, including the Reed Report, which outlined the need to expand the role of nuclear missions against regional adversaries, including a new SIOP to allow for a nuclear expeditionary force with "a handful of nuclear weapons, on alert, day to day" to use against China and other third world states. Another study issued by the navy in mid-1992 (known as STRATPLAN 2010) drew similar conclusions for naval strategy, including a nuclear reserve force with low-yield weapons, "providing a wider range of targeting options for maintaining a credible nuclear deterrence in the new world order." Cited in Kristensen and Handler, *Changing Targets*, p. 6.

1993 also had helped to advance planning innovations to allow for nuclear forces to be flexibly and rapidly retargeted against "spontaneous threats that defy precise preplanning"—so-called adaptive targeting—as well as to add new regional targets into existing plans.[50]

As pressures were mounting on the administration in 1994 to devise a diplomatic agenda that would elicit international support for the indefinite extension of the NPT, to be decided at the final review conference scheduled for April 1995, Pentagon planning was moving steadily toward a redefinition of nuclear missions for regional contingencies. Conventional wisdom was increasingly converging around the idea that whether or not the United States would launch nuclear strikes against a nonnuclear adversary, it was important to retain the ability to threaten nuclear use as part of a credible deterrent. U.S. nuclear forces were needed not just against nuclear states, moreover, or even just against states with chemical or biological weapons, but increasingly to deter the acquisition and development of such capabilities. As General Butler summarized it, U.S. nuclear forces would now be used to deter "any potentially hostile country that has or is seeking weapons of mass destruction."[51]

The tasking to come up with regional military options in the NPR overwhelmed the seriousness of directives issued by Carter to examine whether the United States could move to a policy of no first use. Renouncing the right to use nuclear weapons first, it was quickly concluded, would encourage rather than discourage aggression and proliferation among determined regional adversaries. Although based on scant and sometimes contradictory intelligence and expert reports, assessments of the coalition victory against Iraq, in particular, helped legitimate the importance of nuclear threats in deterring Saddam Hussein from launching chemical and perhaps biological weapons against Western forces and allies. The discovery of nuclear programs in North Korea and the continued intransigence of Iraq in resisting UN inspections helped fuel perceptions that diplomatic arrangements were useless against rogue states, adding to the urgency of developing military countermeasures.

50. Testimony of STRATCOM Commander General Lee Butler, February 1993, cited in Kristensen and Handler, *Changing Targets*, p 6. According to Bruce Blair, the restructuring of SAC into STRATCOM transferred responsibility for planning regional nuclear options from the regional commanders, allowing STRATCOM to take over target planning for strategic and nonstrategic forces against states that have weapons of mass destruction. Using adaptive planning and the reserve force (which can cover an estimated 1,000 targets), STRATCOM could implement a variety of attack options against regional threats in a matter of hours. See Blair, *Global Zero Alert for Nuclear Forces* (Brookings, 1995), p. 8.

51. Quoted in Kristensen and Handler, *Changing Targets*, p 6.

Press reports in March 1994 that the Pentagon was changing long-standing U.S. policy not to target nonnuclear states forced the administration to deny this publicly.[52] "The NGOs [nongovernmental organizations] went ballistic," according to an official, "and we were forced to kick the can."[53] The Non-Proliferation Treaty extension conference was imposing political discipline on the review process, at least temporarily. The NPR was duly silent on the subject of regional targeting, although additional controversies were provoked when Deutch, at the NPR press conference in October 1994 and again in congressional testimony shortly after, referred to the importance of nuclear threats to deter regional aggressors.[54]

By late 1994, U.S. officials, including the president, began to recognize that gaining majority support for NPT extension indefinitely and without conditions was not guaranteed. As part of a concerted strategy to persuade states to extend the treaty indefinitely and without conditions, the United States pledged its leadership on behalf of a series of disarmament measures, including the commitment to achieve a comprehensive test ban by 1996 and a ban on the production and stockpiling of weapons-usable fissile materials. On April 5, 1995, the day before the conference began, the president issued a statement that formally reinforced long-standing U.S. policy to forswear nuclear targeting of nonnuclear states that are parties to the NPT.[55] Taken together, the steps to shore up support for the NPT committed the United States to policies that renounced further nuclear modernization and codified so-called negative security assurances.

52. See "Mr Perry's Backward Nuclear Policy," *New York Times*, March 24, 1994, p. 22.

53. Interview with Pentagon official, May 1996.

54. Deutch also rejected the view that U.S. nuclear policies affect the motivation of states to proliferate. In testimony before the Senate Armed Services Committee, in response to questions from Senator Carl Levin (D-Mich.), he stated that "there is no connection between our nuclear posture and what India and Pakistan do or what Israel does." See *Briefing on Results of the Nuclear Posture Review*, Senate Committee on Armed Services, 103 Cong. 2 sess., p. 42.

55. "Clinton Issues Pledge to NPT Non-Nuclear Weapon States," Presidential declaration, U.S. Information Agency, April 6, 1995, crafted in detailed diplomatic parlance, said, "The United States reaffirms that it will not use nuclear weapons against non-nuclear-weapon states Parties to the Treaty on the Non-Proliferation of Nuclear Weapons except in the case of an invasion or any other attack on the United States, its territories, its armed forces or other troops, its allies, or on a State towards which it has a security commitment, carried out or sustained by such non-nuclear-weapon State in association or alliance with a nuclear-weapon state." A fact sheet that accompanied the president's declaration added, "It is the administration's view that the national statements being issued by all five NPT nuclear-weapon states, their co-sponsorship of a Security Council resolution on security assurances which is under consideration in New York, and the common negative security assurance achieved by four of the five—together comprise a substantial response to the desire of many NPT non-nuclear-weapon states for strengthened security assurances. This outcome reinforces the international nuclear proliferation regime and deserves the support of all NPT parties."

The conciliatory climate and success of the NPT extension conference notwithstanding, the internal security debate in the administration, especially in the Pentagon, was increasingly dominated by images of a Hobbesian world made up of aggressive and reckless rogue governments and terrorists posing ever growing threats to U.S. security, an anarchic world order often characterized as more dangerous than the cold war.[56] Conventional forces were increasingly perceived as insufficient to deter such states or to destroy the hardened underground bunkers being built to protect covert chemical and biological weapons programs, making the idea of a policy of no first use, let alone nuclear delegitimization, imprudent and misguided.

The debate was not fully joined, however, until early 1996, when it was sparked by the successful conclusion of the Africa Nuclear Weapons Free Zone Treaty. This agreement among forty-three African states obligates nuclear states under protocol I not to use or threaten to use nuclear weapons against any African state that is a party to the treaty. The Pelindaba agreement, named after the town in South Africa where a covert nuclear program had been conducted until its termination by President Nelson Mandela, originated as a call by eight African countries in 1960 in the United Nations to respect Africa as a nuclear weapons-free zone. Reinvigorated after the election of President Frederik DeKlerk in 1989, the final treaty was concluded in late 1995 and presented for signature by the nuclear powers.

According to several accounts, the agreement caught senior officials completely by surprise. As a White House official described his initial reaction, "who the hell negotiated this thing?"[57] After thirty-five years of quiet obscurity the ANWFZ was a somewhat ironic catalyst to force the administration to confront the tensions in its own nuclear policies. As a microcosm of the divisions in the administration, however, the deliberations over whether to sign are revealing.

From the outset there were two sets of policy objectives. From a political standpoint, it was assumed that the United States would sign the protocol committing it to a nonnuclear pledge and do so with enthusiasm, a view shared by the State Department, the Arms Control and Disarmament Agency, and, at least initially, the White House. The United States was a staunch supporter of nuclear-free zones and a signatory to similar agree-

56. As described by former Director of Central Intelligence James R. Woolsey, for example, this is a world in which "we have slain the [Soviet] dragon. But we now live in a jungle filled with a bewildering variety of poisonous snakes." Cited in Loch K. Johnson, "Strategic Intelligence and Weapons Proliferation," *Monitor,* Center for International Trade and Security, University of Georgia, vol. 1 (Spring 1995), p. 5.

57. Interview with NSC official, May 1996.

ments for Latin America and the South Pacific.[58] The prospect of using nuclear weapons in Africa was so implausible that it barely warranted consideration. President Mandela's support for the U.S. position at the NPT had been critical in persuading states to agree to its extension. Vice President Al Gore, moreover, was planning a trip to South Africa in April 1996 and wanted to announce U.S. signature of the protocol during his visit.

For Pentagon officials the prospect of signing a binding agreement to forswear the use of or threats to use nuclear weapons was unwise. U.S. policy regarding negative security assurances had never been seen in the Defense Department as legally binding, and it was considered vitally important to protect its status as "just a policy." As a practical matter the Defense Department interpretation was that the United States had always had the right to initiate the use of nuclear weapons in a crisis, a requirement that had grown in perceived importance in response to the spread of chemical and biological facilities in Iraq, Libya, and North Korea.

The timing perhaps could not have been worse. Secretary of Defense Perry had just issued a series of public warnings in March to Libya, a party to the ANWFZ, to stop its construction of an alleged underground chemical facility. The United States intended to prevent its completion, Perry stated in congressional testimony, and "is fully prepared to take more drastic, preventative measures to accomplish this."[59] Taken up in context of the broader discussion that the United States would consider nuclear responses to chemical attacks, Perry's statements were interpreted as a considered policy decision.

It was not just because of Libyan developments that the Pentagon opposed signing the protocol. Whereas other nuclear-free zone agreements had not involved countries with arsenals containing weapons of mass destruction, there was "a trend here," according to a critic, with the United States progressively forswearing its nuclear prerogative without adequate concern for the growing restrictions being placed on U.S. strategy.[60] It was, in some minds, the proverbial slippery slope.[61]

58. The Treaty for the Prohibition of Nuclear Weapons in Latin America (Treaty of Tlatelolco) was opened for signature in 1967 and now has twenty-seven Latin American and Caribbean contracting parties. Argentina, Chile, and Brazil became signatories in 1994. The United States is a party to two protocols to the treaty. The South Pacific Nuclear Free Zone Treaty (Treaty of Raratonga) was opened for signature in 1985 and now has eleven contracting parties. The United States signed the treaty's three Protocols on March 25, 1996.

59. Cited in Spurgeon M. Keeny Jr., "Nuclear Policy in Disarray," *Arms Control Today*, vol. 26 (April 1996), p. 2.

60. Interview with Pentagon official, June 1996.

61. Efforts to extend negative security assurances by formal agreement also sparked internal disputes on more than one occasion. Ambassador Robert Gallucci encountered Pentagon resistance when he proposed extending a binding pledge to North Korea as part of the frame-

In a flurry of ensuing acrimonious interagency discussions, lines were drawn around fundamentally contradictory views about nuclear weapons and U.S. interests in the third world. Officials at the State Department, Arms Control and Disarmament Agency, and National Security Council argued that the political costs of spurning the African countries and backtracking from pledges made at the NPT far outweighed the demand for nuclear options in Africa. The notion that the United States had no recourse to deter or retaliate against Libya without nuclear weapons was not compelling, and there were discussions about the ecological and radiological effects on Europe and the Middle East of nuclear strikes, to say nothing of the political effects on Russia or even Japan of adopting a formal policy of nuclear use against nonnuclear states. ACDA officials argued for signing the treaty without revision as a way to strengthen the trend toward nuclear-free zones internationally and specifically as a way to foreclose preemptive options in U.S. strategy, allowing that the treaty could be violated in any case if security were seriously imperiled.

But the Pentagon flatly opposed American signature of protocol I without a formal reservation that protected the U.S. right to use nuclear weapons in response to "any grave threat to U.S. security," as one participant put it.[62] ACDA's position of signing with the implicit intent to violate if necessary was "irresponsible" according to a critic.[63] One defense official even invoked the need to protect the sanctity of the NATO doctrine of "flexible response" and the threat to the cohesion of the alliance as a compelling reason not to sign.[64]

The Pentagon's demand put the bureaucracy in a quandary—either to "sign a treaty but with constraints that made the agreement a joke," according to one description, or "to be forced to ask the Senate to ratify a treaty that was opposed by the JCS."[65] The latter was considered particularly sensitive in a presidential election year. The interagency discussions that ensued focused on finding a way to finesse this fundamental contradiction.

After months of tortured efforts to find a legal basis for compromise, the bureaucracy produced a "split the difference" resolution that would allow the United States to sign the ANWFZ without a formal reservation but without forswearing nuclear prerogatives. At a White House press briefing on

work agreement to stop the Korean nuclear program, for example, a pledge that had been granted to Ukraine.

62. Interview with Pentagon official, June 1996.

63. Interview with State Department official, August 1996.

64. Interview with NSC official, May 1996.

65. Interview with State Department official, August 1996.

the day the United States signed the agreement, the NSC's senior director for defense policy and arms control, Robert Bell, stated that "under Protocol I, which we signed, each party pledges not to use or threaten to use nuclear weapons against an ANWFZ Party. However, Protocol I will not limit options available to the United States in response to an attack by an ANWFZ party using weapons of mass destruction."[66] The exception was based on the invocation of a little known rule of international "customary" law known as "belligerent reprisal" that allows states to retaliate against illegal acts by adversaries in wartime.[67]

For Bell and others this was an optimal outcome under the circumstances, crafted deliberately to allow the United States to legally suspend its obligations under the treaty in the event of aggression using chemical or biological weapons, but to do so in a "proportionate, limited way" aimed at a specific threat. It tempers the rationale for U.S. nuclear preemption according to this logic: "This is not Curtis Lemay or Rolling Thunder," an NSC official argued, but a way to reinforce U.S. deterrence without jettisoning critical political interests.[68] The likelihood of an American president ordering nuclear strikes against Africa is so remote that it tests credulity, according to this view, but the policy of belligerent reprisal guarantees that enemies will never be sure. Perhaps most important, belligerent reprisal was seen as crucial to a domestic political strategy needed to assure the Senate that in signing the protocol the United States would not find itself helpless in the face of a concerted chemical or biological attack by Libya or anyone else.

In the final analysis the deliberations over the ANWFZ brought to a head the unresolved issues of targeting nonnuclear states that were postponed in the NPR but without concrete resolution or genuine consensus. In the effort to defuse potentially damaging controversy in an election year, civilian officials devised the accepted declaratory rationale for what had become de facto military missions. This policy revision helps formalize concepts of nuclear options for nonnuclear threats, albeit in a modulated and more politically acceptable way than might have otherwise been the case. In the end the decision reinforced ambiguity as the key rationale of U. S. nuclear doctrine.[69]

66. Remarks by Robert Bell, White House press briefing, April 11, 1996.

67. For a detailed discussion, see George Bunn, "Expanding Nuclear Options: Is the U.S. Negating Its Non-Use Pledges?" *Arms Control Today*, vol. 26 (May-June 1996), p. 7.

68. Interview with senior NSC official, May 1996.

69. A week later, Secretary of Defense Perry reiterated this policy, stating that "Anyone who considers using a weapon of mass destruction against the United States or its allies must first consider the consequences. We would not specify in advance what our response would be, but it would be both overwhelming and devastating." Department of Defense press release, April 18, 1996.

Some officials accordingly have begun urging that the United States update its declaratory policy to state that it would never initiate the use of weapons of mass destruction against a potential aggressor. This variation on classical nuclear first-use doctrine is of course misleading, since the United States does not have a chemical or biological force, but is somehow thought by some to be an advantageous political compromise that covers over opposing ideas of nuclear deterrence.

Left unexamined, the drift toward policies for regional nuclear deterrence may test the resilience of decisions not to develop new concepts and designs for nuclear weapons. Deterrence has never been a static concept or one that can be based on "the existential threat." It is a safe bet that an accepted regional deterrent strategy would soon require a commensurate architecture of nuclear operations, including plans for targeting and execution, in order to be "compelling." In such a context the diplomatic agenda for nonproliferation would be tested severely. That the 5 rogue states are considered more significant influences over U.S. policy than the 186 signatories of the NPT to whom the United States has made pledges is a crucial determinant of current thinking.

Lessons for Future Policy?

The Clinton Nuclear Posture Review and its ensuing policy revisions may provide historians with a classic example of how not to attempt innovations in sensitive areas of national security. The NPR had every ingredient of past failures to challenge the nuclear establishment. It included an absent president who seemed painfully intimidated by his lack of clout with the military, the loss of and failure to replace the powerful and politically astute advocate Les Aspin, political appointees operating like Whiz Kids without memory of their predecessors' limitations, an undisciplined Pentagon bureaucracy for whom internal subversion of this initiative was so easy it was not even sporting, and a virtual absence of a domestic political strategy to help defuse predictable congressional opposition.

In retrospect the NPR and the ANWFZ debates were conducted in a domestic political climate that seemed highly promising but was only superficially inclined to accept innovations. Opinion both within the executive branch and in Congress was divided over the desirability of significant alterations in the missions assigned to nuclear forces, at least with respect to the devaluation of nuclear weapons in U.S. strategy. The debate took place before any resolution of more fundamental questions, including how to interpret changes in Russia and the degree to which the United States wanted to pursue a partnership with its former adversary. Any appearance of unanimity within the executive branch proved illusory and subject to constant revision.

The NPT extension, in turn, widely considered a triumph for U.S. leadership, was treated in its aftermath as a vote count, with the goal defined as getting majority support at the review conference, not a successful referendum on the importance and credibility of the nonnuclear regime. To the contrary, the declarations signed by the United States to gain the support of third world countries, especially assuring nonnuclear states that they would never be attacked with nuclear weapons, have been consigned to the background of diplomatic rhetoric, not operational or legal status.

Perhaps there are tactical lessons to be learned from these experiences. Many participants blame individuals for the failures of the NPR, pointing to Aspin for underestimating the resilience of the bureaucracy to sudden changes imposed from the top, to Deutch and Perry for failing to back up their subordinates or assume leadership, to Carter for his managerial inexperience and "Harvard arrogance," to Miller for being an apologist for the nuclear status quo and a skilled saboteur, or to uniformed military officers for their self-interested attachment to outmoded force plans and threat perceptions.

To the extent that officials should be held accountable for failure, however, the real culprits are the president and his closest advisers. A vacuum in senior leadership and White House authority conspired with the reflexive reluctance of career professionals to accept innovations that tested deeply held beliefs. Without any clear directives originating from the president about the critical importance of nuclear innovation, failure was virtually guaranteed.

Based on the bureaucratic arrangements alone, it is also not a mystery that the NPR was transformed from a review of national policy to a force posture exercise which, with modest exceptions, reinforced existing doctrine, targeting plans, and requirements. Participants in the NPR vary in their recollections of events, but they are unanimous in their conclusion that the outcome was a forgone conclusion once Aspin's connections to the president were no longer a factor. Senior officials, beginning with those in the White House, were quick to cave at any hint of controversy. In the end, in the words of one caustic critic, the NPR was "a tar baby," handed to an unwitting and politically inexperienced assistant secretary who "never even had a loyal point man to carry the mandate" internally.[70]

70. One former senior Pentagon appointee who was significant in the NPR denies that this experience is at all significant to guide future efforts. "There are no lessons at all," he said. "It just wasn't the right time for the United States. We had more important priorities and we just could not make changes in this point in history." Interview, January 1997.

For all the NPR's amateurish failings, most agree that Aspin and Carter did attempt to engage in deliberations over nuclear policy at a serious level. Questions raised by Carter went to the heart of the logic of cold war deterrence and its operational assumptions, challenging what had long been understood to be contradictions in force planning. But Aspin's notion of a tabula rasa nuclear review never came close to reality. The analytical exercise was superficially imposed on the planning infrastructure whose momentum was being carried forward by wholly different directives and priorities inherited from preceding administrations. As countless episodes dating back to the 1960s demonstrate, there is a point beyond which even senior officials cannot trespass into protected territory if they are not prepared to take on the consequences.[71]

The anti-Soviet consensus during the cold war had allowed disagreements about political and military objectives in nuclear doctrine to be sublimated under the rubric of deterrence. Deterrence provides a conceptual framework that is sufficiently open-ended and abstract to paper over the most incompatible assumptions. But even at the height of cold war consensus, decisionmakers had never in fact succeeded in formulating clear guidelines about what should be targeted, for what reason, or with what level of destructive force in a way that reflected political as well as military judgments. It was simply not a priority for leaders to expend the time and political capital needed to ensure that war plans and political goals were compatible. A small number of Clinton officials did try, at least for a time, but were not able to withstand the backlash.

Given the way authority is delegated for nuclear policy and planning under current arrangements, it is not wholly accurate to describe the NPR as a victim of intentional sabotage or inept management. The nuclear planning bureaucracy, with minor exceptions, has enjoyed bedrock support (or at least acquiescence) from political authorities for more than four decades. The extreme political sensitivity of nuclear operations, sanctioned by every president since Dwight Eisenhower, required that authority for nuclear war be delegated to a decisionmaking apparatus designed specifically to discourage political intrusion. Nuclear targeting and attack planning evolved into a highly specialized occupation, based on specific skills, computer models, and databases to which only very few had access, let alone oversight. It is a system that by its very nature will oppose radical systemic change, as is its sacred mandate to do.

71. One illustrative case is the political fallout from Robert McNamara's attempts to shift U.S. nuclear doctrine from the first-strike option to mutual assured destruction. Consider also the debacle that followed the Reagan administration's attempt at a unilateral reinterpretation of the ABM Treaty in late 1985. See chapters 2 and 5 in Janne E. Nolan, *Guardians of the Arsenal* (Basic Books, 1989).

It follows that policies that do not meet with the approval of the planning community will be fragile and potentially explosive. Without benefit of informed public discourse, decisions that provoke overt opposition are bound to generate doubts in Congress and the public about the wisdom of elected and appointed officials. The Joint Chiefs, for one, have been entrusted to be the guardians of national security. Direct assaults on military authority provoke an immune reaction in a nation long used to deferring to their judgment in certain areas.

Done carelessly, such actions are far more likely to cast doubts on those seeking innovations than to achieve any positive outcome. Even if a decision cannot be definitively shown to damage national security, any controversy sufficient to undermine the cohesion of the national command authority can be said to be against the national interest. Opposition by the Joint Chiefs, or even the threat of it, has usually been enough to keep the system in check. Indeed, there is reason to believe that the effort to avoid such conflict can be a sufficiently compelling objective that it replaces any interest on the part of senior political authorities to pursue controversial objectives.

Whatever the reasons, President Clinton's stewardship of U.S. nuclear policy is not exemplary. The president's participation in directing nuclear policies has been negligible, and the debates that have occupied his subordinates apparently remain largely unknown to him. It is not clear that the deeper implications for presidential authority of the conduct and outcome of the NPR or the ANWFZ are a matter of conscious concern. Perhaps such concerns were dismissed as not compelling enough to fight over, given the high risk and lack of any apparent political payoff.[72] Involving the president in debates with the military over issues obscure to the public may simply not have been possible when the administration was already besieged by recriminations over questions such as operations in Somalia and Haiti or the debacle over the decision to allow gays to serve in the military.

The Clinton legacy nevertheless stands in sharp contrast to that of his immediate predecessor. Aides to President Bush are unanimous in their admiration for his leadership style, which succeeded in achieving nuclear innovations that provoked no discernible opposition. What accounts for Bush's success? "President Bush never let an important issue drop into the bureaucracy," one of his advisors summarized. "Clinton debates objectives with his subordinates. Bush debated tactics, but never objectives."[73] Bush

---

72. Even with presidential leadership there is no guarantee of success. The episodes of presidents supporting and failing to significantly alter the operational assumptions of nuclear doctrine date back to Truman. For more detailed discussion, see Nolan, *Guardians of the Arsenal*.

73. Interview with former Bush White House adviser, February 1997.

would state his desired outcome: "I want tactical nuclear weapons out of Europe. Gorbachev needs U.S. cover to get their nukes out of the republics before they collapse," according to another description.[74]

In turn Bush could count on his main advisers to carry out his directives, and their unanimity of purpose, political credibility, and bureaucratic skills helped deflect or override opposition. National Security Advisor General Brent Scowcroft, Joint Chiefs of Staff Chairman Colin Powell, and Secretary of Defense Dick Cheney could use their clout with the uniformed military to defuse hawkish opposition, both in the Pentagon and in Congress. They were also astute inside players who knew they could count on the president and one another in the face of opposition.

President Bush, moreover, was involved in what aides call "the heavy lifting" of foreign policy, working directly and tirelessly with congressional and foreign leaders to set the stage for positive reception of U.S. initiatives. "This is simply not something that can be left to staff," said a close aide.[75] Nothing substitutes for direct presidential engagement. In the end Bush also seemed to have a far keener sense for the urgency of unfolding developments in Russia, undoubtedly assisted by his close relationship with Gorbachev.

One is left with several general conclusions about whether there will be a next posture review and whether such a review is prudent in the current political climate. The first is that any serious review has to be a presidentially initiated and supervised initiative. The president has to stake his prestige on the success of the undertaking. The strategy might best begin with a public positioning of the president's objectives: "a ringing endorsement in the State of the Union address that mankind is better off with fewer nuclear weapons, that after forty years of enormous treasure expended and enormous risks endured, it is time for bold action," in the words of former Commander in Chief of the Strategic Command George Lee Butler.[76]

But public exhortations can backfire if they are not accompanied by an effective strategy for defusing elite controversy. Both the Bush and Clinton experiences, as well as earlier efforts at nuclear innovation, highlight the extent to which presidential authority derives from certification by establishment leaders, including those in the military. An interest in innovation has to compete with the risk of being deemed inexperienced, untutored, or just dangerously misguided, as happened to President Carter when he asked innocently in his first SIOP briefing why the United States needed more than

74. Interview with former NSC official, February 1997.
75. Interview with former NSC official, February 1997.
76. Speech delivered by General George Lee Butler (ret.) with question and answer period at the Henry L. Stimson Center's 1996 Award for Public Service Ceremony, Henry L. Stimson Center, Washington, January 8, 1997.

"about 200" survivable missiles. Maintaining credibility as commander in chief is a fragile enterprise, however popular the president may be with the public.

The techniques needed to engage the establishment constructively may vary among presidents but President Clinton, who is neither a war hero like Eisenhower or surrounded by respected military leaders like Bush, is likely to need "someone to give him footing," as a veteran of the policy wars put it. One suggestion is the appointment of a special group of senior and respected advisers to draft the charter for a presidential review, a group that could provide the legitimacy and political cover needed to defuse opposition or protect the president if there were controversy.

The bureaucracy has to be involved and, through its carefully supervised participation, induced to cooperate. The most effective technique recommended by past practitioners and mastered by Henry Kissinger when he was secretary of state and national security adviser is to require agencies to develop options for high-level review, part of a disciplined process for which senior officials are accountable. Creating committees reporting to the senior group could help enforce direction and deadlines. The point is not to impose an expected outcome on the deliberations, which can be disastrous, but to have practical and realistic guidelines put forward for consideration with an implicit conception of where the agenda should come out. Over time the objective is to elicit consensus through concentric circles of decisionmakers managed from the top down.[77]

The bottom line for a domestic strategy is to ensure that the president be given options based on informed analysis, not bureaucratic "findings" born of low-level consensus. As Reagan domestic adviser Martin Anderson, who helped craft the Strategic Defense Initiative while riding on Reagan's campaign plane, commented, new initiatives have to be "protected from the bureaucracy until [they] have some momentum or [they'll] be murdered in their cribs."[78]

Disciplining the bureaucracy to contain opposition is a necessary but not

77. Morton Halperin has suggested a scheme for a future review that includes many of these elements, including the appointment of an interagency task force chaired by a senior Pentagon official to conduct a study of options for the president. The task force would be assisted by personnel from each of the agencies and consult with outside experts, including an experts group appointed by the national security advisor, who would conduct a concurrent study. The final report to the president would include current policy options, options endorsed by particular agencies, and options suggested by the experts group and private reports, each accompanied by analysis of costs and risks but without specific endorsement. Morton Halperin with Leo Mackay, "Terms of Reference," Nuclear Policy Review, Council on Foreign Relations, 1996.

78. Nolan, Guardians of the Arsenal, p 13.

sufficient condition. Public opinion, domestically and internationally, is also crucial. Designing and implementing policies that can win public support may actually prove easier than overriding entrenched interests. Much of the American public seems convinced that nuclear weapons have more or less disappeared. The steadily increasing number of quasi-official pronouncements about the risks and disutility of nuclear weapons, from former military commanders, former heads of state, respected experts such as those engaged in the Canberra Commission, and politicians could be an important influence in setting the context for ambitious change.

Conclusion

The direction of the administration does not provide much confidence in a positive outcome should a review be conducted today. By mid-1999, international events have conspired with a conservative revolution in Congress to deepen official skepticism about the kinds of innovations proposed in this book. The uncertainty of political conditions in Russia, in particular, has become worrisome. Far from prompting further reductions in or de-alerting U.S. forces, the possibility of the collapse of the Yeltsin regime has fueled congressional rhetoric about a resurgent Russian adversary and arguments for greater, not less, nuclear vigilance.

Changes in the size and content of the nuclear forces of recent years have been accepted and implemented in a way that ensures an essential continuity in nuclear strategy. Target lists have been streamlined to reflect decreases in Russian and former Soviet forces and installations, and new types of targeting against emerging rogue states are under development. These modifications notwithstanding, the objective of targeting Russian command centers and nuclear forces with high levels of damage expectancy remains intact. The nuclear posture ratified by the Clinton administration is consistent with that of its predecessors, predicated on the belief that "many thousands of targets must be held at risk with strategic nuclear warheads to achieve deterrence." As former Commander Chiles of the Strategic Command said, "Our mission reflects continuity with the past: to deter major military attack against the United States and its allies, and, if attacked, to employ force."[79]

That said, the administration has achieved reductions in nuclear dangers.

79. Prepared statement of Admiral Henry Chiles, *Department of Defense Authorization for Appropriations for FY95 and the Future Years Defense Program,* Hearings before the Senate Committee on Armed Services, 103 Cong. 2 sess., pt. 1, p. 995.

Its record includes the successful negotiation of the U.S.–North Korean Agreed Framework, signed in October 1994, which averted a catastrophic showdown over nuclear developments, freezing all reprocessing activities and requiring dismantlement of North Korea's nuclear program under stringent international inspections. With U.S. encouragement, the ratification by Brazil and Argentina of the Treaty of Tlateloco and acceptance of full-scope safeguards on their nuclear facilities by the International Atomic Energy Agency showed what can be achieved in rolling back nuclear ambitions. Ukraine has been denuclearized. And the president has demonstrated his obvious interest in the detargeting of U.S. and Russian missiles, an initiative that might be translated into de-alerting agreements. Above all, there seems to be continued, if not especially urgent, interest in helping Russia move beyond the domestic constraints it is encountering in ratifying START II, building on the agreement at the March Helsinki Summit for a framework agreement for lower levels of nuclear weapons to be negotiated under START III.

In late 1996 General Butler, former commander in chief of the Strategic Command, along with fifty-nine other retired senior military officers, issued a statement calling for the United States to take the lead in pressing for global elimination of nuclear weapons. The statement made headlines around the world, the first public excoriation of nuclear weapons by military leaders, many of whom were former architects of nuclear war plans. On the one hand, the statement seems to have stimulated wider and more mainstream debate about the questionable or declining utility of nuclear weapons for modern security challenges. At the same time, critics were quick to dismiss the feasibility and desirability of nuclear elimination, with some trying to depict Butler and his colleagues as delusional and deeply misguided.[80] The publicity the statement has received, however, along with the undeniable expertise of its signers, does seem to have prompted more commentators to support deeper cuts in nuclear arsenals and more progress in de-alerting forces, even if they oppose or question the wisdom of the generals' bolder vision.[81] If motivated mainly by budgetary reasons, moreover, the chairman of the Joint Chiefs testified in Congress in November 1998 that the JCS opposed a return to START I force levels, as is mandated by Congress, despite the Duma's failure to ratify START II.

It is possible that the more active public discussions about nuclear

---

80. See, for instance, Richard Haass, "It's Dangerous to Disarm," *New York Times*, December 11, 1996, p A27; and "Don't Ban the Bomb," *Economist*, January 4, 1997, p. 15.

81. See, for instance, Stephen S. Rosenfeld, "Wake Up—The Nightmare's Not Over," *Washington Post*, January 31, 1997, p. A21.

weapons sparked by Butler and others will prompt a serious national (and international) debate that could force officials to undertake new initiatives. Even more informed analysis of the premises and criteria for nuclear policies could be significant. In the haste to define new nuclear threats and countermeasures, there has been scant opportunity for an adequate evaluation of the legacy of nuclear weapons for global security, let alone time to think about the dangers these weapons posed and may still pose to their traditional possessors. What are the lessons of nuclear deterrence, different operational practices, or the use of nuclear threats for the established powers? Which among these lessons would we want other states to emulate?

PART FOUR

Why Not Abolition?

CHAPTER THIRTEEN

The Road to Abolition: How Far Can We Go?

This chapter contains concise statements of the reasons why many governments and citizens' groups support complete elimination of nuclear weapons and the reasons why weapon state governments wish to retain them. Then it discusses the conditions that may have to be met before these governments decide to eliminate all their nuclear weapons.

In the previous chapters we have described what we believe is a promising approach to achieving minimum nuclear forces. Implementing this deep cuts program would set the stage for decisions on complete elimination of nuclear weapons. Although the political and military implications of these decisions would be great, once small, immobilized arsenals of the five NPT weapon states and the three de facto weapon states—India, Pakistan and Israel—are achieved, eliminating their remaining nuclear weapons would not be difficult in the physical sense. It would be necessary to end the small, free-ranging patrols of the weapons still deployed, dismantle the warheads in the residual arsenals and transfer their fissile material to monitored storage, and destroy their delivery systems. It would also be necessary to close and dismantle all weapon production plants, laboratories, and test sites. Technically, this task is of limited proportions compared with the preceding disarmament measures. But politically, the task is daunting.

Why Nuclear Weapons Should Be Eliminated

In becoming parties to the Non-Proliferation Treaty and its indefinite extension in 1995, the five NPT nuclear weapon states have undertaken a commitment to eliminate all their nuclear weapons. In its July 1996 advisory opinion, the International Court of Justice found unanimously that this commitment constitutes a binding legal obligation that should be brought to its fulfillment. But the NPT does not include a specific time limit or describe prerequisites for completing the elimination. In the UN General Assembly, India and the nonaligned states have repeatedly gained majorities for resolutions urging that the weapon states commit themselves to eliminate their nuclear weapons by a specific date. Among nongovernmental organizations, a large umbrella organization, the Abolition Caucus, has been urging that the nuclear weapon states commit themselves by 2000 to begin negotiation on a convention prohibiting the possession of nuclear weapons.[1]

The nuclear weapon states, led by the United States, have resisted these initiatives, arguing that the weapons are indispensable to national security for the foreseeable future. However, in recent years an increasing number of respected individuals and organizations have joined in advocating the complete elimination of nuclear weapons, although in most cases without specifying a specific time limit. These include the Atlantic Council; the Stimson Center; the Canberra Commission; Nobel Peace Prize–winning Pugwash with Dr. Joseph Rotblat; General Lee Butler, former commander of the U.S. Strategic Air Command; former NATO commander General Andrew Goodpaster; and a group of sixty-one retired generals and admirals from seventeen countries.[2]

In summary, these proposals make the following points.

—There is no legitimate purpose for nuclear weapons aside from deterring their use, an aim that would be more safely and effectively carried out through total elimination of the weapons.

—The existence of these weapons always entails the possibility of a dangerous arms race and even more, of their use, with catastrophic consequences for all humanity.

1. Lawyers' Committee on Nuclear Policy, *Model Nuclear Weapons Convention,* Convention on the Prohibition of the Development, Production, Testing, Stockpiling, Transfer, Use and Threat of Use of Nuclear Weapons and on Their Elimination, October 1996 draft, New York.

2. Joseph Rotblat and others, eds., *A Nuclear Weapons Free World: Desirable? Feasible?* (Boulder, Colo.: Westview Press, 1993). A succinct account of his approach is given by Joseph Rotblat in *Disarmament Times,* vol. 19 (May 1996). See also "An Evolving U.S. Nuclear Posture," Second Report of the Steering Committee Project on Eliminating Weapons of Mass Destruction, Henry L. Stimson Center, Washington, December 1995; and Report of the Canberra Commission on the Elimination of Nuclear Weapons, August 1996. The text of the statement by General Butler and General Goodpaster and the sixty-one retired general officers is included in Craig Cerniello, *Arms Control Today,* vol. 26, no. 9 (1996), pp. 14–15, 18. See also Committee on International Security and Arms Control, National Academy of Sciences, *The Future of U.S. Nuclear Weapons Policy* (Washington: National Academy Press, 1997). (Because knowledge of how to produce nuclear weapons cannot be eliminated, the committee proposes that nuclear weapons be "prohibited" rather than "eliminated.")

—With the end of the cold war the utility of nuclear weapons has sharply declined while the risks associated with their possession have increased.

—Existence of the weapons is a dynamic motivation for proliferation ("if the weapon states consider these weapons necessary for their security and for their international status, why not us?").

—The existence of nuclear arsenals is also a potential direct source of proliferation through forcible seizure, theft, and illegal sale of materials.

—Actual proliferation is inevitable in the absence of the far tighter safeguards regime that would be brought about by eliminating all nuclear weapons.

—This proliferation would threaten the security of all, including the weapon states themselves.

Hitherto, relatively little thought has been given to the circumstances that might induce the weapon states to commit to nuclear weapons abolition. Some advocates of abolition appear to consider that achieving it is a self-contained, autonomous process not dependent on important parallel changes in the international system. Given the current importance of nuclear weapons in international security, this cannot be so.

In contrast, our deep cuts program can be implemented without major changes in the international system. As a necessary part of the program, we call for very high transparency among the weapon states, a treaty ending production of fissile material for weapons, extensive improvement of the safeguards system, and perhaps a treaty restricting production and possession of longer-range ballistic missiles. These would be important achievements, but they would not require major changes in the international system. Eliminating nuclear weapons will almost certainly require such changes. These requirements cannot be legally valid preconditions because the weapon states are already committed in article VI of the Non-Proliferation Treaty, without any conditions, to eliminate their weapons. But the requirements can legitimately be a description of the circumstances these states might want to see created before they are ready to make the decision.

Why Weapon State Governments Want to Retain Their Weapons

It is already apparent that the requirements for eliminating nuclear weapons will be stiff. The perceptions of weapon state governments vary according to their situation, but they appear convinced that possession of nuclear weapons, not their use, brings advantages beyond deterring nuclear attack. These advantages may rest on misconceptions, but the misconceptions are firmly held.

For many U.S. nuclear planners, the advantages include conferring a minimum of order and predictability on an otherwise chaotic international system. Possession of nuclear weapons bolsters the U.S. claim to superpower status and the influence that goes with it. It inhibits large-scale conventional war among the weapon states or between weapon states and others and provides valuable insurance against major armed conflicts that could require U.S. participation. In the view of senior U.S. officials, even in the absence of an explicit U.S. policy to use nuclear weapons to respond to attack by chemical or biological weapons, the mere possession of nuclear weapons can deter use of chemical and biological weapons against the United States, its allies, or U.S. forces overseas.

For Russia, nuclear weapons are its sole claim to great power status. Russia's nuclear weapons provide an obstacle to feared U.S. domination of Russian policy and a persuasive rationale for economic aid to Russia. In addition, in the minds of Russian officials, Russia's nuclear arsenal has become the answer to the collapse of the Soviet Union and of Russia's armed forces and to the nameless threats that arise from that collapse. For China, nuclear weapons have from the outset been a means of countering domination by the Soviet Union and the United States. For India, they are a means of preventing domination by China and of gaining international status; for Pakistan, a means of preventing domination by India; for Israel, a means of preventing mass assault by Arab armies. For France and Britain, nuclear weapons confer international status and a claim on a permanent seat on the UN Security Council as well as some insurance against the recurrent nightmare that the United States, moved by unpredictable domestic political currents, will abandon them in a moment of security crisis, perhaps a crisis involving Russia.

Most of the advantages that weapon state governments perceive from possessing nuclear weapons can be retained in the small, largely immobilized, arsenals we propose in the deep cuts program. But to make possible decisions to eliminate all remaining weapons, it will be necessary to convince nuclear weapon states that the international system can provide other advantages to make up for their loss of perceived nuclear advantages. They must be convinced that it will not diminish their security—that it will in practice increase it—to move beyond these small immobilized arsenals that nonetheless could be used in situations of national emergency to a situation where they will be deprived of this fallback.[3]

Viewed from today's perspective, this would be a giant step. But viewed from the perspective of an already operating system of largely immobilized arsenals, the leap of faith would perhaps not be so great. After nuclear weapons have been eliminated, the weapon states would still have powerful conventional forces for their protection. Their security would also still be backed by the deterrent effect of their continuing capacity to recreate nuclear weapons within a limited time. However, the psychological jump would be a formidable one: they are likely to require a lot of convincing, and all eight nuclear weapon states, including the three de facto weapon states, would have to be convinced. A single holdout could stop the process.

As far as can be seen from the present, preconditions for the decision to eliminate all nuclear weapons would surely be based on the smooth and successful operation of the immobilized 200-warhead nuclear forces proposed under the deep cuts program. This would include the extensive verification and monitoring system associated with nuclear forces, the absence of nuclear crises, a strong, close cooperative relationship among the nuclear weapon states, and an effective world security system with a good performance record in lowering the incidence of regional conflicts that might otherwise involve one or more of the major powers. It would also include conventional arms limitations that satisfied the governments of all the weapon states, effective maintenance of the regimes prohibiting possession or use of chemical and biological weapons, and a nuclear nonproliferation regime that performed with full reliability.

The probable preconditions would also include the existence of dependable machinery to deal with the possibility of a sudden breakout from the regime by a state, especially a former weapon state that had produced or concealed nuclear weapons in considerable number, or by a secret proliferant; and dependable machinery to deal with the possibility of aggressive behavior by a major power using conventional weapons. These contingencies may not be likely, but they will be the toughest challenge a regime free of nuclear weapons is likely to encounter, and weapon state governments

3. The December 5, 1996, statement on nuclear weapons by international generals and admirals says, "It is clear however that nations now possessing nuclear weapons will not relinquish them until they are convinced that more reliable and less dangerous means of providing for their security are in place. It is also clear as a consequence that the nuclear powers will not now agree to a fixed timetable for the achievement of abolition."

will have to be convinced before they move that this problem has been carefully thought through.

Fulfilling these requirements would mean important changes in the international system. All would have to be met for a considerable period of time to absolutely convince nuclear weapon states that they could afford to eliminate their remaining small numbers of nuclear weapons.

Our conclusion is that the weapon states should go as far as they can now. They should reduce to the deep cuts minimum force, operate that regime, and then take stock.

In the remainder of this chapter, we discuss the desiderata for a nuclear weapons–free world in more detail: restrictions on nuclear energy, democratic governments in the weapon states, improvements in the capacity of the world community to lower the level of organized armed conflict, large-scale conventional disarmament, and measures against breakout.

Restrictions on Nuclear Energy

Verifying total nuclear disarmament will require more powerful and intrusive international agencies to prevent proliferation. Even the operation of uranium-fueled nuclear power generators on a "once-through" fuel cycle creates some nuclear weapons capability and will therefore require very tight verification. Existing uranium enrichment technology could be used to make a clandestine enrichment plant. Plutonium in spent fuel might be extracted in clandestine processing plants. Indeed, as long as there is a nuclear power industry, nuclear weapons are only a year away. For these reasons, a number of experts, among them Theodore Taylor, have concluded that in a world free of nuclear weapons, there cannot be nuclear power at all.[4]

We do not go this far, but we do point out that some types of energy production increase the risks of covert weapon production and might have to be eliminated. Reactor-grade plutonium now being recycled in some energy reactors in Europe, and probably soon in Japan, can be used without modification to make nuclear weapons.[5] Given this fact, it may reasonably be a precondition of the nuclear weapon states for eliminating their arms, and a

4. Theodore B. Taylor, "Nuclear Power and Nuclear Weapons," Global Security Study no. 22, Nuclear Age Peace Foundation, July 1996.

5. U.S. Department of Energy, *Non-proliferation and Arms Control Assessment of Weapons-Usable Fissile Material Storage and Plutonium Disposition Alternatives,* draft assessment prepared by the U.S. Department of Energy, Office of Arms Control and Nonproliferation (NN-40), October 1996, pp. 37–39. Committee on International Security and Arms Control, National

concern of many nonnuclear states as well, that the separation of plutonium for use in the civilian fuel cycle be ended and existing separated plutonium be disposed of. This possible requirement means a head-on dispute with the French, British, Japanese, Russian, Indian, and Chinese nuclear establishments, all of which are, in various ways, interested in promoting or exploring plutonium recycling in nuclear power reactors.[6]

The use of highly enriched uranium, a primary component of nuclear weapons for naval reactors and civilian research reactors, would also have to be phased out, and future naval propulsion and research reactors would have to be configured to use low-enriched uranium. In the context of elimination there would also be the problem of finding more secure interim storage sites for the fissile materials from the disarmament process and for world stocks of separated energy plutonium. While these stocks exist in large amounts on the territory of the weapon states and of states that use plutonium for energy, they remain open to forcible seizure by the owner government or others. The question is, are there safer, more isolated modes of storage? With regard to disposition, highly enriched uranium can be blended down to usable low-enriched uranium. The National Academy of Sciences has recommended that separated plutonium be vitrified with radioactive wastes or converted to mixed oxide for use as reactor fuel. The purpose in the second case is not so much to burn up the plutonium as to give it a forbidding shield of highly radioactive materials.

Requirement for Democratic Government

Maintaining a genuinely cooperative relationship among the big powers is the key to world peace with or without nuclear weapons, for only a serious breakdown of this relationship can bring wars of worldwide dimensions. Close cooperation among the major powers will be needed for them to undertake joint action against a successful proliferant or against one of their own

Academy of Sciences, *Management and Disposition of Excess Weapons Plutonium* (Washington: National Academy Press, 1994), chap. 1; and J. Carson Mark, "Explosive Properties of Reactor-Grade Plutonium," *Science and Global Security*, vol. 4, no. 1 (1993), pp. 111–28.

6. Harald Müller argues on this point that instead of total elimination of plutonium recycling, a deeper look at concepts that were dismissed in the 1980s (international ownership, operation, and guarding of facilities; real-time, in-process material accountancy; coprocessing; collocation of reprocessing and MOX fuel fabrication; just-in-time procedures; tight containment measures for bulk facilities) could go a long way to mitigate problems. One could also conceive of an agreement preventing countries that host reprocessing, enrichment, or MOX facilities from also possessing space launch capabilities and production.

number that may covertly retain or redevelop nuclear weapons capability or otherwise commit serious acts of aggression. The nature of the relationships among the big powers will become even more crucial after the elimination of nuclear weapons has removed the restraint, not absolute but important, that these weapons have created in the behavior of the nuclear weapon states toward each other, especially as regards the possibility of conventional war directly among them or of their involvement on opposing sides of regional conflicts.

The requirements for establishing and continuing a productive relationship among the big powers may be very stiff. It is likely that political opinion in the United States, Britain, and France will conclude that enduring good relations among the major powers and enduring cooperation from them in operating systems for nuclear disarmament and world security cannot be certain unless all five weapon states are reliably functioning democracies. China and Russia are key. Russia has made uncertain progress toward pluralism, while China remains an authoritarian, one-party state.

To restate the point more specifically: political opinion in the three Western democracies may conclude that the existence of functioning democratic governments in both Russia and China is a prerequisite both for the operation of a completely dependable verification regime for a world free of nuclear weapons and for enduring cooperation among the former weapon states in maintaining an effective world security system. As regards verification, fear of cheating will be a major obstacle to agreement on elimination of nuclear weapons, ensuring continuing total transparency will be an absolute requirement. Although democracies as well as autocratic states can on occasion be highly secretive on defense and nuclear matters, they appear best able to ensure the ongoing, open discussion of security issues, untrammeled activity of the media, and fully developed system of societal verification (encouragement and protection of civilian whistleblowers) that will be an essential part of a nonweapon world.

Cooperation among the large powers is a categorical requirement for security in a nonnuclear world. Today, active scholarly debate is under way between supporters of the contention that democracies do not go to war with each other and those who do not consider that this idea has substance.[7] What-

7. Christopher Layne, a realist critic of the thesis that democracies do not make war on one another, has a useful review of the literature in "Kant or Cant: The Myth of the Democratic Peace," *International Security,* vol. 19, no. 2 (1994), pp. 5–49. The same issue of *International Security* has an article by David Spiro, "The Insignificance of the Liberal Peace," pp. 50–86, supporting Layne's criticism, and one by John M. Owen, "How Liberalism Produces Democratic Peace," pp. 87–125, supporting the argument that democracies do not war against one another.

ever the historical record, contemporary democracies do appear less likely than other types of states to go to war with one another, primarily because of the institutional restraints on warmaking in democratic states and because of the broad access to information on politics, policies, and personalities that make democracies more dependable partners in verification. Only democracies have the continuing openness and access to information on decisionmaking on defense and security issues that enable early identification of negative trends and present opportunities for outside governments, citizens groups, and individuals to intervene and effectively debate the contested issues. It is this openness of democratic societies that underlies the confidence of national leaders in democracies that they can have reliable information on the considerations that will sway the decisions of the leaders of other nations and therefore that they can afford to trust them. Compare this situation with Western quandaries about decisionmaking in such closed societies as North Korea and China. Factors like these encourage democratic states to prefer democracies as allies and to distrust autocracies.[8]

A benevolent autocracy might for a time provide some of the prerequisites for dependable verification and productive political cooperation, but it cannot provide any assurance against arbitrary change on these points—or on possible breakout.

The forgoing description of democratic government is not intended to describe benefits of democratic government in the abstract. The intention is to make clear why the governments of the United States, France, and the United Kingdom may in the final analysis be unwilling to eliminate their nuclear weapons in their own perceived security interests until they are convinced that the Russian and Chinese governments have some reasonable version of functioning democracy.

This point has a practical consequence. It means that efforts to foster lasting, functioning democracies in China and Russia by carefully thought out means must be a primary objective not only of those promoting human rights for their own sake but also of those seeking to carry out a program of comprehensive nuclear disarmament.

Peacekeeping

According to some estimates, 170 wars have taken place since the end of World War II, leaving up to 35 million dead, the great majority of them

8. Spiro, "The Insignificance of Liberal Peace," suggests that the tendency of democratic states to enter into alliances with each other is also based on the awareness of shared norms.

civilians. More than thirty wars, most of them internal, are now in progress. Most of these are small, but some could spread to become major wars with big-power participation. This continuing tragedy has been a major justification for large military forces and for weapons states' retention of nuclear arsenals. Consequently, it is probable that one requirement of weapon state governments and their allies for eliminating all nuclear weapons would be measurable reduction in the number, size, and frequency of armed conflicts around the world.

The main answer to such a requirement is a combination of improved UN conflict prevention and peacekeeping, strengthened regional security organizations, and radical worldwide reduction in conventional armed forces.

A standing UN readiness force of several brigades, backed if needed by larger assigned forces from member states provided under Articles 43 and 45 of the UN Charter, is a necessity. UN peacekeeping activities should also have an autonomous source of financing so they will not be dependent on the prosperity, budget cycle, or domestic politics of member states. Financing could be from a number of sources approved by national legislatures, such as a tax on air travel, ocean freight, use of communications satellites, or international financial transactions.

The postnuclear world will need a fully developed worldwide network of functional regional security organizations, with at least one in each major region, as the first line of defense against local conflicts and regional wars into which the major powers may be drawn. It will be necessary to encourage the growth of the Organization for Security and Cooperation in Europe, Organization of American States, Organization of African Unity, and other existing regional security organizations to provide each with some conflict prevention and peacekeeping capability. It will also be necessary to establish regional security organizations in areas where they do not now exist: the Near East, South Asia, and Northeast Asia. We can visualize an ultimate world security system as a network of increasingly effective regional security organizations, each with developed conflict prevention and regional peacekeeping capability, backed by a more capable UN, with big-power support when the going gets tough.

The UN Security Council would be reformed by enlarging its membership and by agreement among permanent members that their use of the veto will be limited to issues involving direct threats to their own national security. The reformed Security Council would proactively advise, assist, and warn governments faced by political, social, and economic problems that have the potential to culminate in armed violence. A corps of highly trained experts in mediation and conflict resolution would assist the Security Council and secretary general and be available for field missions in friction areas. UN member governments would agree to refer more international disputes to arbitration or to the International Court of Justice while moving toward compulsory submission of disputes. The members would also bring into force and vigorously use the 1998 treaty creating an International Criminal Court to prosecute war crimes, genocide, and other crimes against humanity. The treaty establishing the court would be broadened to cover crimes involving possession or use of nuclear, chemical, or biological weapons. The Security Council would decide in advance to take action against offenders of this expanded covenant.[9]

Conventional Disarmament

The nuclear weapon states will probably insist that some states undertake deep reductions of their forces as a precondition for their own decision to eliminate their nuclear forces. Conventional disarmament on a regional basis in current areas of confrontation—India and Pakistan; North Korea, if it still exists as a separate state, and South Korea; Iraq and Iran; and Taiwan and China—may be required to reduce the possibility of regional wars that could involve the nuclear weapon states. Russia may call for reduction of Chinese and possibly Turkish forces or NATO forces in general, Israel for reduction of Arab forces in addition to those of Iraq and Iran, and Pakistan for reduction of Indian forces. At this stage the former nuclear weapon states would have destroyed all their nuclear delivery systems. But they still would be permitted to have ballistic missiles with conventional warheads for satellite launch and space exploration, as well as cruise missiles and long-range aircraft equipped to deliver conventional weapons.

It is also probable that some weapon states, especially China and India, and possibly also Russia, will require as a precondition for eliminating their own nuclear weapons that the United States significantly reduce its conventional military capabilities, especially its force projection capability in naval and air forces. It will be a very difficult decision for the United States voluntarily to relinquish its superiority in conventional forces in addition

9. A comprehensive proposal covering these measures and the conventional disarmament in the next section is covered in Randall Forsberg, Jonathan Dean, and Saul Mendlovitz, "Global Action to Prevent War," *Boston Review*, vol. 24, no. 1 (February/March 1999).

to relinquishing its nuclear weapons. The outcome will depend both on the growth of trust among the major powers and the growth of effective world-wide peacekeeping capabilities. Negotiation to rough equality at a lower level in conventional forces of the major powers may be one answer. However, the time may also have come to negotiate force restrictions that make it possible for the major states to cooperate in joint military endeavors but also make it more difficult for them to operate alone or independently to attack each other with their conventional forces. To reach this point, each of the major powers would forgo or sharply reduce one major force component—ground, air, naval, or logistic—whose possession would make it possible for it to project conventional forces capable of attacking and defeating well-equipped conventional forces of another state. These restrictions would make it extremely difficult for major powers to attack each other, although by cooperating they could still field effective forces capable of operating at long range.

Measures against Breakout

Before they decide to eliminate their nuclear weapons, the governments of the nuclear weapon states will have to be convinced that an adequate mechanism exists to cope with potential breakout from the deep cuts regime by a weapon state or a proliferant. When devising such a mechanism is attempted in today's perspective, it is nearly impossible to resolve. But if the task is viewed from the perspective of successful operation of a deep cuts regime and the emergence of functioning democracies in Russia and China, it becomes easier to find a solution.

Although the idea is attractive, it is probably not practical to think of coping with breakout from a zero-nuclear-weapons regime through transferring remaining nuclear weapons to UN control and use of a nuclear weapons force under UN control. The abhorrence against nuclear weapons and the norm against their use is very strong among UN member states. As a consequence, most qualified observers believe that Security Council action against an offender could include economic sanctions and use of conventional force but would not in any circumstances include a decision to use nuclear weapons.

For this reason, as well as skepticism on the part of the nuclear weapon states about the trustworthiness and effectiveness of the United Nations, most plans to put residual nuclear forces at the disposal of the Security Council to enforce a zero weapons regime appear impractical, although an effective Security Council will be an essential requirement for such a regime. The breakout solution will have to be sought elsewhere.

It is probable that a sudden large breakout from a zero-weapon treaty and the deploying of scores of warheads could come only from former weapon states or, less plausibly, from other industrial democracies with extensive nuclear power industries. To accept this risk, states would have to be convinced that any such breakout would be slow and preceded by observable preparatory measures and political indicators so that the major states would have time to prepare and coordinate their countermeasures. This sense of assurance could be had only if all the key states were functioning democracies. This is a further practical reason the three Western weapon states may feel justified in insisting, before they relinquish all their nuclear weapons, on functioning democracy in Russia and China.

If a breakout is not large, but stems perhaps from a smaller rogue state, it is doubtful that action against the proliferator would have to depend on nuclear weapons. Nor would response with nuclear weapons be desirable in a situation in which, despite the breakout, it would be important to maintain the international norm against use of nuclear weapons. In these circumstances the Security Council could decide on joint action under threat to the peace provisions of chapter VII of the UN Charter. If, despite the suspension of veto rights by the permanent five members of the Security Council proposed in chapter 10, a Security Council decision is blocked, one or more major powers would have to act on their own. In reality, this situation would be no worse than that which prevails at present, in which use of U.S. nuclear weapons against a small Middle Eastern or Asian proliferator state is nearly totally excluded for political reasons, and action would have to be through conventional forces. Advance planning to cope with the possibility of a small breakout will strengthen the close habitual cooperation among the former weapon states that is a prerequisite for a world without weapons.

Consideration of possible breakout from a zero nuclear weapons regime after elimination of nuclear weapons would require a new look at the possibility of instituting a regime radically restricting delivery systems with capability exceeding very short ranges, including ballistic and cruise missiles and long-range bombers (described in brief in chapter 10).

Given the increasing lethality of conventional explosives and the continuing possibility that a former weapon state or another country might evade controls on production of nuclear or biological weapons, unrestricted possession of long-range delivery systems would be considered a serious threat, especially by former weapon states like Russia and China. The United States, which could afford both missile defenses and long-range delivery systems, would probably consider that having both would maximize its own security. But having both would also increase the military superiority of the United States over all other states. Other countries, including Russia and China, would not be so fortunate. Consequently, they might either press for global restrictions on delivery systems or for more specific restrictions on U.S. delivery systems. This would be a less far-reaching version of the restrictions on U.S. conventional capability discussed earlier in this chapter.

Conclusions

The requirements described here for moving to complete elimination of nuclear weapons—among them, devising machinery against breakout, achieving failproof verification and developing habitual cooperation among the major powers (which in practice require functioning democratic governments, at least in the five former weapon states), resolution of regional confrontations that could involve nuclear weapon states, much improved peacekeeping on a global and regional level, and large-scale conventional disarmament—are demanding and time consuming but not impossible to achieve.

This does not mean that all the conditions for abolition that may be set out by weapon state governments will have to be met in full before further movement toward abolition from small immobilized arsenals can begin. It may be that countries will come to believe that the danger to civilization posed by nuclear weapons justifies some movement even if all the ideal conditions for a nuclear-disarmed world are not yet in place.

One central point should be made, however. All the nuclear-weapon security establishments will have to become absolutely convinced by the actual performance of the deep cuts program they have agreed to, by the actual performance of improved global and regional security institutions and of nonproliferation regimes for all weapons of mass destruction, and by effective conventional disarmament that they no longer have any need for nuclear weapons. Governments of weapon states will have to come to believe that the advantages they have seen in possessing nuclear weapons have been replaced by changes in the international system that bring even greater advantages for their security. It will take a considerable period of good performance by these other institutions and of international stability without major conflict before the nuclear weapon states can in fact be convinced they can afford to relinquish all their weapons.

We have pointed out that there has been relatively little sustained effort thus far either by officials from weapon states or those urging abolition of nuclear weapons to identify the conditions for total elimination of nuclear weapons or to analyze them.

Much more public discussion of this subject is needed. Officials of weapon state governments should be reminded of their obligation to eliminate their nuclear arsenals and asked to specify the circumstances under which they will be prepared for decisive action. The conditions for action they present should be analyzed as to which have some substance and which are excuses for maintaining the status quo. Where they are shown to be excuses, they can be refuted and the debate over abolition will be simplified. If some conditions, like improved peacekeeping through strengthened regional security organizations or conventional disarmament, have objective justification, they could become common goals both of weapon state governments and those pressing for elimination of all nuclear weapons.

A serious debate along these lines could advance both prospects for elimination of nuclear weapons and for improvement in world security. We hope that this book has made clear that an active process of controlling nuclear weapons will not only reduce the great continuing dangers from these weapons, but can and should provide powerful dynamic impetus for creating an effective world security system. If this can happen through the elimination of nuclear weapons, the invention of these fearsome devices may turn out to have benefited humanity.

International Perspectives

Deep Cuts and De-alerting:
A Russian Perspective

Alexei Arbatov

This book, on issues on which there are already libraries of literature and sets of conferences and workshops on the scale of the Olympic games, is distinguished by its open-minded attitudes, innovative proposals, and at the same time its realism and comprehensiveness in addressing the complex problems of nuclear arms cuts and strategic stability.

In principle, many of the concepts and proposals of the study are acceptable from the Russian point of view, provided that this view is sufficiently liberal (not biologically anti-Western, anti-American, or Soviet revanchist) and professional and broad enough to combine technical, strategic, political, arms control, and economic expertise.

The absolute number of people in Russia that have this combination of virtues is not smaller than in the Soviet Union during the days of Gorbachev's "new political thinking." However, their relative weight in the new Russian political elite and strategic community as well as their ability to find and use an organized decisionmaking system are much weaker than before. They are under the pressure of strong competition from large numbers of outspoken anti-Western professionals and ignorant politicians and organizations, and they are constantly frustrated by the chaotic, unpredictable, bottlenecked and dead-ended patterns of Russia's current government.

Keeping in mind these reservations, which bear heavily on the prospects of practical implementation of nuclear deep cuts and collateral proposals, it is possible to make some comments on the details of the study. The first block of these comments will focus on the core of the deep cuts proposal, dealing with proposed levels, structures, schedules, and techniques of strategic arms reductions and de-alerting. The second block of comments will focus on outer shell issues, including the roles of the ABM Treaty and missile defense systems, the impact of tactical nuclear and conventional forces, the roles of "third" nuclear powers, and warhead dismantling, nuclear materials storage, and the fissile material production cutoff.

Core Issues

The core issues may be divided into two components: those addressing the level of deployed strategic forces at each stage of reduction and those related to nondeployed warheads.

START II and Further Reductions of the Strategic Forces to 2010 and Beyond

The best available basis for assessing Russia's preferences with regard to strategic arms reductions are alternative projections of the natural evolution of its forces. I imagine ten scenarios. All projections are affected by the disintegration of the Soviet Union and its nuclear arms development and production complex; the deep economic and financial crisis in Russia resulting from the failed "reforms" of 1992–96; and disarry in Moscow decisionmaking on strategic programs and arms control talks, which has led to confused priorities in defense policy and wide divergence between force planning and arms control agreements on the one side and budgeting on the other.

As of April 1997 Russia had the following forces.

ICBMs

180 SS-18 (called Russian R-36 and R-36UTTH)

165 SS-19 (UR-100 and UR-100UTTH)

46 SS-24 (RT-23UTTH), including 10 in silos and 36 on railroad launchers

360 SS-25 (RT-2PM)

Bombers

74 Tu-95 (including 10 Tu-95MS, 29 Tu-95MS6, and 35 Tu-95MS16)

6 Tu-160 heavy bombers

Submarines

7 Delta-4 (Project 667 BDRM)

4 Typhoon (Project 941)

11 Delta-3 (Project 667BDR)

4 Delta-1 (Project 667B)

Total Submarine Force: 26 SSBNs, 416 missiles, and 1,824 warheads
Total Baseline Force: 1,241 launchers and 6,214 warheads[1]

The following projections should not be construed as representing actual Russian force planning. They are more illustrations of the logic of major hypothetical options, based on open information on existing forces and weapon programs as well as on simplified financial considerations and commonly known patterns of weapons deployment and withdrawal.

FIRST SCENARIO. By 2003 (the deadline for START II implementation) the natural decommissioning of technically obsolete weapons would probably bring these forces down to 40 SS-18, 120 SS-19, 46 SS-24, and 220 SS-25 ICBMs. The submarine force, for lack of maintenance and overhaul, would probably be drawn down to 3 Typhoon, 7 Delta-4, and 3 Delta-3s.[2] The bomber force may be expected to comprise no more than 20 airplanes, of which 8 would be Tu-160s. Thus the present level of funding, insufficient for adequate maintenance and timely overhaul or life-extension measures, would bring the baseline force to 666 launchers and 3,216 warheads.[3]

By 2010 the baseline force under the same conditions would go down to 50 SS-25 ICBMs, 1 Typhoon SSBN, 3 Delta-4 boats, and no bombers. Altogether, 118 launchers and 442 warheads.[4]

SECOND SCENARIO. Continuation of the present rate of procurement and deployment of SS-25 ICBMs and in a few years its follow-on SS-27 ICBM (RT-2UTTH Topol-M) would add to the baseline force about 70 missiles and warheads by 2003 and 150 by 2010. So by 2003, total warheads could be 3,286, and by 2010 could be 592.

THIRD SCENARIO. Better maintenance, overhaul, and life-extension programs with increased funding (by about 50 percent yearly for strategic forces) could add to the baseline-plus-new-deployment force (BPNDF) 50

1. These data are from Paul Podvig, "Russian Strategic Nuclear Forces, 1990–1997–2007," September 3, 1997. The April 1997 data are from the START I memorandum of understanding.

2. Under START II as well as START III the number of Typhoon submarines will be less than six; there will be at most three or four and maybe fewer. Accordingly, the SS-N-20 (R-39 and R-39UTTH) missiles will not be downloaded from ten to eight warheads, as was planned in the past, when it was expected that under START II six Typhoon, seven Delta-4, and seven Delta-3 SSBNs would be kept in service.

3. The total launchers are 426 ICBMs, 220 SLBMs, and 20 bombers. Total warheads are 1,800 on ICBMs, 1,192 on SLBMs, and 224 on the bombers. From White House, Office of the Press Secretary, "Joint Statement on Parameters on Future Reductions in Nuclear Forces," March 21, 1997.

4. The total launchers are 50 ICBMs, 68 SLBMs, and no bombers. Total warheads are 50 on ICBMs and 392 on SLBMs. From White House, Office of the Press Secretary, "Joint Statement Concerning the Anti-Ballistic Missile Treaty," March 21, 1997.

SS-25 ICBMs, 2 Typhoon SSBNs, and 15 Tu-95 bombers by 2003. This would add 620 warheads to the 3,286 for a total of 3,906.

By 2010 with the same maintenance measures and BPNDF, the forces could have an additional 70 SS-25 missiles, 2 Typhoon and 4 Delta-4 boats, and 8 Tu-160 bombers. These would add 854 warheads to the 592 for a total of 1,446.

The projection could be different if strategic forces are given much higher political priority in the years to come, increasing their yearly share even within the same defense budget by 100 percent. Another possibility is increasing the whole defense budget from the present 3.8 percent to 5 to 6 percent of GNP (from 20 percent to 30 percent of the federal budget) as proposed by some political groups and their partisans in the Duma. Finally, if the Russian economy starts to grow in 1998–99 and the budget revenues go up, this would permit higher spending on defense without increasing its share of the federal budget or GNP.

FOURTH SCENARIO. One of these alternatives or some combination of them might lead to higher rate of procurement of SS-27 ICBMs and the introduction of a new SSBN class (which may be called Delta-5) starting in 2000 at the rate of 2 boats every three years (which was the Typhoon deployment rate in the 1980s) By 2003 this would add to the force about 100 SS-25/27 missiles, and 240 by 2010. Deployment of Delta-5 SSBNs would add 240 SLBM warheads in 2003 and 840 in 2010, bringing the total warhead numbers to 4,246 in 2003 and 2,526 warheads in 2010.

FIFTH SCENARIO. If for whatever reason (for instance, a U.S. decision to deploy a nationwide ABM system) the decision is taken to equip the SS-27 with MIRV warheads, by 2010 a Russian total enhanced force could be as large as 4,100 warheads.

As may be seen, the first five alternatives, defined by various assumptions about funding and technical strategy, span a 25 percent difference in aggregate warhead numbers by 2003 (from 3,200 to 4,250) and an order of magnitude by 2010 (from 442 to 4,100).

Imposing an arms control framework on the above projections complicates the picture and multiplies the number of feasible alternatives. Assuming that START I is observed by both sides, the greatest difference will be made by the presence or absence of START II and III. If START II is not ratified by Russia and nothing is created as a substitute, the Russian strategic forces would most probably evolve along the third scenario. Because the U.S. forces in this case would most probably stay at the START I levels, Russian forces, while naturally degrading, would be turning more and more vulnerable each year. This vulnerablity would transform the first-strike emphasis of Moscow's new military doctrine from a purely political posture to the real and the only available employment option, which would be highly deterimental to strategic stability. Taking into account further degradation of Russia's command-control, early warning, and monitoring systems, this is all the more true.

At a certain point the United States may choose to deploy a nationwide strategic ABM system. Then the Russian response could follow the fifth scenario (revival of a MIRVed ICBM system and a crash modernization effort). All this would imply dire consequences for strategic stability, arms control, and political relations between Russia and the West.

SIXTH SCENARIO. Matching START II with a probable but highly inefficient policy, which is the direct extrapolation of the course of the past five years (the second scenario), would bring the Russian strategic force down to 1,806 warheads, since 1,475 warheads would have to be removed through dismantling and downloading MIRVed ICBMs several years ahead of the end of their service lifetime. The United States by the same time would easily maintain about 3,500 warheads, acquiring a double superiority just through implementation of START II.

SEVENTH SCENARIO. Thus, assuming a five-year extension agreement, which would provide for better maintenance, a smooth dismantling schedule, and a reasonable deployment rate, by 2008 Russian strategic forces could consist of 300 SS-25/27 ICBMs, 3 Typhoon and 7 Delta-4 SSBNs, and about 20 Tu-95/160 bombers. This would add up to 1,668 warheads. A relaxed Delta-5 construction schedule could provide 480 additional warheads for an aggregate level of 2,148 warheads.

EIGHTH SCENARIO. The force would still fall 30 percent short of the START II lower bracket and 40 percent short of the U.S. force level if it were maintained at the permitted maximum of 3,500 warheads. If Russian doctrine would insist on closer parity with U.S. forces, which is quite plausible, there would be two ways of closing the gap. One would be to go for higher ICBM and SSBN deployment rates and reach a force of about 2,500 warheads in 2008.

NINTH SCENARIO. Another option would be to move directly to a START III Treaty, with an aggregate ceiling down to 1,500–2,000 warheads. This would save resources for both the United States and Russia, relieve Russia from high expenditures on new deployments, and undermine the arguments of those in Moscow who call for the revival of MIRVed ICBMs as the only feasible way of matching U.S. force levels. The United States could easily fit under the 1,500 ceiling with 8 Trident SSBNs, 200 Minuteman III ICBMs, and 300 bombers or any other mix of forces.

TENTH SCENARIO. Interestingly enough, for Russia the peculiarity of START III in contrast to START II and all preceding strategic arms reduction treaties, is that it will not require force reductions beyond natural attrition but rather will affect the scale of maintenance efforts and the rate and system types of new deployment programs.

Provided a benign political environment, Russia and the United States could agree on much more radical force reductions under START III or START IV. To achieve much greater Russian savings on maintenance and modernization and U.S. savings on maintenance, after 2010 the parties could go down to a level as low as 1,000 or even 500 nuclear warheads. For Russia, decommissioning to 500 warheads would altogether remove the need for greater maintenance, virtually matching the first scenario of natural force degradation. If the United States agreed to a ceiling of 500 warheads after 2010, both sides might then agree to de-alert and deactivate the remaining forces. This would be as close to a general and comprehensive nuclear disarmament as may be imagined without departing completely from technical and strategic reality.

However, to go in this direction would require reaching a U.S.-Russian agreement on the desirability and feasibility of the reduction within the next two to three years. This is because within this time span Moscow will have to take important long-term decisions on its future nuclear doctrine and strategy, funding levels, maintenance, and modernization directions and rates.

Moving this fast would be a daunting challenge because it would require both countries to address many other complex issues, among them third nuclear weapon states' forces, strategic and theater defenses, tactical nuclear weapons, conventional force balances and capabilities, including counterforce potential of precision-guided systems, and nuclear, chemical, and missile proliferation in the world at large.

The scenarios in table A-1 are to 2010. By 2020, the target date for the deep cuts program to reach third-stage levels, Russia technically would be easily capable of fielding a force of 1,200–1,600 or even 2,000 warheads, largely depending on the rate of Delta-5 submarine construction and the choice of new ICBM and SLBM systems, including decisions on whether to develop a new MIRVed missile. These decisions will be affected by arms control considerations, prospects of strategic defenses, the policies of the middle nuclear weapon states, and general geopolitical trends.

In summary, the deep cuts study-group proposals for the timing, war-

Table A-1. Ten Scenarios of Russian Force Evolution, 2003–2010

Scenarios	Warhead numbers 2003	Warhead numbers 2010
1. Natural degradation	3,216	442
2. Plus current deployment rate	3,286	592
3. Plus adequate maintenance	3,906	1,446
4. Plus higher deployment rate	4,246	2,526
5. Plus new MIRVed ICBM	4,336	4,086
6. Second scenario plus START II	1,806	592
7. Third scenario plus START II extended	3,906	2,148
8. Fourth scenario plus START II extended	4,246	2,526
9. Third scenario plus START III (1,500–2,000)	3,906	1,446–2,000
10. Radical reduction START III, IV	1,806	442–529

Source: Author's calculations.

head numbers, and force structures under consecutive arms reduction treaties seem to be reasonable and acceptable to Russia, provided that more general factors are conducive to deep cuts. Particular corrections or options that could be suggested are of marginal importance and stay within the "noise band" of those more important considerations.

Reserve Warheads and De-alerting Options

Warheads not deployed, whether kept as a reserve force or a result of de-alerting, represent a problem for Russia and raise issues that must be addressed.

THE U.S. BREAKOUT ADVANTAGE. The downloading method of force reduction and the reserve of warheads thus created is a serious problem for START II. It was not missed by opponents in Russia that, in view of the asymmetries in strategic force structures of the two sides, U.S. reductions are to be implemented mostly by downloading U.S. missiles and bombers, while Russia must eliminate launchers and missiles.

America would be permitted to download Trident-1 and Trident-2 SLBMs and Minuteman III ICBMs, while putting its removed warheads and Peacekeeper ICBMs in storage and converting heavy bombers for conventional use, mostly by transporting their nuclear weapons to storage sites no closer than 100 km from the bombers' bases. In contrast, Russia's MIRVed ICBMs of heavy types are to be dismantled, while other MIRVed missiles would be eliminated as well. Putting them in storage would be senseless because their service lives will be over in any case within three to five years. Russian warheads are to be dismantled and their materials disposed of with U.S. help. Most Russian SSBNs and bombers will be withdrawn and dismantled due to obsolence, no bomber conversion is planned, and the SLBMs will be downloaded only marginally if at all.

The specific downloading provisions of START II are much in favor of the United States and provide it with a large superiority in breakout capability by way of uploading. In particular, if the United States were to withdraw from START II, it would be able to quickly upload its deployed ICBMs and SLBMs to 4,956 warheads, which is a higher level than the START I missile warhead ceiling (4,900 warheads).[5] If, in addition, the Peacekeeper ICBMs were returned from storage to their operational bases, this level would rise to 5,306. Together with deployed bomber weapons this would bring U.S. forces to more than 6,300 warheads. Reconverting the 95 B-1B modern heavy bombers back to their former nuclear mission (1,520 warheads) would bring U.S. warheads to more than 7,800.

In contrast, Russia's breakout potential would be only 525 warheads on SS-19 ICBMs.[6] Thus U.S. missile breakout capability would be ten times greater than Russia's. It is imaginable that, if the breakout ratio were reversed, the numbers in the vote for and against the ratification of the START II Treaty in the U.S. Senate (87 for, 4 against) would also have been reversed.

FIXING THE BREAKOUT PROBLEM. Of all the Russian criticisms of START II, the size of the U.S. breakout potential is in my view the most serious. Addressing it and extending the implementation schedule would go a long way in making the treaty more palatable to Russians and also more conducive to strategic stability. One way of doing this might be to use the INF-SRF Treaty precedent: agree to the verified elimination of the reentry shields of removed warheads and eliminate ALCMs associated with bombers converted to conventional missions in the same way GLCMs were eliminated. This would make breakout more costly and delayed and reduce the magnitude of U.S. superiority. Such an agreement might be fixed by adding a protocol to START II without reopening the treaty itself.

Later on, within the framework of the cooperative warhead dismantling and utilization of the nuclear materials, the verified elimination of the "physics packages" of the removed warheads could be added to the arms cuts. They should be dismantled and used under agreed verification procedures and on the basis of technical cooperation of the two sides.[7]

5. About 1,500 warheads on 500 Minuteman IIIs and 3,456 warheads on 18 Trident submarines.

6. Reloading the permitted number of 105 SS-19s from 1 to 6 warheads each.

7. Editor's note: At their March 1997 Helsinki meeting, Presidents Clinton and Yeltsin agreed to include in the START III negotiations, "measures relating to the transparency of strategic nuclear warhead inventories and the destruction of strategic nuclear warheads and

DE-ALERTING. The use of reserve warheads as an upload hedge should not be mixed up with de-alerting agreements, which could also result in a stockpile of warheads in storage. In the case of de-alerting, downloading would become unloading, that is removing all warheads from a delivery vehicle and storing them separately under specific verification procedures. De-alerting is mentioned in the deep cuts study, but it seems that this avenue deserves much greater attention as a supplement and in some cases even a substitute for arms reductions.

De-alerting a relatively small portion of the forces (perhaps 25–30 percent) while keeping the rest on a normal alert status, would not make a lot of sense for reducing surprise-attack capabilities, risk of unauthorized use, or costs. It would not affect nuclear postures enough to be worth the cost and complications of the technical arrangements and verification. Such a small de-alerting would do nothing more than simply transfer part of the force into reserve status and could be done unilaterally to save expenses and relax maintenance requirements.

In fact, as is pointed out in the study, both the United States and Russia presently have in this way "de-alerted" their bomber forces, elements of their C3I systems, and ICBM and submarine forces earmarked for dismantling under START I.

To really matter for its stated purposes and to be worth the trouble, an agreement on de-alerting should envelope a much larger portion of the forces, thus really affecting nuclear postures but permitting the retention of a large reserve of weapons for overt reconstitution of the forces if supreme national interests are endangered. The combat-ready portion should actually serve as a minimum deterrent, while the reserve force would alleviate concerns associated with the minimum-deterrent posture if taken in isolation (the effects of third nuclear powers, strategic defenses, conventional balances, technological breakthroughs, proliferation, requirements of extended deterrence, and so forth). Thus real de-alerting should apply to more than 50 percent of the forces, perhaps even 70 to 80 percent. In such a situation the principal issue would be the methods of de-alerting.

The most effective and easily verifiable method of de-alerting would be to remove and store the warheads separately—perhaps entire "buses" in the case of multiple-warhead missiles—from ICBMs and SLBMs and keep bomber nuclear weapons in depots.

Concerns most frequently raised with regard to this method are the costs,

---

any other jointly agreed technical and organizational measures, to promote the irreversibility of deep reductions including prevention of a rapid increase in the number of warheads."

technical complexities, and safety problems of transporting and storing thousands of nuclear warheads. In addition, there is the predictable vulnerability of the storage sites to nuclear or conventional counter-reconstitution strikes.

Removing the aerodynamic nose cone (or shroud) from the upper stage of the missiles, instead of removing warheads, would have major advantages with regard to costs, safety, and technical complexity. The reconstitution time and possibilities for verification, compared with warhead removal would not be much different. One other important advantage might be the invulnerability of the aeroshells, the location of which could be concealed from the other side. Alternatively, they could be placed in hardened storage locations such as empty missile silos.

Such considerations would mostly affect the postexchange possibilities of reconstituting silo-based and mobile ICBMs becausee all de-alerted bombers and submarines would, in any case, be destroyed in their bases. If de-alerting were implemented before the START II reductions, this would matter for MIRVed ICBMs. After START II, with only single-warhead missiles in service, this method would, for Russia, mean removing warheads themselves and putting them in storage in any case, because the SS-25M aeroshell is integrated with its reentry vehicle. Once again, these stored warheads could be targeted and destroyed by nuclear and conventional strikes.

It is conceivable that, for technical and economic considerations different methods could be applied to single-warhead ICBMs (removing warheads), MIRVed ICBMs and SLBMs (removing aeroshells), and bombers (placing bombs and ALCMs in storage no less than 100 km from bases). If enough storage space is available at naval bases, it might be easier and safer to remove entire SLBMs from submarine tubes.

De-alerting might complement disarmament by going much faster in the same direction of reducing the probability of deliberate or accidental nuclear war at smaller cost. Substantial de-alerting, by its very nature, is an efficient confidence-building and transparency undertaking that would also change traditional modes of operation of nuclear forces and render inadvertent nuclear war less likely. (In particular, submarine patrols and bomber flights without nuclear weapons would be conducted for training purposes only, as would practice dispersals of mobile ICBMs. Much lower armed combat patrol rates of SSBNs, bringing their number at sea during ordinary times down to one or two, would also be an obvious consequence. The probability of environmentally or militarily dangerous accidents would also go down significantly.

In the most optimistic scenario, arms control at levels of less than 1,000 warheads might be achieved by de-alerting a larger and larger portion of the nuclear forces and correspondingly reducing the combat-ready component. In parallel, forces de-alerted at earlier stages might be gradually deactivated. In a first stage, warheads might be partially dismantled, readiness and maintenance standards for weapons relaxed, missile gyros stopped, and flight programs withdrawn from on-board computers. At a second stage the weapon systems might be completely eliminated or just not replaced when their service lifetimes end. Below some very low number of combat-ready nuclear weapons (100–200 warheads), further progress might take the form not of elimination but rather of de-alerting and then deactivation under comprehensive international control and monitoring.

Deep cuts and de-alerting would transform the U.S.-Russia strategic relationship, profoundly affecting deterrence doctrines, nuclear strategies, and targeting. In this connection the policy proposed by the study—to develop alternative attack options but not to publicly reject counterstrikes against cities—seems to be too conservative and lacking in creativity. An alternative would be to substitute a very different strategy for the present strategic logic of vacillation between massive counterforce and counterindustrial strikes.

DE-ALERTED FORCES AS TARGETS. Maintenance of relatively small combat-ready forces (a few hundred warheads) while retaining a vast reconstitution infrastructure would make the primary threat scenario that of a preemptive strike with limited forces to deprive the other side of its reconstitution capability, thereby gaining a monopoly on reconstitution and quickly establishing a clear-cut nuclear superiority.

Each side would therefore probably target its available combat-ready forces against the reconstitution infrastructure of the other side: nuclear warhead and material storage facilities, transportation nodes, maintenance and force-loading facilities, bases of de-alerted forces, final assembly plants, and plutonium production, recycling, and warhead manufacturing enterprises. Also, a much larger proportion of the Russian and U.S. forces might be allocated to targeting third nuclear weapon states and the bases and nuclear production sites in threshold nuclear states. First-strike or first-use strategies or launch-on-warning concepts would become irrelevant and should be renounced, at least in the strategic relationships among the five primary nuclear powers.

Outer Shell Issues

The deep cuts program addresses several issues that, while not directly related to the numbers of strategic weapons allowed at each stage, are nevertheless of paramount importance to the feasibility of achieving deep reductions in nuclear weapons. These issues relate, in particular, to the limits placed on strategic nuclear weapons, limits on the nuclear forces of "third" countries, the treatment of tactical nuclear weapons and conventional forces, and the ways in which a deep cuts regime intersects with the longer-term goal of abolition.

Limits on Strategic Defenses

START II contains a dubious commitment to respect the ABM Treaty and refers simultaneously to the joint U.S.-Russian declaration of 1992 on global antimissile defense. The most effective Russian ABM penetration system, heavy SS-18 ICBMs, would be eliminated under START II. SLBMs and single-warhead ICBMs are much less efficient in countering ABM systems. The actions of the U.S. Congress to expand and accelerate the U.S. strategic ballistic missile defense program to be ready for the initial deployment of a national defense in 2003, when final START II limits are to be implemented, could not have been deliberately arranged to be more convenient to the opponents of START II in Russia.

The U.S. program of theater ballistic missile defense (TMD) has also deadlocked the U.S.-Russian talks at the Standing Consultative Commission on the delineation between strategic and tactical defenses. The Russian concern is that the TMD systems could provide the United States with considerable collateral strategic defense capability and an enhanced technological base for deploying an effective dedicated strategic ballistic missile defense of U.S. territory and abrogation of the ABM Treaty after 2003.

Satisfying both renewed U.S. interest in ABM defenses and the Russian demand for a much stronger linkage of START II and further reductions with the ABM Treaty is no easy task. The way out could be a package deal based on the following main principles and policies.

—Deployment limitations. American proposals for permissive definitions of TMD might be accepted if combined with politically binding commitments to abstain from deployment of such systems in areas beyond the reach of intermediate- or theater-range missiles of any third country and with an understanding that Russia would not consider China's or Israel's intermediate and medium-range missiles a justification for massive TMD deployments on its territory. To facilitate this condition, the United States and Russia would undertake to exchange information on missile programs and deployments of nonaligned third states and to cooperate in monitoring and warning information, systems, and technology.

—Cooperation on TMD. The United States and Russia would commit to a much more ambitious program of technological cooperation in developing TMD systems. This is completely rational because neither side has theater missiles within range of each other's territory or forces and soon neither will have such systems at all. Cooperation would make systems more cost effective and provide additional insurance that they would not be given dedicated strategic capabilities. The primary candidates for a joint venture are obviously the U.S. THAAD and Russian S-400 systems.

—Conditions for amending the ABM Treaty. Both parties would agree that, if longer-range missiles proliferate and seriously threaten their national territories, they would be ready to revise the ABM Treaty. As a first step they could return to its original version, which permitted two ABM deployment areas in each country (reduced to one by a protocol in 1974). Further expansion of permitted ABM coverage or liberalization of qualitative limitations under the treaty would be envisioned if the long-range missile threat from proliferants increased during the next decade. In such a case, as an insurance against each others' ballistic missile defense systems, both sides might agree to allow deployments of limited numbers of warheads on MIRVed ICBMs under START III or START IV. At the same time, both sides would commit not to make unilateral interpretations or revisions of the treaty.[8]

The "Third" Nuclear Weapon States

Making bilateral reductions beyond START II might be unacceptable to the

8. Editor's note: At their March 1997 Helsinki Summit, Presidents Clinton and Yeltsin agreed that "Both sides must have the option to establish and to deploy effective theater missile defense systems [but that]:

—Theater missile defense systems may be deployed by each side which (1) will not pose a realistic threat to the strategic nuclear force of the other side and (2) will not be tested to give such systems that capability.

—Theater missile defense systems will not be deployed by the sides for use against each other.

—The scale of deployment—in number and geographic scope—of theater missile defense systems by either side will be consistent with theater ballistic missile programs confronting that side. . . .

—The sides will exchange detailed information annually on TMD plans and programs. . . ."

The Presidents also agreed that there is considerable scope for cooperation in theater missile defense. They are prepared to explore integrated cooperative defense efforts, inter alia, in the provision of early warning support for TMD activities, technology cooperation in areas related to TMD, and expansion of the ongoing program of cooperation in TMD exercises.

"In resolving the tasks facing them, the Parties will act in a spirit of cooperation, mutual openness, and commitment to the ABM Treaty."

United States or Russia or both, depending on the nuclear arms programs of Britain, France, and China, the third nuclear weapon states (TNWS). But if, as it now appears, the envisioned or suspected force modernization programs of these states are curtailed and a comprehensive test ban is ratified by all five declared nuclear powers, bilateral U.S.-Russian reductions drop to the 2,000 or even 1,000 warheads without bothering about the TNWS. At some later point, however, limitation on the British, French, and Chinese forces would become a necessary condition for further U.S.-Russian arms cuts.

One way of dealing with this problem would be for Russia to reach an agreement on an equal SLBM warhead ceiling with the combined forces of Britain and France. The United States, Russia, and China could agree to an equal ceiling for their ICBM warheads (or, as an option, fixed ICBM warheads). This could satisfy both the TNWS demand for formal equality and the insistence of the United States and Russia on preserving their traditional advantages.

The first goal, equal limits, would be fulfilled by agreeing on equal levels of forces subject to limitation under the treaties. These forces would make up the bulk of the TNWS forces, but the countries would not formally be precluded from expanding other legs of their triads not limited by the agreements. The second goal, preserving the advantages of the United States and Russia, would be achieved by each having a triad (perhaps later a dyad) with a total number of warheads larger than those of any of the TNWS and limited only by their bilateral treaties.

Below the 1,000-warhead level the same compromise between U.S.-Russian and TNWS preferences could be achieved by using innovative de-alerting and deactivation agreements. For instance, a treaty might be concluded to limit U.S., Russian, and French-British combat-ready forces to equal warhead ceilings, while leaving U.S. and Russian dealerted weapons subject only to bilateral limitations. If, as suggested above, the de-alerted portions would constitute as much as 70 to 80 percent of U.S. and Russian overall forces, that would leave them with corresponding superiority in total potential force. For an agreement limiting U.S. and Russian overall force levels to 2,000 warheads, the multilaterally limited parts would then consist of 400-600 deployed warheads. For an aggregate ceiling of 1,000 warheads the limit to be negotiated between the United States, Russia, and TNWS would cap their combat-ready forces at 200-300 warheads.

Procedures for dealerting and deactivation as well as adequate verification provisions would have to be elaborated. Theoretically, the TNWS would be entitled to expand their dealerted forces to match the big two, but

Table A-2. Russian Tactical Nuclear Warheads Subject to Elimination by 2003

Weapons	Total in service in 1991	Subject to elimination in accordance with USSR–Russian commitments	To be eliminated	
			1997 (political)	2003 (technical)
Ground forces				
Rocket forces	4,000	4,000	4,000	4,000
Artillery	2,000	2,000	2,000	2,000
Corps of Engineers (atomic demolition mines)	700	700	500	700
Air Defense (ground-to-air missiles)	3,000	1,500	2,400	3,000
AF Frontal Aviation (bombs, short-range air-to-surface missiles)	7,000	3,500	6,000	7,000
General purpose navy				
Ships and submarines (antiship, antisubmarine, land-attack)	3,000	1,000	1,000	3,000
Naval aviation	2,000	1,000	2,000	2,000
Total	21,700	13,700	17,900	21,700

Source: Author's calculations.

it is highly unlikely that they would use this opportunity. Even if they did, the United States and Russia would be able to retain their latent superiority by agreeing to expand their dealerted force levels too, if they considered it worthwhile.

Reducing Tactical Nuclear Forces

Tactical nuclear forces would acquire greater significance with the reduction of the strategic forces. According to publicly available data, the United States retains about 1,000 tactical nuclear weapons. These include about 600 B-61 gravity bombs, some of which are deployed in Europe, and 350 nuclear-tipped SLCMs in storage. The weapons in Europe could be delivered by U.S. and allied NATO dual-purpose strike aircraft.

The numbers of Russian tactical nuclear munitions are shown in table A-1. Most tactical nuclear munitions earmarked for destruction by 1997, in accordance with the commitments of the Soviet Union and Russian Federation, were to be eliminated anyway by 2003 because their design lives will have expired. This means that the undertakings with regard to tactical nuclear weapons would boil down to the obligation to limit production of new weapons to replace physically obsolete ones.

Whereas in 1991 the USSR had about 22,000 tactical nuclear weapons, at present Russia retains around 3,800, including 200 atomic demolition munitions, 600 air defense missile warheads, 1,000 gravity bombs and short-range air-to-surface missiles, and 2,000 naval antiship, antisubmarine, and land-attack weapons. All those are in the depots of the air force, navy, and air defense or in central storage facilities of the nuclear-technical troops of the Twelfth Main Directorate of the Ministry of Defense. Those that are withdrawn from the active service are in the central storage facilities of the Twelfth Directorate, in the storage facilities of the production-dismantling plants, or in transit to these sites.

Because all available facilities at the four Russian nuclear warhead assembly plants are overburdened by accelerated dismantling of strategic and tactical nuclear munitions (including those withdrawn from other former Soviet republics), assembly of new weapons is proceeding very slowly. It is unlikely that after 2003 there will be more than a few hundred or at most 1,000 tactical nuclear weapons in the Russian armed forces.

Tactical nuclear weapons are extremely controversial in Russia's security debate. Deep reductions in strategic forces make NATO tactical nuclear weapons in Europe a greater threat to Russia. According to the latest Russian military estimates, after 2000 the losses of Russia's land-based missile force caused by a NATO air strike with the weapons could be as high as 70 percent of fixed-based and 20 percent of mobile ICBMs. Much greater damage could be inflicted on naval and airbases, nuclear-support infrastructure, and C^3I facilities. The estimates further consider the hypothetical effect of a coordinated strike of tactical aircraft with nuclear weapons and strategic offensive forces and found them to be 1.5 to 2 times higher than that of a strategic missile strike only.

If NATO expansion continues to central and eastern Europe, and eventually to the Baltic republics, regions in which the Soviet Union developed a dense airfield infrastructure during the cold war (much better and larger than is available in Russia itself), this perceived threat would be much greater.

From this perspective, Russia should be interested in total elimination of tactical nuclear weapons, or at least in their complete withdrawal from Europe. But in view of NATO's vast conventional superiority, which could be increased by NATO expansion, Russia can only rely on tactical nuclear weapons to make up for its conventional inferiority, much as NATO did during the cold war decades. The potential threat from China in the east makes the weapons even more important for Russia's security. Both factors were reflected in the Russian military doctrine adopted in November 1993 that emphasizes a nuclear first-use, first-strike strategy.

The way out of this situation may be a special agreement with full transparency and verification measures on deep reductions and limitations on tactical nuclear weapons. U.S.-Russian cooperation on eliminating nuclear weapons and use of the weapon-grade uranium has in recent years already paved the way toward such an agreement. This new avenue of arms control would also be indispensable for strengthening the security of nuclear weapons and nuclear materials in Russia. As shown in table A-2, the enormous backlog of tactical nuclear weapons and the need for their elimination on an unprecedented scale and in a short time potentially create the greatest threat of this kind.

From this point of view, one possibility considered in the deep cuts study—to mash together "reserve" strategic and tactical nuclear warheads—does not look sound. A much better solution would be to reach a separate agreement to reduce U.S. and Russian tactical nuclear weapons to about 500 by 2003. No more than 100 would be permitted to each side in Europe—in the Conventional Forces in Europe (CFE) Treaty this means the territory from the Atlantic to the Urals. Any type of tactical nuclear deployment would be prohibited in the former East Germany, central and eastern European states, or in any former Soviet republic except Russia. American tactical nuclear weapons should be withdrawn from Turkey. Russia would be banned from their deployment in the North Caucasus and Leningrad military districts (except naval systems on the Kola peninsula). Within the framework of de-alerting, tactical gravity bombs should be prohibited from storage at any airfield depots except those for alerted heavy bombers. Otherwise they should be stored not closer than 100 km from any airbase.

After 2003, in parallel with START II and START III, the number of tactical nuclear weapons could be progressively reduced to 100–200, and depending on the developments in Europe, they might be totally banned from deployment on the Continent. Eventually, if relations with China and the nonproliferation regime develop according to an optimistic scenario, they could be banned altogether. Such an agreement should be multilateral and include all nuclear weapon states.

Conventional Counterforce Capabilities

Another serious issue is the projected vulnerability of strategic forces to conventional counterforce strikes with precision-guided air-launched and sea-launched weapons (SLCMs and carrier aircraft).

According to some military forecasts, about 240 strategic bombers and 5,500 tactical strike aircraft are currently available to NATO worldwide.

By 2000 these numbers may be respectively 180 and 6,500, of which 25 percent of heavy bombers and 5 to 7 percent of tactical aviation may be realistically allocated for conventional strikes against Russian strategic forces. All Russian fixed and mobile missile bases would be within range of converted heavy bombers and about 40 to 50 percent within range of tactical aircraft.

After 2000, with implementation of most of the START II reductions and with planned strategic force modernization complete, NATO aircraft would be capable of destroying 60 percent of Russia's fixed and 15 percent of its mobile ICBM launchers. Much greater damage could be inflicted by conventional strikes on command-control-communication systems, airbases, naval bases, nuclear weapon storage facilities, and support infrastructure.

Conventional counterforce capability favors the United States because Russia virtually lacks conventional, let alone counterforce, strike capability against the U.S. homeland. Although the conventional counterforce threat may seem a negligible problem when both sides have large and combat-ready strategic forces, the situation will appear very different with deeply cut and partially de-alerted nuclear forces. In fact, conventional attacks might effectively deny Russia a reconstitution capability for its de-alerted forces. NATO expansion would further increase the Western preponderance by adding new members' aircraft and bringing the alliance a thousand kilometers closer to Russia's strategic bases and infrastructure.

Thus if the concepts of deep cuts and de-alerting are to be made more palatable to Russia, something should be done to remove NATO's preponderant conventional counterforce capability. This is hard to do because even a follow-on to the CFE Treaty would leave NATO with thousands of strike aircraft, and it would be very difficult to limit their performance and improvements in precision-guided weapons and command-control-information assets.

One way of dealing with this problem might be to elaborate a CFE-2 treaty in such a way that the massive redeployment of U.S. and NATO tactical strike aircraft and converted heavy bombers to eastern Europe would be prohibited. Currently, NATO states are entitled by the CFE to have about 6,700 tactical combat airplanes in the Atlantic-to-the-Urals zone, while Russia is permitted 3,450 aircraft. Former Soviet Warsaw Pact allies may retain 1,650 planes.

One option for CFE-2 could be to reduce these entitlements 50 percent by 2000 or 2003 and, in contrast to the present CFE, place zonal sublimits on aircraft, prohibiting deployment of more than 800 airplanes on the territory of former Soviet allies. To make this limitation palatable to the central European states, the same 50 percent reduction should be applied to Russia, Ukraine, and other former Soviet republics that are parties to CFE. No more than 800 airplanes would be permitted on the territory of Ukraine and other former Soviet republics other than Russia.

Furthermore, no more than 800 airplanes would be based in Russia, in the North Caucasus and Leningrad districts, and the western part of the Moscow military district. National entitlements could in this way be matched with zonal limits.

More stringent confidence-building measures on notification of aircraft redeployments or exercises and on redeployments of naval forces (especially aircraft carriers) would also be conducive to the alleviation of the perceived threat of conventional counterforce attacks.

This logic might indeed be applied to all other weapons covered by CFE. This does not relate directly to strategic arms cuts, but would facilitate European security and cooperation, including U.S.-Russian arms control efforts. If NATO is expanded to the east, CFE-2 and new confidence-building measures, as well as other limiting commitments (for example, on the deployment of tactical nuclear weapons) might at least somewhat reduce the political damage and make revival of cooperative relations between Russia and the West a little easier and earlier. At best, such new agreements, by alleviating security concerns of European states, including Russia, could postpone and eventually freeze NATO extension and military reintegration of post-Soviet states around Russia.

Strategic arms cuts below 1,000 warheads would require more radical reductions and restructuring of the conventional forces in Europe. Their integration along the lines of the Partnership for Peace and assignment exclusively for collective peace-enforcement and peacekeeping operations in Europe, and beyond Europe under the UN mandate, would open the way for further cuts, de-alerting, deactivation, and elimination of nuclear forces and the multilateralization of nuclear arms control.

Abolition

The deep cuts study gives some attention to the sacramental question of whether it is possible to conceive going below 200 nuclear warheads and eventually reaching complete nuclear disarmament. With respect to this question, it should be emphasized that the issue is not just whether it is technically, strategically, or politically possible, but rather whether the United States, Russia, and other states are willing to pay the price for a world free of nuclear weapons. In any case, what is meant by nuclear disarmament is varying degrees of depth of deactivation of nuclear weapons, implying different costs and time delays for reconstitution.

Nuclear weapons are the ultimate instrument and pillar of national sovereignty, and an expensive, dangerous, and provocative instrument at that. That is why so few states acquired nuclear weapons during the first half century of the nuclear age, and this is why those that have done it are so reluctant to give up nuclear arms.

Giving up nuclear weapons without making the world safe for conventional wars or creating too great a risk of nuclear cheating by some state or terrorist group would require enormous sacrifice of national sovereignty by major powers. To fill the gap created by abolishing nuclear deterrence as a primary factor of power politics, they would have to construct effective international organizations for conflict resolution, peacekeeping, and peace enforcement. They should be ready to abide by the decisions of such organizations, even against their perceived national interests. The international hierarchy would change dramatically, which would first affect Russia but eventually the United States as well. The right of veto in world affairs would have to be abandoned by major powers, and they would be severely constrained in their security policies and defense programs. They would have to concede all nuclear industries and dual-purpose technologies to comprehensive controls and possibly international management and profit extraction. They would also have to transfer all missile technologies, programs, and employment to international corporations for use and for exploration of outer space.

Whether nuclear disarmament is worth all this sacrifice and trouble is a philosophical, not technical or strategic, issue. But it brings to mind a joke from Soviet Communist days. A man was being tested for joining the Communist party and being instructed about his duties as a good Communist: to stop drinking, smoking, taking bribes, and having mistresses; and to get rid of his excessive living space, extra dachas, and cars. To everyone's surprise the final demand of the ultimate sacrifice: to be ready, if need be, to give his life for the party, was accepted by him most easily. "What the hell is the sense of such a life?" he explained.

China's Nuclear Disarmament Policy

Li Bin

The evolution of China's nuclear strategy may be divided into three stages. First, when no Chinese nuclear weapon could reach the territories of the Superpowers, China sought to devalue the nuclear threat, as with Mao Zedong's famous likening of nuclear weapons to paper tigers: they look terrible but are not really usable.[1] Then as China's nuclear capacity grew, its nuclear strategy entered a second stage.[2] Given that very few Chinese nuclear weapons could have survived a first nuclear strike by the United States or Soviet Union, China sought to create uncertainty regarding the scale and character of its nuclear arsenal and to instill uncertainty in any country seeking to destroy all Chinese nuclear weapons. In the third stage, which China has now entered, its main focus has shifted to ensuring that a small retaliatory force would survive a first strike by the United States or Russia.

It is unclear how fully China has succeeded in achieving this third-stage goal. It is clear, however, that before it will be able to join a deep cuts regime, it will have to be assured that it has sufficient survivable nuclear weapons

This analysis is the author's personal interpretation.

1. Mao did not believe that a conventional world war would necessarily kill fewer people than a nuclear war. Indeed, he thought that a war in the era before gunpowder could kill as many people as a nuclear war. So he said that there is no need to have a special terror of nuclear weapons. See Lian Shen and others, eds., *The Chinese Diplomacy in the Past 100 Years* (Shenyang, China: Shenyang Publishing, 1995), p. 603.

2. On May 18, 1980, China successfully conducted a missile flight test with a range of more than 9,000 km. The tested missile was a liquid-fuel land-based intercontinental ballistic missile. See Xie Guang and others, eds., *Contemporary Chinese Science and Technology for National Defense* (Beijing, Contemporary China Publishing, 1992), pp. 327–38. A missile with this range could reach almost all the territory of the former Soviet Union and the northern part of the West Coast of the United States.

to deter a nuclear attack. This will depend both on its nuclear forces and the extent of U.S. and Russian nuclear disarmament. Here I try to estimate how far the United States and Russia will have to go in reducing their nuclear forces before China can begin reducing its nuclear arsenal.

In the early 1980s China proposed a disarmament initiative called Three Stops and One Cut. Under this proposal the United States and the former Soviet Union would stop the testing, deployment, and production of nuclear weapons, and they would cut their nuclear arsenals by 50 percent.[3] Once these steps were taken, China favored a one-package approach to a nuclear-weapon-free world; it was not interested in participating in negotiating one-by-one modest nuclear arms control agreements.

Since the late 1980s this policy has changed in two important respects. First, the Chinese government no longer mentions the 50 percent cut; it now asks for more dramatic nuclear reductions by the United States and Russia. Second, China has withdrawn its opposition to step-by-step negotiations; it actively participated in the negotiations on the Comprehensive Test Ban Treaty, and it has promised to join negotiations on a Treaty on the Prohibition of the Production of Fissile Materials for Weapons (Fissile Cut-off Treaty).

The reasons for the change of position may be guessed. When China proposed the Three Stops and One Cut initiative, it believed that if the superpowers could summon the political will to cut their nuclear arsenals by 50 percent, very much deeper nuclear reductions would quickly follow. Events have belied this assumption. It is now clear that negotiations on deep reductions will take time, especially if they are disrupted by changes in political administrations. China's new willingness to negotiate nuclear arms control agreements one by one is probably in large part due to its greater openness in international relations and the rapid growth of its economy. Beijing has realized that its active participation in arms control and disarmament can help build a peaceful and friendly international environment that will benefit economic development. It can be expected that China will adopt a still more active policy on nuclear disarmament in the future as it makes further economic progress.

Conditions to Ensure a Minimum Retaliatory Capability

To understand what would be required to get China to join a global nuclear reductions process, one has to understand how Beijing perceives the role of

3. See Beijing International Strategic Association, *Concise Handbook on Armament and Disarmament in the World* (Beijing: Military Publishing Co., 1986), p. 7.

nuclear weapons. According to the statements of the Chinese government, the sole purpose of China's nuclear weapons is to deter nuclear attack. For this it needs a certain number of nuclear weapons that could survive a first strike and penetrate the attacker's defenses. These weapons should be able to produce intolerable damage in the country of the attacker. In assessments of strategic stability between the United States and Russia, analysts often estimated the minimum number of warheads required to produce intolerable damage to be in the hundreds.[4] For China's deterrence requirements against a U.S. (or Russian) first strike, I suggest a new way to estimate such a number.

In a dispute with China the United States (or Russia) would have three options: peaceful resolution, conventional war, or nuclear war. China must make certain that the United States and Russia are aware that the nuclear option is not acceptable; and because a conventional war between nuclear weapon states could escalate to nuclear war, this option would not be acceptable either.

There were many reasons for ending the wars. One common and important one, however, was that both countries lost tens of thousands of lives.[5] These experiences suggest that the prospect of losing more than tens of thousands of lives in a war would likely deter the United States or Russia from initiating such a war. Specifically, the capability to deliver one or a handful of nuclear warheads in retaliation should be adequate to deter a first nuclear strike launched by the United States or Russia.[6]

To calculate how many deployed strategic warheads are needed to ensure such minimum retaliatory capability, it is necessary to estimate the fraction of China's nuclear weapons that could be destroyed by a first strike or lost in penetrating the defenses of the attacker. Such a calculation is presented in table B-1 under the following assumptions.

—U.S. and Russian nuclear arsenals have similar sizes and configurations,

4. See, for example, Alvin M. Saperstein and Gottfried Mayer-Kress, "A Nonlinear Dynamic Model of the Impact of SDI on the Arms Race," *Journal of Conflict Resolution*, vol. 32 (December 1988), pp. 636–70. In this paper the number of warheads that would produce intolerable damage in the United States and Russia was given as 500.

5. In the Korean War 23,000 U.S. soldiers were killed; in the Vietnam War 56,000 U.S. soldiers were killed. See Yu Zhishen, *History of the U.S.A.* (Shanghai: Huadong Normal University Publishing, 1992), p. 232. In the Afghan War 14,500 Soviet soldiers were killed. See *News Digests*, January 30, 1993.

6. The number of people killed by a nuclear warhead would depend on many factors, especially the yield of the weapon and the population density around its explosion point. Two bombs used against Hiroshima (equivalent to 12.5 kilotons of TNT) and Nagasaki (equivalent to 22 kilotons of TNT) killed approximately 78,000 and 38,000 people, respectively. If we assume a 1 megaton nuclear warhead exploded over a big city with the same population density as Hiroshima and Nagasaki, it would be expected to kill 700,000 people.

Table B-1. Nuclear Weapons Needed by China under Various Assumptions[a]

Warheads in the U.S. arsenal	Numbers of Chinese weapons and hypothetical deployment			
Treaty	Silo-based	One-dimensionally mobile	Two-dimensionally mobile	Submarine-based
START II: Operational and hedge ICBM: 1,400 SLBM: 2,130	1,200	167	22	30
START II : Operational only ICBM: 500 SLBM: 1,680	800	112	18	30
START III Total : 1,000 ICBM: 230 SLBM: 770	430	57	14	30
START IV Total : 500 ICBM: 115 SLBM: 385	250	33	12	30

a. Hardness of silos is assumed to be 140 atmospheres. The hardness of the mobile missiles is assumed to be 2 atmospheres, and the speed of the mobile launchers to be 1 km per minute. It would take 7 minutes for the launcher to escape from a 100 kt warhead, 11 minutes for a 500 kt warhead. For the submarines, it is assumed that one-third will be unlocatable at sea at all times.

and a force sufficient to deter the United States would also be sufficient to deter Russia.

—Only intercontinental ballistic missiles (ICBMs) and submarine-launched ballistic missiles (SLBMs) are used in the first strike against Chinese nuclear weapons. Strategic bombers and tactical nuclear weapons are not considered in the calculation.

—The ratio of the number of warheads on U.S. ICBMs and SLBMs remains the same after the deeper reductions projected for U.S. START II forces.

—Missile defenses are not considered in the calculation (although see below).

—All Chinese nuclear weapons are deployed in a single mode. Four modes are considered: ICBMs based in silos; land-based ICBMs that are one-dimensionally mobile (meaning that the weapons are restricted to moving along a highway or railway, with no opportunity to scatter in other directions); land-based ICBMs that are two-dimensionally mobile (that is, they could travel off roads); and ballistic missiles based on submarines. China would probably choose some combination of all four modes of basing, but the results shown in the table could be adjusted accordingly.

—The parameters of the Chinese nuclear weapons are the same as those of the U.S. and Soviet weapons assumed by Feiveson and von Hippel.[7]

—The number of Chinese nuclear weapons required to survive an attack is ten (if delivered over populated areas or against concentrations of troops, ten nuclear warheads could kill far more than the tens of thousands mentioned).

Table B-1 shows that the number of nuclear weapons needed by China depends significantly on the deployment mode. If China could increase the survivability of its nuclear arsenal without expanding it, it would be able to join a nuclear reductions process much earlier. A move to more survivable basing would also have other benefits: it would reinforce China's no-first-use pledge; it would reduce the incentives of other nuclear weapon states to launch first nuclear strikes against China in a crisis; and it would make it somewhat easier for the United States and Russia to negotiate further nuclear reductions. In fact, China reportedly has acquired mobile and solid-fueled nuclear-armed ballistic missiles that have higher survivability than its first-generation nuclear weapons.[8]

Nevertheless, although START II represents a first step toward substantial nuclear reductions, the treaty by itself does not appear a deep enough cut in the arsenals to create a favorable environment for China to join the nuclear reductions process. As shown in table B-1, if the parties to the treaty maintain a hedge, the situation would look still more unfavorable to China. By contrast, if the U.S.-Russian reductions proceed to the deeper cuts outlined in this book and China moves to more invulnerable basing, it could become confident in its retaliatory capability and join in the reductions.

Such calculations assume no national ballistic missile defense by the United States, however. The development of such defenses would create a serious barrier for China's nuclear disarmament policy. Even a very thin nationwide missile defense system could weaken China's nuclear retaliatory capability, or at least weaken its confidence in its retaliatory capability. Similarly, even systems ostensibly focused on theater missile defense (TMD) will be of concern to China. As shown in chapter 5, some of the TMD systems being developed by the United States could have significant capability against strategic ballistic missiles. It is therefore strongly in China's interests that the United States and Russia maintain strict compliance with an unmodified ABM Treaty.

7. Harold A. Feiveson and Frank von Hippel, "Beyond START: How to Make Much Deeper Cuts."

8. See Xie Guang and others, *Contemporary Chinese Science and Technology*, pp. 301–05.

China's Participation in Nuclear Disarmament

Although China may not yet be ready to join in the deep cuts process, it could still do something to show political support for nuclear disarmament. For example, it could set quantitative limits on its nuclear arsenal and reduce the percentage of vulnerable weapons. China could set quantitative limitations on its nuclear arsenal in one of three ways.

—First, it could state that it would not expand its nuclear arsenal significantly. Although such a statement could not be translated into an accurately quantitative limitation, it could express a political willingness to constrain the scale of its nuclear arsenal. It could increase U.S. and Russian confidence that their bilateral nuclear reductions would not be challenged by a Chinese buildup.

—China could set a ceiling on its nuclear arsenal by negotiating and signing a cutoff treaty. The potential scale of its nuclear arsenal would then be limited by its existing stockpiles of fissile materials for weapons. This limit would be uncertain because of uncertainties about the sizes of these stockpiles and the amounts of fissile material contained in Chinese warheads. Nevertheless, a cutoff treaty would place a meaningful limit on the number of Chinese nuclear warheads, indeed, a much lower limit than those that the United States and Russia will undertake in START II.

—China could unilaterally declare a numerical limit on its nuclear arsenal or negotiate such a number with other countries. If it chose a low ceiling, it would provide significant new information on the scale of its nuclear arsenal.

As I have stressed, China's willingness to take these or similar actions will depend on progress in U.S.-Russian arms reduction. China could also be encouraged to adopt a more active disarmament policy if the United States and Russia made no-first-use commitments. In the past several decades the United States has repeatedly rejected the idea of such a commitment; and Russia has recently withdrawn from the no-first-use pledge undertaken by the Soviet Union. These policies seem shortsighted. The United States in particular has very strong conventional forces and has no need to use nuclear weapons to deter conventional attacks by other countries. The refusal of the nuclear superpowers to adopt no first use raises concern in China that they might use nuclear weapons more readily in a crisis. This is a constraint on China's willingness to take more far-reaching disarmament steps.

Visible Arrangements in a No-First-Use Regime

The nuclear force of a country whose nuclear strategy is indeed based on no first use should have some visible characteristics. People could build some confidence that this country would be unlikely to launch a first nuclear strike by checking these characteristics. In another words, a no-first-use regime could be more attractive if some nonintrusive or not-too-intrusive arrangements are made to constrain the nuclear forces of the nuclear weapon parties to this regime.

Size of the Operational Nuclear Arsenal

The number of nuclear warheads used in retaliation to produce intolerable damage was estimated as hundreds. For the nuclear weapons with high survival probabilities—submarine-launched ballistic missiles (SLBMs) and land-based mobile intercontinental ballistic missiles (ICBMs)—a hundred highly survivable nuclear weapons should be able to deter nuclear strikes. By contrast, the number of nuclear weapons needed in a first strike would have to be much larger. So, a no-first-use regime could set a ceiling of operational nuclear forces for all of its nuclear weapon parties. In such a regime no party would have the capability to launch a preemptive nuclear strike.

Tactical Nuclear Weapons

Tactical nuclear weapons are specially designed to attack military targets. They are not suitable for retaliatory strikes, and they are likely to be more readily used than strategic nuclear weapons. So keeping tactical nuclear weapons in operational nuclear forces is a dangerous sign that the country intends, under some cirucumstances, to use nuclear weapons first.

Multiple Independently Targeted Reentry Vehicles (MIRVs)

Silo-based multiple-warhead missiles are especially good for preemptive strikes, but not so good for retaliation (except possibly against missile defenses). The reason is that a single missile equipped with muliple, independently targeted warheads could destroy many missiles in a preemptive strike. This provides incentive for both preemptive attack and launch on warning. A no-first-use regime should therefore minimize the number of land-based MIRVed missiles.

Antiballistic Missiles (ABMs)

A nationwide ABM system could encourage a country to use nuclear weapons first. Such a system might not be able to defend against a large pre-emptive nuclear strike because of being overwhelmed by attacking missiles. But it might work in defending a retaliatory strike that has much fewer missiles. So the deployment of ABM systems would make the nuclear weapon states worry that they would lose their nuclear retaliatory capabilities if they do not launch nuclear strikes first, and such deployment would therefore be incompatible with a no-first-use regime.

Intrusive Arrangements

A no-first-use regime could also be strengthened by including arrangements such as constraints on accuracy of missiles, separation of nuclear warheads from delivery systems, and other measures to deactivate operational nuclear weapons. However, many of these measures could be very intrusive and sensitive. So, they might not be adopted in the early stage of building a no-first-use regime.

New Stages of Nuclear Disarmament: A European View

Thérèse Delpech

Europe would have been the first victim of a nuclear conflict during the cold war. Deterrence was, in many respects, a European invention. Major disarmament agreements began in Europe at the end of the 1980s with the INF Treaty, which banned a whole class of nuclear weapons from European territory. In a sense, no other region of the world has a comparable experience of the new dimension introduced by nuclear weapons in the strategic arena. No other region of the world is in a better position to witness the consequences of the East-West rapprochement in matters involving nuclear weapons.

It is almost superfluous to recall that the most significant disarmament agreements signed since 1987 would not have been possible without new leadership in Russia, new cooperation between the superpowers. and a radically new strategic environment. Indeed, it is essential to stress that the future relationships among the five nuclear weapon states are central to the feasibility of future arms reductions. These relationships, which will be shaped by domestic and international politics, are likely to be far more important than various technical factors (numbers of nuclear weapons, their pattern of deployment, pace of dismantlement, mode of launching, and the like) that have been the focus of most analyses during as well as after the cold war. Thus, any assessment concerning the pace and feasibility of nuclear disarmament in the next twenty-five years (the period of time considered by this study) has to take into account primarily political factors.

In this respect there are some encouraging developments: the conclusion of new security arrangements in Europe, settlement of most of the Sino-Russian border issues and the signature in May 1997 of the NATO-Russia

Founding Act. In a sense, it was the peace treaty that the end of the cold war needed. There are also less heartening signs, notably the deep internal crisis of Russian society, the continued refusal of the Russian Duma to ratify START II, the increased dependence on nuclear weapons in Russia, the uncertainties about Russia's nonstrategic nuclear stockpiles, the nuclear tests in South Asia, the numerous political tensions in East Asia, the continued improvement of Chinese ballistic missile capabilities, and the fact that China's nuclear objectives remain enigmatic.

The fate of further nuclear arms reductions will largely depend on how well the nuclear weapon states manage their future relationships, the importance they will give to their common commitment to preserve peace and security, and the balance between cooperation and competition they will be able to maintain among themselves. In particular, cooperation among these states in dealing with nuclear proliferation will be essential. In many respects, former enemies share common interests as far as nuclear proliferation is concerned. It is vital that cooperation among them be strengthened and, in particular, that China be encouraged to cooperate more fully in nonproliferation efforts, including its policies in the Islamic world. The major nonnuclear weapon states are also an indispensable part of this cohesion.

As far as the threshold countries are concerned:

—Israel will not change its nuclear policy simply because the United States and Russia sign START III or IV; the future of peace in the Middle East is the key.

—India finds, and accurately so, the current international system more favorable to China than to its own interests, and Pakistan follows India's route.

—Iraq, Iran, and North Korea do not seem particularly impressed by substantial disarmament agreements between the nuclear powers because the heart of their concerns is regional influence or political survival.

The difficulty of solving the complex questions posed by nuclear proliferation in sensitive regions is more apparent today than ten years ago because only the toughest cases remain. The inability of the international community to solve Iraq's and North Korea's equations after years of efforts ranging from cooperation to threats and military action is a matter of concern.

Finally, it seems very relevant indeed to note that, although a large number of purely conventional conflicts have arisen since the end of the cold war, many of the crises or tensions that have occurred have had something, or much, to do with nuclear weapons. But a general and abstract commitment to eliminate them is unlikely to engage the difficult issues involved.

The Europeans, by tradition, give defense discussions a more political bias than the Americans, who are more technologically oriented. An analysis combining the two perspectives is required to grasp the complexities of nuclear disarmament.

Specificity of the European Perspective

Europeans widely consider nuclear weapons to have been a major factor in keeping peace in Europe for the past fifty years. The weapons compelled leaders of the Western and Eastern blocs to exercise caution as soon as there was a possibility that tensions might degenerate into a conflict. The end of the East-West confrontation has opened new debates.

Concerning past Soviet intentions and strategies, military records of the Warsaw Pact that fell into German hands demonstrated beyond doubt that Russian operational plans called for the use of nuclear and chemical weapons in West Germany at the onset of hostilities, even if NATO forces were using only conventional weapons—this at a time when the Russian official doctrine was no first use. The result of the discovery is to suggest that no-first-use pledges constitute a declaratory policy without military significance. The abandonment by Russia in November 1993 of the Soviet no-first-use pledge has been seen as less a reversal of policy than an example of greater candor. In the unlikely event of a no-first-use pledge by NATO, would Russia accept changing its current declared policy? This is less than certain.

On the role nuclear weapons should play in the next century, there is now an extreme diversity of views. Agreement exists, nonetheless, in Europe on the desirability of undertaking deep reductions in the two major nuclear arsenals and to support that objective with additional cuts in the French and British arsenals. The bilateral treaties between the United States and Russia, calling for nuclear reductions to take place at an unprecedented pace and scale, are welcomed in Europe, and their implementation is carefully followed. It would be seen as highly undesirable if the two major powers abandon their joint march to further reductions. France and the United Kingdom have always expressed opposition to the deployment of large nuclear arsenals and therefore support wider adoption of the minimum deterrence doctrine that has long shaped French and British nuclear forces. The evidence so far that the U.S. and Russian defense establishments may also be ready to move toward such a doctrine is slim, however, and even slimmer after Washington's recent decision concerning national missile defense.

European views on nuclear disarmament will indeed take into account the fate of the ABM Treaty. European countries are firmly committed to the treaty and are concerned by U.S. (and possible Russian) initiatives to modify it. At the Helsinki Summit in May 1997, Presidents Yeltsin and Clinton agreed on a joint statement that set forth agreements concerning the demarcation of strategic and theater missile defenses (TMD) and reaffirmed the presidents' commitment to the ABM Treaty. This statement noted that the agreements are consistent with planned U.S. TMD programs, all of which have been certified by the United States as compliant with the ABM Treaty. The NATO-Russia agreement opens the possibility for the United States and Russia to cooperate in the TMD programs. But the situation is dramatically altered with the announcement concerning national missile defense in January 1999. The European countries, in particular France and Britain, were strongly opposed to this move and will carefully follow the implementation of this decision and the possible (even if indirect) consequences on the disarmament process, the nonproliferation regimes, and their own capabilities.

Different sensitivities on the nuclear issue are often related to geography in Europe. The Nordic countries are most interested in the dismantling of Russian nuclear submarines, the environmental conditions of the Kola peninsula, and the security of fissile material stockpiles. The southern countries of Europe are more concerned about ballistic-missile and nuclear proliferation in the Mediterranean area and the absence of any serious protection against a possible attack on their territory. Germany still considers territorial defense and collective defense central to its defense policy, with the consequences this position entails in nuclear matters, but the new government could alter some aspects of this longstanding view. Finally, Britain and France tend to believe that their unilateral contributions to nuclear arms control have already been substantial, since their arsenals are now constrained to 200 or 350 nuclear weapons each. As long as Russia considers it necessary to maintain a substantial nuclear arsenal and to rely heavily on it for its defense, the two countries will deem nuclear forces to be an essential element of stability in Europe. Elections in both countries in May and June 1997, bringing into power left-wing governments, did not modify this belief, as the British *Strategic Defence Review*, published in July 1998, shows.

There is a broad agreement in Europe that nuclear weapons should not be overemphasized, in particular when dealing with NATO enlargement. In the years to come, enlargement promises to be a continuous source of tension between Russia and the West. But Russia should, at least, not be given grounds to argue that enlargement will increase the nuclear threat to it in any way. This was one of the objectives pursued by the NATO-Russia Founding Act, which states that "members of NATO have no intention, no plan, and no reason to deploy nuclear weapons on the territory of new members," repeating the language already adopted unilaterally by NATO members in December 1996. A new commitment has also been undertaken in the Founding Act restricting the establishment of nuclear weapon storage sites in these countries.

The European countries remain determined to build a common European defense policy. Such a policy would not seek to break away from the United States but would have the Europeans assume a more significant share of the collective defense (something the United States has long advocated). The future role of European nuclear weapons in such a perspective is still a matter of discussion and even division in Europe. It is significant nonetheless that France has recently taken steps to secure a rapprochement with NATO (the only alliance its European partners recognize to ensure their defense). To stress the now less than purely "national" purpose of the French nuclear arsenal, France has also initiated discussions with its partners on nuclear issues. Contrary to a widespread perception, however, the purpose of its discussion is by no means to replace the American umbrella with a French or a Franco-British one, but to strengthen the European contribution to the alliance. In this spirit France and the United Kingdom issued a common statement in October 1995 stressing that the two countries could not envision a situation in which the vital interests of one could be threatened without the vital interests of the other being threatened as well. In December 1996 the Franco-German concept of defense explicitly recognized the necessity for the two countries to engage in a dialogue on nuclear issues. The new Social Democratic party–Green party government in Bonn makes this dialogue less easy but even more necessary between the two partners.

The Europeans will also be sensitive to how nuclear reductions could affect extended deterrence. Germany, for example, whose public expresses from time to time strong antinuclear sentiments, still considers American nuclear deterrence the backbone of its security. Before endorsing the study's proposal that the remaining few hundred American nuclear weapons still in Europe be withdrawn, an old Russian objective, one should recognize that the implications of withdrawal go beyond the purely operational role of these weapons. They are there to symbolize the American commitment to European society and to make visible the risk sharing among the NATO allies. Nuclear forces stationed in the United States or at sea would not provide the same political impact. In particular, there must be concern that removal of U.S. nuclear weapons from Turkey would be perceived in Ankara as eroding NATO commitments to its security. Such perceptions could further estrange Turkey, where the feeling of being rejected by Europe is already widespread. Turkey was one of the few states without nuclear weapons to vote against the resolution on nuclear disarmament introduced by Ireland in the first committee of the fifty-third session of the UN General Assembly.

The alliance's New Strategic Concept reaffirmed in 1991 that "nuclear forces based in Europe and committed to NATO provide an essential political and military link between the European and the North American members of the alliance." It seems unlikely that a very different formula could be agreed upon anytime soon. Alliance cohesion is considered essential on both sides of the Atlantic. This being said, the most interesting case concerning extended deterrence is Japan, currently in a much more fragile strategic situation than any country in Europe.

Finally, one merit of the deep cuts study is to give an idea of the complexity of the technical details of nuclear reductions. In particular, the study points out the problems posed by the large uncertainties in the Russian reserve stockpile and by the U.S. hedge strategy to maintain large numbers of warheads in reserve. It is most important to keep the figures for reserve warheads in mind when comparing weapon stockpiles. START I and II could give a misleading view by focusing attention only on deployed warheads. The European countries, which have no nuclear weapons in reserve, do take this important difference with the two major powers into account. In discussing this point it is fair to say that the figures for U.S. reserves are far more precise than those available for Russia and China. The need for greater transparency is therefore essential, particularly for those two states. Implementation of the 1994 U.S.-Russian understanding on transparency would be most appreciated by countries having common borders with Russia. At present, the number of Russian nonstrategic warheads is estimated between 6,000 and 13,000, a huge uncertainty by any account. As far as China is concerned, uncertainties about future plans and deployments DF31, DF61, JL2 are so great that no expert dares to present serious hypotheses.

France: Dramatic Changes in the 1990s

French decisions on nuclear arms control have been dramatic in the 1990s. Three main rationales explain the positions adopted. The strategic environment resulting from the end of the cold war clearly called for more forthcoming arms control measures. France considered it essential to secure the indefinite extension of the Non-Proliferation Treaty. And nuclear forces represent a heavy burden in defense budgets, particularly in France. The decisions made include

—acceding to the NPT after decades of reservations (June 1991);

—halting production of plutonium for weapons purposes (1992), of highly enriched uranium for all purposes (1996), and closing down the Pierrelatte enrichment facility (1996) and the Marcoule reprocessing plant (1997);

—negotiating the Comprehensive Test Ban Treaty (1993), accepting it as banning "any nuclear explosion" (August 1995), putting an end to all French nuclear tests and closing the Muroroa test site (February 1996), and signing the treaty (September 1996);

—signing the relevant protocols of the various nuclear-weapon-free zones—Tlatelolco (August 1992), Raratonga (March 1996), and Pelindaba (April 1996);

—giving positive security assurances under resolution 984 (France was not a signatory of resolution 255 in 1968);

—reducing its nuclear stockpile by dismantling all 18 surface-to-surface ICBMs located on the Albion Plateau and all Hades short-range missiles (1996), leaving the country with only SLBMs, which will be carried by 4 new-generation nuclear submarines instead of 5, and air-to-surface missiles with a nuclear stockpile of 350 warheads according to open sources; and

—detargeting its nuclear weapons (announced in September 1997).

These achievements represent a substantial contribution to nuclear disarmament in a rather short period.

Conclusion

In the future it will be essential to ensure security at each stage of the reductions process and to take into account new actors that have been almost absent from most Western analysis of nuclear weapons during the cold war. We should preserve the nuclear peace we have enjoyed for fifty years, but this task could become more difficult. New players are confronting the chessboard; instability in a large part of the world is generating tensions of all kinds at a time when governments are often too weak to contain or channel them; and proliferation could be driven not only by regional volatility, but also as countries' wishes circumvent the West's technological edge. In these circumstances, three goals are critical: the success of nonproliferation policies, the reduction of nuclear arsenals, and the upholding of an effective doctrine of deterrence (as opposed to war fighting).

A View from Germany

Harald Müller

When defenders of the present U.S. nuclear posture are asked why it is not advisable to reduce the arsenal further, to scrap all tactical nuclear weapons, or to turn to a no-first-use doctrine, the answer "because of the allies" comes quickly. And in a modern version of the "Germans to the front" battlecry, my country is promptly quoted as the "usual suspect" that would seriously consider renouncing its nonnuclear status if the nuclear umbrella would weaken beyond the present state. Germany is thus a pet bogeyman of nuclear pundits to defend the status quo.[1]

There is no doubt that extended deterrence was historically a necessary condition to keep the Federal Republic a nonnuclear weapon state and to persuade a reluctant political elite to acquiesce in the conclusion of the Nuclear Non-Proliferation Treaty. The German government said as much in the notes accompanying the signature (1969) and ratification (1975) of that treaty: accession was contingent on the continued guarantee granted by NATO.[2]

However, history is, for better or worse, no fixed matter. It moves, and it has moved rather mightily during the past ten years with regard to those factors that influence the German attitude toward nuclear weapons and security policy. As a consequence there must now be a strong assumption that the prevailing view on the nuclear issue of a great majority of both the pub-

1. An excellent example of this school, containing a lot of involuntary humor, is Emmet E. Stobbs Jr., "Tactical Nuclear Weapons? Do They Have a Role in the US Military Strategy?" in *Director's Series on Proliferation*, no. 3, edited by Kathleen Bailey (Lawrence Livermore National Laboratory, 1994), pp. 1–14. A more serious argument is found in George Quester and Victor Utgoff, "U.S. Arms Reductions and Nuclear Nonproliferation: The Counterproductive Possibilities," *Washington Quarterly*, vol. 16 (Winter 1993), pp. 129–40.

2. Erwin Häckel, "Die Bundesrepublik Deutschland und der Atomwaffensperrvertrag: Rückblick und Ausblick," *Arbeitspapier zur Internationalen Politik*, vol. 53 (Bonn: Europa-Union Verlag, 1989).

lic and the elite in Germany is and will be under a broad range of possible circumstances independent of changes in the U.S. posture.

For Germany, as for any other country, the attitude toward nuclear weapons is defined by three factors:

—the security situation, that is, the balance of threats, risks, and dangers with due regard to the existing and foreseeable balance of power and forces that obtain, particularly in Europe;

—the international institutional framework within which security policy is being conducted; and

—the political culture of the country, that is, the prevailing feelings, attitudes, and practices as far as nuclear and security issues are concerned.

The German Security Situation

The German security situation is the best ever in its history. Germany is now surrounded by friends and allies. There are no territorial squabbles, no dangerous animosities, no ethnic rivalries, no religious cleavages, or other sources of serious conflict. Instead, there is growing interdependence in economic, cultural, and communication relations, and increasing integration even in the military, with national units assigned to higher multinational formations. War in Germany's immediate neighborhood has become as improbable as in North America.

Germany is Russia's most important and appreciated partner in Europe, to a point that some people in NATO are critical of Germany's apparent advocacy sometimes for Moscow (for example, in the context of the revision of the Conventional Armed Forces in Europe Treaty). Although Germany took a lead in urging NATO enlargement, this has not led to a deterioration in the relationship. It is unlikely that, even with changes in Russia, the hostility of the cold war will reemerge.

And even if it would, the balance of forces in Europe has drastically changed so as to make a risk to German territory impossible. During the cold war seventeen crack Soviet divisions, supported by nuclear and chemical weapons, stood ready with their allies to take the offensive at the outset of an armed conflict between NATO and the Warsaw Treaty Organization. The quantitative superiority of these forces led to a perception in Germany that a war could be quickly lost and would lead to the destruction of the battlefield country. Nuclear weapons were thought to provide the only guarantee that the Soviets would not dare attack.

Today, such fears must be harbored in Moscow rather than Bonn. NATO is quantitatively and, even more strikingly, qualitatively the dominating force on the Continent: compare the performance of Western forces during the Gulf War with that of the Russian Army in Chechnya. Russia is not capable of any long-range conventional attack. In addition, NATO has gained strategic depth and will fortify this depth through enlargement. Warning time is close to eternal. Completely credible options for conventional defense are available. There is simply no military threat emerging from Russia that would require a nuclear counter—with the largely implausible exception of a nuclear threat, exactly the scenario that could be diminished by huge reductions in nuclear weapons and eliminated by nuclear disarmament.

Threats emerging from proliferation are remote in western and central Europe. There are no political conflicts with any rogue state that would plausibly lead to such a threat. Even the fuss with Iran over the Mykonos affair, the accusations against high Iranian officials pronounced by a German court, was more theater than a threat to the substance of an otherwise viable relation. And again, even in the worst case, the threat of fledgling arsenals of weapons of mass destruction can be covered by a much smaller umbrella and by adequate conventional responses. It depends on a clear perspective of how the NATO alliance would react to such threats whether this issue will ever become a prominent topic in national security discourses. Under all foreseeable circumstances, existential nuclear or plausible conventional deterrence would silence European concerns, including German ones. It is thus fair to say that in security terms, nuclear deterrence has become extremely marginal for Germany.

Institutions Affecting German Security

Today, Germany is involved in three institutional frameworks that shape its security policy. The first consists of the various arms control agreements that structure the security situation in Europe: The Conventional Forces in Europe Treaty, the Vienna documents on confidence building, the global agreements such as the Non-Proliferation Treaty, the Chemical Weapons Convention and the Biological Weapons Convention that influence the balance in Europe and, in due course, the Open Sky Treaty that will further improve transparency. These agreements contribute powerfully to the benign security situation, grant early warning long before any threat would become serious, and strengthen trust in the validity and perpetuity of the impossibility of major war.

The second framework consists of the Organization of Security and Cooperation in Europe, the North Atlantic Cooperation Council, and the NATO-Russian Council. These institutions all offer chances to address grievances and emerging conflicts early and to deepen cooperation and common interests between countries that, without these precautions, could develop hostile relationships more easily.

The third framework consists of alliances related to German security: NATO, the Western European Union, and the European Union itself. The European Union, while not (yet) a security alliance, is of pivotal importance to German security: it creates a network of common interests between Germany and those countries it has warred with throughout much of modern history, most of all France. The Union binds Germany and France very closely together, thereby eliminating what has been the major problem for either country for four hundred years. And one has to realize that the EU construction, notably the Franco-German foundation of it, is much more robust than daily newspaper reporting about crises would suggest. (Since I have followed European affairs, there has been permanent crisis—from one step of deepening integration to the next.)

The WEU is presently little more than an organizational skeleton built around a fairly strict mutual assistance commitment in case of an attack. Relying on a division of labor with NATO, the WEU has been left void of an operational body of its own. However, it presents a fallback position should NATO ever crack, and it could be expanded relatively quickly to a full-fledged alliance organization if the member states would feel the need for it. Because everybody (even the French) is eager to preserve NATO and to save costs, this is not likely to occur very soon. But of course, the WEU strengthens security by furthering even more the integration of national security policies among the Europeans.

Finally there is NATO, another unique body that binds together American and European security. Many predicted the demise of the alliance as soon as the Berlin Wall fell: without the cherished enemy, no alliance could hold. Eight years later, NATO is fairly vital, enlarging even its membership. With the full weight of U.S. military power, the alliance makes German security impregnable in today's world.

The three sets of security institutions improve the German situation even beyond what the conventional security analysis would assume. Consequently, nuclear weapons are even more marginalized.

The German Nuclear Discourse

To understand present attitudes toward nuclear weapons, it might be useful to review how they evolved over the past fifty years. Germany emerged from World War II as a country deprived of the right to conduct any nuclear activities, civilian or military. To remove these restrictions became one of the symbols of German political recovery, even though it was realized only in the civilian sector. But this was far from clear at the beginning. When Konrad Adenauer, the first postwar chancellor, renounced the production of nuclear weapons on German soil in the protocol to the Brussels Treaty (in 1954, on the occasion of German accession to the WEU), he viewed this as a temporary setback. In his view Germany would naturally become a nuclear weapon state, commensurate with its status as a medium power, when it would be fully accepted back into the family of Western nations.

Adenauer's defense minister, Franz Josef Strauss, tried to accelerate this process by concluding a secret agreement (though, of course, known to Adenauer) with France and Italy to produce nuclear weapons together. This project fell through during the first days of Charles de Gaulle's presidency in 1958, terminating the most serious German attempt to overcome its nonnuclear status. Later, Germany was very enthusiastic about the U.S. proposal to create a multilateral nuclear fleet, but this project fell victim to a lack of allied enthusiasm (from the United Kingdom, France, Netherlands, and the Scandinavian countries), and the increasing U.S. interest in nonproliferation. Germany had to grudgingly agree to the demise of the multilateral fleet and accept even more grudgingly the conclusion of the Non-Proliferation Treaty. It took a new government to sign this treaty in 1969 because the major partner in the preceding coalition, the conservative Christian Democratic Union–Christian Social Union (CDU-CSU), could not muster the votes within their caucus to grant ratification. Germany ratified six years later by a large majority, including a majority in the conservative caucus, but a sizable minority abstained or objected.

Until the early 1970s Germany was rather a brake on nuclear arms control. Adenauer did not want to give any concessions to Moscow because such signs of weakness could encourage Soviet ventures. Arms control agreements with German Democratic Republic accession would elevate East Berlin's status, and limitations on U.S. weapons in Europe could undermine extended deterrence and the alliance. By the mid-1970s, however, Germany became more active and favorable toward nuclear arms control. Helmut Schmidt's famous London speech that triggered NATO's double-track decision, contained a *double* track, not just a request for deployment. (The double-track system was an effort to neutralize the increasing superiority of Soviet intermediate nuclear forces, caused by the rapid deployment of the SS-20 missiles, either by balancing counterdeployments of equivalent weapon systems or by arms control measures.) After 1989 Germany was the most steady voice calling for implementation of the second arms control track against a very reticent Reagan administration (*Genscherism* became a dirty word in Washington during these years).

A defining moment came in 1987: suddenly, the "zero option," the complete and global elimination of all U.S. and Soviet intermediate-range nuclear systems, became possible, and so too a "double zero," which would include shorter-range intermediate nuclear weapons. But this would include the German army's jewel, the Pershing IA. Operated by the Germans, the missile would receive U.S. nuclear warheads in war and then fly into Warsaw Pact territory. It was the closest the German finger was to any nuclear trigger. Some CDU-CSU defense experts bitterly objected to sacrificing this weapon for arms control. But Chancellor Helmut Kohl, with the applause of a vast majority of the German public and all parties, including his own, decided that the step was worthwhile.[3] Two years later Germany almost single-handedly prevented the modernization of the Lance missile, persuading President George Bush to renounce this step in spring 1989, a very important part of the chain of events that would unfold that year. In 1990 the nonnuclear status of the reunified Germany was sealed into the 2 + 4 Treaty that ended four-power responsibilities for Germany and restored the country's full sovereignty.

The present state of affairs is best characterized by the unanimous Bundestag resolution, adopted in 1994, in favor of indefinite extension of the NPT. No deputy voted against the treaty; there was a broad consensus for continued nonnuclear status. This statement was followed by dedicated, hard work of German diplomats to make indefinite extension happen.

To summarize this long story: there has been a steady evolution of the German attitude in a more and more nonnuclear direction. This evolution took place through very different phases of international affairs: cold war, detente, renewed cold war, renewed detente, and the end of the East-West conflict. These phases did not, apparently, change the direction of the process. Today, nonnuclear status, multilateral security policy, and support for arms control as an integral part of that policy have become part of the German

3. Thomas Risse-Kappen, *The Zero Option: INF, West Germany, and Arms Control* (Boulder, Colo.: Westview 1988).

identity and are doubted or criticized by very few.[4] This is well illustrated by the lackluster response to the French "Eurodeterrent offer," a proposal to extend the scope of the French nuclear deterrent over the territories of the European allies and to create consultations with them. What the previous generation of German defense policymakers would have taken up with a strong appetite met a very measured reception in 1996. Of course, Germany would be interested in discussing nuclear matters with France; but the most daring arrangement that even the most positive statements could put forth was the European equivalent of a Nuclear Planning Group, not more.[5]

Probable Reactions to a Change in U.S. Posture

Given this analysis it is predictable that deep cuts would not lead Germany to a serious reconsideration of its nonnuclear status. To be sure, there would be voices in strategic circles on the right that would discuss this issue. But they would have no chance for obtaining broad-based support even within conservative ranks. The nonnuclear attitude of the public (covering both military and civilian aspects of nuclear energy) would make it suicidal for any serious politician to make a political platform out of this subject.

Extraordinary events affecting all three factors analyzed must come together to change this prediction: the security situation must deteriorate, with a fully reemerged and ostentatiously hostile Russia pushing westward once more; the institutional framework must unravel, with NATO dissolved and the European Union breaking down under a fatal German-French divorce; and the internal balance of political forces must give way to a landmark shift to the far right. The combination of these circumstances appears unlikely, and even then it might take a civil war's equivalent of public unrest before plans of nuclear armament could be realized. The fears of Germany's going nuclear as a "natural" consequence of further nuclear disarmament is thus badly off target, and it is all too easy to see the vested interests behind these unfounded allegations.

The old government's view of nuclear arms control was as follows.[6] Ger-

---

4. Harald Müller and Wolfgang Kötter, *Germany and the Bomb. Nuclear Policies in the Two German States, and the United Germany's Nonproliferation Commitments,* PRIF reports 14 (Frankfurt: PRIF, 1990). For more recent events, I rely on research done by PRIF associate Alexander Kelle in our project on nonnuclear proactivism, funded by the Ford Foundation.

5. See "Le Dôssier: La France, la Dissuasion et l'Europe," *Relations Internationales et Stratégiques,* nr. 21 (Spring 1996).

6. Alexander Kelle in Harald Müller, ed., *Europe and Nuclear Disarmament: Debates and Political Attitudes in 16 European Countries* (Brussels: European Interuniversity Press, 1998).

many is highly interested in steps that reduce the discrimination between nuclear and nonnuclear weapon states. It is, in particular, strongly supportive of measures that improve transparency in civilian and military nuclear complexes, including verification measures. The application of IAEA safeguards in nuclear weapon states is one of the major projects pursued by German diplomacy, be it during the 93 + 2 talks to strengthen the NPT verification system, in the international plutonium regime talks in Vienna, or in the context of a cutoff convention.[7]

The government supports START fully. The Helsinki understanding between Presidents Clinton and Yeltsin was highly welcome. There is nothing in the way of continued support for much deeper cuts as long as the United States keeps an unequivocal security commitment to Europe and NATO is enjoying continued vitality.

Much more conservatism is observable concerning tactical nuclear weapons and NATO's first-use doctrine. Germany was not at all opposed to the enormous reductions in the alliance's nuclear arsenal. But in the Ministry of Defense the old orthodoxy prevails that U.S. weapons in Europe are important to symbolize U.S. commitment. This view is mere stratheology. When tactical weapons were introduced to Europe under the Radford Plan in 1954, the reason was not "coupling" but the austere, budget-balancing policy of the Eisenhower administration. More bang for the buck was to substitute for the otherwise necessary heavy deployments of U.S. forces beyond the considerable burden already shouldered. Germany at first protested because the deployment of tactical weapons seemed to signal a diminished rather than strengthened U.S. commitment.

In the early 1960s, tactical nuclear weapons were the backbone of the new flexible response that was meant to provide the United States with a firebreak between the first shot in Europe and an intercontinental disaster. Again, the first European reaction was fear of a lessening U.S. commitment. It was only with time that the interpretation of tactical nuclear weapons as a symbol of coupling emerged: coupling is not in the nature of the weapons and their deployment, it is in the eye of the beholder.[8] It is predictable that within a very short time, no one in either the United States or Europe will remember the coupling agonies. Officials in the Defense Ministry also believe that the nuclear sharing arrangements are the only way to keep some influence on NATO's and U.S. nuclear policies. In that sense they regard the

7. Annette Schaper, "A Treaty on the Cutoff of Fissile Material for Nuclear Weapons: What to Cover? How to Verify?" PRIF report 48, Frankfurt, 1997.

8. David N. Schwartz, *NATO's Nuclear Dilemmas* (Brookings, 1983).

nuclear warheads deployed in Germany and the nuclear role of the German Air Force envisaged for a (highly improbable) war not as a military asset but as a communication channel.

The new government, composed of the Social Democratic and Green parties, emphasizes continuity, but it is more flexible in the nuclear field and more sympathetic to the idea of nuclear disarmament. The major change in official policy it has announced is the suggestion that NATO's nuclear doctrine be reviewed with the idea of renouncing the option of using nuclear weapons first. The first-use doctrine is probably the most obsolete part of NATO's posture and one extremely damaging to the nuclear nonproliferation regime. How can anybody plausibly explain to any country that it should refrain from acquiring nuclear weapons when the most powerful military organization in the world, not seriously threatened by anyone, cannot even renounce the first use of these weapons? Germany has made it clear that it will not force its new position on its allies but will insist on an in-depth review of NATO's nuclear doctrine in the midterm.

The situation is slightly absurd. Talking to serious German officials, one learns that tactical weapons should remain and the doctrine should not change because the United States would not be willing to keep its soldiers in Europe without the tactical nuclear umbrella close by. Conversations in Washington on the subject reveal that the United States would be ready to withdraw these weapons, but the Germans would panic and possibly do unpredictable (or all too predictable) things. It will take a U.S. initiative, combined with a solemn reaffirmation of its NATO commitment, to overcome it. With the new government it can be surmised that changes might be achieved more easily, and the government may choose a more active role in such changes.

To summarize, changes in the U.S. nuclear posture through very deep cuts are not likely to provoke a reconsideration of Germany's nonnuclear weapon status. The same applies for the elimination of tactical nuclear weapons (or at least their withdrawal from Europe) and a change in NATO doctrine.

The Safety of Russian Nuclear Weapons

Beyond what has been discussed, there are additional measures discussed in this volume that have so far received little attention in Europe. This is ironic because de-alerting would clearly have the most important impact on European security.

The Russian nuclear weapons complex has become a major security concern. So far, only the risk of the diversion of fissile materials or even full warheads by unauthorized actors has attracted full European attention; sometimes too much attention indeed, as the doubtful involvement of journalists and German intelligence services in sting operations would suggest. This is curious. The hair-trigger posture of strategic nuclear forces in Russia entails major risks for all Western allies, including the European ones. It is high time that more attention is focused on this issue.

As a consequence of ignorance, the meaning of de-alerting still escapes even policymakers concerned with security and arms control. If this ignorance could be eliminated, de-alerting might be the most adequate instrument to refocus European attention on nuclear arms control and disarmament because an immediate and obvious security interest is involved. But again, it is likely that some U.S. initiative will be required to trigger this refocusing. Again, with the new government Germany may have become more responsive in this regard. The coalition agreement, the program for the government, contains a line calling for de-alerting measures. Although there have not yet been follow-up steps to implement this request, it can be expected that Bonn would look at any suggestion in this regard with sympathy.

Conclusions

Concerns that Germany would feel increasingly insecure in a world with fewer nuclear weapons are unjustified. Because German security today does not much rely on nuclear weapons and is supported by a broad range of institutional arrangements, there is no risk in involving Bonn in a discourse on bold reductions, elimination of tactical weapons, or de-alerting. It would be advisable to develop such steps through consultation with the European allies. To preempt this process with groundless fears is irresponsible, given both risks of the present nuclear postures and the opportunities offered by the political relationship that obtains (still) between the major powers. With regard to the political culture in Germany, one can expect that a majority of the people and the elite would welcome such steps and strongly support it.

Much more destabilizing than a shrinking nuclear force are trends in the United States toward both isolationism and unilateralism. More than the nuclear umbrella as such, in the long run the U.S. commitment to European security is still a cornerstone of the nonproliferation regime and will remain so. The magnification of economic conflicts, proposals to withdraw all U.S.

soldiers for cost reasons or lack of interest in European security, the contemptuous attitude of certain Republicans to everything multilateral, the increasing difficulties of channeling arms control agreements through Congress—these are much more damaging to the framework of European security than nuclear arms reductions and other disarmament measures.

As to complete nuclear disarmament, there are some sympathies in Germany, but many in the elite are sceptical or opposed. The reasons are not too different from those found elsewhere. First, the residual insurance effect of nuclear weapons against unknown and ominous uncertainties is still appreciated in some quarters. Second, the difficulties of verification and the possibilities of breakout are taken very seriously, particularly by members of the strategic community. Third, the political will of the nuclear weapon states to live up to their commitments under the NPT is in doubt.

The Deep Cuts Group's argument applies here with full force: attitudes will not be the same twenty or thirty years from now. The willingness to take the perceived risks of disarmament and the readiness to believe in its possibilities change as the security framework, the number and density of agreements, the intensity of verification measures, and mutual confidence grow. If we need any proof for the malleability of attitudes toward nuclear weapons, the German example over the last half century is impressive enough.

When the last steps toward a nonnuclear world are seriously considered, we will be in a situation different from the one today. As for now, there is nothing in Germany that would prevent taking not only the first few steps, but going a very long way down the road.

A Nuclear Gordian Knot: South Asia and the Limits of Deep Cuts

Zia Mian and M. V. Ramana

The basic presumption of the deep cuts strategy is the urgent need for new and radical initiatives to contain the threats posed by nuclear weapons. Otherwise, the existing arms control process may begin to come undone. It is hard to disagree. Although the policies of the nuclear weapon states are rightfully the main focus of the strategy, the situation has been made more dangerous and complex by recent events in South Asia.

The dynamics that led to the May 1998 nuclear tests and subsequent developments have created a Gordian knot from the already tangled threads of domestic, regional, and global power that characterise South Asia. Many believe that India's nuclear tests, ordered by a right-wing ultranationalist religious political party with a long-standing commitment to the acquisition of nuclear weapons, incited Pakistan's already desperately insecure leaders to test their own nuclear weapons. The result is a situation in which, for the first time, there are two nuclear-armed but impoverished states with a recent history of war and an unresolved dispute that has led twice to war. With Pakistan's government struggling to administer a state and society verging on social and economic collapse, the situation is grim and in ever present danger of becoming worse. The real complexity of the nuclear knot, however, can be gauged from the Indian government's multiple justifications for its tests. These include a "bitter" Pakistan, a nuclear-armed China, and a long-standing complaint about an inequitable international nonproliferation regime seen as denying India some kind of perverse "right" to have nuclear weapons.[1] To this is added mention of problems with the United States.[2]

The international pressure on the two states following their nuclear tests, combined with a desire on the part of India and Pakistan to restore some appearance of respectability in the international community, may lead to limited arms control or restraint in the deployment of nuclear arsenals. However, the more enduring perspectives are ones that seem to rule out any reasonable possibility of India's acceding to international arms control regimes that would box it into a purely bilateral nuclear relationship with Pakistan or make it the obvious object of nonproliferation policies by the nuclear weapon states. Where India leads Pakistan will follow.

Thus the deep cuts strategy as it is framed here is unlikely to be able to contain or resolve the deeper crisis in South Asia. Success is more likely if the nuclear weapon states unambiguously establish their intention to abolish nuclear weapons. Such a step would create a new context for decision-making, and many existing problems may become more amenable. With abolition as the explicit goal, some of the practical steps proposed in the deep cuts strategy could help ease the situation in South Asia and the transition to a world free from nuclear weapons.

Framing Deep Cuts

Although it purports to be part of a post–cold war revolution in nuclear arms control, the deep cuts proposal builds on some of the same foundations that underlay earlier arms control policies and support existing nuclear arsenals, most notably a commitment to deterrence. This is revealed in the structure of the arguments presented for changing the size, composition, and status of the nuclear arsenals of the nuclear weapon states. In each case change is advocated and then it is shown that the proposed change would not fundamentally affect the strategic purpose supposed to be served by these arsenals. It is pointed out, rather carefully, that the complete implementation of the deep cuts strategy would leave each nuclear weapon state with an arsenal that, although much smaller and largely de-alerted, would still

1. "India's Letter to Clinton on the Nuclear Testing," *New York Times*, May 13, 1998, p. A14; and "Evolution of India's Nuclear Policy," paper laid on the Table of the House, Government of India, May 27, 1998; see http://www.indiagov.org/govt/evolution.htm.

2. See for instance Bharat Karnad, "A Thermonuclear Deterrent," in *India's Nuclear Deterrent: Pokhran II and Beyond*, Amitabh Mattoo, ed. (New Delhi: Har-Anand Publications, 1999).

be capable of inflicting catastrophic damage. At the same time, it is emphasised, the capacity for nuclear retaliation is ensured by these arsenals because they would be not capable of destroying the stored warheads of another weapon state. In effect, the nuclear fat is cut back to the strategic bone.

This result is not altogether surprising. The deep cuts strategy is offered as a cooperative way for the nuclear weapon states to deal with U.S. concerns about the current possibilities of large-scale surprise nuclear attacks and accidental or unauthorized use of nuclear weapons. The strategy is nowhere presented as a necessary step for the abolition of nuclear weapons. The proposal only holds out the hope it may clear the ground for a subsequent decision by the nuclear weapon states to disarm. However, with the danger of massive or accidental nuclear war significantly reduced and each nuclear weapon state confident in its ability to inflict "catastrophic damage," the nuclear weapon states may decide they are safe enough. They could choose to define the residual arsenals as tantamount to being disarmed and simply equate 200 to zero, as Morton Halperin, for example, has already suggested.[3]

Unfortunately, there is little substantive speculation about how to go beyond deep cuts and achieve disarmament or how different a deep cuts program might look if one judged each possible measure by asking how it would affect the goal of a world without nuclear weapons. The reluctance to consider how to go beyond nuclear arms control is presented as emerging from an inability to realistically predict the state of the world beyond the period that the deep cuts program already covers. The apparent practicality of this position is reinforced by claiming that deep cuts can be implemented without major changes in the existing international system, while "far-reaching changes" in the world are required for the abolition of nuclear weapons.[4] There is an obvious if unintended implication in such an argument: that discussing the abolition of nuclear weapons at present is not realistic and not a task for serious scholars.

This is not the only failure of imagination. A second problem with the deep cuts approach is that it fails to take sufficient account of the fact that the overwhelming majority of states have already committed themselves to "far-reaching changes" in the international system when it comes to nuclear weapons. These changes have been taking place steadily over the past nearly thirty years as more and more states (now around 180) have signed the

3. Morton H. Halperin, "Defining 'Eliminating' Nuclear Weapons," *Disarmament Diplomacy*, no. 19 (October 1997), pp. 4–6.

4. See chapter 1.

Nuclear Non-Proliferation Treaty (NPT) as nonnuclear weapon states. Many have gone further and now press for nuclear disarmament as an immediate goal. This new sensibility is reflected in the extensive support for disarmament resolutions at the UN General Assembly. The resolution first presented by Malaysia in 1996 at the UN's First Committee (dealing with disarmament and international security) called for negotiations leading to "an early conclusion of a nuclear weapon convention prohibiting the development, production, testing, deployment, stockpiling, transfer, and threat to use or actual use of nuclear weapons, and providing for their elimination."[5] In 1998, this was supported by 123 states. At the same time, 159 states voted to endorse the unanimous conclusion of the International Court of Justice regarding the existence of a legal obligation to pursue and bring to a conclusion negotiations leading to nuclear disarmament.[6] At the Conference on Disarmament in Geneva, despite resistance from the United States and its nuclear allies, even some members of NATO—Belgium, Germany, Italy, Netherlands, and Norway—have called for discussion of nuclear disarmament.[7]

The strong support at international forums for radical nuclear disarmament measures is noted in the way the deep cuts proposal is framed. Rather than being welcomed as indicative of the international community's urgent desire for disarmament, it is argued that such expressions of dissatisfaction with the slow pace of disarmament if not responded to by something like a deep cuts process could "undermine long-term international support for the nonproliferation regime and the moral and political authority of the United States and other nuclear weapons states in combating proliferation."[8]

There is, however, good reason to doubt this moral and political authority. One need look no further than what was promised by the NPT and how this promise has fared. The preamble to the treaty cites a desire among its signatories to "further the easing of international tension and the strengthening of trust between States in order to facilitate the cessation of the manufacture of nuclear weapons, the liquidation of all their existing stockpiles, and the elimination from national arsenals of nuclear weapons and the means of their delivery."[9] In the treaty the elimination of nuclear weapons and their

5. See Rebecca Johnson, "The Arms Control Agenda at the UN: Breaking New Ground or Breaking Old Habits?" *Arms Control Today*, vol. 26 (January 1997), pp. 8–13.

6. John Burroughs, *The (Il)legality of Threat or Use of Nuclear Weapons: A Guide to the Historic Opinion of the International Court of Justice*, International Association of Lawyers against Nuclear Arms (Münster: LIT Verlag, 1997).

7. Rebecca Johnson, "Agenda but No Program of Work (Yet)," Geneva Update, *Disarmament Diplomacy*, no. 33, December 1998–January 1999.

8. See chapter 1.

9. *Treaty on the Non-Proliferation of Nuclear Weapons, 1968.*

delivery systems is to be brought about by the nonnuclear weapon states abjuring nuclear weapons in exchange for the nuclear weapon states agreeing "to pursue negotiations in good faith on effective measures relating to cessation of the nuclear arms race at an early date and to nuclear disarmament, and on a treaty on general and complete disarmament under strict and effective international control."[10]

Although the nonnuclear weapons states have almost without exception kept their end of the bargain, they have seen the nuclear weapon states conduct innumerable nuclear weapons tests and increase the size and destructive power of their arsenals. According to one estimate in 1968 when the NPT was negotiated there were some 40,000 nuclear weapons in the world, and that this number increased to 70,000 in 1987 before falling back to around 36,000 in 1998.[11] It is clear that the NPT was not sufficient to prevent increases in nuclear arsenals or their modernization. This only ended with the end of the cold war and the collapse of the Soviet Union. However, the numbers of warheads still in existence nearly a decade later, despite the complete disappearance of the justification offered for these nuclear arsenals for the past fifty years, do not suggest that the nuclear weapon states will keep their side of the bargain by eliminating their nuclear arsenals.

The NPT is not the only example of the difference between what the nonnuclear weapon states thought they were getting and what the nuclear weapon states gave them. At the talks on the Comprehensive Test Ban Treaty (CTBT), which were the first opportunity the nuclear weapon states had to show a new approach toward disarmament after the indefinite extension of the NPT, it was the same old story. The U.S. ambassador to the CTBT negotiations explained the difference in expectation and intention: "It is important to recognise that the motivation of the 38 countries that joined together in this negotiation is not the same. The majority believes, as I understand it, that the banning forever of all nuclear tests in all environments will bring about, and bring about rapidly, the deterioration and decay of all existing nuclear weapons stockpiles. As I understand it, all five nuclear weapon states believe that without testing we can nevertheless maintain for the foreseeable future the viability, the safety, and the reliability of our nuclear stockpiles."[12] The construction of major new facilities for nuclear weapon

10. Ibid.

11. Natural Resources Defense Council, *Global Nuclear Stockpiles, 1945–1996*, http://www.igc.org/nrdc/worldview/index.html; and William Arkin, Robert Norris, and Joshua Handler, *Taking Stock; World Nuclear Deployments 1998* (Washington: Natural Resources Defense Council, 1998).

12. Andrew Lichterman and Jacqueline Cabasso, *A Faustian Bargain: Why Stockpile Stewardship Is Incompatible with the Process of Nuclear Disarmament* (Oakland, Calif.: Western States Legal Foundation, 1998), p. 13.

research and the production of key nuclear weapon materials, especially by the United States, suggest this "foreseeable future" may be intended to last a long time.[13]

This leads to the third problem with the deep cuts strategy: it seems to assume that although proliferation is a threat to the nuclear weapon states, the nuclear weapon states threaten only each other. The nuclear weapon states have never committed unambiguously to refrain from using nuclear weapons against a nonnuclear weapon state, and some are known to have threatened to do so on numerous occasions. Most recently, there is evidence that in the U.S.-led war against Iraq in 1991 the use of U.S. nuclear weapons was considered by the military and the secretary of defence to the extent that some of its allies "were beginning to believe that the U.S. did intend to employ nuclear weapons."[14] Since then, there have been clear indications that the United States has been considering the use of nuclear weapons in response to attack by chemical and biological weapons from third world states as well as in preemptive attacks against facilities suspected of manufacturing chemical and biological weapons in such states.[15]

International resistance to the spread of nuclear weapons is further undermined by policies such as the long-standing complicity by the United States and other nuclear weapon states in both allowing and privileging Israel's nuclear arsenal, currently estimated at about 100.[16] The position of the nuclear weapon states regarding Israel's existing arsenal and the imprisonment of Mordechai Vanunu, the Israeli nuclear technician who revealed its scale and sophistication, is in sharp contrast to the near hysteria about Arab states and the possibility of their acquiring weapons of mass destruction. Israel has received $70–$80 billion (in current dollars) of U. S military and economic aid over the past two decades, and currently receives more than

13. Christopher E. Paine and Matthew G. McKinzie, *End Run: The U.S. Government's Plan for Designing Nuclear Weapons and Simulating Nuclear Explosions under the Comprehensive Test Ban Treaty* (Washington: Natural Resources Defense Council, 1997; and Charles Ferguson and Frank von Hippel, "U.S. Tritium Production Plan Lacks Strategic Rationale," *Defense News* (December 7–13, 1998).

14. Barry Posen, "U.S. Security Policy in a Nuclear Armed World," *Security Studies*, vol. 6 (Spring 1997), p. 20.

15. Bruce Blair, *Global Zero Alert for Nuclear Forces* (Brookings, 1995). See also Steven Lee Myers, "U.S. 'Updates' All-out Atom War Guidelines," *New York Times*, December 8, 1997, p. A13; and Hans Kristensen, *Nuclear Futures: Proliferation of Weapons of Mass Destruction and U.S. Nuclear Strategy*, BASIC research report 98-2 (London: British American Security Information Council, 1998).

16. David Albright, Frans Berkhout and William Walker, *Plutonium and Highly Enriched Uranium 1996* (Oxford University Press, 1997).

$3.5 billion a year.[17] It is never asked to sign the NPT nor rebuked or sanctioned for its nuclear weapons and ballistic missiles, while Iraq has been subject to a murderous regime of sanctions and repeated military attacks in the wake of the 1991 war. Iran is, it seems, being lined up as the next target. Because of such behavior, in the eyes of some states, and certainly for the peace movements around the world, the United States and other nuclear weapon states have no moral and political authority when it comes to combating proliferation.

India

This reading of the deep cuts proposal may sound unsympathetic if not hostile. Nevertheless, it is one that will be widely shared in India, especially by those opposed to the recent nuclear tests and the prospect of India's further developing and deploying nuclear weapons. The story of how things came to be this way and the associated history of India's nuclear weapons programs is sufficiently well known that there is no need to recapitulate it here. What does need to be stressed is that Indian leaders since independence have been concerned about the implications of living in a world where only some states had nuclear weapons. In parallel with diplomatic proposals for nuclear disarmament, Jawaharlal Nehru, the first prime minister of India, took pains to create and support a nuclear infrastructure that could lead to the manufacture of nuclear weapons, should the need ever arise.

In addition to concerns about national security in a nuclear armed world, there were also compulsions of prestige and self-esteem about India's place in the world. The Nuclear Non-Proliferation Treaty, with its formalization of the status of states into nuclear weapon states and nonnuclear weapon states only served to strengthen Indian perceptions of the consolidation of "nuclear apartheid," as it was sometimes called. This was thrown into sharp relief by Prime Minister Atal Behari Vajpayee's statement shortly after the tests that nuclear weapons were the "due of one-sixth of humanity" and the words of India's Minister of Science and Technology that the tests "reflected India's endeavors to find a rightful place among the world's powers."[18] But it must be remembered that the core of this sense is more one of India's not being accorded its rightful place in the world than it is some uni-

17. Duncan L. Clarke, Daniel B. O'Connor and Jason D. Ellis, *Send Guns and Money: Security Assistance and U.S. Foreign Policy* (Praeger, 1997).
18. "Options of More Detonations Open: Joshi," *Hindustan Times*, May 13, 1998.

versal ethical principle about the unacceptability of discrimination in international relations.

The May 1998 tests marked a rupture with several decades of successive Indian governments supporting the development of the nuclear weapon infrastructure but concerned about whether the time was right to undertake nuclear tests or deploy nuclear weapons.[19] What distinguishes the Bharatiya Janta party (BJP), which made the decision to test, from other major Indian political parties and traditions is that its politics are based on a violent intolerance of religious and ethnic minorities and a determination to forge a new Hindu India.[20] Just as the party has not hesitated to use violence for achieving domestic ends, it regards the development of military might as the means to ensure that it gets its way in international affairs. This is at the core of its decision to move so decisively and quickly after coming to power and order the nuclear tests.

The BJP may not settle for anything less than a fully nuclear India, one with deployed nuclear weapons. Reports of work on a new longer-range Indian missile and a nuclear submarine suggest the possibility that a nuclear force with a triad structure is being pursued.[21] The budget of the Department of Atomic Energy (responsible for the nuclear weapons program) has been increased by 68 percent since the May 1998 tests. In the Indian parliament Prime Minister Vajpayee stated: "While our decision is to maintain the deployment of a deterrent which is both minimum and credible, I would like to reaffirm to this House that the government will not accept any restraints on the development of India's R&D capabilities."[22]

A non-BJP government inheriting such programs—which command significant support among scientific, bureaucratic, and military elites—may be able to do little more than keep them at the level of research and development. This, combined with the current levels of development of nuclear weapons and ballistic missiles, makes it unlikely that India's quest for a nuclear arsenal will be ended soon. Only if the nuclear weapon states genuinely moved to eliminate nuclear weapons would any Indian government be able to command support for significant nuclear restraint on its part. India, then, in the eyes of the Indian elite, would have a status equal to that of the great powers.

19. See, for instance, the statement by former prime minister H. D. Deve Gowda, "Real Motive Was Political, Not Military, Says Gowda," *Hindustan Times*, May 20, 1998; and Shekhar Gupta "Road to Resurgence," *Indian Express*, May 12, 1998.

20. Achin Vanaik, *The Furies of Indian Communalism: Religion, Modernity and Secularization* (London: Verso Books, 1997).

21. "India's Nuclear Submarine to Be Ready by 2004," *Rediff on the Net*, June 27, 1998; and Shishir Gupta, "Longer Range Agni Test-Fire Soon," *Hindustan Times*, September 5, 1998.

22. Brahma Chellaney, "Expert Comment: New Nuclear Clarity with Old Waffle," *Hindustan Times*, January 3, 1999.

Given this background, the likely response to the deep cuts proposal by future Indian governments, and more generally supporters of nuclear weapons in India, is easy to see. Although they are likely to support the massive reductions in nuclear arsenals of the nuclear weapon states, they are unlikely to accept preemptive restraints on India's programs.

It should be said, however, that there are some among India's nuclear hawks, who have consistently espoused acquiring a full-fledged nuclear arsenal and opposed any restraint, that now see value in participating in arms control agreements that they had previously decried. Such participation now would, in their view, consolidate the gains they feel India made by carrying out its nuclear tests. India's hawks may become its arms controllers.[23]

The position of Indian opponents of nuclear weapons is a far more principled one. In a recent comment Praful Bidwai, a leading antinuclear intellectual and activist, condemned India's nuclear tests as "strategically irrational, politically outrageous and morally repugnant" and then went on to argue that India "should avoid the temptation of looking for devious bargains that . . . perpetuate nuclear weapon states' hegemonies and legitimize machtpolitik."[24]

Pakistan

Pakistan's leaders have far simpler motivations and far smaller ambitions. For decades they have engaged in fearful competition with India, no matter how self-destructive. Pakistan's nuclear weapons were presented first as a counter to India's nuclear weapons, but have since become seen also as an "equalizer" against India's conventional military superiority.[25] In the wake of India's tests and the attendant belligerence by the BJP government, Pakistan's leaders took the opportunity offered to them, an opportunity some of them had long hoped for, and followed suit. It is now hard to see Pakistan's leaders giving up nuclear weapons without some sense of maintaining parity with India, and even insisting on creating such parity when it comes to conventional weapons. Pakistan's refusal to agree to a no first use of nuclear weapons proposal offered by India is a result of this perceived imbalance.

23. See for example, C. Raja Mohan, "Rethinking CTBT and FMCT (Nuclear Diplomacy-II)," *Hindu*, June 16, 1998, p. 13.

24. Praful Bidwai, "India Defiled, Indians Diminished," *Frontline*, June 5, 1998.

25. See for instance Zia Mian, "Renouncing the Nuclear Option," in *Pakistan and the Bomb*, Samina Ahmed and David Cortright, eds. (University of Notre Dame Press, 1998).

It is in this light that the linkage Pakistan's leaders make between their nuclear weapons and the Kashmir dispute needs to be seen. Kashmir is undoubtedly a major flashpoint; it has generated crises between India and Pakistan many times before and led to wars. As the continued shelling across the line of control separating the two armies in Kashmir indicates, demonstrating nuclear capabilities has not stopped the low-intensity battle there; only the stakes have been raised.[26] A settlement of the Kashmir dispute therefore seems vital as a way of reducing the risk of the conflict escalating, perhaps inadvertently, into nuclear war.

However, there is a lesson to be learned from the persistence of massive nuclear arsenals in the United States and Russia after the collapse of the Soviet Union: even when the apparent source of conflict between two states is removed, if these states have nuclear weapons, the weapons remain and so does the danger. The settlement of the Kashmir dispute may leave the same legacy. Settling Kashmir will also not remove the risk of war. The last war between India and Pakistan had nothing to do with Kashmir and resulted in the largest number of casualties of any Indo-Pakistan war, the creation of Bangladesh from the former East Pakistan, and 90,000 Pakistani prisoners of war.

Despite these reasons, if India does put caps on its nuclear program, Pakistan may well be forced to follow suit. Pakistan's smaller infrastructure and economy is simply not capable of living up to the international pressure that is sure to ensue in the event that India acquiesces to the various arms control proposals suggested. The announcement of even limited sanctions after its nuclear tests was sufficient to trigger a near collapse of the Pakistani economy and has caused widespread hardship.

Sanctions have served to compound a more enduring crisis in Pakistan. The last decade has seen the country start to show signs of a deep crisis of legitimacy as a state and in its social order. The polity is fragmenting into warring religious and ethnic sectarian groups who battle out their differences on the streets of its cities amid collapsing infrastructure and lack of even basic social services. Sanctions have only led to further erosion of state authority, an increase in the popularity of religious nationalist groups, and government efforts to regain some authority by attempting to placate them. In particular, the government has sought support by proposing a new amendment to the Constitution that calls for the enforcement of strict Islamic law in the country.

In this context it is significant that the radical Islamist groups were the most

26. On the continuing battle, "Pakistan Firing Toll Rises to 34," *Hindu*, August 3, 1998.

vociferous in demanding that Pakistan conduct nuclear tests and they have subsequently adopted the bomb as their own. What is important is that many within the Pakistani state, the military, and the nuclear weapons program have sympathies with one or the other of these groups. In such a situation, the state may not be able to ensure control over its nuclear weapons. This is in addition to the dangers of technical failures of command and control.

In light of the dangers created by the Indian state's insistence on some kind of parity with the nuclear weapon states, even if it is in name only, and the compulsions on Pakistan to follow despite socioeconomic collapse, it seems that the challenge to the nuclear weapon states and those who would propose nuclear policies to them is to accept explicitly the need for nuclear disarmament and to begin fighting for it. This is undoubtedly a difficult challenge, but not as difficult as it once was. The peace movement and the non-nuclear weapon states, which have struggled for decades to be heard, now find their arguments echoed by the likes of the former head of U.S. Strategic Command, General George Lee Butler, and other senior military and political figures from the nuclear weapon states. It is also worth noting that on May 28, 1998, following the first set of nuclear tests by Pakistan, President Clinton said, "I cannot believe that we are about to start the 21st century by having the Indian subcontinent repeat the worst mistakes of the 20th century, when we know it is not necessary to peace, to security, to prosperity, to national greatness or personal fulfillment."[27] This is perhaps the closest a U. S. president has come to officially stating, albeit grudgingly and not focussing on U. S. policies, that nuclear weapons are not necessary for peace or security.

In the context of abolition, the deep cuts strategy could become the first step, "but certainly not the last," on a road clearly sign-posted as leading to nuclear disarmament. There could then be a role in South Asia for some of the ideas outlined in the proposal. But to reiterate, such measures are only going to gain a sympathetic hearing in India and Pakistan if they are seen as a stopgap while the battle for abolition is being fought. Moreover, by being part of an abolition program, these steps may gain support from the majority of nonnuclear states and so help India and Pakistan comply. This factor should not be underestimated. Much of the public opinion in both India and Pakistan has seen demands and sanctions by the nuclear weapon states as hypocritical bullying.

27. Office of the Press Secretary, the White House, "Remarks by the President on the Patients' Bill of Rights," May 28, 1998.

A Disarmament Bricolage

There are a few possibilities that may usefully integrate parts of the deep cuts strategy with the urgent need to address the dangers to the people of South Asia inherent in the present situation.[28] The first involves keeping nuclear weapon systems off alert and separate from their delivery systems.

It should be clear that the present Indian government and probably any successor would refuse any move to do this on a bilateral basis with Pakistan. A wider agreement will be required. With this in mind, it is possible to build on the proposal offered by the deep cuts strategy of a verified system of de-alerting the nuclear warheads of the nuclear weapon states. It may be fruitful to invite India to participate in the verification of such de-alerting. This would meet some of its aspirations for recognition by engaging it in a process otherwise restricted to nuclear weapon states: India would be a participant-observer in the disarmament process. It may also put to rest some of the BJP government's claimed concerns about China.

For its part, India could be asked to make an unverified commitment to keep its nuclear weapons demated as well as stop the testing and deployment of missiles, in particular the Agni missile, which has been tested a few times and is still under development and which may allow India to threaten the territories of the nuclear weapon states. The fact that some nuclear weapons will be kept mated and deployed by the nuclear weapon states and that India's arsenal is relatively small means that India may be unlikely to accept full reciprocity in verification. In the current climate, if nuclear weapon states demand reciprocal verification, India may well opt out of an agreement.

An Indian agreement with the nuclear weapon states that would freeze further development and deployment of India's long-range missiles is likely to be seen as irrelevant by Pakistan. The contiguous border and the size and shape of Pakistan ensure that nearly all its major cities and military installations are within range of India's short-range Prithvi missile. There would therefore need to be a parallel but overlapping bilateral agreement between India and Pakistan covering such missiles.

One possibility would be for India to agree to move its Prithvi missiles to monitored storage far away from the border. In exchange, Pakistan would commit not to test or deploy long-range missiles, such as the intermediate-range Ghauri and Shaheen, which are justified by Pakistan's government as

28. Some of these possibilities are elaborated in Zia Mian and M. V. Ramana, "Beyond Lahore: From Transparency to Arms Control," *Economic and Political Weekly*, vol. 34, April 17–24, 1999.

a response to Prithvi. The difference in size between India and Pakistan means such an arrangement could remove the immediate threat to Pakistan's major cities, while ensuring that Pakistan could not threaten any major part of India. The value of such a step for India is that despite public rhetoric in Pakistan, it is highly unlikely, with only limited testing so far, the Ghauri and Shaheen would be ready for deployment; halting future tests would be significant.

The limited means available to both states and the importance they still attach to ambiguity about the numbers of nuclear weapons and missiles would make verification of such an agreement difficult. However, the absence of even limited trust between the two states makes verification vital, especially since it is claimed Pakistan may have short-range Chinese-made M-11 missiles that it has so far chosen not to deploy. One possibility would be for a single cooperative monitoring center, or two co-located ones, with international satellites providing Indians and Pakistanis identical high resolution imaging data from a swath several hundred kilometers wide on both sides of the border. The exact width could be such as to ensure that neither Prithvi nor the M-11 could be deployed close enough to the border to be able to threaten significant areas of the other state without being detected.

Because both India and Pakistan could deliver their nuclear weapons by aircraft, any arrangement would have to cover not just missile development and deployment, but also airbases. India and Pakistan could simply agree to monitor activity at airbases through inspections.

Following India's tests, the prime minister declared a moratorium on further nuclear tests. After its tests, Pakistan made the same announcement. This culminated in the announcement at the United Nations by the respective prime ministers that they would, in effect, sign the Comprehensive Nuclear Test Ban Treaty before the September 1999 deadline for entry into force. Indian opposition parties responded by demanding that the BJP stick to the "national consensus" reached in 1996, on the basis that the treaty was discriminatory and did not further India's traditional disarmament goals. There is, however, considerable international and domestic pressure that all of India's leaders be seen to be politically responsible on this question. The fall of the BJP government in April 1999 and scheduling of fresh elections for autumn 1999 makes it unlikely that India will sign the treaty by the September deadline. However, the moratorium on testing may well remain in place.

In Pakistan, while accession to the treaty is opposed by hard-line Islamist groups, there seems to be little doubt that the severe economic crisis in the country will force the government to sign. The only question may be whether it should sign before or with India.

While signing the CTBT by India and Pakistan would certainly be welcome, their doing so should not be interpreted as a lessening of the dangers created by the nuclear tests and the nuclear nationalism they unleashed. The enmity and fears on both sides will persist, and there are signs of an imminent conventional arms race. The dispute over Kashmir persists, and South Asia will remain a stumble away from catastrophe.

It is possible to imagine that with direct nuclear arms races closed off by a combination of de-alerting and nondeployment agreements and accession to the CTBT, India and Pakistan's nuclear and military establishments may displace their competitive urges to filling their respective "fissile material gaps." India's stocks of fissile material are estimated to be less than 500 kilograms of weapons grade plutonium. It would take the country fifteen years to double this stock at the estimated present rate of production. Even then, the stockpile would be about half or less that of the United Kingdom, which is now the smallest of the nuclear weapon states. Pakistan's fissile stocks are estimated to be a few hundred kilograms of highly enriched uranium with an annual production capacity of 25–50 kilograms. Limited plutonium production may have started.[29] However, although the stocks of fissile material of India and Pakistan are small, it is possible that both states could accelerate production, with the attendant damage to the environment and people's health. Indian plans for a new plutonium reactor may be the first step.[30]

One way to address this concern would be through the proposed Fissile Material Treaty (FMT). The Conference on Disarmament now seems to be in a position to begin negotiations, after getting India, Pakistan, and Israel to agree to talks. India dropped its long-standing condition that the FMT be linked to a time-bound program of nuclear disarmament, and Pakistan agreed to negotiate on a treaty that would not consider past stockpiles. Presumably both agreements are part of an effort to establish credibility as responsible nuclear states in the aftermath of their tests. However, Pakistan's ambassador at the Conference on Disarmament has said "as regards the FMCT, for Pakistan this issue is now dependent on India's nuclear status, its degree of weaponization, and size and quality of its fissile material stockpiles. Pakistan cannot afford to allow India to once again destabilize the balance of deterrence in the future through asymmetry in the level of stockpiles."[31]

Both India and Pakistan have categorically rejected any possibility of a moratorium on fissile material production before the conclusion of the talks.

29. Albright, Berkhout, and Walker, *Plutonium and Highly Enriched Uranium, 1996.*
30. "BARC Planning New Dhruva-type Reactor," *Hindustan Times*, April 28, 1999.
31. Statement by Ambassador Munir Akram at the Special Session of the Conference on Disarmament on June 2, 1998, available from Pakistan Permanent Mission to the UN, Nuclear Testing in South Asia.

Moreover, negotiations over such a treaty are likely to take a long time, especially given the difficulties that are bound to arise in India and Pakistan over verification and inspections. In the interim, there may well be a fissile material race.

A way around this problem is, first, for the nuclear weapon states to commit to a deadline for the talks. This would set a limit to the stocks of fissile material that could be produced during the talks as well as concentrate diplomatic resources on the negotiations. As part of preparing the ground for speeded-up negotiations, the nuclear weapon states could formalize their existing moratoriums on fissile material production, declare the sizes of their present stockpiles, and begin to place significant fractions of their fissile material under international safeguards. This would address India's long-standing concerns that safeguards were discriminatory unless the nuclear weapon states allowed their facilities to be inspected.[32]

At the same time, India could be asked to cancel its planned plutonium production reactor and to put its nuclear power reactors under safeguards. Without the possibility of running its power reactors at low burn-up, Indian capacity to produce large amounts of fissile material and thus quickly build up its stocks is limited. This step gains in importance if it can be done soon, since India is scheduled to start reprocessing power reactor fuel at the new Kalpakkam Reprocessing Plant in the near future.[33] In exchange for such a restriction on India's fissile material production capability, Pakistan could be asked to suspend operation of its new Kushab plutonium production reactor.

A fissile material treaty that only stopped the future production of material would, like the Comprehensive Test Ban Treaty and the NPT, leave nuclear weapon states holding whatever nuclear capabilities they had for as long as they wanted. By agreeing to a process that would place their stocks of nuclear material under safeguards the nuclear weapon states could demonstrate an intention to abolish nuclear weapons.

Conclusion

The deep cuts strategy cannot help but reflect its genealogy. As an arms control measure, albeit a radical one, deep cuts would preserve the capacity for nuclear weapon states to wreck devastation through the use of such weapons and leave unchallenged the doctrine of nuclear deterrence.

32. This argument was developed in the context of the NPT but Indian hawks have implicitly attacked safeguards in general. The fact that the FMT as envisioned currently would involve safeguards on the weapon states also is simply glossed over. See for example, Brahma Chellaney, "Fanged Safeguards, Hanging Fissbans," *Pioneer,* May 21, 1997, p.10.

33. John Cherian, "The BJP and the Bomb," *Frontline,* vol. 15 (April 11–24, 1998).

In South Asia the measures advocated by the deep cuts program for the weapon states are likely to be welcomed as a form of strategic self-restraint. But the suggested restrictions on the Indian and thus the Pakistani programs are unlikely to be given a sympathetic hearing. Recognizing this and that the dangerous dynamics at work in the region cannot be left to work themselves out in the hope that time will eventually yield some kind of solution, there needs to be a more thoroughgoing alternative.

One possibility is for the deep cuts strategy to be recast as part of a radical transformation in arms control and thinking about nuclear weapons. The arms control process should now explicitly embrace the abolition of nuclear weapons.

Pakistan and the Deep Cuts Regime

Pervez Hoodbhoy

Pakistan stands close to the bottom of the nuclear hierarchy. In all probability, therefore, the impact on the Pakistani nuclear program of deep cuts in nuclear arsenals by the five nuclear weapon states will be felt largely via the effects that these will have on its larger neighbor and adversary, India. However, one can expect some direct effects as well.

Evidence can easily be adduced to the contention that Pakistan's acquisition of nuclear weapons has been driven solely by the desire to counter India's nuclear and conventional might. Pakistan's five nuclear tests coming in the wake of India's five demonstrate this clearly. But even before the tests Pakistan's development of nuclear weapons was clearly aimed at India. In a poll conducted in 1996 by the Kroc Institute of International Studies, every respondent who supported the bomb saw the reason as being fairly and squarely India.[1] Contrary to popular belief in the West, Islamic solidarity was not stated to be a motive. The principal motivations, ordered according to their importance, for Pakistan's nuclear weapons program appear to be based on the following.

—Pakistan's assumption that relations between the two countries will always be hostile, and a fear that, as in 1971, India's massive conventional military could succeed again in dismembering Pakistan.

—Pakistan's desire to provide a nuclear shield that would permit it to maintain its support for Kashmiri militants while protecting it from attack by India. Although this is not officially acknowledged as a motive, there is no doubt that it is extremely important in strategic planning.

—Pakistan's obvious fear of India's nuclear weapons program, which came into view in 1974.

1. Samina Ahmed and David Cortright, eds., *Pakistan and the Bomb* (University of Notre Dame Press, 1998).

—The nationalistic fervor that nuclear weapons provide.

While pursuing the nuclear program, civil and military leaders have also been aware of the need to show flexibility before the international community. Therefore, at the diplomatic level, Pakistan has sought negotiations and made several attempts to bring India to the nuclear bargaining table. These include proposals for bilateral nuclear talks, a five-nation conference, and a South Asian nuclear weapon–free zone (NWFZ). Proposed by Pakistan to the UN General Assembly, the nuclear weapon–free zone has been repeatedly endorsed, most recently on December 9, 1997, when 153 states voted for the resolution and only 3 against (India, Bhutan, and Mauritius). The Indian position is that nuclear-free zones are illusory and promoters of the status quo, and that India is prepared to work for a nuclear-free world instead.

Pakistan's various offers for talks are usually dismissed by Indian commentators as insincere and are said to be merely a diplomatic stick with which it seeks to beat India. Pakistan's statement that it will sign the Non-Proliferation Treaty if India agrees to do the same is also claimed to belong to this category because it knows that India will not sign the treaty and therefore such declarations carry little real risk. Of course, one cannot fairly comment with certitude on abstract ideas of sincerity. However, the significant point is that India has not made any attempt to call Pakistan's bluff. The reason is fairly obvious; India now perceives itself as the emerging regional giant of South Asia. With the maturation of the Prithvi missile program and the first successful launch of the Agni missile in 1989, India joined an exclusive club hitherto dominated by the world's technological and military giants.

The coming to power in 1998 of the Hindu nationalist Bharatiya Janata party (BJP), albeit as the leader of an unstable fourteen-party coalition, has also affected India's changed position. The BJP policy of inducting nuclear weapons into India's military arsenal is of long standing and was the only one of its manifesto promises to make it through the interparty negotiations of the National Agenda, which is supposed to represent the common platform of the governing coalition. Its decision to test should have come as no surprise.

It is likely that India's fierce and quite newly found nuclear nationalism will not respond readily to global disarmament measures even if the cuts are as deep and wide as can be realistically hoped. Indian attitudes have undergone a profound change in the past five decades. Although it had supported a test ban as far back as 1952, India finds much fault with the Comprehensive Test Ban Treaty, and even though it has now tested, it remains a hold-out. During the protracted and painful negotiations in 1996, India raised numerous technical objections to the CTBT and, most importantly, insisted on a time-bound framework for global nuclear disarmament, a position that drew wide condemnation as a treaty killer. This position has been reaffirmed after the tests. The rhetoric of many Indian leaders and commentators is that they will accept nothing short of parity with the nuclear weapon states because to do otherwise would be to accept nuclear colonialism.

Nevertheless, India does recognize that a global move toward nuclear arms reductions cannot leave it untouched: through trade and aid it is well integrated into the global economy (the United States is now the largest foreign investor in India). One may therefore reasonably speculate on, or perhaps demand, the direction in which India moves following an agreement between the five nuclear states to implement measures such as those proposed by the Deep Cuts Group. This will be discussed at some length later.

Pakistan's nuclear stance will be largely a reaction to India's. Should India make significant nuclear concessions, such as agreeing to the NPT or CTBT or some regional denuclearization measure, Pakistan is likely to respond in kind. However, even if there is no significant change in the Indian nuclear posture, Pakistan will feel the impact of deep global cuts because they will inevitably lead to a changed international environment much more hostile to nuclear proliferant states. Because of its economic, political, and military dependencies, Pakistan is intrinsically more susceptible to external pressures than India. In fact, there are reasons to believe that its economic and technological weakness will impose increasingly stringent, perhaps crippling, constraints on the growth of its defense capabilities. It is therefore likely that in years to come Pakistan's nuclear program will cap itself even if the country's political or military forces wish otherwise. Two factors virtually dictate that this be so.

First, there is very little money available for the social and health services that are desperately wanting in the country. In a population of 130 million, about 38 percent are literate, newspaper circulation is less than one for every seventy persons, clean drinking water is unavailable to the majority of the populace, and on the Human Development Index (HDI) Pakistan now ranks 138 out of 174 countries.[2] It is clear that the Pakistani state is spending close to every penny that it possibly can on social services and health. Further squeezing this or cutting back on subsidies or administrative expenditures

2. UN Development Programme, *Human Development Report: Consumption for Human Development* (1998).

may yet yield another few percent increase for defense but at the cost of severe social disruption. Pakistan is under continuous pressure for debt payments from the International Monetary Fund and the World Bank, which are pressuring it to scale back defense spending. Although the present loans have not been made conditional on specified reductions, future loans may be subject to strict terms. Britain, which is part of the Aid-to-Pakistan Consortium, has already indicated that it may tie future aid to reductions in Pakistan's military spending.[3]

Five decades of high defense spending have sharply reduced Pakistan's ability to defend itself because the spending has drained away resources from a reservoir that is the source of strength of every modern country: its educational system and a pool of highly skilled people. Today the poor quality of scientific and technical education in Pakistan, and thus the generally poor quality of scientists and engineers employed in national technical institutions, places fundamental limitations on Pakistan's efforts for a defense based on high technology. The indications are that higher education, particularly in the sciences, is in a fast downward spiral.

The result is that although Pakistan, like India, has tested nuclear weapons, the weapons are likely to be based on an imported (Chinese) design. Otherwise they would be crude in design and manufacture, rather large, and with uncertain reliability. Anyway, the numbers are likely to be small, and boosting the explosive yield, miniaturization, permissive action links (PAL), and other sophistications are ruled out. Pakistan's failure to develop the Khalid tank and, more significantly, to successfully match India's Prithvi missile with an indigenously developed missile, the Hatf, are principally due to lack of technical and scientific expertise. The first test of the Ghauri, a new missile with a 1,500-km range, while presented as a major advance for Pakistan's military capability, may offer further eveidence for this lack of scientific capability. The missile seems to be based on a North Korean design rather than being a development of the earlier indigenous Hatf missiles. This has resulted in Missile Technology Control Regime (MTCR) sanctions being applied by the United States on Pakistan and North Korea.[4]

One may therefore surmise that changes in the global security environment, such as those under consideration by the Deep Cuts Group, will inevitably put severe pressure on Pakistan to respond. Further, given that it

3. Nasir Malick, "UK Threatens to Cut Off Aid to Pakistan," *Dawn* (March 26, 1998).

4. David Wright, "An Analysis of the Pakistani Ghauri Missile Test of 6 April 1998," *Science & Global Security* (1998); and Tim Weiner, "U.S. says North Korea Helped Develop New Pakistani Missile," *New York Times*, April 11, 1998, p. 3.

is a weakened and weakening power, the government may even welcome the opportunity to at least partially disengage from a race it is losing. Pakistan is not in a position to match India's development of intermediate-range ballistic missiles (without considerable assistance by North Korea or China) or contest it in developing satellite surveillance, both of which decisions have recently been taken in India.[5] These elements will be decisively important for all future military strategies, including those relying on nuclear weapons as a last resort. Thus, while a full-fledged nuclear race would be bad for both countries, Pakistan would stand to lose far more.

It would be dangerous to assume, however, that Pakistan will bow out of the race; it and India are locked into a zero-sum game, and simple knee-jerk actions substitute for planning and strategy. As long as the two continue to view each other as hostile aggressors, violent conflict will be just around the corner. Therefore, only political dialogue and resolution of conflicts through negotiation can ensure a peaceful future.

Improving the Security Environment

We shall now consider those actions by the five nuclear weapon states and by Pakistan and India that would have the greatest beneficial impact on the subcontinent's security environment.

Cutting Conventional Arms Exports

The five nuclear weapon nations, in addition to their special nuclear status, also have the dubious distinction of being the biggest exporters of conventional weapons. According to the Stockholm Peace Research Institute, between 1993 and 1997 the aggregate exports of the top six exporters, five of them being the nuclear weapon states, neared $100 billion, the United States leading the way with conventional exports amounting to more than $50 billion. In the same years India and Pakistan imported $4.4 billion and $3.0 billion, respectively, worth of weapons, with the bulk being from the nuclear weapon states.[6]

The high returns in the export of conventional arms, with profits accruing to domestic arms industries, makes it a lucrative business. The cost, both

5. Shishir Gupta, "Government Decides to Develop Missile System," *Hindustan Times*, May 5, 1998; and "India to Launch Spy Satellite Next Year," *Dawn*, April 17, 1998.
6. Stockholm Peace Research Institute Arms Transfers project, July 17, 1998.

in economic terms and lost opportunities for peace, are borne by the consumer. Today South Asia is awash in arms ranging from hand-held weapons and mines to submarines and the most sophisticated fighter aircraft. It would be disingenuous to cook up formulas for peace that concentrate entirely on reducing or eliminating nuclear weapons from the subcontinent; the fact is that India and Pakistan have already fought three wars with conventional weapons imported almost exclusively from the nuclear weapon states and may well fight a much more destructive one in the future with more of them. Therefore, the deep cuts strategy must include large reductions, and eventually total prohibition, in allowable exports of major weapon systems by the industrialized countries. One formula might be to demand that the total volume exported each year be 10 percent less than the previous year.

De-alerting and Reducing Warheads

As argued by the Deep Cuts Study Group, there is plenty of room for further reductions by the nuclear weapon states without compromising their national security. Also, the Deep Cuts Group emphasizes the importance of de-alerting the forces, principally by separating warheads from missiles and bombers or by removing other key components from missile delivery systems. The hope is that, with the reductions and de-alerting of the nuclear forces of the nuclear weapon states, pressure could be brought to bear on Israel, India, and Pakistan to keep their nuclear forces effectively demated and eventually to put their unsafeguarded fissile materials in predesignated storage facilities. Although there seems little prospect of the threshold countries formally adopting such a posture soon, there may be other actions they could take to lower levels of nuclear alert.

Perhaps the most urgent task is to reduce the threat posed by Indian and Pakistani intermediate-range ballistic missiles. India possesses the indigenously manufactured Prithvi, an IRBM. In a *Defence News* report the Prithvi project director, Vijay Kumar Saraswat, was quoted as saying, "The development program of Prithvi missile is over, and production of the 150 km missile has begun."[7] The report stated that missile production started in mid-1996 and sixty out of the one hundred that have been ordered have already been built. Each missile costs more than $1 million. Indian Defense Ministry sources are reported as saying that it will be for frontline battlefield support and carry a fuel-air explosive warhead or a prefragmented war-

7. *Defence News* (March 10–16, 1997).

head for destroying airstrips. However, a recent study of Prithvi suggests that its use with such warheads in a counterforce strike would have limited effect.[8] It is therefore not surprising that Retired General K. Sundarji, now an influential defense analyst, has written that the Prithvi "though primarily designed and developed for delivering sophisticated advanced conventional munitions, can in the case of need be modified to carry a nuclear warhead."[9] He also noted, "The nuclear pits that are to go into the aircraft bomb casing or the missile warhead compartment have to be successfully miniaturised and with only the proverbial 'last wire' yet to be connected by teams of suitably qualified scientists. I expect we are in that state now."

Pakistani missile capabilities are much more limited. The only comparably reliable missiles are the M-11s, with specifications similar to the Prithvi. The Ghauri, having had only one test, constitutes little more than a proof of concept. It may take the better part of a decade to develop it into a reliable delivery system, if Pakistan can get help with the missile guidance system.

Given the essentially zero warning time of missiles and the near impossibility of an effective missile defense system, the deployment of IRBMs by the two adversaries is bound to provoke tensions and induce instability. However, so far there are no credible reports that the Prithvi has been deployed in significant numbers or that the M-11s have been taken out of their crates at Sargodha Airforce Base. This state of affairs should be prolonged as long as possible. If the missiles are deployed, the two sides should try to reach an agreement that they would be kept out of range of each other's territory. Although the missiles are mobile, a suitable verification agreement could allow the two countries to gain a margin of safety and move away from the brink.

The impact on the subcontinent of deep cuts in warhead numbers by the nuclear weapon states is more difficult to assess. Effects on Pakistan would arise from the general hardening of the global environment against proliferant states, but it is difficult to be more specific. In principle India could demand that it be given parity with the nuclear weapon states and therefore be entitled to the 200-warhead level at the third stage of reductions outlined by the Deep Cuts Group. This would allow India to increase its present arsenal several times over before it reaches the prescribed limit. Although Indian hawks are likely to make such demands, in all probability

8. Z. Mian, A. H. Nayyar, and M. V. Ramana, "Bringing Prithvi Down to Earth," *Science & Global Security*, vol. 7 (1998).

9. K. Sundarji, "Imperatives of Indian Minimum Nuclear Deterrence," *AGNI: Studies in International Strategic Issues*, vol. 2, pp. 17–22, published in New Delhi by the Forum for Strategic and Security Studies.

a deep cuts regime would put tremendous pressure on India to respond by cutting back in some appropriate way. What could that way be? Joining a worldwide fissile materials cutoff would be the most significant.

Agreeing to a Fissile Materials Cutoff

Estimates exist for the inventories of fissile materials held by India and Pakistan. How good they are is a matter of speculation, but having numbers provides some basis for devising guidelines for a possible cutoff of fissile materials production.

According to the most current estimates by David Albright and his colleagues, Pakistan possesses 210 kg of highly enriched uranium (with an error margin of plus or minus 50 kg).[10] This was produced via the centrifuge enrichment process at Kahuta between 1986 and 1991. Assuming that 25 kg is used per weapon, Pakistan's arsenal is eight to thirteen bombs the size of that dropped on Hiroshima. Under pressure from the United States, in 1991 Pakistan promised not to enrich uranium beyond the 5 percent limit but refused to allow on-site verification. Therefore, the quantity and quality of low-enriched uranium feedstock that can be rapidly converted to HEU is not known (although one estimate suggests that it may be sufficient to double the existing estimated stock of HEU).[11] This may have happened in association with the nuclear tests.

Albright and colleagues also list India's inventory. A steady source of weapon-grade plutonium is provided by its two largest research reactors located at the Bhabha Atomic Research Centre in Bombay. Additionally, it has unsafeguarded CANDU power reactors that can provide plutonium of any desired level of isotopic purity, although there is no evidence that India has produced weapon-grade plutonium in this way. The country has had the capacity to reprocess plutonium from spent fuel since 1964, and the Pokhran test of 1974 established that it had acquired adequate knowledge of fission explosives. The estimated inventory of weapon-grade plutonium at the end of 1995 was 330 kg with an error of plus or minus 15 kg. This translates into sixty bombs at 5 kg per weapon.

On a possible fissile cutoff the present positions are as follows: India has rejected a regional cutoff and seems determined to follow its policy at the

10. David Albright, Frans Berkhout, and William Walker, *Plutonium and Highly Enriched Uranium, 1996: World Inventories, Capabilities, and Policies* (Oxford University Press, 1997).

11. A. H. Nayyar, A. H. Toor, and Z. Mian, "Fissile Material Production Potential in South Asia," *Science & Global Security*, vol. 6 (1997).

Comprehensive Test Ban Treaty talks and tie any global cutoff to negotiations on time-bound nuclear disarmament. In fact, after these talks then Indian Prime Minister I. K. Gujral compared the Fissile Material Cutoff to the NPT and CTBT explicitly and declared India would not sign it. In a reversal of an earlier position, India has indicated that it now may be willing to consider including existing stocks of fissile materials in such negotiations if they are held in the context of larger nuclear disarmament talks. This is very similar to Pakistan's position.

Although supporting a cutoff, Pakistan has long insisted that existing unequal fissile material stocks be addressed by treaty, proposing that, for example, stocks be equalized at the lowest possible levels by the transfer of the excess to safeguarded civilian use. Pakistan's other long-standing concern is on-site verification of any nuclear agreement. This has been evident in its dispute with the United States over freezing of uranium enrichment mentioned earlier, and during the CTBT talks. The small size of its nuclear stockpile has put a premium on the ambiguity surrounding it. Taken together, these mean that even if India were to sign a cutoff, Pakistan might not automatically follow.[12]

The Indian and Pakistani stands must be seen as bargaining positions that could change dramatically should there be a cessation of fissile material production by the nuclear weapon states as the result of a multilateral, but not necessarily global, agreement. In particular, one can imagine a situation in which India is persuaded to put its power-reactor plutonium and Pakistan its low-enriched uranium under international safeguards.

Altering Targeting Practices

Nuclear strategists have long debated the virtues of counterforce, countervalue, and counterpower targeting of nuclear weapons (see, for example, chapter 4). Sometimes the argument is given that assured destruction of enemy cities requires fewer and less accurate bombs, makes military planners less nervous about losing command and control centers, and hence that countervalue targeting is superior to counterforce targeting as a means of achieving deterrence. However, in the context of the subcontinent, I argue

12. *News* (Islamabad), November 1996; M. V. Ramana, "The Hawks Take Flight—The Fissile Cutoff and the Indian Nuclear Debate," *INESAP Bulletin*, no. 13 (July 1997), pp. 10–12; and statement by Ambassador Munir Akram at the INESAP "Workshop on Fissile Materials and Tritium: How to Verify a Comprehensive Production Cut-off and Safeguard All Stocks," Geneva, June 29–30, 1995.

later that nuclear weapons can be made relatively less destabilizing by an agreement to limit nuclear attacks to counterforce targets only.

Although Pakistan is estimated to have no more than eight to thirteen weapons, because of interception and reliability problems, no more than two to four could be reasonably expected to get to the target and explode properly. Since Pakistan is an undeclared nuclear state, it has never enunciated a nuclear doctrine on how such a number of nuclear weapons could be used; and nuclear targeting has never been publicly discussed. However, there is a general line of argument that, instead of "wasting" these few weapons against military formations or installations, it should theaten high-value targets—Delhi, Bombay, and other Indian cities within the range of its delivery aircraft. The Indians are presumably not willing to pay this price, according to the Pakistani calculation, so an invasion by a more powerful adversary will have been deterred.

There are, however, counterarguments to this line of reasoning. First, the actual use of nuclear weapons by Pakistan against an Indian city would be suicidal because of the much larger number of Indian weapons that would then surely be used against Pakistani cities. Thus the Pakistani threat might lack credibility. To the extent that it was credible, the Indian temptation to launch a preemptive strike to save its cities might become irresistible in a crisis. There are some indications that the Indian Air Force is preparing a capability to do just this through its acquisitions of "smart bombs" for use against Pakistani air bases.[13]

Far better for Pakistan and India would be to reach agreement not to target each other's cities while freezing their nuclear stockpiles at the present levels. Allowed targets could include military concentrations, dams, nonnuclear power stations, and other targets of high economic value, but not population centers.

There is an example of a nuclear targeting agreement between Pakistan and India that gives encouragement for such a step. The two countries agreed in December 1990 not to attack each other's nuclear installations. This is the first, and so far only, nuclear agreement between the two. It entered into force on January 1, 1991, and lists of nuclear installations have been exchanged every year since then.[14] Each country has occasionally accused the other of cheating in the lists, but the agreement has survived.[15]

13. Eric Arnett, "Nuclear Stability and Arms Sales in India: Implications for U.S. Policy," *Arms Control Today*, vol. 27 (August 1997).

14. Carnegie Endowment for International Peace, *Tracking Nuclear Proliferation* (Washington, January 1991), p. 98.

15. How well such agreements can be expected to hold is anybody's guess, however. The chief of the Pakistan Air Force, Air Marshal Abbas Khattak, in an interview said, "an agreement of no-attack on each other's nuclear installations would not hold good in case of outbreak of war." *News* (Islamabad), April 9, 1997.

Agreeing to No First Use

If the nuclear weapon states could agree never to use nuclear weapons first (or more particularly, not to use nuclear weapons against nonnuclear states), it would be highly likely that significant progress along similar lines could be made on the subcontinent as well. A treaty between Pakistan and India that neither country will initiate the use of nuclear weapons against the other would be an important confidence-building measure. India had proposed this idea, but Pakistan rejected it. Pakistan's reasoning, following NATO doctrine in relation to the former Warsaw Pact countries, is that its use of nuclear weapons would be to protect its territory against invasion by a larger adversary. The implication is that if necessary it will use nuclear weapons even if it is attacked by conventional arms. Support for this can be inferred from remarks by former prime ministers and senior military officers who have claimed that Pakistan's nuclear weapons are a deterrent against overwhelming Indian conventional forces. Former Prime Minister Benazir Bhutto has argued that in fact a South Asian nonproliferation regime will not be durable until the threat of Indian conventional attack has been removed.

Should this issue be brought formally to the negotiating table and an agreement reached, Pakistan would stand to gain much. It makes no sense at all for it to use nuclear weapons under any conditions; while a couple of Indian cities could be severely damaged, the Indian response would leave every single Pakistani city in ruins. To suggest that nuclear weapons can defend Pakistan is dangerous folly. On the contrary, Pakistan's agreement to no first use could lead to a substantial decrease in nuclear tensions and force India toward bilateral nuclear discussions, which it has so far spurned.

Signing the Comprehensive Test Ban Treaty

The CTBT does not prohibit any country from possessing nuclear weapons, increasing their numbers, improving aircraft and missile delivery systems, making weapons more effective and reliable, simulating them on computers, developing new types based on the principles of fission and fusion, or even testing most components. The single prohibition is that no test involving nuclear materials can go beyond zero yield, or in plain language, no nuclear explosion whether small or big is allowed.

Although it has not formally acquiesced to signing the CTBT, Pakistan almost certainly will do so before September 1999. This seems to be the quid pro quo for the lifting of U.S. sanctions imposed after the May 28, 1998, tests in Pakistan. One must bear in mind, however, that the CTBT is largely redundant for fission weapons of the type Pakistan possesses.

As was made evident by the May tests by India and Pakistan, testing produces a psychological climate of anxiety, fear, and aggression in the populace. On May 11 in Delhi, and then two weeks later in Pakistan, huge crowds gave vent to extreme emotions. A ban on further testing is, therefore, important for stopping a further increase in India-Pakistan tensions.

It is still an open question as to when, and under what conditions, India will sign the CTBT. However, growing international pressure may force it to relinquish its present rigid position.

Conclusion

Implementation of the Deep Cuts Program by the nuclear weapon states could substantially decrease the intensity of nuclear competition between India and Pakistan. Drastic reductions in the number of warheads held by the five atomic powers, de-alerting their missiles and bombers, cutting off fissile material production, agreeing to no first use, forgoing further nuclear testing, and declaring that nonnuclear states will not be targeted cannot fail to have a profound impact on the subcontinent. But this is not enough. These same powers must immediately cease, and accept responsibility for, their immoral business of selling conventional weapons with immense destructive capabilities to sworn enemies who have used them three times in fifty years to make war on each other.

Back to Sanity: An Israeli View of the Effects of Deep Reductions

Shai Feldman

D eep reductions in U.S. and Russian nuclear arsenals, in contrast with total nuclear disarmament, would indicate two judgments about the efficacy of nuclear deterrence and its requirements. First, that it is important to retain some capacity for ultimate or existential deterrence, namely, the ability to deter threats to the state's basic security and survival. And second, that such deterrence can be achieved by possessing no more than a small arsenal of nuclear weapons. The resulting change from the cold war arsenals should be seen as a giant step away from the insane post–World War II nuclear arms race.

Thus, the proposed deep cuts in U.S. and Russian nuclear arsenals would represent a move back to common sense. Indeed, it was difficult to believe that the two nations' political leaders would ever have authorized the use of nuclear weapons in any of the complicated scenarios concocted by strategic analysts as requiring large and complex nuclear forces. By contrast, it was fairly reasonable to assume that the same leaders would order the use of such weapons if their nation's very survival were threatened. Yet for this purpose a small arsenal that would have targeted a small number of high-value adversary assets would have been more than sufficient. Thus, deep cuts would imply that the nuclear powers would possess small nuclear forces that are associated with a reasonable doctrine of ultimate or existential deterrence.

The de-alerting of nuclear force structures suggests a third judgment about the new political and strategic environment: that in the post–cold war era, the United States and Russia need no longer fear a surprise attack from

When I wrote this article I was senior research fellow at the Belfer Center for Science and International Affairs at the John F. Kennedy School of Government.

one another. Consequently, they no longer require the means for instant retaliation and can afford a separation and distancing of warheads from their delivery vehicles. Indeed, as fears of a nuclear Pearl Harbor seem increasingly irrelevant, there is no justification for continuing to maintain nuclear forces on hair-trigger alert. In turn, de-alerting would markedly diminish the danger of mistaken or unauthorized launching of nuclear weapons.

Deep cuts in U.S. and Russian nuclear forces would have direct as well as indirect implications for Israel. At first glance, Israel should only benefit from such deep reductions, primarily as they relate to Russia's nuclear arsenal. Russia borders on the Middle East, and in the past the Soviet Union had some grounds for viewing Israel's "nuclear option" as a threat. As a long-time opponent of Russia's allies in the region, Israel cannot exclude the possibility that it remains the target of some Russian atomic missiles.

More specifically, because Moscow supported Arab countries that engaged Israel in battle, if these countries were ever to pose a serious threat to Israel's survival, the Soviet Union could not exclude an Israeli attempt to end the threat by threatening the USSR directly. Consequently, it would not be surprising that some parts of the Soviet nuclear force—what in 1990 became Russia's nuclear arsenal—was targeted against Israel. Indeed, it is quite possible that this remains the case: the U.S. and Russian pledges to refrain from targeting one another have not been extended to a promise to avoid targeting other countries.

As a result, an accidental launch of a nuclear-tipped Russian ballistic missile could cause tremendous damage, directly or through fallout, to Israel's small population, resulting in hundreds of thousands of casualties and the destruction of the country's economic and industrial infrastructure. Indeed, the widely held views regarding the poor state of controls that Russia currently exercises regarding these missiles cannot leave Israeli defense planners sanguine regarding the danger that one of the missiles might be launched accidentally. Given Israel's highly exposed population, this level of damage would mean the end of the state in its present form. Any measure aimed at diminishing such danger should be more than welcomed by Israel. The most dramatic such measure is deep cuts.

A similar but more reversible effort to reduce the dangers of an accidental launch focuses on de-alerting the superpowers' nuclear arsenals by separating warheads from their delivery vehicles. Thus even if a ballistic missile were launched accidentally, the effect would be minimal: it would be limited to the effects of the blast created by the impact of a missile without a warhead. Thus Israel should exert its influence to encourage such a change.

Yet the net effect of the proposed changes in the two powers' nuclear arsenals on Israeli security would depend on the manner in which they were carried out. Israel would clearly benefit if the warheads removed from their delivery systems in the framework of deep cuts would be destroyed and the fissile material they contained transformed into non-weapons-grade material. Israel would also benefit if de-alerting would result in storing the removed warheads in well-secured installations invulnerable to theft and smuggling.

Conversely, Israeli security would diminish if deep reductions would merely result in the destruction of delivery systems or if de-alerting would result in storing the removed warheads in installations that were not properly secured, leaving them much more vulnerable to theft and smuggling to one of the more radical governments in the Middle East. Under such circumstances Israel might be wise to prefer that Russia keep its warheads aboard their delivery vehicles and that deep cuts and de-alerting be avoided.

More generally, the possibility that the United States and Russia would carry out deep reductions in their nuclear arsenals and de-alert their remaining forces provides an opportunity to reflect on the much more impressive restraint exercised so far by the so-called threshold states: Israel, Pakistan, and India.[1] Although the nuclear policies of the three countries have been very different, they have all avoided the pitfalls of the U.S.-Soviet and NATO–Warsaw Pact nuclear arms race. Indeed, the restraint they have exercised is impressive even in comparison with China, which continues to develop and deploy ever more usable weapons, ones that have more compact and lower-yield warheads.

Despite perceived threats to their basic security and survival, the three threshold states have resisted the adoption of explicit nuclear deterrence and its associated declaratory policy. They have also refrained from integrating nuclear weapons into their armed forces and from adopting a nuclear war-fighting doctrine. Thus they have avoided making nuclear weapons a central feature of their defense policy, thereby minimizing the danger that their conventional armed forces would become less vigilant. They have further refrained from issuing specific nuclear threats and from testing nuclear weapons and warheads. And they have certainly avoided the production and deployment of huge quantities of nuclear weapons. Finally, nuclear policy in the three countries has remained remarkably stable and constant despite changes in almost every other feature of their political circumstances and behavior.

1. Editor's note: these comments were written before the Indian and Pakistani nuclear tests in May 1998.

This general restraint has been exercised consistently by very different Israeli governments and despite serious challenges to the state's security: the success of the Egyptian and Syrian assaults during the initial stage of the 1973 war as well as the Iraqi Scud ballistic missile attacks during the 1991 Gulf War. Moreover, unlike India, Israel has never challenged the rationale of the global nuclear nonproliferation regime. Rather, it has merely argued that its strategic environment, the violent nature of the Middle East, has not permitted it to join the 1968 Nuclear Non-Proliferation Treaty. At the same time, it has joined other dimensions of the global nuclear nonproliferation regime. It joined the UN General Assembly consensus that instructed the Conference on Disarmament to negotiate a ban on fissile material production, and it is an original signatory to the Comprehensive Test Ban Treaty (CTBT).

Israel's nuclear policy can be summarized in simple terms: a state whose existence is still anathema to important regional powers such as the present governments of Iran and Iraq and whose security is continuously challenged requires an ultimate insurance policy. Implicitly, Israel's approach is that a nuclear option is to be exercised only under the most extreme circumstances. Having developed a nuclear option and having said very little about it, the country can be described as a nuclear minimalist.

By cutting their nuclear forces dramatically, the nuclear powers would be diminishing the gap between their approach to nuclear weapons and Israel's. Indeed, in contrast to complete disarmament, deep cuts would bring U.S. and Russian approaches to nuclear weapons more in line with those of the three threshold states because such cuts will lead to the adoption of minimal deterrence that Israel, Pakistan, and India have exercised for three decades. Also, the U.S. and Russian defense doctrines would increasingly avoid identifying specific countries as targets for their residual nuclear deterrence, thus surrounding their nuclear doctrine with far more ambiguity. This would also bring their approach to nuclear deterrence more in line with the ambiguity surrounding the nuclear policies of the threshold states. Finally, the United States (and, possibly to a lesser extent, Russia) would increasingly view nuclear deterrence primarily as a hedge against the possible use of weapons of mass destruction by rogue states, a view that would enjoy much implicit sympathy in Israel.

One aspect of deep reductions that Israel may find worrisome is the possibility that they might be associated with a growing tendency to view nuclear weapons as illegitimate and as having no utility except for deterring other countries' use of them. The extent to which the region's record supports this proposition is debatable. Indeed, it would be difficult to deny that perceptions of Israel's nuclear option have contributed to compelling the neighboring Arab states to accept Israel as a permanent feature of the Middle East. Also, it would be difficult to refute the proposition that these perceptions helped deter Sadam Hussein from employing chemical and biological warheads against Israel's population centers during the 1991 Gulf War.

Another implication of this attitude—that nuclear threats are not useful for deterring the use of chemical and biological weapons—is that U.S. military forces stationed in the Middle East may become increasingly exposed to such threats. Since Israel views nuclear deployments as essential for guaranteeing the region's stability, it would be concerned about any development that might diminish U.S. confidence in the ability to protect its troops abroad.

In addition, Israel may fear that a successful effort to carry out deep cuts in U.S. and Russian nuclear forces—eventually involving some changes in the nuclear force structures of China, France, and Britain—might be associated with some pressures on Israel to reciprocate. Israel would then face a difficult dilemma: any contractually based reciprocity would need to be accompanied by some verification mechanisms. But such mechanisms cannot be implemented without further eroding whatever ambiguity still surrounds Israel's nuclear option.

These understandable concerns notwithstanding, the odds that Israel would be faced with pressures to reciprocate to deep cuts implemented primarily by the United States and Russia are not very high. Such pressures are unlikely to originate from Washington, partly because the United States has no interest in contributing to any erosion in the ambiguity surrounding Israel's nuclear program and partly because of the more general conviction that Israel should not be pressed to compromise its nuclear option until all major Arab states have concluded peace agreements with it.

Still, it is possible that a decision by the United States and Russia to de-alert their nuclear forces would lead them to press Israel, as well as India and Pakistan, to keep their nuclear forces effectively demated and eventually to put their unsafeguarded fissile materials in predesignated storage facilities (see appendix F). The only way that Israel could respond to such pressures without compromising its nuclear option is by issuing a unilateral statement announcing that it has decided to scale back the size of its nuclear option or to de-alert it by demating its components. Such a nonbinding statement is likely to be dismissed by Israel's Arab neighbors and legally focused nonproliferation zealots as meaningless. Nevertheless, while preserving

Israel's nuclear ambiguity, such a statement may demonstrate good will and would illustrate that Israel is in tune with global sentiments.

Yet even a relatively benign unilateral statement will only be made following a serious internal debate. Key members of Israel's defense establishment are likely to argue that a statement of this type would yield a limited payoff while its associated risks are considerable: that Israel might face a general demand to convert its promise to a verifiable operational action plan. Israel will wish to avoid such pressures until the Middle East political environment would allow and justify a major reinvention of the country's nuclear option.

Under what conditions is Israel likely to reciprocate more fully to a move by the nuclear powers to implement deep cuts and to de-alert their nuclear forces? Such reciprocity, implying a major change in Israel's nuclear posture, is likely to take place only after the underlying factors that have propelled it to adopt its nuclear deterrence posture are removed. This means an end to the hostility of Arab and non-Arab Muslim states and to the perception of some of the region's governments, publics, and elites that Israel is an illegitimate entity. Thus Israel would be able to implement verifiable deep cuts and de-alerting only after people-to-people peace with the neighboring Arab states has taken root and a regional security system established. Such changes will provide Israel with the requisite confidence that the peace process will not be reversed and that the Jewish state will never again face threats to its basic security and survival.

Contributors

Alexei Arbatov
*State Duma of the Russian
  Federation Defense Committee*

Li Bin
*Beijing Institute of Applied
  Physics and Computational
  Mathematics*

Bruce G. Blair
Brookings Institution

Jonathan Dean
Union of Concerned Scientists

Thérèse Delpech
Commisariat à l'Energie Atomique

Harold Feiveson
Princeton University

Shai Feldman
Tel Aviv University

Steve Fetter
University of Maryland

James Goodby
*Brookings Institution
Carnegie Mellon University*

Pervez Hoodbhoy
Quaid-e-Azam University

George N. Lewis
*Massachusetts Institute of
  Technology*

Zia Mian
Princeton University

Harald Müller
Peace Research Institute

Janne E. Nolan
Twentieth Century Fund

Theodore Postol
*Massachusetts Institute of
  Technology*

M. V. Ramana
Princeton Universtiy

Frank N. von Hippel
Princeton University

Index

A-5 attack aircraft, 139
ABM Treaty. *See* Treaty on the Limitation of Anti-Ballistic Missile Systems
Abolition of nuclear weapons, 15; calls for, 287–88; conventional disarmament and, 297–98; deep cuts proposal and, 287, 289, 291, 355, 363; democratic government as requirement for, 293–95; efforts of nonnuclear states, 355–56; nuclear energy production and, 292–93; preconditions for, 287, 289, 291–301; prevention of breakout, 298–300; prospects for, 300–01, 323–24, 355, 363; rationale, 288–89; reduced risk of armed conflict as requirement for, 295–97; South Asian nuclear forces and policies and, 354, 363; state government resistance to, 289–92; in U.S. strategic interests, 32–33n
Accidental launch, 3–4, 71–72; benefits of de-alerting, 102, 127; Israeli concerns, 382; potential scale of, 72; risk in counterforce retaliatory doctrine, 49–51; risk in Russia, 104–07, 111; Y2K problem, 106
Adaptive targeting, 55–57, 269
African Nuclear Weapons Free Zone Treaty, 243, 271–74
Agni missile, 69, 364
Anderson, Martin, 280
Arbatov, Alexei, 266
Argentina, 33, 282
ASMP missiles: French arsenal, 137, 138; START V deployment, 152
Aspin, Les, 32, 246–47, 248–49, 250,

276, 277
Assured destruction, 52
Aziz, Tarik, 39

B-*1B* bombers, 132–33
B-2 bombers: de-alerting, 118; refurbishing, 130; staged reductions, 24; START II compliance, 132; START III reductions, 146; START IV reductions, 149; START V deployment, 151
B-6 bombers, 139
B-*52* bombers, 24
B-52H bombers: carrying capacity, 132–33; START III reductions, 146; START IV reductions, 149
B-*61* earth-penetrating bombs, 118, 159
Ballistic missile defense: boost-phase intercept, 77; China's concerns, 196; cold war strategy, 63; countermeasures, 81–84, 95; cruise missile threat, 84; cuing information for, 88–89; current applications, 66; deep reduction scenario, 199–200; deterrence and, 85–86, 96; effectiveness, 64, 81–84, 96–97; first strike policy and, 65; as impetus to increase offensive capacity, 64, 87–88; inadequacy of, 96–99; indications of no first-use policy, 331; intercontinental, 66; international cooperation on systems, 91–93; international response to U.S. or Russian deployment, 90–91; medium-range, 66; national, 63, 72–74, 78; national, thin, 86–88, 89;